D0948704

# THE MARQUIS DE SADE
# THE MAN, HIS WORKS,
# AND HIS CRITICS

GARLAND REFERENCE LIBRARY
OF THE HUMANITIES
(VOL. 469)

# THE MARQUIS DE SADE
# THE MAN, HIS WORKS,
# AND HIS CRITICS
### *An Annotated Bibliography*

Colette Verger Michael

GARLAND PUBLISHING INC. • NEW YORK & LONDON
1986

**Library of Congress Cataloging-in-Publication Data**

Michael, Colette Verger, 1937–
  The Marquis de Sade.

  (Garland reference library of the humanities ;
v. 469)
  Includes index.
  1. Sade, marquis de, 1740–1814—Bibliography.
I. Title.  II. Series.
Z8775.14.M53  1986    016.843′6    83-49313
[PQ2063.S3]
ISBN 0-8240-8998-7 (alk. paper)

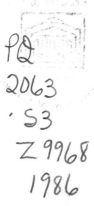
Printed on acid-free, 250-year-life paper
Manufactured in the United States of America

# CONTENTS

ACKNOWLEDGMENTS

I would like to acknowledge the financial support provided by Northern Illinois University Graduate School as well as the scholarly research undertaken through the good office of NIU's Founders Library and the Deans of the College of Liberal Arts and Sciences. Through their combined help, I was able to secure the services of a research assistant and special funding allocations. My gratitude also goes to Karen Blaser, director of the College of Liberal Arts & Sciences Word Processing Center of Northern Illinois University who provided, with numerous members of her staff, able help and technical assistance.

Thanks also go to my three sons, Alan, David, and especially Gérard, for the help they gave me. Without them it would have been impossible to collect the material scattered in so many different libraries, in so many foreign lands.

C.V.M.

# INTRODUCTION

Donatien Alphonse François--Marquis de Sade, Squire de la Coste
and Saumaune, Cavalry Colonel, Lieutenant Général of the prov-
inces of Bresse, Bugey, and others--was born in Paris in 1740.
Educated first by his uncle, the Abbey de Sade d'Ebreuil, then
by the Jesuits, he was only 23 when he married, with royal
blessings, Renée Cordier de Launay de Montreuil, the oldest
daughter of Président de Montreuil. She bore three children.
His wife's devotion, quite apparent from their published correspondence, was counteracted by the venomousness of his mother-
in-law, the Présidente de Montreuil, who went so far as to
write a "lettre de cachet," an arbitrary warrant of imprisonment that resulted in the Marquis' being incarcerated for the
first time at Vincennes in 1777.

During each of his stays in prison, which totalled some
thirty years of his life, he wrote profusely. Novels, short
stories, plays, political essays, and treatises on the theater
and on the novel are included in his monumental output. Most
notable among these are *Justine ou les malheurs de la vertu*,
*Les 120 Journées de Sodome, Florville et Courval,* and *Dialogues
entre un prêtre et un moribond.* An impressive array of scholars has commented on his work: Baudelaire, Maurice Heine,
Georges Bataille, Apollinaire, Simone de Beauvoir, Mario Praz,
Roland Barthes, Maurice Blanchot, to name but a few. And, perhaps not too surprisingly, Gilbert Lély stated that were it not
for the connotation of his name, the Marquis de Sade's novel
*Aline et Valcour* (1795) would be inscribed side by side with
such immortal works of fiction as the *Decameron, Don Quixote,*
and *Gulliver's Travels.*

In Sade, man's inhumanity to man becomes a metaphysical
question: how could such evil be possible? His writings explain, almost predict, the possibility of the horrors of
Hitler's holocaust; but, with ironic overstatement, Sade puts
a distance between us and his prose so that his contentions are
not painful. In the words of Hannah Arendt, in another context, he sets us face to face with the "banality of evil." Incestuous orgies, meaningless torture, and wanton cruelty fill
some of his books--not all of them--but these horrendous

ix

descriptions, quite foreign to us, are so clinically atrocious
that they take on a cosmic dimension.  Yet, this aspect of his
work has completely overshadowed some of the qualities of his
production: the modern technique of his one-act morality plays,
his talent as a short story writer, the radical eloquence of
his writings, the uncanny appraisal of the historian in
*Histoire secrète d'Isabelle de Bavière* (first published in
1952), his unfailing belief in the integrity of the self, his
defense of personal liberties, and his avant-garde sociology.
In *Les 120 Journées de Sodome*, the work which is largely re-
sponsible for the reputation he has acquired, he wrote systematically about sexual aberration.  The "sadistic" aspect of
some of his writings has overshadowed the fact that he wrote
about deviant behavior more than a century ahead of Sigmund
Freud, which in essence means that he can be considered a genuine precursor of modern sexology.

The intent of this bibliography is to list as fully as
possible works by and about the Marquis de Sade, the man and
the writer.  To date, there exist only unannotated bibliographies on Sade, i.e., *D.A.F. de Sade* by Gilbert Lély, 16 v.
(Paris: Cercle du Livre précieux, 1966-67), and E. Pierre
Chanover, *The Marquis de Sade: A Bibliography* (Metuchen, N.J.:
Scarecrow Press, 1973).  Both of these works are first-rate but
out of date.  Other valuable sources include Françoise Rosart
in the journal *Obliques 12-13,* published in Paris in 1977, and
the critical bibliography compiled by Michel Delon entitled
"Dix ans d'études sadiennes (1968-1978)" and  published in *Dix-
huitième siècle*.  Also important is the study made by Giorgio
Cerruti, "Il Marchese di Sade: la sua recente fortuna e gli
ultimi studi critici (1958-1968)," and published in *Studi
francesi* (1969).

An attempt has been made to include all material published
on the Marquis de Sade until the year 1983.  To gather the material for these pages, I consulted all the standard reference
works known to me and examined many periodicals and books in
several libraries in France, as well as in the United States.
Through the good office of Northern Illinois University, a
Dialog Search was instituted.  In Europe, books and articles
were obtained from the Bibliothèque Nationale in Paris, the
Bibliothèque Municipale in Marseille, and the Bibliothèque
Publique et Universitaire in Geneva, Switzerland.  Forty-three
basic tools for bibliographical research are mentioned in the
short section titled "Reference Works Consulted."

This bibliography is organized into three main parts--two
sections of primary sources, and one section of annotated secondary sources--followed by a single index which includes names
of authors, editors, translators, titles, and those of charac-

ters in novels or plays mentioned in the annotated items.

The listing of primary sources--the works by the Marquis
de Sade himself, including those published anonymously--was
prepared from the works cited as "Reference Works Consulted"
and cannot claim independent authority or comprehensiveness.
The first section lists the works of the Marquis de Sade in
alphabetical order. An attempt has been made to give the first
date of publication of the work in question. The second section in "Primary Sources" should not be considered as a complete listing of editions of Sade's works. Whenever possible,
translations of specific works have been included.

Books, articles, and reviews listed in the main section of
this book, "Secondary Sources," are followed by my annotations.
Notices of reviews are inserted directly below the article or
book listed. I have placed the entries under a subject heading
which emphasizes some of Sade's interests as well as the critics' preoccupations. Admittedly, the selection of subject
divisions is arbitrary and subjective; these divisions were intended to highlight the many different facets of Sade's works
and of his critics, but not to exhaust them. For extra conve-
nience, a section of foreign criticism has been compiled and
listed alphabetically by language. It is not annotated.

Of special help to me in compiling this section were some
Sade's scholars' bibliographies which were used as cross-refer-
ences. I cannot name here all the works consulted but would
like to acknowledge a special debt to A. Laborde's *Sade,
romancier* and E. Pierre Chanover's *The Marquis de Sade: A Bibliography*.

The Marquis de Sade
The Man, His Works,
and His Critics

# I. REFERENCE WORKS CONSULTED

1. Barbier, Antoine-Alexandre. DICTIONNAIRE DES OUVRAGES ANONYMES. Paris: Daffis, 1877-1879.

2. Bassan, Fernande; Breed, Paul F.; and Spinelli, Donald C. AN ANNOTATED BIBLIOGRAPHY OF FRENCH LANGUAGE AND LITERATURE. New York: Garland Publishing, 1977.

3. Belin, Jean-Paul. LE COMMERCE DES LIVRES PROHIBES A PARIS DE 1750 A 1789. Paris: Belin, 1913.

4. Bibliothèque Nationale. CATALOGUE GENERAL DES LIVRES IMPRIMES DE LA BIBLIOTHEQUE NATIONALE. Paris: Imprimerie Nationale, 1897.

5. Brenner, Clarence. A BIBLIOGRAPHICAL LIST OF PLAYS IN THE FRENCH LANGUAGE, 1700-1789. Berkeley, 1947.

6. British Museum. Department of Printed Books. GENERAL CATALOGUE OF PRINTED BOOKS. London: Trustees of the British Museum, 1965-1966.

7. _____. TEN-YEAR SUPPLEMENT, 1956-1965. London: 1968.

8. Cabeen, David C. CRITICAL AND SELECTIVE BIBLIOGRAPHY OF FRENCH LITERATURE. Vol. IV: THE EIGHTEENTH CENTURY. Edited by George R. Havens and Donald F. Bond. New York: Syracuse University Press, 1968.

9. _____. Ibid. Vol. IV-A: THE EIGHTEENTH-CENTURY SUPPLEMENT. Edited by Richard A. Brooks. New York: Syracuse University Press, 1968.

10. Cerruti, Giorgio. "Il Marchese di Sade: La sua recente fortuna e gli ultima studi critici (1958-1968)." STUDI FRANCESI 39 (1969): 420-441.

11. Chanover, E. Pierre. THE MARQUIS DE SADE: A BIBLIOGRAPHY. Metuchen, N.J.: Scarecrow Press, 1973, 252 p.

12. Cioranescu, Alexandre. BIBLIOGRAPHIE DE LA LITTERATURE FRANCAISE DU XVIIIe SIECLE. Paris: Editions du Centre National de la Recherche Scientifique, 1969.

1

13.  Cordié, Carlo.  AVVIAMENTO ALLO STUDIO DELLA LINGUA  E
     DELLA LETTERATURA FRANCESE.  Milan:  Carlo Marzorati,
     1955, pp. 406, 419, 430, 940, 1011-1012.

14.  Delon, Michel.  "Dix ans d'études sadiennes (1968-1978)."
     DIX-HUITIEME SIECLE 11 (1979):  393-426.

15.  DIALOG  INFORMATION RETRIEVAL SERVICE for  PHILOSOPHERS'
     INDEX,  HISTORICAL  ABSTRACTS and SOCIAL  SCIENCE
     RESEARCH data bases.

16.  DISSERTATION  ABSTRACTS  INTERNATIONAL.  Ann  Arbor,
     Michigan: University Microfilms.  All volumes.

17.  Fromm, Hans.  BIBLIOGRAPHIE DEUTSCHER UBERSETZUNGEN AUS
     DEM  FRANZOSICHEN 1700-1948.  Vol. V.  Baden-Baden:
     Kunst und Wissenschaft, 1950, p. 386.

18.  Gay, Jules.  BIBLIOGRAPHIE  DES  OUVRAGES  RELATIFS  A
     L'AMOUR,  AUX FEMMES, AU MARIAGE, CONTENANT LES TITRES
     DETAILLES DE CES OUVRAGES,  LES NOMS DES  AUTEURS,  UN
     APERCU DE LEUR SUJET,  LEUR VELEUR ET LEUR PRIX,  DANS
     LES  VENTES,  L'INDICATION  DE  CEUX  QUI  ONT  ETE
     POURSUIVIS  OU  QUI  ONT  SUBI  DES  CONDAMNATIONS.
     Paris: J. Gay, 1864.

19.  Giraud, Jeanne.  MANUEL DE BIBLIOGRAPHIE LITTERAIRE POUR
     LES  XVIe,  XVIIe,  ET XVIIIe SIECLES FRANCAIS  (1946-
     1955).  Paris: Nizet, 1970.

20.  Gottschalk,  Louis.  "Studies since 1920 of French
     Thought  in  the Period of the  Enlightenment."  THE
     JOURNAL  OF MODERN HISTORY 4 (1932):  242-260.

21.  Klapp, Otto.  BIBLIOGRAPHIE DER FRANZOSISCHEN LITERATUR-
     WISSENSCHAFT/BIBLIOGRAPHIE  D'HISTOIRE  LITTERAIRE
     FRANCAISE.  Frankfurt am Main: Klostermann, 1956-1973.

22.  Laborde, Alice.  SADE ROMANCIER.  Neuchâtel:  Editions
     de la Baconnière, 1974, pp. 171-192.

23.  Lanson, Gustave.  MANUEL  BIBLIOGRAPHIQUE  DE  LA
     LITTERATURE FRANCAISE MODERNE, XVIe, XVIIe, XVIIIe, ET
     XIXe SIECLES.  Paris: Hachette, 1921.

24.  Laporte,  Antoine.  BIBLIOGRAPHIE  CLERICO-GALANTE;
     OUVRAGES GALANTS OU SINGULIERS SUR L'AMOUR,  LES

FEMMES, LE MARIAGE, LE THEATRE, ETC., ECRITS PAR DES ABBES, EVEQUES. . . CARDINAUX ET PAPES. Paris: 1879.

25. Lély, Gilbert. OEUVRES COMPLETES. Paris: Cercle du livre précieux, 1966.

26. Lemonnyer, J. BIBLIOGRAPHIE DES OUVRAGES RELATIFS A L'AMOUR, AUX FEMMES ET AU MARIAGE ET DES LIVRES FACETIEUX, PANTAGRUELIQUES, SCATALOGIQUES, SATYRIQUES. Paris: Lemonnyer, 1894.

27. Le Petit, Jules. BIBLIOGRAPHIE DES PRINCIPALES EDITIONS ORIGINALES D'ECRIVAINS FRANCAIS DU XVe AU XVIIIe SIECLE. Paris: 1927.

28. Martin, Angus; Mylne, Vivienne G.; and Frautschi, Richard. BIBLIOGRAPHIE DU GENRE ROMANESQUE FRANCAISE, 1751-1800. London: Mansell, 1977.

29. MLA INTERNATIONAL BIBLIOGRAPHY. New York: Modern Language Association of America, 1922.

30. Monglond, André. LA FRANCE REVOLUTIONNAIRE ET IMPERIALE. ANNALES DE BIBLIOGRAPHIE METHODIQUE ET DESCRIPTION DES LIVRES ILLUSTRES. Grenoble: 1930-1949.

31. NATIONAL UNION CATALOG. PRE-1956 IMPRINTS. Vol. 310.

32. Osburn, Charles B. RESEARCH AND REFERENCE GUIDE TO FRENCH STUDIES. Metuchen, N.J.: Scarecrow Press, 1968.

33. Peloux, Charles du. REPERTOIRE GENERAL DES OUVRAGES MODERNES RELATIFS AU XVIIIe SIECLE FRANCAIS, 1715-1789. Paris: 1926.

34. Quérard, Joseph-Marie. LES SUPERCHERIES LITTERAIRES DEVOILEES. GALERIE DES ECRIVAINS FRANCAIS DE TOUTE L'EUROPE QUI SE SONT DEGUISES SOUS DES ANAGRAMMES, DES ASTERONYMES, DES CRYPTONYMES, DES INITIALISMES, DES NOMS LITTERAIRES, DES PSEUDONYMES FACETIEUX OU BIZARRES. Paris: Maisonneuve et Larose, 1964.

35. Rancoeur, René. BIBLIOGRAPHIE DE LA LITTERATURE FRANCAISE DU MOYEN AGE A NOS JOURS (1968). Paris: Armand Colin, 1969.

36. REPERTOIRE        INTERNATIONAL      DES      TRADUCTIONS/INDEX
    TRANSLATION/INTERNATIONAL        BIBLIOGRAPHY         OF
    TRANSLATIONS.  Paris: Presses de l'UNESCO, 1949-.

37. Rochebilière,   Antonin.   BIBLIOGRAPHIE  DES  EDITIONS
    ORIGINALES    D'AUTEURS  FRANCAIS  DES XVIe,  XVIIe  ET
    XVIIIe   SIECLES;   rédigée   avec   des   notes   et
    éclaircissements  par  A.  Claudin et corrigé  par  J.
    Place.  Paris: 1930.

38. Ryland,  Hobart.  "Recent Developments in Research on the
    Marquis de Sade."  FRENCH REVIEW 25 (1951): 10-15.

39. Talvart, Hector, and Place, Joseph.  BIBLIOGRAPHIE  DES
    AUTEURS   MODERNES   DE  LANGUE   FRANCAISE.   Vol.  X.
    Paris: Chronique des lettres françaises, 1950.

40. Tchémerzine,  Avenir.   BIBLIOGRAPHIE       D'EDITIONS
    ORIGINALES ET RARES D'AUTEURS FRANCAIS DEX XVe,  XVIe,
    XVIIe  ET  XVIIIe SIECLES,   CONTENANT  ENVIRONS  600
    FACSIMILES  DE TITRES ET DE  GRAVURES.   Paris:  1927-
    1934.

41. Zylberstein, Jean-Claude.   "Bibliographie chronologi-
    que."  OEUVRES COMPLETES DU MARQUIS DE SADE.   Paris:
    Cercle du livre précieux, 1967.


                 SPECIAL ISSUES OF THE FOLLOWING REVIEWS

42. CAHIER DU SUD 285 (1947).

43. L'ESPRIT CREATEUR, Winter 1975.

44. EUROPE, October 1972.

45. MAGAZINE LITTERAIRE, No. 114, June 1976.

46. OBLIQUES, 12-13 (1977).

47. PRESENCE DU CINEMA 6/7, December 1960.

48. REVUE DU CINEMA:  IMAGE ET SON, No. 272, May 1973.

49. TEL QUEL, Winter 1967.

50. YALE FRENCH STUDIES (1965).

II.  PRIMARY SOURCES

A.  ALPHABETICAL LISTING OF PUBLISHED WORKS

51.  ADELAIDE OF BRUNSWICK.  Translated by Hobart Ryland from an unpublished manuscript recently discovered among papers left by the Marquis de Sade.  Washington: Scarecrow Press, 1954.

52.  ADRESSE D'UN CITOYEN DE PARIS AU ROI DES FRANCAIS. Girouard, imprimeur, rue du Bout-du-Monde.  Paris: 1791, 16 p.

53.  L'AIGLE, MADEMOISELLE. . . .  Lettres publiées pour la première fois sur les manuscrits autographes inédits avec une Préface et un Commentaire par Gilbert Lély. Paris:  Les Editions Georges Artigues, 1949. FRONTISPICE de Jacques Hérold dans les exemplaires sur grand papier.  XLVIII + 222 p.

54.  ALINE ET VALCOUR, OU LE ROMAN PHILOSOPHIQUE.  Ecrit à la Bastille un an avant la Révolution de France.  Orné de quatorze gravures.  Par le citoyen S***.  A Paris, chez Girouard, libraire rue du Bout-du-Monde, No. 47, 1793.  4 vol. XIV + 315, 503, 575, 374 p.

55.  ALZONDE ET KORADIN.  Paris:  Cerioux, an VII.

56.  LES AMIS DU CRIME.  Paris: n.d. (Excerpt from L'HISTOIRE DE JULIETTE.)  (With lithograph on wood plate by Clelio.)

57.  "Les antiquaires."  Play in OEUVRES COMPLETES. Vol. XXXIII.  Paris: J. J. Pauvert, 1970, pp. 341-420.

58.  "Attrapez-moi toujours de même."  In HISTORIETTES, CONTES ET FABLIAUX.  Paris: Société du Roman philosophique, 1926.  340 p.

59.  "Augustine de Villefranche, ou le stratagème de l'Amour."  In HISTORIETTES, CONTES ET FABLIAUX. Preface by Gilbert Lély.  Paris: Union générale d'éditions, 1968, pp. 116-136.

60.  L'AUTEUR DES CRIMES DE L'AMOUR A VILLETERQUE, FOLLICULAIRE.  Paris: Massé, An IX.  19 p. (Listed by P. Lemonnyer [item 26], vol. I, p. 304.)

61. Aux stupides scélérats qui me tourmentent, avec une note
    par Gilbert Lély.    NEON (1949).    (Letter also
    published in L'AIGLE, MADEMOISELLE.)

62. "Aventure incompréhensible." In HISTORIETTES, CONTES ET
    FABLIAUX.    Preface by Gilbert Lély.    Paris: Union
    générale d'éditions, 1968, pp. 49-55.

63. LES AVENTURES GALANTES. N.p.:  Ed. Schmid, n.d.

64. Avertissement (première version de l'IDEE SUR LES
    ROMANS) (pp. lv-lxvi);  sur Retif de la Bretone
    (pp. lxxv-lxxvi);  deux passages d'EUGENIE DE FRANVAL
    (pp. 150-154  et 209-210) n'ayant pas figuré dans LES
    CRIMES   DE  L'AMOUR.  -- OEUVRES  CHOISIES  ET  PAGES
    MAGISTRALES du marquis de Sade publiées et  commentées
    par Maurice Heine. Paris: Editions du Trianon, 1933.

65. "Le Boudoir."  Play in OEUVRES COMPLETES.    Vol. XXXIII.
    Paris: J. J. Pauvert, 1970, pp. 341-420.

66. LE BORDEL    DE    VENISE,  nouvelle  édition,    ornée
    d'aquarelles  scandaleuses de  Couperyn.    [Notice de
    Louis Perceau.] N.p.:n.d.

67. CAHIERS PERSONNELS 1803-1804.    Publiés pour la première
    fois  sur les manuscrits autographes inédits avec  une
    préface et des notes par Gilbert Lély.

    [En appendice:  I.  Projet de Séide.--II. Notes sur M.
    de  Sade,  par le Dr. L.-J. Ramon.] Paris:    Corréa,
    1953.  130 p.

68. "Le capricieux."  Play.    In OEUVRES COMPLETES.    Vol.
    XXXIV.  Paris: J. J. Pauvert, 1970, pp. 315-455.

69. LE CARILLON DE VINCENNES, Lettres inédites publiées avec
    des notes par Gilbert Lély.  Paris: Arcanes, 1953.

70. LES  CARNETS  D'UN  LIBERTIN,  HISTORIETTES,  CONTES  ET
    FABLIAUX.    Bruxelles:  Club  Mondial du livre,  1956.
    (Listed by F. Rosart in OBLIQUES 12-13 [1977].)  (Item
    46)

71. CENT  ONZE NOTES POUR LA NOUVELLE JUSTINE.  Paris:  Le
    Terrain Vague, 1956.    159 p.  Eau-forte de Bona dans
    les exemplaires sur Montgolfier.

72. LES 120 JOURNEES DE SODOME OU L'ECOLE DU   LIBERTINAGE.
    Publié pour la première fois d'après le manuscrit
    origine avec des annotations scientifiques par le
    Docteur Eugen Duhren. Paris: Club des Bibliophiles,
    1904. VIII + 543 p.

73. "La Châtelaine de Longeville, ou la femme vengée." In
    HISTORIETTES, CONTES ET FABLIAUX. Preface by Gilbert
    Lély. Paris: Union générale d'éditions, 1968,
    pp. 294-305.

74. Cinq lettres à Mlle Colet. In LES CAHIERS DE LA
    PLEIADE, printemps--été 1951.

75. "Le Cocu de lui-même, ou le raccommodement imprévu." In
    HISTORIETTES, CONTES ET FABLIAUX. Preface by Gilbert
    Lély. Paris: Union générale d'éditions, 1968,
    pp. 252-267.

76. "La Comtesse de Sancerre, ou la rivale de sa fille,
    anecdote de la Cour de Bourgogne." In LES CRIMES DE
    L'AMOUR. Vol. IV. Paris: Massé, An VIII.

77. CONTES LICENCIEUX. Genève: Editions crémille, 1973.
    (Listed by F. Rosart in OBLIQUES 12-13 [1977], item
    46.)

78. CORRESPONDANCE INEDITE DU MARQUIS DE SADE. De ses
    proches et de ses familiers, publiée avec une
    introduction, des annales et des notes, par Paul
    Bourdin. Paris: Librairie de France, 1929.

79. Couplets chantés à Son Eminence le cardinal Maury, le 6
    octobre 1812, à la maison de santé près de Charenton.
    REVUE RETROSPECTIVE, 1833.

80. LA COURTISANE ANAPHRODITE, ou la pucelle libertine.
    Avignon, 1787. (Listed by F. Rosart in OBLIQUES 12-13
    [1977], item 46.)

81. LES CRIMES DE L'AMOUR. [Juliette et Raunai, ou la
    Conspiration d'Amboise.] Précédé d'un Avant-propos
    [Avis aux éditeurs, signé: G.D.], suivi des IDEES SUR
    LES ROMANS, de l'Auteur des Crimes de l'amour ;à
    Villeterque, d'une Notice bio-bibliographique du M[is]
    de Sade . . . et du Discours prononcé par le M[is] de

Sade à la Section des piques. Bruxelles: Gay et
Douvé, 1881.

82.  LES CRIMES DE L'AMOUR, Nouvelles héroïques et tragiques
     précédées d'une IDEE   SUR LES ROMANS et ornées de
     gravures,   par D.-A.-F. Sade, auteur d'ALINE   ET
     VALCOUR.  A Paris, chez Massé, éditeur-propriétaire,
     An VIII.  4 vol. XLIII-228, 274, 256 et 246 p. Quatre
     frontispices. Tome I.  JULIETTE ET RAUNAI, ou LA
     CONSPIRATION D'AMBOISE, NOUVELLE HISTORIQUE; LA DOUBLE
     EPREUVE.  Tome II.  MISS HENRIETTE STRALSON, OU LES
     EFFETS DU DESESPOIR,  nouvelle anglaise; FAXELANGE OU
     LES TORTS DE L'AMBITION;  FLORVILLE ET COURVAL, ou le
     Fatalisme. Tome III.  RODRIGUE, OU LA TOUR ENCHANTEE,
     conte allégorique; LAURENCE ET ANTONIO, nouvelle
     italienne; ERNESTINE, nouvelle suédoise.  Tome IV.
     DORGEVILLE, OU LE CRIMINEL PAR VERTU; LA COMTESSE DE
     SANCERRE, OU LA RIVALE DE SA FILLE, anecdote de la
     Cour de Bourgogne; EUGENIE DE FRANVAL.

83.  "Les  Dangers  de  la  bienfaisance  (Dorci.)"   In
     HISTORIETTES,   CONTES ET FABLIAUX. Paris: Société du
     Roman Philosophique, 1926, 340 p.

84.  Deux lettres à Goupilleau de Montaigu. In CORRESPONDANCE
     LITTERAIRE, 1859.

85.  Deux Lettres du marquis de Sade, avec des notes par
     Gilbert Lély. LES CAHIERS DE LA PLEIADE, Autumn 1948-
     Spring 1949.  (Lettres publiées ensuite dans L'AIGLE,
     MADEMOISELLE. . . .)

86.  Deux lettres inédites du marquis de Sade à sa femme.  -
     Morceaux choisis de D.-A.-F. de Sade, par Gilbert
     Lély. Paris: P. Seghers, 1948, pp. 125-131.

87.  Deux lettres sur les représentations théâtrales de
     Charenton. REVUE ANECDOTIQUE, nouvelle série, vol. I,
     1$^{er}$ semestre 1860, pp. 103-106.

88.  DIALOGUE ENTRE UN PRETRE ET UN MORIBOND. Publié pour la
     première fois sur le manuscrit autographe inédit, avec
     un avant-propos et des notes par Maurice Heine.
     Paris: Stendhal et Compagnie, 1926.  62 p.

89.  Discours prononcé à la Fête décernée par la Section des
     Piques aux mânes de Marat et de Le Pelletier, par
     Sade, citoyen de cette Section et membre de la Société

populaire (29 September 1793).    De l'Imprimerie de la
Section des Piques, rue S.-Fiacre, No. 2.   S.d.  8 p.

90.  "Documents et lettres à propos de la vente du château de
     Lacoste  en  1796:  L.  Peise Rovère et le marquis  de
     Sade." REVUE HISTORIQUE DE LA REVOLUTION FRANCAISE ET
     DE L'EMPIRE, July-September, 1914.

91.  DORCI,  OU  LA BIZARRERIE DU SORT,  conte inédit par le
     marquis  de  Sade,  publié sur le manuscrit  avec  une
     notice  sur l'auteur [signée A. F. (Anatole France)].
     Paris:  Charavay frères, éditeurs, 1881.  Frontispice
     de G. Charpentier.  64 p.

92.  "Dorgeville,  ou le Criminel par Vertu."  In LES  CRIMES
     DE L'AMOUR.  Vol. IV.  Paris: Massé, An VIII.

93.  "La Double épreuve."  In LES CRIMES DE L'AMOUR.  Vol. I.
     Paris:  Massé, An VIII.

94.  ECRITS  POLITIQUES;  SUIVIS DE OXTIERN.  Sceaux:  J.  J.
     Pauvert, 1957.  180 p.

95.  "L'égarement  de  l'infortune."   Play.   In  OEUVRES
     COMPLETES.  Vol. XXXIII.  Paris:  J. J. Pauvert, 1970,
     pp. 271-339.

96.  "Emilie  de  Tourville,  ou la cruauté fraternelle."   In
     HISTORIETTES,  CONTES ET FABLIAUX.  Preface by Gilbert
     Lély.  Paris: Union générale d'éditions, 1968, pp. 76-
     115.

97.  "L'Epoux  complaisant."  In HISTORIETTES,   CONTES   ET
     FABLIAUX.  Preface  by Gilbert  Lély.   Paris:  Union
     générale d'éditions, 1968, pp. 47-48.

98.  "L'Epoux corrigé."  In HISTORIETTES, CONTES ET FABLIAUX.
     Preface  by  Gilbert  Lély.   Paris:  Union  générale
     d'éditions, 1968, pp. 273-282.

99.  ERNESTINE.  Avec 10  eaux-fortes de  Sylvain  Sauvage.
     Paris:  J. Fort, 1926.

100. L'ETOURDI.  Lampsaque, 1784.  (Also attributed to Andréa
     de  Nerciat.  Listed by F.  Rosart in OBLIQUES  12-13
     [1977], item 46.)

101. EUGENIE DE FRANVAL. Avec huit illustrations par Valentine Hugo. Paris: G. Ar, 1948.

102. "L'Evêque embourbé." In HISTORIETTERS, CONTES ET FABLIAUX. Preface by Gilbert Lély. Paris: Union générale d'éditions, 1968, pp. 32-33.

103. "Extrait des registres des délibérations de la section des Piques (12 juillet 1793.)" In OPUSCULES ET LETTRES POLITIQUES. Preface by Gilbert Lély. Paris: Union générale d'éditions, 1979, pp. 113-119.

104. "Fanni." Play. In OEUVRES COMPLETES. Vol. XXXIII. Paris: J. J. Pauvert, 1970, pp. 203-269.

105. "Faxelange, ou les Torts de l'ambition." In LES CRIMES DE L'AMOUR. Vol. II. Paris: Massé, An VIII.

106. "La fête de l'amitié." Play. In OEUVRES COMPLETES. Vol. XXXV. Paris: J. J. Pauvert, 1970, pp. 377-454.

107. "Les filous." In HISTORIETTES, CONTES ET FABLIAUX. Preface by Gilbert Lély. Paris: Union générale d'éditions, 1968, pp. 306-315.

108. "La Fleur de Chataignier." In HISTORIETTES, CONTES ET FABLIAUX. Preface by Gilbert Lély. Paris: Union générale d'éditions, 1968, pp. 56-60.

109. "Florville et Courval, ou le Fatalisme." In LES CRIMES DE L'AMOUR. Vol. II. Paris: Massé, An VIII.

110. "Fragments de lettres et couplets provençaux." La Marquise de Sade (suivie de Un Amour platonique du marquis de Sade), par Paul Ginisty. Paris: Fasquelle, 1901.

111. "Fragments inédits d'un roman perdu de Sade: LE PORTEFEUILLE D'UN HOMME DE LETTRE." Edited by J. Vercruysse. In REVUE D'HISTOIRE LITTERAIRE DE LA FRANCE, 1968.

112. FRANCAIS, ENCORE UN EFFORT: extrait de LA PHILOSOPHIE DANS LE BOUDOIR précédé de l'inconvenance majeure par Maurice Blanchot. Paris: Pauvert, 1965.

113. LA FRANCE FOUTUE, tragédie lubrique et royaliste en trois actes et en vers. 1796.

114. "Franchise et trahison." Play.   In OEUVRES COMPLETES.
     Vol. XXXII. Paris: J. J. Pauvert, 1970, pp. 355-420.

115. "Les Harangueurs provençaux." In HISTORIETTES,   CONTES
     ET FABLIAUX.   Preface by Gilbert Lély.   Paris: Union
     générale d'éditions, 1968, pp. 39-43.

116. "Henriette   et   Saint-Clair."   Play.   In   OEUVRES
     COMPLETES.  Vol. XXXV.  Paris: J. J. Pauvert, 1970,
     pp. 141-249.

117. "L'Heureuse   Feinte."   In HISTORIETTES,   CONTES   ET
     FABLIAUX.   Preface  by Gilbert Lély.   Paris: Union
     générale d'éditions, 1968, pp. 22-25.

118. HISTOIRE DE JEROME.   Illustrée d'eaux-fortes originales
     par  un  artiste  inconnu.   Paris:  Chez  tous  les
     libraires, 1936.  (Listed by J. Rosart in OBLIQUES 12-
     13 [1977], item 46.)

119. HISTOIRE  DE  JULIETTE, ou Les prospérités du vice.
     Illustrée de soixante gravures et . . . En Hollande,
     1797.

120. HISTOIRE  DE JUSTINE,   OU LES MALHEURS DE LA VERTU.  En
     Hollande, 1797.

121. HISTOIRE DE SAINVILLE ET DE LEONORE.   Introduction par
     Gilbert Lély.  Paris: Union générale d'éditions, 1962.

122. HISTOIRE SECRETE D'ISABELLE DE BAVIERE, reine de France
     (dans  laquelle  se  trouvent  des  faits  rares  et
     inconnus,  ou restés dans l'oubli jusqu'à ce jour,  et
     soigneusement  étayés  de  manuscrits  authentiques,
     allemands,  anglais  et  latins).   Publié  pour  la
     première fois sur le manuscrit autographe inédit  avec
     un  avant-propos de Gilbert Lély.   Paris:  Librairie
     Gallimard, 1953.  336 p.

123. HISTORIETTE,  CONTES  ET  FABLIAUX.   Publiés pour la
     première  fois sur les manuscrits autographes  inédits
     par Maurice Heine.   A Paris, pour les membres de  la
     Société  du  Roman philosophique,  1926.   340   p.
     Frontispice de Henry Chapront.   HISTORIETTES:  Le
     Serpent;  La Saillie gasconne;  L'heureuse Feinte;  le
     M. . . puni;   l'Evêque embourbé;  le Revenant;  Les
     Harangueurs provençaux; Attrapez-moi toujours de même;

L'Epoux complaisant; Aventure incompréhensible; La
Fleur de Châtaignier. CONTES ET FABLIAUX:
L'Instituteur philosophe; La Prude, ou la Rencontre
imprévue; Emilie de Tourville, ou la Cruauté
fraternelle; Augustine de Villeblanche, ou le
Stratagème de l'Amour; Soit fait ainsi qu'il est
requis; Le Président mystifié; La Marquise de Télème,
ou les Effets du Libertinage; Le Talion; Le Cocu de
lui-même, ou le Raccommodement imprévu; Il y a place
pour deux; L'Epoux corrigé; Le Mari prêtre, conte
provençal; La Châtelaine de Longueville, ou la Femme
vengée; Les Filous. APPENDICE: Les Dangers de la
bienfaisance (Dorci).

124.  Idée sur le mode de Sanction des Loix. S.L.: De
      l'Imprimerie de la rue Saint-Frère, 1792. 16 p.

125.  IDEE SUR LES ROMANS. Paris: Rouveyre, 1878.

126.  "Il y a place pour deux." In HISTORIETTES,  CONTES  ET
      FABLIAUX.   Preface by Gilbert Lély.   Paris: Union
      générale d'éditions, 1968, pp. 268-272.

127.  "Un inédit du marquis de Sade, Isabelle de Bavière."
      (Fragments), published by Gilbert Lély.  In ARTS, 15-
      21 August 1953.

128.  LES INFORTUNES DE LA VERTU.  Texte établi sur le
      manuscrit original autographe et publié pour la
      première fois avec une introduction par Maurice Heine.
      Paris:  Editions Fourcade, 1930.  (First version of
      JUSTINE.) liv + 206 p.

129.  "L'Instituteur philosophe." In HISTORIETTES, CONTES ET
      FABLIAUX.   Preface by Gilbert Lély.   Paris: Union
      générale d'éditions, 1968, pp. 61-64.

130.  "Jeanne Lainé."   Play.   In OEUVRES   COMPLETES.
      Vol. XXXII. Paris: J. J. Pauvert, 1970, pp. 113-279.

131.  JOURNAL INEDIT.  Deux cahiers retrouvés du journal
      inédit du marquis de Sade (1807, 1808, 1814) suivis en
      appendice d'une notice sur l'hospice de Charenton par
      Hippolyte de Colins.  Publiés pour la première fois
      sur les manuscrits autographes inédits avec une
      préface de Georges Daumas.  Paris: Gallimard, 1970.
      185 p.

132. "Juliette et Raunai, ou la Conspiration d'Amboise." In
     LES CRIMES DE L'AMOUR. Vol. I. Paris: Massé, An
     VIII.

133. "Les jumelles." Play. In OEUVRES COMPLETES. Vol.
     XXXII. Paris: J. J. Pauvert, 1970, pp. 281-354.

134. JUSTINE, OU LES MALHEURS DE LA VERTU. En Hollande, chez
     les Libraires associés, 1791.    2 vol.    283 et 191 p.
     Frontispice de Chéry, gravé par carrée.

135. "Laurence et Antonio, nouvelle italienne." In LES
     CRIMES DE L'AMOUR. Vol. III. Paris: Massé, An VIII.

136. LEONORE   ET   CLEMENTINE;   OU,   LES   TARTUFFES   DE
     L'INQUISITION; avec une notice bibliographique par
     Louis Perceau.    Edition ornée de quatre eaux-fortes
     par Viset. Paris: Au Cabinet du livre, 1930.

137. Lettre.    L'AMATEUR D'AUTOGRAPHE, 1866.

138. Lettre à Madame de Sade publiée par Gilbert Lély.    LA
     NEF (Almanach surréaliste du demi-siècle), March 1950.

139. Lettre à Madame de Sade,   publiée par Gilbert Lély.    LA
     REVOLTE EN QUESTION, 1, February 1952.

140. Lettre à Mlle de Lauris;   chanson sur la même.    In LA
     TABLE RONDE, No. 40, April 1951.

141. Lettre à   Marie-Dorothée de Rousset publiée et   annotée
     par Gilbert Lély.    LES   CAHIERS   DE   LA   PLEIADE,
     Spring/Summer 1951.

142. Lettre;   fragments de lettres;   fragment extrait du
     manuscrit, non encore publiée à ce jour, des notes du
     marquis de Sade pour la rédaction de son   roman LES
     JOURNEES DE FLORBELLE OU LA NATURE DEVOILEE, suivies
     des Memoires de l'abbé de Modose et des Aventures
     d'Emilie de Volnange servant de preuve aux assertions;
     texte complet du 5$^e$ paragraphe du testament de Sade.
     In LE VRAI VISAGE DU MARQUIS DE SADE, par Jean
     Desbordes.    Paris:   Nouvelle Revue critique, 1939.
     330 p.

143. Lettre inédite du marquis de Sade (à Martin Quiros), 4
     octobre   1779,   publiée par Maurice   Heine.    LE

SURREALISME AU SERVICE DE LA REVOLUTION, no. 2, October 1930.

144. Lettre sur un spectacle donné à La Coste en 1772. PETITE GAZETTE APTESIENNE, 11 décembre 1911.

145. Lettres à Monsieur Rose, Notaire Royal. MERIDIENS, No. 1, 1929.

146. LETTRES AUX FEMMES. Paris: Tchou, 1965.

147. Lettres et fragments de Lettres. REVUE INDEPENDANTE (Le marquis de Sade, par ***, passim), 1885.

148. Lettres et fragments de Lettres. Correspondance inédite du marquis de Sade, de ses proches et de ses familiers, publiée par Paul Bourdin, Paris: Librairie de France, 1926.

149. Lettres et fragments de Lettres. La Vérité sur le marquis de Sade (par Charles Henry). Paris: E. Dentu, 1887, passim.

150. "Le M. . . puni." In HISTORIETTES, CONTES ET FABLIAUX. Preface by Gilbert Lély. Paris: Union générale d'éditions, 1968, pp. 26-31.

151. "Le Mari Prêtre, conte provençal." In HISTORIETTES, CONTES ET FABLIAUX. Preface by Gilbert Lély. Paris: Union générale d'éditions, 1968, pp. 283-293.

152. "Le mariage du siècle." Play. In OEUVRES COMPLETES. Vol. XXXII. Paris: J. J. Pauvert, 1970, pp. 79-111.

153. LA MARQUISE DE GANGE. Paris: Béchet, libraire, quai des Augustins, no. 63, 1813. 2 vol. of XII + 258 and 298 p.

154. LA MARQUISE DE THELEME ou les Effets du libertinage. Viry-Châtillon: S.E.D.I.E.P., 1965.

155. "Mettres et couplets provençaux." In P. Ginisty, UN AMOUR PLATONIQUE DU MARQUIS DE SADE. Paris: Fasquelle, 1901.

156. "Le misanthrope par amour." Play. In OEUVRES COMPLETES. Vol. XXXV. Paris: J. J. Pauvert, 1970, pp. 9-139.

157. "Miss Henriette Stralson, ou les effets du désespoir."
     In LES CRIMES DE L'AMOUR. Vol. II. Paris: Massé, An
     VIII.

158. MON ARRESTATION DU 26 AOUT. Lettre inédite suivie des
     Etrennes philosophiques. Avec un double frontispice
     de Hans Bellmer. Paris: J. Hughes, 1959. 45 p.

159. MONSIEUR LE 6. Lettres inédites publiées et annotées
     par Georges Daumas. Preface by Gilbert Lély. Paris:
     Julliard, 1954, 285 p.

160. MORCEAUX CHOISIS de Donatien-Alphonse-François Sade,
     publiés avec un prologue, une introduction et aide
     mémoire biographique, une bibliographie, treize hors
     texte et deux lettres inédites du marquis. Paris: P.
     Seghers, 1948.

161. Note sur LES MALHEURS DE LA VERTU citations du
     Portefeuille d'un homme de Lettres note sur la Ruse
     d'amour trois Lettres à Laporte, souffleur de la
     Comédie-Française (p. 35). L'OEUVRE DU MARQUIS DE
     SADE de publiée par Guillaume Apollinaire. Paris:
     Bibliothèque des Curieux, 1912.

162. LA NOUVELLE JUSTINE, OU LES MALHEURS DE LA VERTU.
     Ouvrage orné d'un frontispice et de quarante sujets
     gravés avec soin. En Hollande, 1797. 4 vol. of IX +
     347, 351, 351, 356 et 366 p. Suivent 6 volumes dont le
     titre devient JUSTINE OU LES INFORTUNES DE LA VERTU.

163. LA NOUVELLE JUSTINE, OU LES MALHEURS DE LA VERTU.
     Suivie de l'HISTOIRE DU JULIETTE, sa soeur [ou les
     Prospérités du vice]. Ouvrage orné d'un frontispice
     et de cent sujets gravés avec soin. En Hollande,
     1797. 6 vol. of 371, 360, 357, 371, 370, and 352 p.

164. NOUVELLES EXEMPLAIRES. Choix, notices et introduction
     de Gilbert Lély. Paris: Le Club français du livre,
     1958. (Listed by F. Rosart.)

165. "Observations présentées à l'assemblée administrative
     des hôpitaux (28 octobre 1792.)" In OPUSCULES ET
     LETTRES POLITIQUES. Preface by Gilbert Lély. Paris:
     Union générale d'éditions, 1979, pp. 89-92.

166.  OEUVRES COMPLETES.  Paris: Jean-Jacques Pauvert, 1970.

      Contents:  Vol.  I - Les Infortunes de la vertu; Vols.
      II,  III - Justine;  Vols.  IV,  V, VI - Les Crimes de
      L'amour;  Vol. VII.  - Historiette, Contes et Fabliaux,
      Dorci,  Séide;  Vol.  VIII - Dialogue, Oxtiern, Ecrits
      politiques;  Vols.  IX, X, XI, XII - Aline et Valcour;
      Vol.  XIII - Cahiers personnels,  Adelaide; Vol. XIV -
      La marquise de Gange;  Vols.  XV à XVIII - La nouvelle
      Justine; Vols. XIX à XXIV - Histoire de Juliette; Vol.
      XXV - La  philosophie dans le boudoir;  Vols.  XXVI  à
      XXVIII - Les 120 journées de Sodome; Vols. XXIX, XXX -
      Lettres  de Vincennes et de la Bastille;  Vol.  XXXI -
      Histoire secrète d'Isabelle de Bavière;  Vols. XXXII à
      XXXV - Théâtre.

167.  OPUS SADICUM; a philosophical romance for the first time
      translated  from the original French (Holland,  1791)
      with  an engraved  frontispiece.  Paris:  I.  Liseux,
      1889.  (This is a poor translation of JUSTINE.)

168.  OPUSCULES  ET LETTRES POLITIQUES.  Preface de  Gilbert
      Lély.  Paris: Union générale d'éditions, 1979.

169.  OXTIERN  OU LES MALHEURS DU LIBERTINAGE,  drame en trois
      actes et en prose par D.-A.-F.S. Représenté au théâtre
      Molière,  à Paris,  en 1791 et à Versailles, sur celui
      de la Société Dramatique,  le 22 frimaire,  l'an 8 de la
      République.  A Versailles, chez Blaizot, Libraire, rue
      Satory, An VIII.  48 p.

170.  PAGES CURIEUSES, recueillies et préfacées par  Balkis.
      Illustration  de  Maurice  l'Hoir.   Paris:   Les
      Bibliophiles libertins, 1929.

171   PAULINE ET BELVAL, ou les Victimes d'un amour criminel.
      Anecodote récente,  avec Romances et figures.  Par M.
      R** , d'après  les  corrections  faites  par  l'auteur
      d'Aline et Valcour.  A Paris, chez Chambon, libraire,
      rue de Seine-Saint-Germain,  No.  26, 1812. 2 vol. of
      XII + 268 and 270 p.  Deux frontispices par Giraud.
      (Roman  d'un auteur inconnu corrigé par le marquis  de
      Sade.)

172.  Pensée inédite de D.-A.-F. de Sade, publiée par Maurice
      Heine. LE SURREALISME AU SERVICE DE LA REVOLUTION, No.
      3, December 1931.

173. Petites feuilles in{dites de D.-A.-F. de Sade (carton de 4 pages clandestin), publi{es par Maurice Heine. LE SURREALISME AU SERVICE DE LA REVOLUTION, No. 5, November 1933.

174. Pétition de la Section des Piques aux repr{sentants du peuple français. De l'Imprimerie de la Section des Piques, rue S.-Fiacre, No. 2. Signe: <<Sade, rédacteur>>. In fine: <<5$^e$ jour de la III$^e$ décade du 2$^e$ mois de la 2$^e$ année de la République française une et indivisible>>, 17 novembre 1793, 8 p.

175. Pètition de la Section des Piques aux repr{sentants du peuple français. [Signé:] Sade, rédacteur. Ce 5$^e$ jour de la III$^e$ décade du 2$^e$ mois de la 2$^e$ année de la République français, une et indivisible [15 novembre 1793]. De l'Imprimerie de la Section des Piques. 8 pp.

176. "Pétition des Sections de Paris à la Convention nationale (juin 1793.)" [Signé:] Pyron, président de la Commission. Sade, secrétaire. De l'Imprimerie de la Section des Piques. S.d. [juin 1793]. 4 p.

177. "Le Philosophe soi-disant." Play. In OEUVRES COMPLETES. Vol. XXXII. Paris: J. J. Pauvert, 1970, pp. 35-77.

178. LA PHILOSOPHIE DANS LE BOUDOIR. Ouvrage posthume de l'Auteur de Justine. A Londres, aux dépens de la Compagnie, 1795. 2 vol. of 180 and 214 p. Frontispice et quatre gravures érotiques.

179. "Un poème inconnu du marquis de Sade, suivi d'une lettre de Mme de Sade. Textes présentés par Jean Chaumely. In LES LETTRES NOUVELLES, April 1953. (Listed by F. Rosart in OBLIQUES 12-13 [1977], item 46.)

180. LE PORTEFEUILLE DU MARQUIS DE SADE. Edited by Gilbert Lély. Paris: Editions de la Différence, 1977, 280 p.

181. "Le Président mystifié." In HISTORIETTES, CONTES ET FABLIAUX. Preface by Gilbert Lély. Paris: Union générale d'éditions, 1968, pp. 141-244.

182. "Le prévaricateur." Play. In OEUVRES COMPLETES. Vol. XXXV. Paris: J. J. Pauvert, 1970, pp. 251-375.

183.  Projet de pétition des Sections de Paris à la Convention
      Nationale.  De l'Imprimerie de la Section des Piques,
      rue S.-Fiacre, June 1793.  4 p.

184.  "La Prude,  ou la rencontre imprévue."  In HISTORIETTES,
      CONTES ET FABLIAUX.  Preface by Gilbert Lély.  Paris:
      Union générale d'éditions, 1968, pp. 65-75.

185.  Quatre  lettres aux Comédiens français   (pp. xlv-xlviii)
      et Lettre sur Justine (pp. xxix-xxx,  en note).    IDEE
      SUR   LES   ROMANS, publié  par  O.  Uzanne.   Paris:
      Rouveyre, 1878.

186.  REFLEXIONS, NOTES ET PROJETS (1803-1804) publiés sur les
      manuscrits autographes inédits avec un avant-propos et
      des  notes  par  Gilbert Lély et suivis du  projet  de
      Séide et d'un mémoire inédit du docteur L. J. Ramon.

187.  "Le  Revenant."  In HISTORIETTES,   CONTES ET  FABLIAUX.
      Preface  by  Gilbert  Lély.   Paris: Union  générale
      d'éditions, 1968, pp. 34-38.

188.  "Rodrigue, ou la tour enchantée, conte allégorique."  In
      LES CRIMES DE L'AMOUR.  Vol.  III.  Paris:  Massé,  An
      VIII.

189.  "La  Saillie gasconne."  In HISTORIETTES,   CONTES   ET
      FABLIAUX.   Preface  by Gilbert  Lély.   Paris:  Union
      générale d'éditions, 1968, pp. 20-21.

190.  SARA ou la dernière aventure d'un homme de quarante-cinq
      ans.   Préface de Maurice Blanchot.   Paris:  Delamain
      et Boutellenu, n.d., XIVV + 205 p.

191.  "La  Section  des  Piques.   Extrait des  Régistres  des
      délibérations de l'Assemblée générale et permanente de
      la Section des Piques.  Du 12 juillet 1793, l'an II de
      la République françoise,  une et indivisible. [Signé:]
      Pyron,  président.  Girard,  vice-président.  Artaud,
      Sade,  Clavier,  secrétaries.   De l'Imprimerie de  la
      Section des Piques.  8 p.

192.  "La Section des Piques.  Idée sur le mode de la sanction
      des  Loix;  par  un  citoyen de  cette  Section.   De
      l'Imprimerie de la rue Saint-Fiacre, No. 2, 2 November
      1792.  16 p.

193. "La Section des Piques à l'Assemblée administrative des hôpitaux. 28 October 1792. [Signé:] Sade, rédacteur. Guzman, président. Ternois, secrétaire. De l'Imprimerie de la Section des Piques, rue Saint-Fiacre, No. 2. 4 p.

194. "La Section des Piques à ses Frères et Amis de la Société de la Liberté et de l'Egalité, à Saintes, département de la Charente-Inférieure. Paris, le 19 juillet 1793, l'an II de la République françoise, une et indivisible. [Signé:] Pyron, président. Girard, vice-président. Artaud, Sade, Clavier, secrétaires. De l'Imprimerie de la Section des Piques [etc.]. 4 p.

195. "Séide." Conte moral et philosophique (Projet), publié par Gilbert Lély. LE MERCURE DE FRANCE, No. 1070, October 1952.

196. "Le Serpent." In HISTORIETTES, CONTES ET FABLIAUX. Paris: Union générale d'éditions, 1968, pp. 17-19.

197. "Soit fait ainsi qu'il est requis." In HISTORIETTES, CONTES ET FABLIAUX. Preface by Gilbert Lély. Paris: Union générale d'éditions, 1968, pp. 137-140.

198. Le Suborneur (1972). Play attributed to Sade by Lemonnyer, item 26. Vol. III, p. 1154.

199. Sujet de <<Zélonide>>, comédie en cinq actes et en vers, publié par Maurice Heine. LE MINOTAURE, No. 1, February 1933.

200. "Le Talion." In HISTORIETTES, CONTES ET FABLIAUX. Preface by Gilbert Lély. Paris: Union générale d'éditions, 1968, pp. 245-251.

201. "Tancrède." Play. In OEUVRES COMPLETES. Vol. XXXIII. Paris: J. J. Pauvert, 1970, pp. 161-201.

202. LE TARTUFFE LIBERTIN OU LE TRIOMPHE DU VICE. A Cythère, chez les gardiens du temple. (Attributed to Sade by Gay, item 18 and listed by F. Rosart in OBLIQUES 12-13 [1977], item 46.)

203. "Testament." In J. Janin. LE LIVRE, ONZIEME JOURNEE. Paris: Plon, 1870. (Listed by F. Rosart in OBLIQUES 12-13 [1977].)

204.  "La tour enchantée." Play. In OEUVRES COMPLETES.
      Vol. XXXIV. Paris: J. J. Pauvert, 1970, pp. 9-97.

205.  "Trente-huit lettres ou textes divers." VIE DU MARQUIS
      DE SADE, par Gilbert Lély, Paris: Librairie
      Gallimard, 1952.

206.  "L'union des arts." Play. In OEUVRES COMPLETES.
      Vol. XXXIV. Paris: J. J. Pauvert, 1970, pp. 99-313.

207.  VALMOR ET LYDIA ou Voyage autour du monde de deux amants
      qui se cherchaient. Paris: Pigoreau et Leroux, an
      VII.

208.  LA VANILLE ET LA MANILLE, lettre inédite à Madame de
      Sade écrite au donjon de Vincennes en 1783. Cinq
      eaux-fortes originales de Jacques Hérold. [Paris]:
      Collection Drosera, 1950.

209.  LA VERITE, publié du manuscrit autographe par Gilbert
      Lély. Paris: J. J. Pauvert, 1961.

210.  "Vers pour le buste de Marat." In OPUSCULES ET LETTRES
      POLITIQUES. Preface by Gilbert Lély. Paris: Union
      générale d'éditions, 1979, pp. 128-129.

211.  ZOLOE ET SES DEUX ACOLYTES ou Quelques décades de la vie
      de trois jolies femmes, Histoire véritable du siècle
      dernier, par un contemporain. A Turin. Se trouve à
      Paris chez tous les marchands de nouveautés. De
      l'Imprimerie de l'auteur, messidor an VIII. XII +
      142 p. Frontispice gravé par Lepagelet.

   B.  ALPHABETICAL LISTING OF UNPUBLISHED MANUSCRIPTS
       DESTROYED OR LOST BUT MENTIONED IN THE CATALOGUE
       RAISONNE OF 1788, IN THE REFLEXIONS, NOTES ET PROJETS,
       OR CONFISCATED ON THE 15 VENTOSE, AN IX (6 MARCH
       1801).

212.  ADELAIDE DE MIRAMAN OU LE FANTASME PROTESTANT,
      historiette.

213.  L'ANE SACRISTAIN ou le nouveau Salomon.

214.  LES APPARENCES TROMPEUSES, Conte.

215.  Omitted.

216. LE BOCCACE FRANCAIS. (Mentioned by G. Lély in Preface to CAHIERS PERSONNELS, item 67.)

217. LE BOUDOIR, comédie reçue au théâtre Favart en 1791. (Manuscript first mentioned in the BIOGRAPHIE UNIVERSELLE DE MICHAUD. Listed by G. Lély, item 25.)

218. CAHIERS de notes, pensées extraites, chansons et mélanges de vers et de prose.

219. MES CAPRICES, ou un peu de tout, ouvrage politique.

220. LE CAPRICIEUX ou l'Homme inégal, comédie en cinq actes et en vers (titres primitifs: Le Métamiste, puis L'Inconstant.) Mentioned in the CATALOGUE RAISONNE OF 1788. Listed by G. Lély, item 25.

221. Catalogue raisonné des oeuvres de M. de S*** à l'époque du 1er octobre 1788. Manuscript belonging to the Marquis Xavier de Sade. (Listed by G. Lély, item 25.)

222. CLEONTINE OU LA FILLE MALHEUREUSE, drame en trois actes. (Manuscript first mentioned in the BIOGRAPHIE UNIVERSELLE DE MICHAUD. Listed by G. Lély, item 25.)

223. CONFESSIONS. Portrait en frontispice. (Mentioned by G. Lély in the Preface to CAHIERS PERSONNELS, item 67.)

224. CONRAD OU LA JALOUX EN DELIRE. Tiré de l'histoire des Albigeois. (Mentioned by G. Lély in the Preface to CAHIERS PERSONNELS, item 67.)

225. "Les Conversations du château de Charmelle." (First draft for LES JOURNEES DE FLORBELLE.)

226. LA CRUAUTE FRATERNELLE.

227. LE CURE DE PRATO, tale.

228. LES DELASSEMENTS DU LIBERTIN OU LA NEUVAINE DE CYTHERE.

229. Devis raisonné sur le projet d'un spectacle de gladiateurs. (Manuscript first mentioned in the BIOGRAPHIE UNIVERSELLE DE MICHAUD. Listed by G. Lély, item 25.)

230. DISSERTATIONS HISTORIQUES, OITIQUES, CRITIQUES ET PHILOSOPHIQUES SUR LES VILLES DE FLORENCE, ROME, NAPLES ET LEURS ENVIRONS (notes préparatoires). (Manuscripts belonging to the Marquis Xavier de Sade.)

231. LA DOUBLE INTRIGUE, comedy in prose. (Attributed to Sade by J. Lemonnyer, Vol. II, p. 36, who reports that M. de Soleinne had in his possession the manuscript of this 95-p. play, No. 3078 of his catalog.)

232. "L'ECOLE DES JALOUX OU LA FOLLE EPREUVE. (One-act play.) (Mentioned in Sade's CATALOGUE RAISONNE OF 1788. Listed by G. Lély, item 25.)

233. L'EGAREMENT DE L'INFORTUNE, drame (en trois actes) et en prose.

234. L'EPREUVE, comédie en un acte et en vers, saisie en 1782 par le lieutenant de police Le Noir. (Manuscript first mentioned in the BIOGRAPHIE UNIVERSELLE DE MICHAUD. Listed by G. Lél, item 25.)

235. FANTOMES. (Listed by G. Lély as a possible introduction to the REFUTATION DE FENELON.)

236. LA FILLE MALHEUREUSE, one-act play.

237. LA FINE MOUCHE, tale.

238. LA FORCE DU SANG, tale.

239. FRAGMENTS LITTERAIRES ET HISTORIQUES. Manuscript located in the Bibliothèque de l'Arsenal (Archives de la Bastille, No. 12456). (Listed by G. Lély, item 25.)

240. L'HEUREUX ECHANGE, tale.

241. L'HOMME DANGEREUX OU LE SUBORNEUR, comédie en 1 acte et en verse de dix syllabes. (Performed at the Théâtre Farvar in 1790. Listed by Dr. Jacobus X, item 1278.)

242. L'HONNETE IVROGNE, historiette.

243. LES INCONVENIENTS DE LA PITIE.

244. JEANNE LAISNE ou le Siège de Beauvais, tragédie en cinq actes et en vers.

245. JOURNAL (Détention de l'auteur à Vincennes, à la Bastille et à Charenton, 1777-1790.) Treize cahiers, dont une partie rédigée en chiffres. (Manuscript first mentioned in the BIOGRAPHIE UNIVERSELLE DE MICHAUD. Listed by G. Lély, item 25.)

246. LES JOURNEES DE FLORBELLE, ou la Nature d{voil{e, suivies des Mémoires de l'abbè de Modose et des Aventures d'Emilie de Volange servant de preuves aux assertions, ouvrage orné de deux cents gravures. Ce roman, qui devait former la matiére de dix tomes, fut achevé par Sade le 25 avril 1807. Son titre primitif {tait: Valrose ou les Egarements (variante: Les Ecarts du Libertinage). (Manuscript first mentioned in the BIOGRAPHIE UNIVERSELLE DE MICHAUD. Listed by G. Lély.)

247. JULIA, ou le mariage sans femme. Vaudeville, one act. Attributed to the Marquis de Sade by M. P. Lacroix. (Listed in Lemonnyer, item 26, Vol. II, p. 746.)

248. LES JUMELLES OU LE CHOIX DIFFICILE, comédie en deux actes et en vers.

249. LA JUSTICE VENITIENNE, historiette.

250. LIBER SADICUS. Listed by J. Lemonnyer, item 26, Vol. II, p. 734.

251. LA LISTE DU SUISSE, historiette.

252. MADAME DE THELEME (second version).

253. MARCEL OU LE CORDELIER. (Mentioned by G. L{ly in Preface to CAHIERS PERSONNELS, item 67.)

254. LA MARQUISE DE THELEME, conte.

255. MES CONFESSIONS.

256. LA MESSE TROP CHERE, historiette.

257. LA NATURE DEVOILEE, cent quatre-vingts cahiers. (Mentioned by G. L{ly in Preface to CAHIERS PERSONNELS, item 67.)

258.  NOTE RELATIVE A MA DETENTION.    (Mentioned by G. Lély in
      Preface  to CAHIERS PERSONNELS.)  (Listed by G.  Lély,
      item 67.)

259.  NOTES LITTERAIRES.

260.  "NOTES  pour  la  rédaction du roman  LES  JOURNEES  DES
      FLORBELLE,  etc."   Manuscrit  dont  il  existe  une
      reproduction   photographique   à   la   Bibliothèque
      Nationale  (fonds Maurice Heine).   Exact location  of
      the original unknown.

261.  N'Y ALLEZ JAMAIS SANS LUMIERE, historiette.

262.  OEUVRES DIVERSES (1764-1769).   Lettres galantes; lettres
      diverses couplets; Le Philosophe soidisant, comédie en
      un  acte;   Voyage  de  Hollande,  etc.    Manuscripts
      belonging to the marquis Xavier de Sade.    (Listed  by
      G. Lély, item 25.)

263.  PLAN D'UN ROMAN PAR LETTRES.    (Mentioned by G.  Lély in
      preface to CAHIERS PERSONNELS, item 67.)

264.  LE PORTEFEUILLE  D'UN  HOMME  DE  LETTRES,  formant  la
      matière de quatre volumes.  Il subsiste de ce recueil,
      outre  neuf  contes  publiés  par  Maurice  Heine
      (Historiettes,  Contes  et  Fabliaux),  le  Voyage  de
      Hollande  (Section V,  No.  58) et differents  petits
      texts.

265.  Projet de création de lieux de prostitution,  organisés,
      entretenus et dirigés par l'Etat.

266.  REFUTATION DE FENELON.    (Mentioned in CATALOGUE GENERAL
      of 1803-1804.)

267.  Les Reliques, tale.

268.  LA RUSE DE L'AMOUR,ou Les six spectables, comédie formée
      de 5 épisodes:   Euphéie de Melun ou le siège d'Alger.
      Le Suborneur.   La fille malheureuse.   Azelis ou  la
      Coquette  punie.   La  Tour  enchantée.   Le  Ballet
      pantomine. (Listed by A. Laborde, item 22).

269.  TANCREDE,   scène  lyrique  (en  un  acte  et)  en  vers
      alexandrins (mêlé de musique).

270.  LA TOUR MYSTERIEUSE,  opéra-comique en un acte.  (Listed
      by G. Lély, item 25.)

271.  Travail destiné au Conseil général de la Commune de
      Paris  et relatif au changement des noms de  certaines
      rues.  (Archives nationales Fond 4775.)

272.  LE TROUBADOUR PROVENCAL.    (Mentioned by Jean Desbordes
      in LE VRAI VISAGE DU MARQUIS DE SADE, item 688.)

273.  VALROSE  OU  LES  EGAREMENTS.    See  LES  JOURNEES  DE
      FLORBELLE.

C. LISTING OF PUBLISHED WORKS BY TOPICS

## 1. COLLECTED EDITIONS

274. L'OEUVRE DU MARQUIS DE SADE: ZOLOE, JUSTINE, JULIETTE, LA PHILOSOPHIE DANS LE BOUDOIR, OXTIERN ou LES MALHEURS DU LIBERTINAGE. Pages choisies. . . . Introduction, essai bibliographique et notes par Guillaume Apollinaire. Paris: Bibliothèque des curieux, 1909. 259 p.

275. OEUVRE DU MARQUIS DE SADE. Pages choisies contenant des morceaux inédits et des lettres publiées pour la première fois, tirées des archives de la Comédie française; introduction, bibliographique et notes par Guillaume Apollinaire. Paris: Bibliothèque des curieux, 1912.

276. OEUVRES CHOISES ET PAGES MAGISTRALES du Marquis de Sade, publiées, commentées et annotées, par Maurice Heine. Paris: Editions du Trianon, 1933. 254 p.

277. OEUVRES COMPLETES. Sceaux: J. J. Pauvert, 1948.

278. MORCEAUX CHOISIS de Donatien-Alphonse-François Sade, publiés avec un prologue, une introduction et aide-mémoire biographique, une bibliographie, trois hors-texte et deux lettres inédites du marquis. Paris: P. Seghers, 1948.

279. OEUVRES. Introduction de Jean-Jacques Pauvert. JUSTINE OU LES MALHEURS DE LA VERTU. DIALOGUE ENTRE UN PRETRE ET UN MORIBOND. EUGENIE DE FRANVAL. IDEE SUR LES ROMANS. L'AUTEUR DES CRIMES DE L'AMOUR A VILLETERQUE, folliculaire. Suivis d'un ESSAI SUR SADE, par Pierre Klossowski. Illustré par Giani Esposito. Paris: Club français du livre, 1960. 739 p.

280. OEUVRES. Introduction by Jean-Jacques Pauvert. Illustration by Giani Esposito. Paris: Club français du livre, 1961.

281. OEUVRES COMPLETES DU MARQUIS DE SADE, Edition definitive. Paris: Cercle du livre précieux, 1962.

1. Gilbert Lély. VIE DU MARQUIS DE SADE avec un examen de ses ouvrages. Nouvelle édition. Postface d'Yves Bonnefoy. Vol. 1, 1962. 661 p.

2.  Gilbert Lély.   VIE DU MARQUIS DE SADE,   avec  un
examen  de ses ouvrages.    Nouvelle édition.   Postface
d'Yves Bonnefoy.  Vol. 2, 1962.   699 p.

3.  JUSTINE  OU LES MALHEURS DE LA VERTU.   Préface du
Dr. A. (Ange-Louis-Marie) Hesnard et de Maurice Heine.
Suivi de LA PHILOSOPHIE DANS LE BOUDOIR.   Préface  de
Pierre Klossowski.  1963.   563 p.

4.  ALINE  ET  VALCOUR  OU  LE  ROMAN   PHILOSOPHIQUE.
Préface de Jean Fabre.   Vol. 1, 1962.   XXXII + 383 p.

5.  ALINE ET VALCOUR OU LE ROMAN PHILOSOPHIQUE.    Vol.
2, 1962.  449 p.

6-7.  LA NOUVELLE JUSTINE OU LES MALHEURS DE LA VERTU,
suivie  de L'HISTOIRE DE JULIETTE,  SA SOEUR,   OU  LES
PROSPERITES DU VICE. 1963. 2 vol. 479, 465 p.

8-9.  HISTOIRE DE JULIETTE. 2 vol. 583, 609 p.

10.  LES  CRIMES  DE L'AMOUR,  NOUVELLES HEROIQUES  ET
TRAGIQUES, suivies de L'AUTEUR DES CRIMES DE L'AMOUR A
VILLETERQUE,  folliculaire.   Préfaces de Jean Fabre et
de Pierre Klossowski.   1964.   LXII + 529 p.

11.  LA  MARQUISE DE GANGE.   Précédée  des  OPUSCULES
POLITIQUES   et   d'OXTIERN   ou   LES   MALHEURS   DU
LIBERTINAGE.   Préfaces de Pierre Naville,  de Camille
Schuwer et de Gaëtan Picon. 1964.   433 p.

12.  CORRESPONDANCE,  1759-1814.   Préface et postface
de Gilbert Lély.  1964.   657 p.

13.  LES   120  JOURNEES  DE  SODOME  OU  L'ECOLE   DU
LIBERTINAGE.   Préface de Maurice Heine, de A. Hesnard,
de Henri Pastoureau et de  Pierre  Klossowski.   1964.
LXXVIII + 447 p.

14.  OPUSCULES.  HISTORIETTES, CONTES ET FABLIAUX. LES
INFORTUNES DE LA VERTU.   Préfaces de Maurice Heine et
d'Antoine Adam. 1963.   475 p.

15.  HISTOIRE  SECRETE D'ISABELLE DE BAVIERE REINE  DE
FRANCE, précédée des NOTES LITTERAIRES, des Notes pour
les  JOURNEES DE FLORBELLE et d'ADELAIDE DE BRUNSWICK,
princesse de Saxe.   Notes sur M.  de Sade, par le Dr.

L.-J.   Ramon.    Postface  de  Jean-Jacques  Brochier.
1964.   537 p.

282.  OEUVRES COMPLETES.    Paris:   Edition J. J. Pauvert 1962-
      1970.   35 vol.

283.  OEUVRES COMPLETES.   Geneva:   Slatkine, 1966-1968.

284.  OEUVRES    DIVERSES.     Deux  lettres  à  Martin  Quiros.
      ETRENNES PHILOSOPHIQUES.    DIALOGUE ENTRE UN PRETRE ET
      UN MORIBOND.    LES INFORTUNES DE LA VERTU.    LA VERITE
      FAXELANGE.    AUGUSTINE DE VILLEBLANCHE.    FLORVILLE ET
      COURVAL.    EUGENIE DE FRANVAL.    Introduction et notice
      biographique de Gilbert Lély. Paris:   le Club français
      du livre, 1967.   489 p.


TRANSLATION:  DANISH

285.  MARKIS DE SADE ANTOLOGI.    Translated by Albert  Larsen.
      Kobe Thaningand Appel, 1966.


TRANSLATION:  DUTCH

286.  EEN SELECTIE,   et Beauvoir (Simone de):   Moeten Wij Sade
      Verbrand?   Translated  by C.  Verman and Jenny  Tuin.
      Amsterdam: Van Ditmar, 1963-1964.

287.  SADE-VITSPRAKEN.    Translated by F.-J.   Schmidt and A.C.
      Wiemeyer.   Gravenhage: Boucher, 1965.


TRANSLATION:  ENGLISH

288.  SELECTED  WRITINGS.    Selected and translated by Leonard
      de Saint-Yves.   London:   P. Owen, 1953.

289.  SELECTIONS FROM WRITINGS.   Chosen and translated by Paul
      Dinnage.    In  "The  Marquis  de  Sade,"  an  essay  by
      Simone  de Beauvoir translated by  Annette  Michelson.
      New York: Grove Press, 1953.

290.  SELECTED  WRITINGS.    Selected and translated by Léonard
      Saint-Yves.   New York: British Book Center, 1954.

291.  SELECTED  WRITINGS.   Selected and translated by Leonard
      de Saint-Yves.  New York:  Castle Books, c1954.

292.  DE SADE  QUARTET.   Translated  by  Margaret  Crosland.
      London: Owen, 1963.

293.  SELECTED WRITINGS.   Selected and translated by Margaret
      Crosland.  Revised edition, London:  P. Owen, 1964.

294.  THE  COMPLETE JUSTINE,  PHILOSOPHY IN THE  BEDROOM,  and
      other  writings.   Compiled and translated by  Richard
      Seaver  & Austryn Wainhouse.   With  introductions  by
      Jean  Paulhan & Maurice Blanchot.   New  York:   Grove
      Press, 1965.

295.  THE  COMPLETE MARQUIS DE  SADE.   Edited, adapted, and
      translated  from  the original French text by Paul  J.
      Gillette.   With an introduction by John S. Yankowski.
      Los Angeles:  Holloway House Pub. Co., 1966.

296.  THE 120 DAYS OF SODOM, AND OTHER WRITINGS.  Compiled and
      translated  by  Austryn Wainhouse and Richard  Seaver.
      With  introductions  by Simone de  Beauvoir &  Pierre
      Klossowski.  New York:  Grove Press, 1966.


TRANSLATION:  GERMAN

297.  AUSGEWAHLTE WERKE.  Hamburg:  Merlin, 1962-1965.

298.  AUSGEWAHLTE WERKE, übers, mit Dokumentation und Nachwort
      von Gerd Henniger.  Basel:  K. Desch, 1965.

299.  WERKE.   Translated  by Gerd Henninger.   Basel: DESCH,
      1965.

300.  LE MARQUIS DE SADE, SELBSTZEUGNISSEN UND BILDDOKUMENTEN.
      Dargestellt von Walter Lennig.   Reinbek bei  Hamburg:
      Rowohlt  Taschenbuch Verlag (Rowohlt  Monographien,
      108), 1967.

301.  DIE  120  TAGE VON SODOM.   DIE PHILOSOPHIE IN  BOUDOIR.
      JUSTINE.   DIE GESCHICHTE DER  JULIETTE.   Vol.  I.
      Stuttgart: Dt. Bücherbund, 1973.

302.  DIE  NEUEN  JUSTINE ODER DAS UNGLUCK DER  TUGEND.    III
      Notizen  sur  Neuen  Justine.   Aline  und  Valcour.

Verbrechen dee Liebe, etc. Vol. II. Stuttgart: Dt.
Bücherbund, 1976.

303. VERBRECHEN DER LIEBE UND ANDERE WERKE. Zurich: Neue
Schweizer Bibliotek, 1976.


TRANSLATION: ITALIAN

304. OPERE. Translated by Elemire Zolla, Gianna Manzini et
al. Milano: Lon-Ganesi, 1961.

305. OPERE SCELTE. Edited and with an introduction by Gian
Piero Brega. Translated by Pino Bava. Milano:
Feltrinelli, 1962.

306. OPERE SCELTE. Translated by Pino Bava. I. ETRENNES
PHILOSOPHIQUES. II. DIALOGUE ENTRE UN PRETRE ET UN
MORIBOND. III. LES 120 JOURNEES DE SODOME. IV.
ALINE ET VALCOUR. V. LA PHILOSOPHIE DANS LE BOUDOIR.
VI. HISTOIRE DE JULIETTE. VII. JUSTINE. VIII. LES
CRIMES DE L'AMOUR. Milano: Feltrinelli, 1967.


TRANSLATION: JAPANESE

307. HISAN MONOGATARI. Translated by Tatsuhiko Shibusawa.
Tokyo: Gendai Schichó-Sha, 1976.


TRANSLATION: SPANISH

308. TEXTOS ESCOGIDOS Y PRECEDIDOS PAR UN ENSAYO. "El
libertino y la revolución," por Jorge Gaitán Durán.
Bogotá: Ediciones Mito, 1960.


TRANSLATION: SWEDISH

309. MARKIS DE SADE. Translated by Lars Bjurman. Stockholm:
Prisma-Solnaseelig, 1969.


TRANSLATION: TURKISH

310. SADE. Türköe Kilavuzu. Ankara: Turk Tarik Kumuru
Basimevi, 1960.

## 2.  ALINE ET VALCOUR

311.  ALINE ET VALCOUR,  OU LE ROMAN PHILOSOPHIQUE.  Ecrit à la
      Bastille,  un an avant la Révolution de France.  Paris:
      V. Girouard, 1795.

312.  ALINE ET VALCOUR,  OU LE ROMAN PHILOSOPHIQUE; écrit à la
      Bastille,   un  an  avant  la  révolution  de  France.
      Bruxelles:  J.J. Gay, 1883.

313.  ALINE ET VALCOUR, OU LE ROMAN PHILOSOPHIQUE.  Preface by
      Pierre Klossowski.  Paris:  Jean-Jacques Pauvert, 1956.

314.  ALINE ET VALCOUR;  OU,  LE ROMAN PHILOSOPHIQUE.  Ecrit à
      la Bastille un an avant la Révolution de France.
      Paris:  J. J. Pauvert, 1956.

315.  ALINE ET VALCOUR.  Preface by Béatrice Didier,  Paris:
      Livre de poche, 1976.

TRANSLATION:  ENGLISH

316.  ALINE ET VALCOUR.   New York:  Lenchet European, 1976,
      480 p.

TRANSLATION:  GERMAN

317.  IN NAMEN DER REPUBLIK (Flugschrift).   Translated by
      Joachim Klünner.  Wiesbaden: Limes Verlag, 1961.

318.  ALINE  UND  VALCOUR oder  der  Philosophische  Roman.
      Translated by Hannelore Wichmann.  Hamburg:  Merlin
      Verlag, 1963.

TRANSLATION:  ITALIAN

319.  ALINE  ET  VALCOUR  OVVERO  IL  ROMANZO  FILOSOFICO.
      Translated by Aurelio Valesi.  Milano: Sugar, 1969.

TRANSLATION:  JAPANESE

320.  SHOKUJIN-KOKU  RYOKO-KI.  Translated  by  Tatsuhiko
      Shibusawa.  Tokyo: Chogen-Sha, 1963.

TRANSLATION:  SPANISH

321.  HISTORIA  DE ALINE Y VALCOUR.  Translated  by  Fernando
      Montes.  Madrid: Fundunucontos, 1976.

### 3.  CAHIERS PERSONNELS

322.  CAHIERS  PERSONNELS (1803-1804) publiés pour la première
      fois  sur les manuscrits autographes inédits avec  une
      préf.  et des notes par Gilbert Lély.  Paris:  Corrèa
      1953.  128 p.

323.  CAHIERS PERSONNELS et Notes sur Monsieur de Sade (par le
      Dr. L.-J.  Ramon).  Préface de Gilbert Lély.  Notes
      pour  les  "Journées  de  Florbelle."  Adélaïde  de
      Brunswick.  Paris:  J.-J.  Pauvert, 1966.  XVIII +
      403 p.

### 4.  CENT VINGT JOURNEES

324.  LES  120  JOURNEES DE SODOME OU L'ECOLE DU  LIBERTINAGE,
      Publié  pour  la première fois d'après  le  manuscrit
      original  avec  des annotations scientifiques  par  le
      Docteur Eugen Duhren.  Paris:  Club des Bibliophiles,
      1904.

325.  LES 120, i.e., CENT VINGT JOURNEES DE SODOME; ou l'Ecole
      du libertinage.  Ed.  critique,  établie  sur  le
      manuscrit  original  autographe par Maurice Heine.
      Paris:  S. & dépens  des bibliophiles  souscripteurs,
      1931-1935.

326.  LES,  120 i.e. CENT VINGT JOURNEES DE SODOME. Bruxelles:
      n.p., 1947-1948.

327.  LES,  120  i.e.,  CENT  VINGT JOURNEES  DE  SODOME;  ou,
      L'ECOLE DU LIBERTINAGE.  Paris:  J.-J. Pauvert, 1953.

328.  LES 120, i.e., CENT VINGT JOURNEES DE SODOME, OU L'ECOLE
      DU LIBERTINAGE.  Préface de Maurice Heine.  Paris:
      Cercle du livre précieux, 1964.

TRANSLATION:  DUTCH

329.  DE 120 DAGEN VAN SODOM.     Translated by Claude C.
      Krijgelmans. Antwerpen: W. Soethoudt, 1968.

330.  DE 120 DAGEN VAN SODOM OF DE SCHOOL DER LASBANDIGHEID,
      Translated by Hans Warren.  Gravenhage:  Daamen, 1969.

331.  DE 120 DAGEN VAN SODOM of De school der losbandigheid.
      Translated by Hans Warren. Amsterdam:  Bakker, 1977.


TRANSLATION:  ENGLISH

332.  THE 120 DAYS OF SODOM; or, The romance of the school for
      libertinage.   Being an English rendering done by
      Pieralessandro Casavini, with an essay by Georges
      Bataille.  Paris:  Olympia Press, 1954.

333.  THE 120 DAYS OF SODOM,  or the Romance of the school for
      libertinage.   Translated by Pieralessandro Casavini,
      with an essay by Georges  Bataille.   Paris:  Olympia
      Press, 1954.

334.  THE  120 DAYS OF SODOM or the Romance of the school for
      libertinage, translated together with a prefatory
      essay by Georges Bataille and Pieralessandro Casavini.
      Paris: Olympia Press, 1957.

335.  THE 120 DAYS OF SODOM; or, The romance of the school for
      libertinage; being an English rendering of Les 120
      journées de Sodome done by P. Casavini, with an essay
      by G. Bataille. Paris:  Olympia Press, 1957.

336.  THE  120 DAYS OF SODOM.    Sade, Donatien Alphonse
      François, comte, called Marquis de, 1740-1814. New
      York: Grove Press, 1966.

337.  THE 120 DAYS OF SODOM.  N. Hollywood: Brandon, 1967.


TRANSLATION:  JAPANESE

338.  SODOME  NO  HYAKUNIJU-NICHI traduit en japonais par
      Masafumi Óba.  Tokyo: Shinryu-Sha, 1962.

339.  SODOM  NO  HYAKU HATSUKA,  Translated by  Masafumi  Obâ.
      Tokyo:  Shinryu-Sha, 1965.

340.  SODOM  HAYAKU  NIJUNICHI-HISAN  MONOGATARI.      Zoloé  to
      Fujari  no  Jijo,  Translated by Tatsuhiko  Shibusawa.
      Tokyo: Togen-Sha, 1966.

341.  SODOME  120 NICHI.    Translated by Tatsuhiko  Shibusawa.
      Tokyo: Kadokawa Shoten, 1976.


                      5.  CORRESPONDANCE


342.  DOCUMENTS ET LETTRES à propos de la vente du château  de
      Lacoste  en  1796:  L.  Peise Rovère et le marquis  de
      Sade . . . Largentière,  Impr.  de Mazel et  Plancher,
      1915.   In REVUE HISTORIQUE DE LA REVOLUTION FRANCAISE
      ET DE L'EMPIRE, July-September, 1914.

343.  CORRESPONDANCE  INEDITE DU M^{is}  DE SADE,  de ses proches
      et  de ses familiers,  publiée avec une  introduction,
      des annales et des notes,  par Paul  Bourdin.     Paris:
      Librairie de France, 1929.

344.  LE CARILLON DE VINCENNES; lettres inédites publiées avec
      des notes par Gilbert Lély.    Ed.  originale.    Paris:
      Arcanes, 1953.

345.  MONSIEUR LE 6; LETTRES INEDITES (1778-1784) annotées par
      Georges Daumas.  Avant-propos Lély.  Paris:  Julliard,
      1954.

346.  MARQUIS DE SADE.  LETTRES CHOISIES.   Préfaces de Gilbert
      Lély.  Paris: J.-J. Pauvert, 1963.  272 p.

347.  CORRESPONDANCE, 1759-1814.  Préf. et postface de Gilbert
      Lély.  Paris: Cercle du livre précieux, 1964.

348.  LETTRES AUX FEMMES.   Paris: Tchou (impr.  Blanchard),
      1965.  191 p.

349.  LETTRES AUX FEMMES PAR SADE.  Paris: Tchou, 1965.

350.  LETTRES  ECRITES  DE VINCENNES ET DE LA  BASTILLE. . . .
      Préface d'Antoine Adam.  Paris:  J.-J. Pauvert, 1966.
      2 vol. XXII + 287, 303 p.

351. LETTRES CHOISIES DU MARQUIS DE SADE. Préface de Gilbert
     Lély. Paris: Union générale d'éditions, 1969.
     191 p.

352. CORRESPONDANCE inédite du marquis de Sade de ses proches
     et de ses familiers, publiée avec une introduction et
     des annale notes, par Paul Bourdin. Genève:
     Reprints, 1971. 450 p.


TRANSLATION: ENGLISH

353. SELECTED LETTERS by the Marquis de Sade. Preface by
     Gilbert Lély. Translated by W. J. Strachan. Edited
     by Margaret Crosland. New York: October House, 1966,
     c1965.

354. SELECTED LETTERS. Preface by Gilbert Lély. Translated
     by W. J. Strachan. Edited by Margaret Crosland.
     London: P. Owen, 1965.


TRANSLATION: GERMAN

355. BRIEFE. Translated by Hilda von Born-Pilsach.
     Düsseldorf: Ranch, 1962.

356. BRIEFE. Ausgewählt und mit einem Vorwort hrsg. von
     Gilbert Lely. Aus dem Französischen übertragen von
     Hilda von Born-Pilsach. Frankfurt am Main: Fischer,
     1965.


TRANSLATION: SPANISH

357. CORRESPONDENCIA. Translated by Meneme Gras. Barcelona:
     Anagrama, 1975.


6. LES CRIMES DE L'AMOUR

358. LES CRIMES DE L'AMOUR, Nouvelles heroiques precedes
     d'UNE IDEE SUR LES ROMANS, et gravures. Par D.A.F.
     Sade Paris: Massé, 1800.

359. LES CRIMES DE L'AMOUR. [Juliette et Raunai, ou la
     Conspiration d'Amboise.] Précédé d'un Avant-propos
     [Avis aux éditeurs, signé: G.D.], suivi des Idées sur

les romans, de l'Auteur des Crimes de l'amour à
Villeterque, d'une Notice bio-bibliographique du M$^{is}$
de Sade . . . et du Discours prononcé par le M$^{is}$ de
Sade à la Section des piques. Bruxelles: Gay et
Doucé, 1881.

360.   LES CRIMED DE L'AMOUR. 2 vol. Sceaux: Editions du
       Palmugre, 1948. Listed in E. Pierre Chanover, item
       11.

361.   LES CRIMES DE L'AMOUR et HISTORIETTES, CONTES ET
       FABLIAUX. Saint-Amand (Cher): Sagittaire, 1950.

362.   LES CRIMES DE L'AMOUR: IDEE SUR LES ROMANS, FAXELANGE
       EUGENIE DE FRANVAL, DORGEVILLE, A VILLETERQUE,
       folliculaire, précédé d'une note bibliographique.
       Paris: J. J. Pauvert, 1952.

363.   LES CRIMES DE L'AMOUR. Paris: J. J. Pauvert, 1955.

364.   LES CRIMES DE L'AMOUR. Introduction de Gilbert Lély.
       Paris: J. J. Pauvert, 1961. 3 vol. XXIV + 319, 352,
       233 p.

365.   LES CRIMES DE L'AMOUR, nouvelles héroïques et tragiques,
       suivies de L'AUTEUR DES CRIMES DE L'AMOUR A
       VILLETERQUE, folliculaire. Paris: Cercle du livre
       précieux, 1964.

366.   LES CRIMES DE L'AMOUR, EUGENIE DE FRANVAL.
       Lithographies originales de Xavier Saint-Justh.
       Paris: 1966. 138 p.

367.   LES CRIMES DE L'AMOUR. Paris: Editions Baudelaire,
       1967, VIII + 552 p.

368.   LES CRIMES DE L'AMOUR. Viry-Chatillon: S.E.D.I.E.P.
       1969. 221 p.

369.   LES CRIMES DE L'AMOUR. Paris-Londres-New York: Sambel;
       Paris: Editions Bel Air, 1969.


TRANSLATION: ENGLISH

370.   THE CRIMES OF LOVE; three novellas. Translated by
       Lowell Blair. With an introduction by Aldous Huxley.
       New York: Bantam Books, 1964.

371. CRIMES OF PASSION. Edited and translated by Wad Baskin. New York: Castle Books, 1965.

372. THE CRIMES OF LOVE. Three novellas, translated by Lowell Blair. New York: Bantam Books, 1967.

TRANSLATION: GERMAN

373. VERBRECHEN DER LIEBE. Translated by Christian Barth. München: Kindler, 1964.

374. VERBRECHER DER LIEBE und andere Werke. Zürich: Neue Schweizer Bibliotek, 1976.

TRANSLATION: ITALIAN

375. I CRIMINALI DELL'AMORE. Translated by Giorgio Vorstein. Milano: Corno, 1966.

376. LA DOPPIA PROVA. Translated by Giorgio Vorstein. Milano: Corno, 1966.

377. I CRIMINI DELL'AMORE. Translated by Adriano Spatola and Marcella Sampietro. Bologna: Sampietro, 1968.

TRANSLATION: JAPANESE

378. KOI NO KAKEHIKI. Translated by Tatsuhiko Shibusawa. Tokyo: Kawade Shobo, 1955.

379. KOI NO TSUMI. Translated by Tatsuhiko Shibusawa. Tokyo: Chogen-Sha, 1963.

380. KOI NO TSUMI. Translated by Tatsuhiko Shibusawa. Tokyo: Togen-Sha, 1966.

## 7. DIALOGUE ENTRE UN PRETRE ET UN MORIBUND

381. DIALOGUE ENTRE UN PRETRE ET UN MORIBOND, publié, pour la première fois, sur le manuscrit autographe inédit, avec un avant-propos et des notes, par Maurice Heine. Paris: Stendhal, 1926.

382. DIALOGUE ENTRE UN PRETRE ET UN MORIBOND.    Paris:
     Presses littéraires de France, 1949.

383. DIALOGUE ENTRE UN PRETRE ET UN MORIBOND,  suivi  d'une
     Pensée.  Sceaux: J. J. Pauvert, 1953.

384. DIALOGUE  ENTRE  UN PRETRE ET  UN  MORIBOND,  et  autres
     opuscules.   Préface de Maurice Heine.   Paris:  J. J.
     Pauvert, 1961.

385. DIALOGUE  ENTRE  UN  PRETRE  ET UN  MORIBOND  ET  AUTRES
     OPUSCULES.    Préface  de  Maurice  Heine.    OXTIERN.
     ECRITS  POLITIQUES.    Préface  de  Maurice  Blanchot.
     Paris: J.-J. Pauvert, 1966. 315 p.

TRANSLATION:  DUTCH

386. GESPREK TUSSEN EEN PRIESTER EN EEN STERVENDE,  EN ANDERE
     TEKSEN.    Translated  by  Flamand  par  Herwig  Leus.
     Brugge, De Galge, 1965.

387. GESPREK  TUSSEN  EEN  PRIESTER  EN   EEN   STERVENDE.
     Translated by Hersig Leus.   Amsterdam:  Polan en  Van
     Gennep, 1965.

TRANSLATION:  ENGLISH

388. DIALOGUE  BETWEEN  A  PRIEST AND A DYING  MAN,  from  an
     unpublished  manuscript,  edited with an  introduction
     and  notes  by Maurice Heine,  translated  by  Samuel
     Putnam.  Chicago:  P. Covici, 1927.

8.  DORCI

389. DORCI, OU LA BIZARRERIE DU SORT, conte inédit par le M^is
     de Sade,  publié sur le manuscrit, avec une notice sur
     l'auteur [par Anatole France].    Paris:   Charavay
     frères, 1881.

390. DORCI; OU,  LA BIZARRERIE DU SORT.  Suivi de Dialogue
     entre  un prêtre et un moribond.   Avec un notice  sur
     l'auteur. Paris: Pernette, 1957.

## 9.  ECRITS POLITIQUES

391.  PROJET DE PETITION DES SECTIONS DE PARIS A LA CONVENTION
      NATIONALE.  Paris:  impr.  de  la Section des piques,
      1793.

392.  PETITION   DES   SECTIONS  DE  PARIS  A  LA   CONVENTION
      NATIONALE.  [Signé:  Pyron, Sade.]  Paris:  impr. de
      la Section des piques, 1793.

393.  SECTION  DES  PIQUES.   DISCOURS  PRONONCE  A  LA  FETE
      DECERNEE PAR LA SECTION DES PIQUES AUX MINES DE  MARAT
      ET  DE  LE PELLETIER,  par Sade. . . .  (29 septembre,
      1793).  Paris:  impr. de la Section des piques, 1793.

394.  SECTION   DES   PIQUES.   Extrait  des  registres  des
      délibérations de l'Assemblée générale et permanente de
      la Section des piques,  du 12  juillet  1793.  Paris:
      1793.

395.  A L'IMMORTALITE.   FRANCAIS!   ENCORE  UN EFFORT SI VOUS
      VOULEZ   ETRE   REPUBLICAINS   ET   LIBRES   DE   VOS
      OPINIONS.  Paris:  au chef-lieu du Globe, 1848.

396.  ECRITS POLITIQUES; SUIVIS DE OXTIERN.  Sceaux:  J. J.
      Pauvert, editor, 1957.

397.  MON ARRESTATION DU 26 AOUT [1778], lettre inédite suivie
      des Etrennes philosophiques.  [Note de Gilbert Lély.]
      Avec  un  double frontispice gravé au burin  par  Hans
      Bellmer.  Paris:  J. Hugues, 1959.  45 p.

398.  FRANCAIS,  ENCORE UN EFFORT:   extrait de LA PHILOSOPHIE
      DANS  LE BOUDOIR précédé de L'INCONVENANCE MAJEURE par
      Maurice Blanchot.  Paris:  Pauvert, 1965.


TRANSLATION:  ITALIAN

399.  SCRITTI UTOPISTICI ET POLITICI.  Translated by Luigi  de
      Nardis.  Milano: La Goliardica, 1967.


TRANSLATION:  SPANISH

400.  ESCRITOS POLITICOS.  Montevideo: El Timon, 1966.

401.  ESCRITOS    FILOSOFICOS    Y  POLITICOS.    Translated  by
      Alfredo Juan Alvarez.   Barcelona: Grijalbo, 1976.

### 10.  EMILIE DE TOURVILLE

402.  EMILE DE TOURVILLE;  OU,  LA CRUAUTE FRATERNELLE.    Deux
      eaux-fortes  originales  de  Denise  Lannes.    Paris:
      Librairie Le François, 1945.

TRANSLATION:  ITALIAN

403.  EMILIA DE TOURVILLE o la crudeltà Fraterna.    Translated
      by  Michel  Rago,  Oreste de  Ruono  et al.    Milano:
      Bompiani, 1951.

### 11.  ERNESTINE

404.  ERNESTINE,  avec  10  eaux-fortes  de  Sylvain  Sauvage.
      Paris:  J. Fort, 1926.

405.  ERNESTINE.   (Suivi  de:    FLORVILLE  ET  COURVAL  OU  LE
      FATALISME.)    Paris:    Editions  féminines  françaises
      1966.

### 12.  EUGENIE

406.  EUGENIE  DE  FRANVAL.    Avec  huit par  Valentine  Hugo.
      Paris:  G. Ar, 1948.

TRANSLATION:  ENGLISH

407.  EUGENIE  DE FRANVAL and other stories.    Translated  and
      introduced by Margaret Crosland.    London:    Spearman,
      1965.

TRANSLATION:  JAPANESE

408.  HISAN  MONOGATARI.    Translated by Tatsuhiko  Shibusawa.
      Tokyo: Gendai-Schicho-Sha, 1958.

TRANSLATION:  SWEDISH

409.  EUGENIE 15 AR.    Translated by V. Alvifore.  Stockholm:
      Seelig, 1965.


13.  FLORVILLE ET COURVAL

410.  NOVELLE AMOROSE Translated by Vito Romaniello.    Torino:
      Ed.  Dell'Abero,  1967.    For English and French
      versions, see LES CRIMES DE L'AMOUR, item 359-372.


14.  HISTOIRE DE JULIETTE

411.  HISTOIRE DE JULIETTE, OU LES PROSPER DU VICC.  Illustrée
      de soixante gravures et . . . En Hollande, 1797.

412.  HISTOIRE  DE JULIETTE,  ou les prosperites du vice.    En
      Hollande:  n.p., 1797.

413.  HISTOIRE DE JULIETTE.  Sceaux:  Pauvert, 1948.

414.  LES  PROSPERITES  DU  VICE.    Paris:   Union  générale
      d'éditions, 1969. 320 p.


TRANSLATION:  ENGLISH

415.  THE STORY OF JULIETTE,  OR VICE AMPLY REWARDED (Histoire
      de  Juliette,  ou les prospérités du vice),  being  an
      English rendering  from the French by  Pieralessandro
      Casavini.  Paris:  Olympia Press, 1958.

      1.  1958 287 p.
      2.  1959 169 p.
      3.  1960 183 p.
      4.  1960 204 p.

416.  JULIETTE.   Translated by Austryn Wainhouse.  New York:
      Grove Press, 1968.


TRANSLATION:  FLEMISH

417.  JULIETTE.  Translated by Rene Gysen, C.C. Krijgelmans et
      al. Antwerpen: W. Soethoudt, 1966.

TRANSLATION:  GERMAN

418.  GESCHICHTE  DER JULIETTE,  oder die Wonnen des  Lasters,
      eingeleitet  durch eine Biographie des Verfassers  und
      eine Inhalts-übersicht.  Bucharest:  Cesareano, 1892.


TRANSLATION:  ITALIAN

419.  I PIACERI DEL CRIMINE.  Milano: Editus, 1975.


TRANSLATION:  JAPANESE

420.  JULLIET.  Translated  by  Zen'ichiro  Shimada.  Tokyo:
      Murasaki Shobo, 1952.

421.  AKUTOKU  NO SAKAE.  Translated by Tatsuhiko  Shibusawa.
      Tokyo: Gendai Schicho-Sha, 1959.

422.  AKUTOKU  NO  HAE.  HISAN  MONOGATARI.  Translated  by
      Tatsuhiko Shibusawa.  Tokyo: Togen-Sha, 1964.

423.  AKUTOKU NO HAE (Zoku), JULIET NO HENREKI.  Translated by
      Tatsuhiko Shibusawa.  Tokyo: Gendai Schicho-Sha, 1964.

424.  AKUTOKU  NO SAKAE.  Translated by Tatsuhiko  Shibusawa.
      Tokyo: Togen-Sha, 1965.

425.  AKUTOKU  NO SAKAE.  Translated by Tatsuhiko  Shibusawa.
      Tokyo: Kadodawa Shoten, 1966.


        15.  HISTOIRE DE SAINVILLE ET DE LEONORE

426.  HISTOIRE  DE SAINVILLE ET DE LEONORE, Introduction par
      Gilbert Lély.  Paris:  Union général d'éditions, 1962.
      379 p.


        16.  HISTOIRE SECRETE D'ISABELLE DE BAVIERE

427.  HISTOIRE SECRETE D'ISABELLE DE BAVIERE, REINE DE FRANCE.
      Publiée  pour  la  première  fois  sur  le  manuscrit
      autographe dit, avec un avant-propos par Gilbert Lély.
      Paris: Gallimard, 1953.

428. UN INEDIT DU MARQUIS DE SADE. ISABELLE DE BAVIERE
     (fragments), edited by Gilbert Lély. In ARTS, 15-21
     août 1953.

429. HISTOIRE SECRETE D'ISABELLE DE BAVIERE, reine de France.
     (Avant-propos de Gilbert Lély.) Paris: Club français
     du livre 1964. XL + 285 p.

430. HISTOIRE SECRETE D'ISABELLE DE BAVIERE, reine de France,
     par le marquis de Sade. Texte établi et presenté par
     Gilbert Lély. Paris: Union générale d'éditions,
     1968. 317 p.

TRANSLATION: ITALIAN

431. STORIA SEGRETA D'ISABELLA DI BAVIERA, regina di Francia,
     Translated by Marisa Vassale. Milano: Sugar, 1964.

TRANSLATION: SPANISH

432. HISTORIA SECRETA DE ISABEL DE BAVIERA, reina de Francia.
     Translated by Angeles Santana. Barcelona: Taber,
     1969.


                     17. HISTORIETTES

433. HISTORIETTES, CONTES ET FABLIAUX publiés pour la
     première fois, sur les manuscrits autographes inédits,
     par Maurice Heine. Paris: les membres de la Société
     du roman philosophique, 1926.

434. HISTORIETTES, CONTES ET FABLIAUX, publiés sur le texte
     authentique de la Société du roman philosophique, avec
     un avant-propos par Maurice Heine. Paris: S. Kra,
     1927.

435. LES CARNETS D'UN LIBERTIN, historiettes, contes et
     fabliaux. Bruxelles: Club Mondial Du Livre, 1956.

436. HISTORIETTES, CONTES, ET FABLIAUX; DORCI. Sceaux:
     Jean-Jacques Pauvert, editor, 1957.

437. OPUSCULES. Historiettes, contes et fabliaux. Les
     infortunes de la vertu. Préfaces de Maurice Heine et

d'Antoine Adam. Paris: Cercle du livre précieux, 1963.

438. LES INFORTUNES DE LA VERTU. Suivi des HISTORIETTES, CONTES ET FABLIAUX, par le marquis de Sade. Introduction par Gilbert Lély. Paris: Union générale d'éditions, 1965. 505 p.

439. LA CHATELAINE DE LONGEVILLE OU LA FEMME VENGEE. Châtillon (Val-de-Marne): SEDIEP, 1968. Listed by E. Pierre Chanover, item 11.

TRANSLATION: ENGLISH

440. De Sade quartet: Four Stories from CONTES ET FABLIAUX. Translated by Margaret Crosland. London: Owen, 1963.

TRANSLATION: GERMAN

441. DIE KASTANI IN BLUTE UND ANDERE ERZALHUNGEN. Translated by Christian Barth. München: Kindler, 1964.

TRANSLATION: ITALIAN

442. STORILLE, racconti e folklore. Translated by Pino Bava. Milano: Veronelli, 1957.

443. LA DONNA LUDICA e Altri racconti d'Amore. Translated by Francis Cecosk. Firenze: ed. Arno, 1963.

444. HISTORIETTE. Translated by Gianni Frati. Milano: Corno, 1966.

TRANSLATION: SPANISH

445. CUENTOS, HISTORIAS Y FABULAS COMPLETAS. Madrid: Felmar, 1976.

18. IDEE SUR LES ROMANS

446. IDEE SUR LES ROMANS publiée avec préfaces, notes et documents inédites par Octave Uzanne. Paris:

Rouveyre, 1878 (extrait des CRIMES DE L'AMOUR).
Quatre lettres aux comédians français et lettre sur le
roman, in: IDEE SUR ROMANS, Paris: Rouveyre, 1878.

447. IDEE SUR LES ROMANS. Sceaux: Palimigre, 1948.


19. JUSTINE OU LES MALHEURS DE LA VERTU

There exist three different versions of JUSTINE. The
first, LES INFORTUNES DE LA VERTU, was published in
1787; the second, JUSTINE OU LES MALHEURS DE LA VERTU,
in 1791, and the third, LA NOUVELLE JUSTINE OU LES
MALHEURS DE LA VERTU, in 1797. For the best
comparative studies of these three texts, see chapter
III of SADE ROMANCIER, by A. Laborde, item 1374.

448. JUSTINE, OU LES MALHEURS DE LA VERTU. Reproduction
textuelle de l'édition originale. En Hollande: n.p.,
1791.

449. JUSTINE, OU LES MALHEURS DE LA VERTU. En Hollande: Les
Libraires associés, 1791.

450. HISTOIRE DE JUSTINE, OU LES MALHEURS DE LA VERTU, En
Hollande [i.e., Paris]: n.p., 1797.

451. LA NOUVELLE JUSTINE, OU LES MALHEURS DE LA VERTU, suivie
de L'HISTOIRE DE JULIETTE, sa soeur. Tome 3e. En
Hollande [i.e., Paris]: n.p., 1797. 356 p.

452. LA NOUVELLE JUSTINE, OU LES MALHEURS DE LA VERTU; suivie
de L'HISTOIRE DE JULIETTE sa soeur. Ouvrage orné d'un
frontispice. En Hollande [i.e., Paris]: 1797.

453. JUSTINE, OU LES MALHEURS DE LA VERTU [par Louis-François
Raban], with a preface by the Marquis de Sade. Paris:
Olivier, 1836.

454. LES INFORTUNES DE LA VERTU, texte établi sur le
manuscrit original autographe et publié pour la
première fois, avec une introduction, par Maurice
Heine. Paris: Fourcade, 1930.

455. LES INFORTUNES DE LA VERTU. Avec une notice de Maurice
Heine, une bibliographie de Robert Valençay, et une
introduction par Jean Paulhan. Paris: Editions du
Point du jour, 1946.

456.  LES  INFORTUNES  DE  LA  VERTU.  Preface  de  Thierry-
      Maulnier.  Paris:  J.  Valmont,  1947.

457.  JUSTINE OU LES MALHEURS DE LA VERTU.  Sceaux:  J.  J.
      Pauvert,  1949.

458.  JUSTINE;  OU,  LES  MALHEURS DE LA VERTU.  Gravures sur
      cuivre  de  Gastoa  Barret.  Paris:  Editions  de  La
      Vieille France, 1950.

459.  JUSTINE;  OU,  LES  MALHEURS DE LA VERTU.  Préface  de
      Georges Bataille.  Tomes 1 et 2.  Paris:  Le Soleil
      noir, 1952.

460.  LA NOUVELLE  JUSTINE  OU  LES  MALHEURS  DE  LA  VERTU.
      Sceaux:  J.  J.  Pauvert, 1953.

461.  LES INFORTUNES DE LA VERTU.  Sceaux:  J.  J.  Pauvert,
      1954.

462.  JUSTINE;  OU,  LES MALHEURS DE LA VERTU.  Préf. de Georges
      Bataille.  Paris:  J.J. Pauvert, 1955.

463.  CENT ONZE NOTES POUR LA NOUVELLE JUSTINE.  Paris:  n.p.,
      1956.

464.  LES INFORTUNES DE LA VERTU.  Edition nouvelle, précédée
      de  la Douteuse Justine ou les Revanches de la pudeur,
      par Jean Paulhan.  Paris:  J. J. Pauvert, 1959. 203 p.

465.  LA NOUVELLE JUSTINE OU LES MALHEURS DE LA VERTU,  suivie
      de  L'HISTOIRE DE JULIETTE,  sa soeur,  ou  Les
      prospérités  du vice.  Préfaces de Maurice  Blanchot,
      Georges Bataille,  Pierre Klossowski et Maurice Heine.
      Paris:  Cercle du livre précieux, 1963.

466.  JUSTINE  OU  LES INFORTUNES DE  LA  VERTU.  Paris:
      Editions féminines françaises, 1965. 191 p.

467.  LES  INFORTUNES DE LA VERTU.  Suivi des HISTORIETTES,
      CONTES  ET  FABLIAUX.  Introduction be Gilbert Lély.
      Paris:  Union générale d'éditions, 1965.  505 p.

468.  LES  INFORTUNES  DE LA VERTU.  Suivi de LA MARQUISE DE
      GANGE.  Paris:  Editions de la Renaissance, 1966.

469. LES INFORTUNES DE LA VERTU. Paris:    Editions
     Baudelaire, 1967.

470. JUSTINE OU LES MALHEURS DE LA VERTU.    Paris:    Editions
     de la Renaissance, 1967. 413 p.

471. JUSTINE    OU LES INFORTUNES DE LA    VERTU.    Viry-
     Châtillon: S.E.D.I.E.P., 1967. 207 p.

472. LES INFORTUNES DE LA VERTU.    Chronologie et préface par
     Jean-Marie Goulemot.    Paris:    Garnier-Flammarion,
     1969. 189 p.

473. LES INFORTUNES DE LA VERTU.    Paris, London, New York:
     Editions Bel Air, 1969. 352 p.


TRANSLATION:    DANISH

474. ULYKKERNE FOLGER DEN DYDIGE ELLER  JUSTINE.    Translated
     by Kamma Albretchtsen Kobenhavn:    Biilnan og  Eriksen,
     1965.


TRANSLATION:    DUTCH

475. JUSTINE OF DE TEGENSPOED DER DEUGDZAAMHEID,    Translated
     by Gemma Pappot.  'sGravenhage: Bakker-Daanen, 1967.

476. JUSTINE,  OF DE TEGENSPAED DER DEUGDZAAMHEID, translated
     by Gemma Pappot.  'sGravenhage:  Dammen, 1969.


TRANSLATION:    ENGLISH

477. JUSTINE,  OR THE MISFORTUNES OF VIRTUE.  OPUS SADICUM; a
     philosophical  romance  for the first time  translated
     from  the original French  (Holland,  1791).  With an
     engraved frontispiece.  Paris:  Isidore Liseux, 1889.

478. JUSTINE; OR, THE MISFORTUNES OF  VIRTUE.  New York:  The
     Risus Press, 1931.

479. JUSTINE; OR, THE MISFORTUNES OF VIRTUE.  Introduction by
     Iwan Bloch.  New York:  The Risus Press, 1935.

480. JUSTINE, OR GOOD CONDUCT WELL CHASTISED.  Translated by
     Pieralessandro Casavini. Paris: Olympia Press, 1953.

481. THE MISFORTUNE OF VIRTUE. Translated by Harriet Sohmers. Paris: Obelisk Press, 1953.

482. JUSTINE or Good conduct well chastised. Translated by Pieralessandro Casavini. Paris: Olympia Press, 1959.

483. JUSTINE OR THE MISFORTUNE OF VIRTUE. New York: Castle Books, 1964.

484. JUSTINE, OR THE MISFORTUNES OF VIRTUE. A faithful and unexpurgated translation from the original manuscript of 1787, together with expansions and selected variants from the editions of 1791 and 1797. Notes, bibliography and introduction by Allan Hull Walton. London: N. Spearman, 1964.

485. JUSTINE; OR, THE MISFORTUNES OF VIRTUE. A complete and unexpurgated translation by Allan Hull Walton. London: Transworld Publishers, 1965.

486. JUSTINE OR THE MISFORTUNES OF VIRTUE. Translated by Helen Weaver. New York: Putnam's Sons, 1966.

TRANSLATION: GERMAN

487. DAS MISSGESCHICK DER TUGEND. Translated by Katarina Hock. Hamburg: Merlin Verlag, 1963.

488. JUSTIN. Translated by Christian Barth. München: Kindler, 1964.

489. JUSTINE ODER VOM MISSGESCHICK DER TUGEND. Translated by W. Tritzche. Frankfurt: Velstein, 1967.

TRANSLATION: ITALIAN

490. LE DISGRAZIE DELLA VIRTU. Translated by Giorgio Vorstein. Milano: Corno, 1966.

491. LE AVENTURE DELLA VIRTU. Translated by Emilio Carizzoni. Milano: Sugar, 1967.

492. LE DISGRAZIE DELLA VIRTU. Translated by Adriana Spatola. Bologna: Sampietro, 1967.

493. JUSTINE O LE SVENTURE DELLA VIRTU. Translated by Emilio
     Carizzoni. Milano: Club degli editori, 1974.

494. LE SVENTURE DELLA VIRTU. JUSTINE. Translated by Emilio
     Corizzoni. Milano: Longanesi, 1975.

TRANSLATION: JAPANESE

495. JUSTINE. Translated by Tatsuhiko Shibusawa. Tokyo:
     Shoko Shoin, 1956.

496. JUSTINE. Translated by Tatsuhiko Shibusawa. Tokyo:
     Tozai Gogatsu-Sha, 1960.

497. BITOKU NO FUKO. Translated by Tatsuhiko Shibusawa.
     Tokyo: Togen-Sha, 1962.

498. SHIN JUSTINE. Translated by Tatsuhiko Shibusawa.
     Tokyo: Togen-Sha, 1965.

499. JUSTINE. BITOKU NO FUKO. Translated by Tatsuhiko
     Scibusawa. Tokyo: Togensha, 1969.

TRANSLATION: PORTUGUESE

500. JUSTINE A CRUELDADE FORTERNA. Translated by Carlos
     Brito. Lisbon: Ag. Port. de Reurstas, 1976.

TRANSLATION: SPANISH

501. JUSTINE. Translated by Pilar Calvo. Madrid:
     Fundamentos, 1976.

502. JUSTINE. Translated by Mercedes Costellanos.
     Barcelona: A.T.E., 1976.

503. LOS INFORTUNIOS DE LA VIRTUD. Translated by Juana
     Bignozzi. Madrid: Edol, 1977.

504. LOS INFORTUNIOS DE LA VIRTUD. Translated by Imma
     Baycurri. Barcelona: Mundilibro, 1977.

## 20.  LA MARQUISE DE GANGE

505.  LA MARQUISE DE GANGE.  Paris:  Béchot, 1813.

506.  LA MARQUISE DE GANGE, roman.  Texte conforme à l'édition
      unique de 1813.  Avant-propos de Gilbert Lély.  Paris:
      P. Aimot, 1957.

507.  LA MARQUISE  DE GANGE.   Introduction de  Gilbert  Lély.
      Paris:  Jean-Jacques Pauvert, 1961.

508.  LA MARQUISE DE GANGE,  précédée des OPUSCULES POLITIQUES
      et D'OXTIERN, OU LES MALHEURS DU LIBERTINAGE.  Préfaces
      de  Pierre  Naville,  de Camille Schuwer et de  Gaëtan
      Picon.  Paris:  Cercle du livre précieux, 1964.

509.  LA MARQUISE DE GANGE.   Paris:  Editions Esprit et joie,
      1964, 225 p.

510.  LA MARQUISE  DE  GANGE.   Introduction de  Hubert  Juin.
      Paris:  P. Belfond, 1965. 225 p.

511.  LA MARQUISE  DE  TELEME OU LES EFFETS  DU   LIBERTINAGE.
      Viry-Châtillon:  S.E.D.I.E.P., 1965.  181 p.

512.  LA MARQUISE   DE   GANGE.    Viry-Châtillon,   Essonne:
      S.E.D.I.E.P., 1967.  239 p.


TRANSLATION:  GERMAN

513.  DIE MARQUISE DE GANGE.  Translated by Ludwig Man and Ute
      Hamburg: Merlin Verlag, 1967.


TRANSLATION:  ITALIAN

514.  LA MARCHESA  DI  GANGE.  Translated by Nicoletta  Dudan.
      Milano:  n.p., 1966.

515.  LA MARCHESA DI GANGE.  Translated by Antonietta Cavanca.
      Milano:  1966.


## 21.  LA PHILOSOPHIE DANS LE BOUDOIR

516.  LA PHILOSOPHIE  DANS LE BOUDOIR; ou,  LES INSTITUTEURS
      LIBERTINS; dialogues destinés à l'éducation des jeunes

demoiselles.   London:   Aux  dépens de la   Compagnie,
1795.

517.  LA PHILOSOPHIE  DANS LE BOUDOIR.   Bruxelles:   Chez Les
       Marchands de nouveautés, 1890.

518.  LA PHILOSOPHIE DANS LE BOUDOIR, précédée d'une étude sur
       le  marquis  de Sade  et  son  oeuvre,   par  Helpey,
       bibliographe poitevin.   Vincennes:   Pour le Group des
       études sadistes, 1948.

519.  LA PHILOSOPHIE DANS LE BOUDOIR.   Paris:  J. J. Pauvert,
       1953.

520.  FRANCAIS,  ENCORE UN EFFORT,  extrait de la  PHILOSOPHIE
       DANS  LE  BOUDOIR Précédé de "'Inconvenance  majeure,"
       par Maurice Blanchot.   Paris:   J.-J.  Pauvert, 1965.
       176 p.

TRANSLATION:  DANISH

521.  SADISTISK TESTAMENTE.   Kobenhavn:  Olympia  Press  and
       Obelisk, 1967.

TRANSLATION:  ENGLISH

522.  THE BEDROOM PHILOSOPHERS.   Translated by Pieralessandro
       Casavini.  Paris:  Olympia Press, 1953.

523.  THE BEDROOM PHILOSOPHERS.   Translated by Pieralessandro
       Casavini.  Paris:  Olympia Press, 1957.

524.  THE BEDROOM PHILOSOPHERS.  Being an English rendering of
       La Philosophie dans le boudoir, done by Pieralessandro
       Casavini.  Introduction by Irving Shulman.  San Diego,
       California:  Greenleaf Classics, 1965.

525.  PHILOSOPHY IN THE BEDROOM in THE COMPLETE JUSTINE.   New
       York:  Grove Press, 1965.

TRANSLATION:  GERMAN

526.  PHILOSOPHIE  IN BOUDOIR.   Translated by Barbara  Ronge.
       München: Willing, 1967.

TRANSLATION: JAPANESE

527. KEIBO TETSUGAKU. Translated by Hachirō Shiraishi.
Tokyo: Murasaki Shobo, 1952.

528. KEIBO TETSUGAKU SHO. Translated by Tatsuhiko Shabusawa.
Tokyo: Shoko Shoin, 1956.

529. KEIBO TETSUGAKU. Translated by Tatsuhiko Shibusawa.
Tokyo: Togen-Sha, 1962.

530. KEIBO TETSUGAKU, Translated by Tatsuhiko Shibusawa.
Tokyo: Kadokawa Shoten, 1976.

TRANSLATION: PORTUGUESE

531. A FILOSOFIA NA ALCOVA. Translated by Manuel Joào Gomes.
Lisbon: Afrodité, s.d.

TRANSLATION: SPANISH

532. LA FILOSOFIA EN EL TOCADOR. Translated by Ricardo
Pochtor. Barcelona: Brugura, 1977.

## 22. ZOLOE

533. ZOLOE ET SES DEUX ACOLYTES; OU, QUELQUES DECADES DE LA
VIE DE TROIS JOLIES FEMMES. Paris: Bibliothéque des
curieux, 1910.

534. ZOLOE ET SES DEUX ACOLYTES OU QUELQUES DECADES DE LA VIE
DE TROIS JOLIES FEMMES. Paris: Bibliotheque des
curieux, 1922.

535. ZOLOE ET SES DEUX ACOLYTES, OU QUELQUES DECADES DE LA
VIE DE TROIS JOLIES FEMMES. Paris: Bibliothèque des
curieux, 1926.

536. ZOLOE ET SES DEUX ACOLYTES, OU QUELQUES DECADES DE LA
VIE DE TROIS JOLIES FEMMES, précédé d'une étude bio-
bibliographique, de Fernand Mitton. Paris: Librairie
intermédiaire du bibliophile, 1928.

537. ZOLOE ET SES DEUX ACOLYTES; OU, QUELQUES DECADES DE LA
VIE DE TROIS JOLIES FEMMES. Ed. illustrée de 12 eaux-
fortes de Lue Lafnet. Paris: Bibliothèque des
curieux, 1932.

538. ZOLOE ET SES DEUX ACOLYTES, OU QUELQUES DECADES DE LA
VIE DE TROIS JOLIES FEMMES. Sceaux: Jean-Jacques
Pauvert, 1954.

TRANSLATION: JAPANESE

539. ZOLOE. Translated by Tatsuhiko Shibusawa. Tokyo: Shoko
Shoin, 1957.

III.   SECONDARY SOURCES

A.   BIBLIOGRAPHICAL ESSAYS

540.   Apollinaire,   Guillaume;  Fernand  Fleuret;  and  Louis
Perceau.    L'ENFER   DE  LA  BIBLIOTHEQUE  NATIONALE.
Paris:    Mercure  de  France,  1913,  pp.  73,  77,  240-254,
375-377.

Presents a critical bibliography of all the works kept
in the "Enfer" of the Bibliothèque Nationale in Paris.
Lists numerous works of Sade kept there;   for instance
(p.  240,  No.  500):   "ALINE ET VALCOUR OU LE  ROMAN
PHILOSOPHIQUE.    Ecrit  à  la Bastille un an avant  la
Révolution  de  France.    Orné  de  seize  gravures.--A
Paris,   chez  la  veuve  Giouard,   libraire,   maison
Egalité, Galerie de Bois, No 196, 1795.

--1 volume in-12 de 503 p.  Demi-reliure,  veau fauve,
plats marbrés, dos orné pièces, tranches peigne.  Tome
II  seulement  contenant  la  3e  et  4e  partie.    Avec  8
figures gravées non libres.

--Par le marquis de Sade.

--Destruction  ordonnée  pour  outrages  à  la  morale
publique  et aux bonnes moeurs,  par arrêt de la  Cour
royale  de  Paris,   en  date  du  19  mai  1815  (pas
d'insertion au MONITEUR).

--Cet ouvrage a aussi été mis à l'index, par mesure de
police, en 1825.

--Malgré ces condamnations,  on ne s'explique guère le
classement  à  l'ENFER  de  cet ouvrage,  où  il  y  a
beaucoup  de  traits  autobiographiques."    (See  item
613.)

541.   Apollinaire, Guillaume.  L'OEUVRE  DU MARQUIS DE  SADE.
Paris:  Bibliothèque des curieux, 1909.

"Though superseded by Nadeau,  work remains important
for long introduction,  largely biographical with many
bibliographical   references  and  interspersed   with
general  comment  on Sade who was to become a  god  to
later surrealists."  (Quoted from Cabeen, item 8.)

542. Arban, D. "Débat sur Sade entre gens sérieux." FIGARO LITTERAIRE 290 (10 November 1951): 5.

Reviews the trial occasioned by the publication in 1949 of the unexpurgated text of LA PHILOSOPHIE DANS LE BOUDOIR by the Editions Premières, and subsequent condemnation and appeal. Quotes Matarasso, attorney for the defense, and Turlan, the prosecuting attorney. Findings of the Court are not reported.

543. Assezat. "Justine ou les malheurs de la vertu." L'INTERMEDIAIRE DES CHERCHEURS ET CURIEUX 152 (September 1874): 515-516.

Comments on an edition of JUSTINE supposedly published in 1786 but was instead published in 1794--after the Revolution.

544. Becourt, Daniel. LIVRES CONDAMNES, LIVRES INTERDITS. Paris: Le Cercle de la librairie, 1972, pp. 302, 322, 404-405, 453, 501.

Lists all the works of the Marquis de Sade condemned to censorship: ALINE ET VALCOUR, LES AVENTURES GALANTES (Ed. Schmid), LE BORDEL DE VENISE, CENT VINGT JOURNEES DE SODOME, CRIMES DE L'AMOUR, DIALOGUES ENTRE UN PRETRE ET UN MORIBOND, HISTOIRE DE JULIETTE, JUSTINE, LA NOUVELLE JUSTINE OU LES MALHEURS DE LA VERTU, OXTIERN OU LES MALHEURS DU LIBERTINAGE, LA PHILOSOPHIE DANS LE BOUDOIR, ZOLOE ET SES DEUX ACOLYTES. Includes a most interesting history of censorship.

545. Bégis, Alfred. LE REGISTRE D'ECROU DE LA BASTILLE DE 1782 A 1789. Paris: Imprimerie de G. Chamerot, 1880.

This is listed in Pierre Chanover's bibliography, item 557, but is not available at the Bibliothèque Nationale in Paris. It is unlikely that it could be available in book form, since it is only a short article.

546. Bégis, Alfred. "Notes de police." NOUVELLE REVUE, November 1880, p. 528.

Although listed in E. Pierre Chanover's bibliography, item 557, there is no such article on p. 528 of the November-December 1880 issue of LA NOUVELLE REVUE.

547.  Bellour, Raymond. "Les exigences de l'oeuvre complète.
      Notes sur l'oeuvre et sa critique." LES LETTRES
      FRANCAISES, 17 January 1968, pp. 9-10.

      Brings to light a legal suit between two publishers,
      the Cercle du Livre Précieux and the Cercle du
      Bibliophile, after both had advertised as forthcoming
      the complete works of Emile Zola. However, the Cercle
      du Bibliophile only published approximately 20% of the
      known works of Zola (only what was approved by Zola
      during his lifetime). This, states the author,
      creates a problem for the critics and leads to
      questioning of whatever constitutes the complete
      works: "Il y a une exigence proprement actuelle qui
      veut l'oeuvre complète, joue de l'idée comme d'un sort
      inéluctable, parfois jusqu'au mensonge et toujours
      jusqu'au paradoxe." Concludes with the case of Sade's
      works as an example of choice by necessity: some of
      Sade's writings are of poor quality.

548.  Bonneau, Alcide. "La première édition de JUSTINE OU
      LES MALHEURS DE LA VERTU. CURIOSITES LITTERAIRES ET
      BIBLIOGRAPHIQUES. Paris: Liseux, 1<sup>re</sup> série, 1880,
      pp. 130-141.

      Outlines three separate theses in JUSTINE:  1) virtue
      is a ridiculous weakness of timid souls who get what
      they deserve when they encounter misfortune;
      2) compassion is a vice which should get severely
      punished; 3) cruelty is the necessary seasoning to
      pleasure. Denies the possibility that the marquis was
      insane and insists that he quite clearly defined his
      system, which is based on the belief that sensuous
      pleasure is increased or caused by inflicting pain.

549.  Bordeaux, Fr.-M. JUSTINE OU LES MALHEURS DE LA VERTU.
      Paris: Olivier, 1835.

      Even though this work has the famous title of a work
      by Sade, it was not written by the marquis. It does,
      however, include part of a preface written by Sade for
      his novel. According to J. Lemonnyer, this work is
      much less reprehensible than that of Sade.
      Nevertheless, the publisher of this book was condemned
      to six months in jail and fined 3,000 francs on 15
      March 1836. A report appeared in the MONITOR of 26

June 1836 on the passage that had been deemed not acceptable.

550. Brenner, Clarence. A BIBLIOGRAPHICAL LIST OF PLAYS IN THE FRENCH LANGUAGE, 1700-1789. Ann Arbor, Michigan: Edwards Brothers, Inc., 1947, p. 123.

Lists three plays by Sade, LE PERE DE FAMILLE, in three acts; L'EGAREMENT DE L'INFORTUNE, in three acts; and HENRIETTE ET SAINT-CLAIR, OU LA FORCE DU SANG, drama in five acts.

551. Breton, André. "Boite alerte, missives lascives." CATALOGUE DE L'EXPOSITION INTERNATIONALE DU SURREALISME, 1959-60, reprinted in LE SURREALISME ET LA PEINTURE. Paris: Gallimard, 1965.

Another publication which shows the surrealists' important influence in the popularization of Sade's works.

552. Brochier, Jean-Jacques. "Sur deux éditions de Sade." LE MAGAZINE LITTERAIRE 6 (April 1967): 21.

Reviews two new complete editions of the works of Sade. The first is a re-edition of "Cercle du livre précieux," originally published in 1962 and 1964; the second, a new edition in thirty volumes from J. J. Pauvert. Comments that Pierre Naville is justified in saying that Sade has replaced Kafka in modern sensibility.

553. Brousson, Jean-Jacques. "Le Dossier Sade." NOUVELLES LITTERAIRES, 10 (March 1930): 3.

Reviews of the book CORRESPONDANCE INEDITE DU MARQUIS DE SADE, edited by Paul Bourdin. Contrasts Rouseau's theories to those of Sade: "Le génial benêt [Rousseau] n'avait pas eu d'enfants sous les yeux. Il n'apprit jamais à des Emile à la bavette, le licite et l'illicite; le décent et le scabreux. Sade répond, et comme un théologien: 'Tout est mal au sortir des mains du Créateur.'" Concludes with an appraisal of the collection of letters published by Bourdin: "Grâce à lui, nous savons plus de choses sur les Sade que n'en savait peut-être Sade lui-même."

554.  Brunet, Pierre Gustave. LE MARQUIS DE SADE: L'HOMME ET
      SES ECRITS. Sadopolis:    Chez Justin Valcourt à
      l'enseigne de la "vertu Malheureuse" l'an 000.
      Brussels: Jules Gay, 1866.

      Contains as an appendix Le Discours prononcé à la
      section des Piques.

      Only one hundred-fifty copies of that work were
      printed.    Attempts to give biographical and
      bibliographical details on Sade.   Harshly reviewed by
      J. Piazzoli, CATALOGUE D'UN COLLECTION DE LIVRES
      ANCIENS (Milan: Lib. Dumolard, 1878), pp. 394-395.

555.  Brunet, Pierre Gustave. "Zoloé et ses deux acolytes."
      In FANTAISIES BIBLIOGRAPHIQUES.    Paris:   Jules Gay,
      1864, pp. 63-68.

      Short review of ZOLOE.    Attributes this book to Sade.
      ZOLOE would be the Empress Josephine, born in 1763.
      She would have been thirty-eight years of age when
      ZOLOE was written.   States in the last paragraph: "We
      have painted men of a century which no longer exists.
      May the next century produce better ones and lend to
      my brushes the charms of virtue."  What was described
      in that book were several decades in the lives of
      three pretty women.

556.  Cerruti, Giorgio.  "Il Marchese di Sade: La sua recente
      fortuna e gli ultimi studi critici (1958-1968)."
      STUDI FRANCESI 13 (1969): 420-441.

      Very thorough bibliography of the critical works
      published during the decade 1958-1968.   Includes an
      interesting section on the influence of Sade on movies
      and the theater.

557.  Chanover, E. Pierre.    THE MARQUIS DE SADE:    A
      BIBLIOGRAPHY.   Metuchen:   Scarecrow Press,   1973.
      252 p.

      Lists studies on Sade (588 items) and gives twenty-
      five pages of works by Sade with numerous re-editions.
      Not up-to-date on latest published works but a
      conscientious compilation and a useful starting point.
      Also includes eleven-page bibliography of works in
      translation and 115 items of writings on sadism.

Reviewed by William Mead in FRENCH REVIEW 47 (1974): 991-992.

558.  Cohen, Henry.  GUIDE DE L'AMATEUR DE LIVRES A GRAVURES DU XVIIIe SIECLE.  Paris: P. Rouquette, 1886, pp. 528-531.

Presents a biblio-iconography of Sade's works.

559.  COLLOQUE  D'AIX-EN-PROVENCE SUR LE MARQUIS DE SADE,  19 and 20 February 1968.  Paris:  Librairie Armand Colin, 1968.  305 p.

Introduction by André Bourde, Bernard Guyon, Jean Fabre;  articles by André Boüer, "Lacoste, laboratoire du sadisme";  Michel Vovelle, "Sade, Seigneur de village";  Maitre Marcel Parrat,  "L'Affaire de Marseille et le parlement d'Aix"; André Bourde, "Sade, Aix, et Marseille:  un autre Sade;" Pierre Guiral, "Un noble provençal contemporain de Sade, le marquis d'Antonelle"; Henri Coulet, "La vie intérieure dans JUSTINE";  Jean Biou,  "Deux oeuvres complémentaires: LES LIAISONS DANGEREUSES et JULIETTE";  Jean-Marie Goulemot,  "Lecture politique d' ALINE ET VALCOUR"; Jean Molino, "Sade devant la beauté"; Jean-Jacques Brochier,  "La circularité de l'espace";  Jean Deprun, "Sade et la philosophie biologique de son temps"; Jean Tulard,  "Sade et la censure sous le premier empire"; Claude Duchet, "L'Image de Sade à l'époque romantique";  Raymond Jean,  "Sade et le surréalisme"; Jean Fabre,  "Sade et le roman noir"; Docteur Jacques Cain,  "Le fantasme sadique et la réalité"; and Pierre Naville, "Sade et l'érotisme d'aujourd'hui."

Reviewed by J. Vercruysse in DIX-HUITIEME SIECLE 3 (1971): 387-388.

560.  Costa, Corrado.  "Sextrapolazioni."  QUINDICI 11 (15 June 1968): viii.

Discloses some of the interesting steps taken by censoring editors and gives as an example the manipulation of some of the most recent works of Sade, especially Sugar's translation of JUSTINE.

561.  Delon, Michel.  "Dix ans d'études sadiennes (1968-1978)." DIX-HUITIEME SIECLE 11 (1979): 393-426.

Erudite study of the state of Sadian scholarship.
Covers a ten-year period, 1968-1978, divided into
assorted topics: biography, academic criticism,
textual analysis, feminism, etc. Concludes with a
section on theater and movie adaptations of Sade's
works.

562. Delon, Michel. "Indications bibliographiques." EUROPE
522 (1972): 148-149.

Short bibliographical information presenting nothing
new on Sade or his work.

563. Delon, Michel. Review of LE PORTEFEUILLE DU MARQUIS DE
SADE, textes rares et précieux reunis et presentés par
Gilbert Lély. DIX-HUITIEME SIECLE 10 (1978): 470.

Reviews this collection of assorted documents
published in 1977 by the Editions de la Différence.
States: "Nul ne peut mettre en doute la remarquable
compétence de Gilbert Lély, ni contester sa fascinante
dévotion à l'égard du marquis; mais on
peut . . . lire Sade autrement que (du point de vue)
qui nous apprend à mieux le connnaître."

564. Didier, Béatrice. "Sade: Du conte philosophique au
roman épique et romantique." In LE PREROMATISME:
HYPOTHEQUE OU HYPOTHESE? Edited by Paul Viallaneix.
(Colloque organisé à Clermont-Ferrand les 29 et 30
juin 1972 par le Centre de recherches Révolutionnaires
et Romantiques de l'Université.) Paris: Klincksieck,
1975, pp. 209-218.

States that the BIBLIOTHEQUE NATIONALE Manuscript No.
4010, a draft of the second version of LES INFORTUNES
DE LA VERTU, contains several tales (later published
in LES CRIMES DE L'AMOUR and some in HISTORIETTES) and
a draft of the main theme for JUSTINE and JULIETTE:
"Deux soeurs, l'une trés libertine vit dans le
bonheur, dans l'abondance et la prospérité, l'autre,
extrèment sage tombe dans mille panneaux qui finissent
enfin par entrainer sa perte." The style chosen for
this first version is flowery and elliptical, quite
different from what is a normal Sadian style. The
second version (1791) addresses itself to a new
reader, one avid of "roman noir." "De la première à
la seconde version on est passé du Mal tel que le

concevait la philosophie des Lumières, au Mal tel que l'entendra la philosophie romantique. . . . Mais de la seconde à la dernière version, ce n'est pas seulement la masse romanesque qui s'est amplifiée: elle a presque triplé. . . . Des INFORTUNES aux MALHEURS, Sade avait évolué du conte au roman romantique noir des MALHEURS à la NOUVELLE JUSTINE, la transformation est tout aussi frappante. Avec la troisième JUSTINE, nous assistons à une sublimation, à un éclatement du roman noir."

565. Drach, Albert. IN SACHEN DE SADE. Dusseldorf: Claassen, 1974. 354 p.

This is a translation into German of Sade's diary for the years 1807, 1808, and 1814. It includes in an appendix some details on the insane asylum of Charenton. Reviewed by Joachim Schondorff, in LITERATUR UND KRITIK XI (1976): 182-183.

566. Drujon, Fernand. CATALOGUE DES OUVRAGES POURSUIVIS DEPUIS LE 21 OCTOBRE 1814 JUSQU'AU 31 JUILLET 1877. Paris: Edouard Rouveyre, 1879, pp. 215-216.

Lists JUSTINE as one of the works condemned between 21 October 1814 and 31 July 1877.

567. Eluard, Paul. "Sur Sade." L'EVIDENCE POETIQUE. DONNER A VOIR. Paris: Editions de la Nouvelle Revue Française, 1939. Also LA VIE IMMEDIATE. Paris: Gallimard, 1968, pp. 9-17.

Fragment of a conference presented in London on 24 June 1936 at the surrealist exhibit organized by Roland Penrose. States that Sade wanted to give back to man the strength of his primitive instincts. Compares him with Lautréamont: "Ils ont mené tous deux la lutte la plus acharnée contre les artifices, qu'ils soient grossiers ou subtils, contre tous les pièges que nous tend cette fausse réalité besogneuse qui abaisse l'homme."

568. L'ESPRIT CREATEUR 15, 4 (1975): 403-459.

This special issue of L'ESPRIT CREATEUR includes the following articles on Sade:

Béatrice C. Fink, "Sade and Cannibalism";
Nancy K. Miller, "JULIETTE and the Posterity of
Prosperity";
Anne Lacombe, "Les INFORTUNES DE LA VERTU, le Conte et
la Philosophie";
Alice Laborde, "Sade: l'érotisme démystifié";
Jenny H. Batlay and Otis E. Fellows, "Diderot et Sade:
Affinites et divergences."

569.    EUROPE 522 (October 1972):  3-149.

This  special  issue  of EUROPE includes the  following
articles on the marquis de Sade:

Pierre Abraham, "Le lecteur de Sade";
Hubert Juin, "Sade entier";
Jean-Claude Montel, "Sade, encore un effort";
Nelly Stephane, "Morale et nature";
Michel Delon, "Sade face à Rousseau";
Dr.  Janine  Neboit-Mombet,  "Un  logicien de   la
deraison";
Beatrice Didier, "Le château intérieur de Sade";
Catherine Claude, "Une lecture de femme";
Maurice Tourn, "Les mythes de la femme";
Raymond Jean, "L'imitation de Sade";
Jean-Pierre  Han and Jean-Pierre  Valla,  "Le  système
philosophique de Sade";
Michel Delon, "Sade, maitre d'agression";
Jean-Claude Izzo, "Sade marquis de Lacoste."

570.    Fabre, Jean.   Preface  to ALINE ET  VALCOUR.   OEUVRES
COMPLETES DU MARQUIS DE SADE.  Vol. IV.  Paris: Cercle
du livre précieux, 1964, pp. xi-xxiii.

States  that ALINE ET VALCOUR was originally scheduled
to  be  published by the "citoyen Girouard," who  was
arrested  before he could finish the job.  During  the
seven-year period which followed,  Sade corrected  and
revised the manuscript for this "roman philosophique,"
intended to be his masterpiece.   His aim, rather than
to  emulate Rousseau as many of his contemporaries had
done,  was "de rappeler par un dernier feu d'artifice,
les  enchantements de celui qu'en dépit de la mode  il
tient  toujours pour le createur et le grand homme  du
genre  romanesque,  l'auteur de CLEVELAND."    Also
believes  that ALINE ET VALCOUR was a means of  escape
for the marquis,  at least from his obsessions and his
fears, which he treated as ingredients of an adventure

novel. Concludes that in ALINE ET VALCOUR, Sade has made "une contribution inoubliable et un apport decisif . . . c'est à la dignité de l'homme qu'il en appelle, par la voix de Zamé pour lui rappeler son premier devoir:   Tout est à prendre dans le coeur de l'homme quand on veut se mêler de la conduite. . . ."

571. Faure, Maurice. "Compte-rendu d'ouvrages sur Sade." GAVROCHE (1948):12.

Gives a good review of several publications on Sade; deals especially with SADE MON PROCHAIN by P. Klossowski.

572. Felkay, Nicole. "Quelques documents sur le marquis de Sade aux archives de Paris." ANNALES HISTORIQUES DE LA REVOLUTION FRANCAISE 43 (1971):   130-143.

Lists several documents kept at the Archives de Paris, in particular a manuscript written in 1812 by Hyppolite de Colins, giving precise descriptions of life at Charenton while Sade was imprisoned there. Also includes a copy of Sade's death certificate and an inventory of Sade's possessions at Charenton. Among them, sold at auction, were thirty-one pamphlets, twenty-one unidentified items and a trunk.

573. Fink, Béatrice. "Colloque 'Sade, écrire la crise,' Centre cultural International de Cerisy-la-Salle, 19-29 June 1981." BULLETIN DE LA SOCIETE FRANCAISE D'ETUDE DU XVIIIe SIECLE 39 (October 1981):   22, 23.

Gives a good review of the colloquium of June 1981. Collection of papers presented was published by Pierre Belford in 1983.

574. Fiorioli, Elena. "La fortuna di Sade in Italia." CULTURE FRANCAISE (BARI) 24 (1977): 3-10.

States that the theater performance of MARAT/SADE, a play by Peter Brook translated into Italian by Ippolito Pizzetti, focused interest on Sade's works and that the marquis's popularity increased because his writings furnished material for research in several areas: "Il significato letterio del testo, la scrittura nella sua autonomia e nelle sue conseguenze, l'evoluzione del pensiero sadiano, il tessuto storico-

sociologico, l'erotismo con le sue deviazioni come
caso patologico o complessar freudiano, e cosi via."

575.   Fleuret, Fernand; Guillaume Apollinaire; and Louis
       Perceau.  "Bibliographie des oeuvres de Sade et
       jugements sur lui et son oeuvre."  L'ENFER DE LA
       BIBLIOTHEQUE NATIONALE.  Paris: Mercure de France,
       1913.

       See annotation under Apollinaire, Guillaume [540].

576.   Fraxi, Pisanus (pseudonym for Spencer H. Ashbeen).
       "Notes sur Sade et ses ouvrages."  In INDEX LIBRORUM
       PROHIBITUM, NOTES BIO-BIBLIOICONOGRAPHICAL AND
       CRITICAL ON CURIOUS AND UNCOMMON BOOKS.  London:
       Privately printed, 1877.  Facsimile reprints--London:
       1960; and New York:  n.p., 1963.

       Analyzes the novel ALINE ET VALCOUR using some
       biographical details, pp. 30-39; analyzes ZOLOE, pp.
       406-410; also gives description of the manuscript of
       LES 120 JOURNEES DE SODOME.

577.   Garagnon, Jean.  "Sur une annotation marginale de Sade."
       STUDI FRANCESI 24 (1980):  288-289.

       Interprets two annotations written by Sade in the
       margin of a letter to his wife, circa 1785/1786, and
       suggests that Sade took meticulous care to organize
       the chronology of his novel, ALINE ET VALCOUR.

578.   Garçon, Maurice.  L'AFFAIRE SADE.  Paris: Editions Jean-
       Jacques Pauvert, 1947.

       Recounts the trial which took place 15 December 1956
       in Paris in the suit brought against the Editions
       Jean-Jacques Pauvert, which had published LA
       PHILOSOPHIE DANS LE BOUDOIR (1 v.), LA NOUVELLE
       JUSTINE (4 v.), JULIETTE (6 v.), and LES 120 JOURNEES
       DE SODOME (3 v.).  "La Commission du livre,
       considèrent que ces volumes mêlaient à des propos sur
       la société du temps des descriptions de scènes
       d'orgies, des cruautés les plus répugnantes, et des
       perversions les plus variées, et contenaient
       intrinsiquement un ferment détestable et condamnable
       pour les bonnes moeurs, émit l'avis qu'il y avait lieu
       à poursuites pour les quatre titres" [above].
       Prosecution attorney was M. Maynier.  Maurice Garçon,

who wrote this book, was the attorney for the defense.
Witnesses for the defense included Georges Bataille,
Jean Paulhan, and André Breton.

579.  GAZETTE DE LAUZANNE, 6 February 1965, pp. 17-20.

This special issue of the GAZETTE DE LAUZANNE includes
the following articles on Sade (listed by E. Pierre
Chanover, item 11).

Franck Jotterand, "Sade";
Jean-Jacques Brochier, "Le langage et la démesure:  le
    poète";
Gilbert Lély, "Panorama de Sade";
Odette Renaud-Vernet, "La machine infernale de
    Sodome";
Henri-Charles Tauxe, "Le divin marquis et son siècle."

580.  Goulemot, Jean-Marie.  "Mort et libération de Sade."
LES NOUVELLES LITTERAIRES 2591 (30 June 1977):  6.

Gives a very good review of the special issue on Sade
of OBLIQUES published in 1977:  "Ce qui me fascine
dans ce numéro d'OBLIQUES ce sont les produits en
résonance de l'effet Sade:  ce réseau iconographique
et textuel, ces créations de peintres et d'écrivains
constituées en équivalence de l'oeuvre du marquis."

581.  Grossel, Hans.  "Das Denken von Sade."  NEUE DEUTSCHE
HEFTE 20 (1973):  176-180.

Reviews German translations of works by/on Sade:
AUSGEWAHLTE WERKE I-VI (Frankfurt:  Eisher, 1972); DER
GREIS IN CHARENTON (Munich:  Hanser, 1972).

582.  Guerre, Pierre.  "Variétés."  CAHIER DU SUD 290 (1948):
187.

Reviews the MARQUIS DE SADE, MORCEAUX CHOISIS by
Gilbert Lély, published by Seghers.  Compliments Lély
for his erudition and his presentation of Sade's
selected writings, which serve well to acquaint the
reader with the truthful aspects of Sade:  "L'homme
perd de sa monstruosité et le précurseur, le pionnier
des problèmes de l'amour physique se montre sous son
joug véritable."  Regrets, however, that Lély was
prompted for one reason or another to delete certain
passages which were relatively inoffensive.  Concludes

that, in any case, this little book has "je ne sais
quelle valeur spéciale, et fait que Sade vraiment y
apparait."

583. Guyon, B. "Allocution." In LE MARQUIS DE SADE. Paris:
Librairie Armand Colin, 1968, p. 9.

Proceedings of the colloquium on the Marquis de Sade,
Aix-en-Provence, 19 and 20 February 1966. Brief words
of welcome from the dean of the faculté des lettres
d'Aix.

584. Hassan, Ihab. THE DISMEMBERMENT OF ORPHEUS: TOWARD A
POSTMODERN LITTERATURE. Madison, Wisc.: University
of Wisconsin Press, 1982, pp. 24-47.

Chapter I of this book was first published as an
article in TRI-QUARTERLY in 1969. See annotation to
"Sade: Prisoner of Consciousness" (Item 1775).

585. Hayn, Hugo. BIBLIOTHCA GERMANORUM EROTICA. Leipzig:
Verlag von Albert, Unflad, 1885, p. 267.

Gives titles and publishers of some of Sade's works in
German translation and JUSTINE UND JULIETTE, ODER DIE
GEFAHREN DER TUGEND UND DIE WONNE DES LASTERS, which
is not a translation but a thorough discussion of
Sade's novels with a biography of the author.

586. Heine, Maurice. "Commentaire à seize notes pour la
nouvelle JUSTINE--Actualités de Sade III." LE
SURREALISME AU SERVICE DE LA REVOLUTION, 15 May 1933,
pp. 4-10.

Gives many details concerning the composition of the
JUSTINE OF 1791. And furnishes a complete outline,
divided into sixteen different parts found in a one
hundred eleven separate sheets sold at auction in
Paris on 1 June 1926.

587. Heine, Maurice. Preface to CENT ONZE NOTES POUR LA
NOUVELLE JUSTINE. Paris: Le Terrain Vague, 1956, no
pagination.

Reprints the notice published on the occasion of the
auction at the Hotel Drouot, 1 June 1926, of the
Marquis de Sade's manuscript entitled LA NOUVELLE
JUSTINE OU LES MALHEURS DE LA VERTU. This manuscript

was made up of one hundred eleven notes on as many
sheets of paper and was, up to that time, unknown to
bibliographers and researchers.

588. Heine, Maurice.   Preface  to  INFORTUNES DE LA  VERTU.
Paris: Editions Fourcade, 1930, pp. 1-24.

Describes  the  1797 version of LA  NOUVELLE  JUSTINE,
first  discussed  by Guillaume  Apollinaire  in  1909
following  the latter's discovery in the  BIBLIOTHEQUE
NATIONALE of the manuscript numbered 4010.  Includes a
"plan  primitif," details of the manuscripts making up
the HISTORIETTES, CONTES ET FABLIAUX, and mentions the
CATALOGUE of 1788.

This  preface was also published as a chapter in  SADE
(Gallimard, 1950), pp. 45-69.

589. Hoefer.  "Article Sade  par Jean Morel.   In  NOUVELLE
BIBLIOGRAPHIE GENERALE.  Paris: Firmin-Didot, 1863.

Presents a short biography of Sade.   Adds nothing new
to what was already known in 1863.

590. Jacob, [Paul La Croix].  "La Vérité sur les deux procès
criminels  du marquis de Sade."  LA REVUE DE PARIS  38
(1837): 135-144.

Reprinted in CURIOSITES DE L'HISTOIRE  DE FRANCE:  LES
PROCES CELEBRES.  Paris:  1858.

591. Jannoud, Claude.  "L'Affaire Sade."  LA VIGIE MAROCAINE,
24 March 1957, p. 6.

Reassesses  the  merits  of  Sade's  works  after  the
condemnation of the publisher J. J. Pauvert, who had
reedited  several  of Sade's novels.   Insists on  the
relativity  of evil; whereas some authors--Rimbaud,
Baudelaire,  Verlaine--had a short stay in the "enfer"
of libraries,  Sade is condemned to remain imprisoned.
It  seems  that society cannot forgive him his  thirst
for freedom: "Avec Sade, pour la première fois depuis
Lucrèce,  l'homme est réellement seul dans  l'univers.
Il  assume  les conséquences de cette solitude et  ses
vestiges  avec  une  frénésie,  une  soif  de  liberté
décuplées par la detention où se trouvait l'auteur."

592.  Jannoud,  Claude.  "Sade reste un nom lourd à  porter."
      FIGARO LITTERAIRE 1145 (31 March 1968): 24.

      Describes the castle,  Chateau-Thierry,  in  Conde-en-
      Brie,  now  occupied  by  Xavier  de  Sade,  a  direct
      descendant of the Marquis de Sade,  where archives and
      papers  once  belonging to his infamous ancestor  were
      found.

593.  Kemp,  Robert.  "Eros et Psyché."  LES  NOUVELLES
      LITTERAIRES, 3 September 1953, p. 3.

      Reviews the publication in 1953 of L'HISTOIRE  SECRETE
      D'ISABELLE  DE  BAVIERE (Paris,  Gallimard,  333  p.).
      With an introduction by Gilbert Lély.

594.  Larnac,  Jean.  "La  littérature  française  de  la
      décadence."  LA PENSEE 31 July-August  (1950):  110-
      117.

      Comments on the controversy created by the publication
      in  1949  of LA PHILOSOPHIE DANS LE BOUDOIR  (Editions
      premières).

595.  Lély,  Gilbert.  "Un cahier inédit de D. A. F. de Sade."
      TEL QUEL 81 (Fall 1979):  98-99.

      Describes  in  detail the contents  of  the  QUATRIEME
      CAHIER  DES  NOTES  OU  REFLEXIONS  EXTRAITES  DE  MES
      LESTURES OU FOURNIERS PAR ECRIT, written in the prison
      at  Vincennes  between  12 June and  21 August  1780.
      Implied  in  this  find  is  the  existence  of  three
      anterior "cahiers," apparently now lost.

596.  Lély, Gilbert.  "Introduction aux CENT VINGT JOURNEES DE
      SODOME."  MERCURE DE FRANCE 331 (1957): 497-504.

      Explains  that  the  original manuscript  of  the  120
      JOURNES  DE  SODOME,  a roll of  paper  about  twelve
      centimeters by twenty meters long, was found by Arnoux
      de  Saint-Maximin  and held by his  family  for  three
      generations;  it  was  then  sold  to  a  Berlin
      psychiatrist,  Iwan  Bloch  (Dr.  Eugene  Duhren),  who
      published  it  with so many mistakes as  to  make  the
      enterprise useless.  The manuscript was later acquired
      by Maurice Heine and published by him between 1931 and
      1935; this must be considered the original edition.

597. Lély, Gilbert. "Notes historiques sur deux lettres du marquis de Sade." LES CAHIERS DE LA PLEIADE 6 (Winter 1948): 12.

Discusses two letters, dated November 1777, which are in essence "double." They contain two texts, one written in black ink and another written between the lines with lime juice. This second text remains invisible unless the paper is heated.

598. Lély, Gilbert. "Présentation de dix-sept lettres inédites du marquis de Sade aux officiers de la Bastille." OBLIQUES 12-13 (1977): 90-110.

Publishes seventeen hitherto unknown letters, ten addressed to M. de Losme, two to the Chevalier du Puget, one to the officers of the Bastille, one to the Chevalier de Saint-Sauveur, and three to unknown addressees.

599. Lély, Gilbert. "Réflexions sur la morale et la liberté de l'homme." LES CAHIERS OBLIQUES 1 (1980): 7-8.

Unpublished manuscript written by Sade found in a booklet entitled NOTES ET EXTRAITS--QUARTRIEME CAHIER. The first page, which was begun on 12 June 1790, bears the inscription "De cahier des notes ou réflexions extraites de mes lectures içi ou fournies par elles." The last page bears the notation: "fini le 21 Août 1780." (Facsimile from ms 12456 "Fonds Bastille" de la Bibliothèque de l'Arsenal.)

600. Lély, Gilbert. "Réportoire des oeuvres du marquis de Sade." REVUE DES SCIENCES HUMAINES 70 (June 1953): 133-147.

Very erudite work concerning Sade's publications. Includes a synoptic table and a listing of some of Sade's known works compiled according to the bibliography made by Sade himself. Does not mention most of the plays written by Sade but not published until fairly recently.

601. Lély, Gilbert. "Sade n'est pas l'auteur du pamphlet de Zoloé." MERCURE DE FRANCE 328 (1956): 182-184.

Denies that the pamphlet attacking the empress Josephine, Tallien, Bonaparte, and entitled "Zoloe"

was the work of Sade. States that because the
pamphlet was erroneously attributed to him, Sade
became the victim of Bonaparte, who had him imprisoned
for life.

602. MAGAZINE LITTERAIRE, 114 (June 1976): 8-25.

Includes these articles:

Jean-Jacques Brochier, "Sade à notre horizon," pp. 8-
17;
Xavier de Sade, "Sade et sa famille," p. 18;
Pascal Pia, "Lire Sade au XIXe," pp. 19-21;
Alain Robbe-Grillet, "L'ordre et son double," pp. 22-
23;
Jean-Jacques Brochier, "Un grand rhétoricien des
figures érotiques. Entretien avec Roland Barthes,"
pp. 24-25.

603. Masson, André. "Six dessins et une gravure pour
l'édition allemande de LA PHILOSOPHIE DANS LE
BOUDOIR." In NAME DER REPUBLIK. Wiesbaden: Ed.
Limes Verlag. 1961.

Reproduces six drawings and one engraving included in
the German edition of THE PHILOSOPHY IN THE BEDROOM.

604. Mead, William. Review of THE MARQUIS DE SADE: A
BIBLIOGRAPHY by Pierre Chanover. FRENCH REVIEW 47,
no. 5 (1974): 991-992.

States: "The body of the work is scrupulously done,
rationally arranged, and attractively printed and
bound. . . . It might perhaps also have been wished
that some attempt had been made to distinguish what is
inane among the 588 listings in the literary
bibliography from what, still quite exceptionally, is
not."

605. Nadeau, Maurice. "Sade au goût du jour." LA QUINZAINE
LITTERAIRE 232 (1976): 15.

On the occasion of the publication of SADE: LA
PHILOSOPHIE DANS LE PRESSOIR, by Philippe Roger; SADE:
UNE ECRITURE DU DESIR, by Beatrice Didier; and L'AMOUR
EST UNE FETE, by Sylvia Bourbon, discusses the
contemporary popularity of Sade. Considers the work
of Philippe Roger, "un bondissant ouvrage" and that of

Beatrice Didier, "bien conventionnel et tranquille," but by contrast labels Sylvia Bourbon, "une exhibitionniste de haut vol et véritable machine à jouissance boulimique qui aime prendre son plaisir de préférence en public et sous les projecteurs, mais aussi à pied, à cheval, et en voiture, en épelant de A à Z l'alphabet de ce que hier encore on appelait les perversions. . . ."

606. N.D.L.R. "Etudes sadiennes: 1100 pages d'inédits." LES CAHIERS OBLIQUES 1 (1980): 10.

Announces the publication (by Ed. Borderie) of two big volumes of unpublished works by Sade, entitled MARQUIS DE SADE. LETTRES ET MELANGES LITTERAIRES ECRITS A VINCENNES ET A LA BASTILLE, AVEC DES LETTRES DE MADAME DE SADE, DE MADEMOISELLE MARIE-DOROTHEE DE ROUSSET ET DE DIVERS CORRESPONDANTS. The work is annotated by G. Daumas and G. Lély. A third volume, CENT-QUATRE VINGT QUATRE LETTRES INEDITES DU MARQUIS DE SADE, constitutes the last of the collection belonging to Count Xavier de Sade.

607. Nodier, Charles. "De quelques livres satyriques et de leur clef." BULLETIN DU BIBLIOPHILE ET DE L'AMATEUR 7 (1834): 3-11.

Reviews the hypothetical publication of a book entitled MANIPULUS CLAVIUM OU TROUSSEAU DE CLEFS which would give the "keys" to some of the best known satirical publications. Among many others, mentions Voltaire, Beaumarchais, Molière, Sterne, La Fontaine, Rabelais, La Bruyère, and, in a very derogatory fashion, Laclos and Sade, who gets "the disgusting prize of cynicism."

608. Paraz, Albert. "Sur le procès Sade." DEFENSE DE L'OCCIDENT, October 1957, pp. 37-39.

Reports on the trial in Paris of the J. J. Pauvert publishing firm, which had edited the works of the Marquis de Sade and was subjected to a long litigation for advocating a philosophy "contraire aux principes fondamentaux de la morale."

609. Pastoureau, Henri. Notes for CENT ONZE NOTES POUR LA NOUVELLE JUSTINE. Paris: Eric Losfeld, 1956, pp. 1-4.

In the "Avertissement de l'Editeur," discusses several of the notes published under the title "Actualité de Sade" in LE SURREALISME AU SERVICE DE LA REVOLUTION by Maurice Heine.

610.  Perceau, Louis.   "Notice bibliographique."  LEONORE ET CLEMENTINE OU LES TARTUFFES DE L'INQUISITION.   Paris: Au cabinet du livre, 1930, pp. 5-9.

Gives bibliographical information concerning the publication of LEONORE ET CLEMENTINE (1793), a fragmented part of ALINE ET VALCOUR written in all likelihood at the Bastille. Concludes: "On retrouvera dans l'histoire de LEONORE ET CLEMENTINE ces dissertations philosophiques qui font de Sade un rude démolisseur de préjugés, un véritable révolutionnaire; on y retrouvera aussi les qualités de composition et de style qui placent l'auteur de JUSTINE au rang de nos meilleurs écrivains."

611.  Petrucci, Antonio.   "Quasi un diario."  L'OSSERVATORE ROMANO, 22 October 1966, p. 3.

Announces the Italian translation of the Marquis de Sade's works.

States that in spite of the problems encountered by the editions J. J. Pauvert (condemnation of LA PHILOSOPHIE DANS LE BOUDOUR, LA NOUVELLE JUSTINE, JULIETTE, LES 120 JOURNEES DE SODOME) following the complaint and trial brought in 1955 by the Commission du Livre, one hundred thirty thousand volumes of Sade's works have been sold. Says the Italian translation is intended "for adults only." Also notes that "sadism" has invaded the theater and movies and is now part of our contemporary image. Concludes with a quote from R. Queneau, who finds the world of Sade a staggering depiction of what was to come with the Gestapo, its tortures and its concentration camps. And comments: "No, le discussioni e le analisis dei filosofi e dei letterati non hanno 'pastorizzoto' Sade, gli hanno dato un certificato de libera circolazione per cui domani il mondo sara forse pui turpe di quanto non sia oggi."

612.  Pia, Pascal.   "Dans l'enfer de la Nationale."   LE MAGAZINE LITTERAIRE 21 (September 1968):  38-39.

Gives bibliographical information concerning the first
royal indictment against Sade's publications.  Notes
an error made by many bibliographers:  this indictment
should be dated 19 May 1825 and not 19 May 1815, since
that period falls during the "Cent Jours"--the Hundred
Days, when there were no Royal Courts. Attacks some of
the  fables  of  Jules  Janin  and  gives  credit    to
Baudelaire  and  Flaubert  for bringing  Sade  out  of
"Enfer" (the very classified section of libraries).

613.  Pia, Pascal.   LES LIVRES DE L'ENFER DU XVIème SIECLE A
      NOS JOURS.   Paris:   C.  Coulet &  A.  Faure,  1978,
      pp.  14,   15, 29, 67, 129, 130, 181-184, 269, 430, 498,
      580,  618-621,  671,  675-678, 681-686, 735, 738, 819,
      927, 939-942, 955, 959, 989, 1045-1048, 1057, 1099.

      Gives  bibliographical  data on Sade's  works  in  the
      "Enfer"  of the Bibliothèque Nationale.    Follows  the
      format adopted by G.  Apollinaire,  F. Fleuret, and L.
      Perceau in L'ENFER DE LA NATIONALE (item 540) and,  in
      some cases,  reprints verbatim what was already in that
      now out-of-print publication.

614.  Piazzoli, Jacques. Review of LE MARQUIS DE SADE, L'HOMME
      ET SES ECRITS,  by Gustave Brunet.   In CATALOGUE D'UNE
      COLLECTION  DE  LIVRES ANCIENS ET MODERNES,  RARES  ET
      CURIEUX.   Milan:   Librairie Dumolard Frères, 1878, pp.
      394-395.

      Reviews Sade and his work harshly:  "l'un des fous les
      plus  extraordinaires  et  en  même  temps  les  plus
      repoussants."   Gives  a bibliography of  other  works
      dealing with Sade and also includes a list of names of
      men  who have surpassed Sade (in  his  monstrousness):
      Maréchal de Rays,  Gilles de Saval,  Valentino Borgia,
      Bernabo Visconti, Pier Luigi Farnese, etc.

615.  Pigoreau, Alexandre.   PETITE BIBLIOGRAPHIE BIOGRAPHICO-
      ROMANCIERE,  OU DICTIONNARIE DES  ROMANCIERS.   Paris:
      Pigoreau, 1821.

      Lists Sade,  with short biographical details and short
      bibliography.

616.  Poultier,  François-Martin.   "Sade."   LE   TRIBUNAL
      D'APOLLON  OU  LE JUGEMENT EN DERNIER RESSORT DE  TOUS
      LES AUTEURS VIVANTS:   LIBELLE INFURIEUX,  PARTIAL, ET
      DIFFAMATOIRE,  PAR UNE SOCIETE DE PYGMEES LITTERAIRES.

Vol. II. Paris: Marchand Libraire, 1799, pp. 193-197.

This article, published anonymously, is attributed to F. Poultier by Vincenzo Barba in INTERPRETAZIONE DI SADE. States that Sade's name alone has a cadaverous odor which destroys virtue and infuses readers with horrors. Goes on to discuss the "monstrosity" of Sade's works.

617. Profühl, Gaston. "Notes bibliographiques pour les ECRITS POLITIQUES et OXTIERN." Paris: J. J. Pauvert, 1957.

Gives some bibliographical informations on Sade's political writings not published during author's lifetime. Also acknowledges a debt to the serious work done by Paul Bourdin. Recounts some of the events that led to the production on 21 October 1791 of OXTIERN at the Theatre Molière. The play was directed by Jean-François Boursault.

618. Rosart, Françoise. "Bibliographie." OBLIQUES 12-13 (1977): 277-310.

Important bibliography which lists Sade's works in chronological order of publication. Includes some translations. Also includes twenty-page listing of studies on Sade and his works.

619. Rousseau, Hervé. "Sade." In LE DIEU DU MAL. Paris: Presses universitaires de France, 1963. 130 p.

This book is listed in Chanover's bibliography item 505 does not have a section on Sade, or even a reference to the marquis.

620. Roy, J. H. Review of LE MARQUIS DE SADE, by Maurice Heine. In TEMPS MODERNES 5 (June 1950): 2255-2256.

Reviews LE MARQUIS DE SADE, by Maurice Heine, edited by Gilbert Lély and published by Gallimard in 1950. Reports that Heine was the first scholar to bring the infamous marquis out of oblivion and successfully draw attention to him: "Il l'a défendu avec d'autant plus de chaleur qu'il se heurtait à une opposition presque unanime. Ses articles, ses introductions et ses notes, réunis par Gilbert Lély, nous font déplorer qu'il n'ait pas pu mener sa recherche jusqu'au bout et l'unifier."

621. Ryland, Hobart. "Recent Developments in Research on the Marquis de Sade." FRENCH REVIEW 25 (1952): 10-15.

Gives a very scholarly review of the state of research on Sade (1951). Concludes with a prophecy: "Certainly it should be recognized that Sade occupies a fairly important place in the philosophy and literature of the eighteenth century. There is reason to believe that during the next half century a more tolerant attitude towards his violent pornography may result in a better appreciation of his daring originality." Discusses the renewed interest in Sade, especially as promoted by Maurice Heine and Gilbert Lély; but the article is outdated since it was published in 1952, before the publication of most of the new works of and on Sade.

622. Sade, Xavier de. "Sade reste à découvrir. Entretien avec Xavier de Sade." MAGAZINE LITTERAIRE 21 (September 1968): 40-41.

Reports on the discovery, in the library and in the attic of the Castle of Condé, of twenty trunks filled with archives and family papers. The contents of two trunks had been catalogued at the time of this writing; they contained two works by Sade (ADELAIDE DE BRUNSWICK, ISABELLE DE BAVIERE), many letters, and all the plays written at Lacoste (with the exception of TANCREDE and L'EGAREMENT DE LA FORTUNE, which are apparently lost).

623. Seaver, Richard. "From: JUSTINE by D. A. F. de Sade" and "A Note about Justine." EVERGREEN REVIEW 36 (June 1965): 57-60, 89.

Recounts the history of the original publication of JUSTINE, first printed anonymously in 1791. Within the next ten years it was reprinted six times. Quotes Sade as claiming that it is wrong to get the impression from his works that "virtue is a barren cul-de-sac whose only possible issue is onto the lush plain where vice abounds and flourishes." Includes in translation a passage from JUSTINE.

624.  Shimpachiro, Miyata.  "The Marquis on Trial."  JAPAN
      QUARTERLY 8 (1961): 494-496.

      Discusses the long battle--1950 to 1957--waged in
      Japanese courts over the question of whether the
      Japanese version of D. H. Lawrence's LADY CHATTERLEY'S
      LOVER was a work of art or of pornography and
      investigates the fate of Sade's novel JULIETTE, the
      Japanese translation of which was indicted in January
      1961.  Does not mention the outcome of the trial.

      Reports also on the trial in Paris stemming from the
      publication by the Edition Pauvert of the works of the
      Marquis de Sade.  Repercussions went far beyond the
      confines of France and were closely followed as far
      away as Japan.

625.  Stéphane, Roger.  "Marquis de Sade: OEUVRES."  LA NEF
      43 (1948): 122-123.

      Reviews the COLLECTED TEXTS of Sade, edited by Maurice
      Nadeau (Jeune Parque, 1948).  Though Nadeau's
      enterprise may seem presumptuous--to summarize in one
      volume the thoughts originally published in more than
      twenty works--it seems that his choice was wise.  "Son
      choix semble bon.  On l'aurait préféré plus abondant
      et peut-être moins axé sur les théories sadiques."

626.  TEL QUEL 28 (1967):

      This special issue of TEL QUEL, entitled "La Pensée de
      Sade," includes the following articles:  Pierre
      Klossowski, "Sade ou le philosophe scélérat"; Roland
      Barthes, "L'arbre du crime"; Philippe Sollers, "Sade
      dans le texte"; Hubert Damisch, "L'écriture sans
      mesures"; and Michel Tort, "L'effet Sade." This issue
      of TEL QUEL was translated into German and published
      under the title DAS DENKEN VON SADE (Munich:  Teihe
      Hanser, 1969).

627.  Tourné, Maurice.  "Compte rendu:  Le marquis de Sade.
      Actes du colloque d'Aix en Provence."  REVUE
      D'HISTOIRE LITTERAIRE DE LA FRANCE, September-December
      1970, pp. 1074-1079.

      Reviews the proceedings published by the editor Armand
      Colin of the Colloquium on the Marquis de Sade held at
      Aix-en-Provence on 19-20 February 1966.  States: "Les

dix-sept communications présentées dans ce recueil
sont regroupées en trois corps distincts, dont on
pourrait dire, en schématisant leur riche teneur,
qu'ils envisagent successivement, I, L'Homme, II,
L'Oeuvre, III, La Postérité." And concludes: "Il est
louable qu'un centre comme celui d'Aix, loin de
reculer devant les syllabes maudites du nom de Sade,
ait abordé l'homme et son oeuvre comme un objet de
critique scientifique et sereine, en refusant aussi
bien de les rejeter en enfer que de les exalter
gratuitement, avec le seul souci de redonner à Sade sa
place dans l'histoire de la littérature, dans
l'histoire des idées."

628.   Tulard, Jean. "Sade et la censure sous le premier
       empire." In LE MARQUIS DE SADE. Paris: Librairie
       Armand Colin, 1968, pp. 209-217.

       Proceedings of Colloquium on Marquis de Sade, Aix-en-
       Provence, 19 and 20 February 1966. Discusses the
       police's arbitrary measures under Napoléon's regime.
       States that books were confiscated, censured, and
       distributed to friends by the police, who often
       accused writers of insanity simply to get them out of
       the way. The role of censorship was not clearly
       defined and seems to have been based on whim.
       Napoléon's hostility toward Sade stemmed perhaps from
       a dislike of the marquis's work; yet, it does not seem
       to have any correlation with Sade's arrest: "Deux
       motifs ont justifié son internement sans jugement: le
       prétexte de la folie et les demandes réitérées de la
       famille même du célèbre écrivain."

629.   Ullrich, Crucitti. Review of J. Vercruysse, "Fragments
       inédits d'un roman perdu de Sade: LE PORTEFEUILLE
       D'UN HOMME DE LETTRES." In REVUE D'HISTOIRE
       LITTERAIRE DE LA FRANCE 68 (1968): 633-637; also
       published in STUDI FRANCESI 38 (1969): 357.

       States that these fragments have been found in Belgian
       archives and that they are tied together by letters
       which give them the shape of a novel.

630.   Vercruysse, J. "Fragments inédits d'un roman perdu de
       Sade: LE PORTEFEUILLE D'UN HOMME DE LETTRES." REVUE
       D'HISTOIRE LITTERAIRE DE LA FRANCE 68 (1968): 633-
       637.

Mentions a lost epistolary novel of Sade, LE
PORTEFEUILLE D'UN HOMME DE LETTRES, and includes an
unpublished fragment, the thirtieth letter, titled
"Pholoé à Zenocrate." Briefly reviewed by F. B.
Crucitti Ullrich, STUDI FRANCESI 38 (1969): 357.

631.  Wainhouse, Austryn. "On Translating Sade." EVERGREEN
REVIEW 42 (1966): 50-56.

Recounts, in short story style, the events that led
authors to translate the edition of the complete works
of the Marquis de Sade published by Grove Press.

632.  Zylberstein, J. C. "Bibliographie chronologique." In
OEUVRES COMPLETES. Paris: Club du livre précieux,
1967.

One of the best bibliographies to date of Sade's works.

## B. BIOGRAPHIES

633. Almeras, Henri d'. LE MARQUIS DE SADE, L'HOMME ET L'ECRIVAIN. Paris: Albin Michel, 1906. 374 p.

Biography of Sade largely superseded by that of Lély, yet contains interesting chapters on Sade and Rétif de la Bretonne, on Sade, the politician, and on ZOLOE ET SES DEUX ACOLYTES, which author calls a roman à clef. Also contains an annotated bibliography of Sade's work, for the most part a reproduction of Michaud's BIOGRAPHIE UNIVERSELLE ANCIENNE ET MODERNE, pp. 1811-1828.

634. Amer, Henry. "Sur le marquis de Sade." NOUVELLE REVUE FRANCAISE, 1 April 1958, pp. 724-727.

Reviews vol. II of VIE DU MARQUIS DE SADE by Gilbert Lély. Comments on the strange destiny of the marquis and on the labor of love done by his biographers, first Maurice Heine and now Gilbert Lély. States that the true greatness of Sade does not lie in his literary efforts but in the fact that he went beyond literature, writing without indulging in games. Rather, he described situations without any coating, thereby putting a tremendous distance between himself and the writers of the standard erotic novel. Concludes that one finds in Sade a deliberate effort to unmask the real truth about mankind. "Si cette oeuvre est scandaleuse par essence, c'est qu'elle dénonce et annihile, presque sans littérature, les efforts patients des sociétés et des génératijons pour masquer et dissimuler l'horrible vérité que l'homme est né pur le crime."

635. Amiaux, Mark. LA VIE EFFRENEE DU MARQUIS DE SADE. Paris: Editions de France, 1936. 235 p.

"Generally good biography but much of dialogue is imaginative or reconstructed and is, unfortunately, often sensational. Documentation scarce and sources almost never given. Some distortion of Sade's wife and mother-in-law in their favor. Good use of Sade's correspondence for psychological reconstructions. No notes; no bibliography; no index." (Quoted from Cabeen, item 8.)

636.  Anonymous.   "A  Name  to  Conjure  With."   THE  TIMES
      (London), 14 December 1961, 17.

      Reviews  briefly  a translation into English  by  Alec
      Brown  of  Gilbert  Lély's THE  MARQUIS  DE  SADE:   A
      BIOGRAPHY  and states that Lély's book "is not one  to
      be  left alone.   It demands and repays attention  for
      its  close  portrayal  of a career  that  will  always
      baffle common understanding."

637.  Apollinaire, Guillaume.   "Portrait de Sade."  OBLIQUES
      12-13 (1977):  133-140.

      Comments  on  the  appearance  of  the  marquis.  This
      article,  originally  published as an introduction  to
      L'OEUVRE  DU  MARQUIS  DE  SADE.   (Bibliothèque  des
      Curieux,  1909,  item 274), begins with an  assertion
      that  there  are  no  authentic  portraits  of   Sade
      available  and  that  those  which  are  currently  in
      circulation  are phony.   Among the false ones are the
      one  on the cover of the biography by Jules  Janin,  a
      portrait  from the collection of M.H. of Paris  which
      portrays Sade as a young man surrounded by demons, and
      a  version of a medallion by M. de la Porte to  which
      were added fauns, a dunce-cap, and a prison scene.

638.  Baccolo,  Luigi.   "Un Turista di nome  Sade."   NUOVA
      ANTOLOGIA 506 (1968): 245-254.

      Retraces  the steps of the Marquis de Sade in Italy  in
      1775.   He  traveled  with  his  sister-in-law,  Anne
      Prospére  de Launay,  and wrote mostly about solitude;
      people  disturbed him,  and at times he  could  barely
      stand  the presence of others.   States that Sade  was
      influenced  by the revitalizing factor of the  Italian
      climate and concludes:  "L'Italia non e la patria dei
      fantasmi lieti,  chisto non è forse o' paese d'o sole?
      Lo fu anche per Sade,  infatti.   Ha ragione Pieyre de
      Mandiarguer  di  dire che  le invensioni  italiane  di
      Juliette  son  le sole dove il sadismo mostri  qualche
      volta un aspetto 'gioioso.'"

639.  Bachaumont, François de.  MEMOIRES SECRETS POUR SERVIR A
      L'HISTOIRE  DE  LA  REPUBLIQUE DES LETTRES  EN  FRANCE
      DEPUIS  1762  JUSQU'A  NOS  JOURS  OU  JOURNAL   D'UN
      OBSERVATEUR.   London:   John  Adamson,  1777-1789,
      pp. 162-163.

This article was re-edited in MEMOIRES SECRETS . . .
EDITES ET CONTINUES PAR PIDANZAT DE MAIROBERT ET
MOUFLE D'ARGENVILLE, REVUS ET PUBLIES AVEC DES NOTES
PAR P. L. JACOB, BIBLIOPHILE (Paris: Adolphe Delahaye,
1859).

Deals with the Marseille Affair. Listed under the
date 27 July 1772.

640. Bagot, Michel. "Les bruits de la ville." REALITES,
June 1970, p. 34.

Reviews very briefly Jeanine Delpech's book on the
Marquise de Sade, LA PASSION DE LA MARQUISE DE SADE.

641. Barthelot, M. "Article Sade." LA GRANDE ENCYCLOPEDIE.
Vol. 29. Paris: Société anonyme de la Grande
Encyclopédie, n.d., p. 47.

Gives a short biography of Sade and an appraisal of
his literary production which he labels "the
extravagant production of a delirious imagination."
States: "l'analyse d'un de ses livres présente une
accumulation de crimes, de viols, d'incestes, à chaque
page, on dresse des chevalets, on brise des cranes, on
dépouille des hommes de leur peau fumante, on
blasphème, on s'arrache le coeur de la poitrine. La
plupart de ces ouvrages sont illisibles."

642. Bataille, Georges. "Vue d'ensemble: Sade 1740-1814."
CRITIQUE 9 (1953): 989-996.

Interesting comparison between Don Juan and Sade, both
of whom recognized the limits of the possible and its
conditions. Death for Don Juan, thunderstruck, is the
great dialectical moment of life, when the
authenticity of pleasure is built on the impossible.
Therefore, author feels that we should be grateful to
Sade, who pointed out that sensual pleasure, with or
without consent, is the only truth and the only
measure outside of the boundaries of the possible:
"La volupté est à ses yeux la partie de l'homme qui a
franchi les bornes du possible."

643. Beauvoir, Simone de. "Sade." In LES ECRIVAINS
CELEBRES. Vol. II. Paris: Lucien Mazenod, 1951, pp.
226-229.

Suggests that it is high time to give Sade all the
honors due him as a writer. And gives him credit for
understanding, before Freud and beyond Freud, the
importance not only of sexuality but also of hitherto
ignored sexual aberrations. Fascinated by, as well as
afraid of, his own peculiarities, Sade wrote as much
to justify himself as to exploit his own discoveries,
and "sa sincérité passionnée fait de lui, á defaut
d'un artiste consommé ou d'un psychologue cohérent, un
grand moraliste." Concludes that Sade accepted only
those truths confirmed by his own experience even if
that did contest radically the ideas of reciprocity:
"il a refusé les faciles et fausses promesses de la
vertue et du bonheur; dans la solitude des cachots il
a réalisé une nuit éthique analogue à cette nuit
intellectuelle où s'est plongé Descartes: s'il n'en a
pas fait jaillir une réponse sûre, du moins a-t-il
opposé aux principes abstraits et à leur cortèges
d'abstraites hécatombes cette interrogation
tragiquement concrète qu'a été sa vie même."

644.  Bégis, Alfred. "Le Registre d'écrou de la Bastille de
      1782 à 1789." LA NOUVELLE REVUE, November-December
      1880, pp. 522-547.

      Describes the Bastille and gives information
      concerning procedures. Names of prisoners were not
      included on the registers but, rather, men were called
      by floor number and location. Gives appellations of
      numerous inmates including that of Sade. The last
      page of that register is dated 10 and 12 July 1789.
      On 14 July of that year only seven persons were left
      at the Bastille. Sade was not one of them. He had
      been transferred to Charenton on 4 July by Sieur
      Quidor. His room was then sealed.

645.  Belaval, Yvon. "La vanille et la manille." LES CAHIERS
      DE LA PLEIADE 12 (1951): 156-159.

      Publishes a letter dated 1783 from Sade to his wife
      and discusses the possible meaning of that letter,
      which tends to be ambiguous. Sade complains to his
      wife about the personal problems created by his
      imprisonment and lets her know about some of the
      solutions he has found.

646.  Béliard, Octave (Dr.) LE MARQUIS DE SADE. Paris:
      Edition du Laurier, 1928. 315 p.

Partly apocryphal biography of Sade. Romanticized
version of the life of the marquis, but interesting
reading. Divided into three parts: 1) his youth,
2) his life as a prisoner, and 3) his old age.
Reviewed by Emile Magne, MERCURE DE FRANCE 206
(1928): 654-655.

647. Benoît, Jean. "Notes concernant l'exécution de
testament Sade." In BOITE ALERTE. MISSIVES LASCIVES.
Catalog of internationale l'exposition surréaliste,
1959-1960, of the Galerie Daniel Cordier.

648. Bey, A. "Sur les dernières années du marquis de Sade."
LE TEMPS, 4 January 1912, p. 12.

Does not present anything new on the last years of
Sade spent at Charenton.

649. Biberstein, H. PORTRAIT FANTAISISTE DU MARQUIS DE SADE.
(frontispice de la correspondance de Mme Gourdan,
1806). (Listed by F. Rosart in OBLIQUES 12-13
[1977]).

Confirms that there exists no known portrait of Sade.

650. Billioud, Edouard. "Le Fort l'Ecluse au temps où le
Marquis de Sade en était gouverneur." VISAGES DE
L'AIN, September-October 1968, pp. 29-31.

Explains how Donatien de Sade became governor of
Bresse, Bugey, Gex and Valmorey, an estate which, on
13 August 1764, brought him 8,750 pounds. Sade lost
this "charge" on 2 May 1778; it was turned over to his
cousin, Jean-Baptiste de Sade d'Eygueres.

651. Biou, Jean. "D.A.F. de Sade: Lettre à Melle de
Rousset." LETTRES NOUVELLES, March-April 1967,
pp. 55-67.

Discusses file 12456, located at the Library of the
Arsenal in Paris, which contains numerous documents
hitherto ignored by researchers. Publishes a letter
from that file written by Sade to Mademoiselle de
Rousset on 7 May 1779 and which ends with a long
passage in bastard Provençal: "Ave dise mignote le
voules donc sapre lou second effet, escouta mi bin,

quand un canon es trop cargai que faut faire per lou
libera, lou faou descarga. . . ."

652. Biou, Jean. "Sade à la Bastille." LES LETTRES
NOUVELLES, January-February 1967, p. 10.

Recounts some of the highlights of the five and a half
year stay of Sade in the Bastille prison. Good resume
but brings no new development in the life of the
famous marquis.

653. Blanchot, Maurice. "Quelques remarques sur Sade."
CRITIQUE 3-4 (1946): 239-249.

On the occasion of the publication by Palimurge (1946)
of Sade's IDEE SUR LES ROMANS (preface by Frederic
Prince), reviews some general conceptions about Sade.
Stresses the fact that the marquis was very much a
product of his time but cautions against attributing
to him only the main characteristics of his social
class and epoch. States that there is in him
something more terrible than the Terror, "une bassesse
qui n'est celle ni de sa société ni de la plus basse
société, une vulgarité qui n'est pas contraire aux
raffinements, mais qui, à certains moments,
s'expriment en des hurlements de sauvage, en des cris
perçants et barbares dont la Nature semble confondue."

654. Bloch, Iwan (Dr.) (pseudonym for Eugen Dühren). LE
MARQUIS DE SADE ET SON TEMPS. Geneva: Slatkine,
1970.

First published in Berlin by H. Barsdorf in 1901.
Translated from the German by Dr. A. Weber-Riga.
Preface on "L'idée de sadisme et l'érotologie
scientifique" by Octave Uzanne. In this important but
somewhat outdated study on the eighteenth century and
the life of the Marquis de Sade, author gives detailed
analysis of JUSTINE, JULIETTE, and LA PHILOSOPHIE DANS
LE BOUDOIR. Includes a chapter on sadism in
literature and on the influence of the works of the
Marquis de Sade. Also attempts to pinpoint the
precise philosophy of Sade. Long table of contents
and complete index. Reviewed by E. Locard in ARCHIVES
D'ANTHROPOLOGIE CRIMINELLE, etc., 17 (1902): 568-569
and Dr. Paul Voivenel, LE PROGRES MEDICAL 7 (Februar
1917): 7-14.

655. Bonmariage, Sylvain. LA SECONDE VIE DU MARQUIS DE SADE. Lille: Mercure de Flandre, 1927.

Apocryphal and of little interest. Contains some rather mild love stories of libertinage.

656. Bonnefoy, Yves. "La Cent vingt et unième journée." Postface to VIE DU MARQUIS DE SADE, by Gilbert Lély. In OEUVRES COMPLETES DU MARQUIS DE SADE. Vol. II. Paris: Cercle du livre précieux, 1962, pp. 677-685.

Comments not so much on Lély's work, VIE DU MARQUIS DE SADE, but on Lély himself, a former poet who devoted much of his life to research connected with the writings of Sade and who convinced Sade's descendants to publish some of Sade's correspondence. States: "Lély a séparé de ses équivoques sadiques l'intuition sadienne de l'être. Il étend, comme il le dit dans sa VIE DU MARQUIS DE SADE, le 'merci' du langage 'sur les proies délicieuses ressuscitées à l'aube de la 121e journées."

This essay was first published in CRITIQUE 132 (1958): 389-395.

657. Borel, Pétrus. MADAME PUTIPHAR. 1839; Paris: Régine Desforges, 1972.

Nineteenth-century novel which borrows a lot from Sade's biography. The author attempts to criticize a system of justice which condones continued and unjustified imprisonment. Includes three prefaces, one by Béatrice Didier, another by Jules Claretie, and the third by Jean-Luc Steinmetz.

658. Bouër, André. "La Coste, Laboratoire du sadisme." In LE MARQUIS DE SADE. Paris: Librairie Armand Colin, 1968, pp. 15-20.

Proceedings of Colloquium on the Marquis de Sade, Aix-en-Provence, 19 and 20 February 1966. Describes the château of La Coste, giving minute details of location of doors, windows and number of rooms in each wing. Also presents an analogy with the Château de Silling, the setting for the book LES CENT VINGT JOURNEES DE SODOME, which apparently had identical apartments to those of Lacoste. First published in CORRESPONDANCES

4 (1956-1957):  60-67 under title, "Mystère et lumière de La Coste, Laboratoire du sadisme."

659.  Bourde, André J.  "Sade, Aix-en-Provence et Marseille. Un autre Sade."  In LE MARQUIS DE SADE.  Paris: Libraire Armand Colin, 1968, pp. 59-71.

Proceedings of Colloquium on the Marquis de Sade, Aix-en-Provence,  19 and 20 February 1966.  Uncovers some hitherto  overlooked  facts  concerning  Joseph  Henri Véran de Sade who, like his famous cousin, Donatien de Sade,  was  imprisoned because of a lettre de  cachet. Both  men owe much of their torment to their  mothers-in-law:  the Marquise de Causans and the Presidente de Montreuil,  respectively.   Also  discusses  several causes célèbres,   including the cases of Gaufridy, La Cadière,  and  that of the Marquise de  Ganges,  later used by Sade in one of his books.

660.  Bourgeade,     Pierre.     "Portrait     imaginaire . . . le marquis de Sade."  LE MONDE, 17 July 1983, Supplément, p. 1.

Calls   himself  a  "sadophile."   Investigates  some discrepancies in Sade's JOURNAL,  published by Gilbert Lély in 1953.   In the apocryphal fill-in that follows the  missing  days  in Sade's diary are a tale  of  an escape from the asylum where Sade was confined at  the time,  a visit to Teresa d'Avila's grave, and a return to Sainte-Pelagie, the mental institution.

661.  Bouvel, Emile.  "Les trois châteaux du marquis de Sade." REVUE DU TOURING CLUB DE FRANCE,  June 1956,  pp. 312-316.

This  article  was  cited by Giorgi Cerruti  in  STUDI FRANCESI 39  (1961):  432 but was  not  available  as listed.

662.  Brenner, Jacques.  "Sur le marquis de Sade de  Maurice Heine." PARIS-NORMANDIE, 6 June 1950, p. 12.

Gives  recognition to Maurice Heine,  a  scholar,  who appraised  Sade's  works and successfully brought  him out of the "Enfer" where he had been confined.

663.  Breton, André.  "The Grand Cérémonial Restored to Us at Last  by  Jean Benoît."  SURREALISM  AND  PAINTING.

Translated by Simon Watson Taylor. New York and London: Harper & Row, 1972, pp. 386-389.

Numerous references to Sade throughout the book, and reproduces especially important painting by Jean Benoît entitled COSTUME FOR EXECUTING THE TESTAMENT OF THE MARQUIS DE SADE. (1959). About the fact that Sade's first will and testament was ignored, comments in surrealist terms: "We know the rest: the unshakable faith manifested in the burning passion with which poets (Borel, Swinburne, then Apollinaire) gazed upon those dagger-ripped purple robes which accuse the future, the very slow rehabilitation of a memory towards which biology and a still inarticulate moral science will eventually be compelled to acknowledge their debt."

664. Breton, André. "Enfin Jean Benoît nous rend le grand cérémonial." OBLIQUES 12-13 (1977): 169-173.

Attempts to extract from Sade's testament and the mode of his burial a global meaning to his life. Finds a rapprochement with the sculptures of Jean Benoît.

665. Brierre de Boismont, Alexandre (Dr.). "Remarques médico-légales sur les perversions de l'instinct génésique." GAZETTE MEDICALE DE PARIS 29 (21 July 1849): 559-560.

Deals with the Rose Keller affair.

666. Brochier, Jean-Jacques. "Sade à notre horizon." MAGAZINE LITTERAIRE 114 (June 1976): 8-17.

Publishes two letters with biographical and historical interest and precedes them with another account of Sade's life. Nothing new added to what has already been said by Paul Bourdin, Jean Desbordes, and Gilbert Lély.

667. Bury, R. de. "Sur le séjour de Sade à Charenton." MERCURE DE FRANCE 45, no. 95 (1912): 634-637.

Recounts some of the details published in TEMPS of January 1815 related to Sade's stay in Charenton. They were drawn from the collected archives at Charenton, a mental institution directed by M. de Coulmier when Sade was first interned there.

668.  Cabanes,    Auguste.   "La    prétendue   folie   du    divin
      marquis."   In LE CABINET SECRED DE L'HISTOIRE,   Paris:
      Michel, 1905, pp. 417-490.

      "Appearing first in 1900,  this article published many
      documents  for the first time,  especially those  from
      archives  of  hospitals at Charenton.   Still of  real
      value  and  has been used as a source  by  many  later
      biographers.   Far from supporting title, refutes it."
      (Quoted from Cabeen, item 8).

669.  Campion, Leo.  SADE, FRANC-MACON.  Paris:  Cercle des
      Amis de la bibliothèque initiatique, 1972.  163 p.

      Sees  a "Franc-maçon" as a member of a society  having
      at   least   two facets—on the one hand,  a society  of
      philosophers  attempting to ameliorate the  world,   on
      the other, a society of mystics and believers in magic
      and   alchemy   opposed   to   the   ideals   of   the
      Encyclopedists.    Feels that much in Sade follows  the
      ideology  advocated  by  the  Franc-maçons.   Gives  a
      cursory  biography of Sade.   Concludes with a chapter
      of quotes from A.  Breton, M. Blanchot, P. Klossowski,
      and others.

670.  Capuletti,  Joseph-Manuel.   SADE PRISONNIER.  Dessin et
      lavis.  N.p.:n.p., 1959.

      Not available.

671.  Cellard,  Jacques.   "Des lieux,  des hommes.   Sade, de
      châteaux en cachot.  Un grand seigneur méchant homme."
      LE MONDE DES LIVRES, 6 August 1976, p. 10.

      Describes  several castles and fortresses where  Sade,
      "a bad man," spent some time.

672.  Chapsal, Madeleine.  "Tout Sade est amour." L'EXPRESS,
      24-30 January 1966, pp. 67-70.

      Reviews the re-edition of Gilbert Lély's book,  VIE DU
      MARQUIS DE SADE by the Editions J. J. Pauvert.  States
      that  Sade's  biography was largely a continuation of
      the  work  began  by Maurice Heine and  was  based  on
      numerous  letters published as L'AIGLE, MADEMOISELLE
      (1949),   LA VANILLE ET LA MANILLE (1953),   LE CARILLON
      DE  VINCENNES (1953),  MONSIEUR LE 6 (1945),   and  MON

ARRESTATION DU 26 AOUT (1959). Concludes that, in spite of an obvious passion for his subject, Lély's book is well worth reading: "Le miracle veut que tous ces excès tournent ici en avantages: cet échafaudage passionné tient en équilibre sur une documentation que l'on ne saurait prendre en défaut."

673. Cherasse, Jean A. and Guicheney, Geneviève. SADE: J'ECRIS TON NOM LIBERTE. Préface de Xavier de Sade. Paris: Pygmalion, 1976. 286 p.

In this two-part book, discuss the adult life of Sade. See Sade as belonging to two worlds, that of the aristocrat and that of the libertine, at a time when the king was setting a bad example. Also analyzes the praxis of a person walled-in alive. In the second part stresses the militant aspect of Sade's undertaking, his contribution as a driving force in the theater at Charenton. Concludes with a chapter on "the sperm of liberty."

Reviewed by Michel Delon, DIX-HUITIEME SIECLE 9 (1977): 460.

674. Clouard, Henri. Review of LA PASSION DE LA MARQUISE DE SADE, by Jeanie Delpech. LA REVUE DES DEUX MONDES (July 1970): 154-156.

Reviews Jeanine Delpech's LA PASSION DE LA MARQUISE DE SADE, which describes the pathetic loyalty demonstrated by the marquise toward her husband. Yet, in the end, Madame de Sade gave in to the pressure exercised by her mother, and the book ends with her request for separation from the marquis.

675. Colins, Hippolyte de. "Notice sur l'hospice de Charenton." JOURNAL INEDIT. Paris: Gallimard, 1970, pp. 121-164.

Describes the unsanitary conditions prevalent at Charenton hospital for the insane during Sade's stay there. States that no medical records were kept and that patients were often mistreated, abused, even tortured. Admission to the asylum was not necessarily dependent on the mental state of the person involved but often the result of a power move on the part of influential relatives wishing to get rid of a bothersome individual. Also attacks the

establishment's director who apparently was on very
friendly terms with the Marquis de Sade.

676.  Conroy,  Peter V., Jr.  Review of THE MARQUIS DE SADE by
      Donald S. Thomas.  In THE EIGHTEENTH CENTURY:  A
      CURRENT  BIBLIOGRAPHY,  edited  by Robert  R.  Allen.
      Goleta,  California:  AMS Press, Inc., 1979, pp. 372-
      373.

      States that "Donald Thomas has produced a highly
      readable biography of the Marquis de Sade.  He paces
      his story well, ending chapters in dramatic fashion or
      bringing  us  quickly--unexpectedly--to  familiar
      episodes such as the story of Rose Keller.  Briefly
      but accurately, Thomas picks out unprincipled, immoral
      rakes--like the Duc de Richelieu--who provide living
      models for Sade's literary fantasies as well as his
      personal conduct.  Plates and engravings accompany the
      text--some  are eighteenth-century illustrations for
      Sade's novels.  Others provide eloquent evidence on
      the times that nourished these novels:  miniature
      erotic scenes painted in lockets; suggestive and
      lascivious  drawings  by  Fragonard  for  private
      customers."  Continues with an interpretation of
      Thomas's work on Sade,  intended more for the general
      reader than for the scholar.  Concludes that for
      Thomas, "Sade's life resembles a 'macabre farce'
      rather than the stuff of high philosophic moment."

677.  Corput, V. D. (Dr.).  "Le marquis de Sade était-il fou?"
      L'INTERMEDIAIRE  DES  CHERCHEURS  ET  CURIEUX 43 (15
      February 1901):  263-266.

      Feels that an affirmative answer to this question
      would be the kindest to Sade's memory.  Denies that
      Sade could have been victim of assorted persecutions.
      Stresses Sade's monomania, a type of mental aberration
      in which the patient stresses only one type of idea or
      inclination:  "C'est  précisement  un  phénomène
      caractéristique chez la plupart des monomanes
      instinctifs ou des invertis, de chercher à excuser les
      actes les plus désordonnés et les plus répréhensibles,
      les faits les plus révoltants, avec une logique
      déconcertante et une lucidité fallacieuse, bien propre
      à induire en erreur sur leur état mental véritable des
      profanes, ou même des médecins experimentés dans les
      arcanes si abstruses de la psychopathie."

678. Crépieux-Jamin, M., and Lecerf, André. "Etude graphologique sur le marquis de Sade." In LE VRAI VISAGE DU MARQUIS DE SADE. Paris: Nouvelle revue critique, 1939, pp. 9-11.

Studies the marquis's handwriting and affirms "L'écriture du marquis de Sade ne révèle point la folie morale dont on l'a souvent taxé. Il faut y voir l'union peu commune d'une intelligence très cultivée et l'hypertrophie de l'instinct sexuel. . . . Tout dans cette écriture plaide pour l'équilibre."

679. Cruickshank, John, ed. "Libertinism and the Novel." FRENCH LITERATURE AND ITS BACKGROUND. London: Oxford University Press, 1968, pp. 148-162.

Sees Sade as a male chauvinist who denounces all generous impulses in man but defends nature, which would not have impulses harmful to it. States that Sade's ideas, "based on the motive force of egoism and the destructive impulses of the individual, are essentially antisocial, denying both Christian values and the subservience of the individual's interests to the common good."

680. Dalmas, André. "Sur la vie du marquis de Sade par G. Lély." TRIBUNE DES NATIONS, 2 January 1953, p. 9.

Author of A LA RECHERCHE DES LIAISONS DANGEREUSES gives a good review of Lély's VIE DU MARQUIS DE SADE.

681. Daumas, Georges. "Sur la vie du Marquis de Sade, par G. Lély." REVUE DES SCIENCES HUMAINES, June 1953, pp. 183-184.

This brief book review is not signed but only initialed "G.D." Gives a favorable account of Lély's work. Concludes: "Par son contenu ce livre assure de façon décisive de nouvelles conquètes dans la connaissance objective du marquis de Sade, et par sa forme il n'est pas indigne de l'homme qu'Apollinaire aima et qui figure comme le démon de la liberté dans les mythes du Surréalisme.

682. Daumas, Georges. Preface to JOURNAL INEDIT. DEUX CAHIERS RETROUVES DU JOURNAL INEDIT DU MARQUIS DE SADE 1807, 1808, 1814. Paris: Gallimard, 1970. 183 pp.

Publishes Sade's diaries for the years 1807, 1808, and
1814 (until Sade's death on 2 December 1814).
According to this journal, Sade would have had, at age
74, an affair with a sixteen-year-old girl, Madeleine
Leclerc. Includes (pp. 117-164) in an appendix a long
report written by Hippolyte de Colins, of the hospital
at Charenton.

683. Dauzat, Albert.   DICTIONNAIRE ETYMOLOGIQUE DES NOMS DE
FAMILLE ET PRENOMS DE FRANCE. Paris: Larousse, 1951.

Lists the following under the heading "SADE (de)":
"Famille avignonnaise, connue dès le XIIIe siècle, de
SADDES, hameau de L'Herault (Avene).   Cf: aussi le
surnom SADE, agréable (proprement 'SAVOUREUX')."

684. Delon, Michel. "Chronologie." EUROPE 522 (1972): 139-
147.

Lists the main events in the life and the society of
the Marquis de Sade, from his birth on 2 June 1740
until his death on 2 December 1814.

685. Delon, Michel. Review of QUI ETAIT LE MARQUIS DE SADE?
by Janine Neboit-Mombet.   DIX-HUITIEME SIECLE 6
(1974):   414-415.

Points to some minor flaws in this book and stresses
Sade's actuality.   Recapitulates: "L'auteur rappelle
le contexte historique (chap. I), la biographie de
Sade (II), le contenu de ses oeuvres (III et IV),
avant d'analyser les axes principaux de sa pensée (V)
et son comportement (VI).   La monographie se termine
par un aperçu des lectures successives de l'oeuvre, de
J. Janin à G. Bataille (VII).   Cette synthèse évite
les jugements moralisateurs et l'enthousiasme des
thuriféraires."

686. Delon, Michel. Review of LE MARQUIS DE SADE, BIOGRAPHIE
ILLUSTREE, by Donald Thomas.   DIX-HUITIEME SIECLE 11
(1979):   514-515.

Reviews the French translation by A. M. Garnier,
published by Seghers in 1976.   Comments dryly:
"Donald Thomas a composé une biographie romancée qui,
au prix de quelques inventions et de beaucoup de
confusions, présente une image familière et rassurante
de l'écrivain. . . ."   However, author is more

generous toward the production of the book which, he
says, "ne laisse rien à désirer."

687. Delpech, Jeanine.   LA   PASSION DE LA MARQUISE DE SADE.
Paris: Planète, 1971.   158 p.

Writes a compassionate biography of the Marquise de
Sade. Persecuted because of her love for her husband,
she was the first to believe in his genius.   Recounts
the story of an extraordinary conjugal love which, in
essence, proves the marquis to be a different kind of
person than is generally believed.   Also pays a great
tribute to the marquise, who apparently had quite a
personality of her own and an unqualified devotion to
her husband.

Reviewed by H. Clouard, LA REVUE DES DEUX MONDES, July
1970, pp. 154-156, and Michel Bagot, REALITES, June
1970, p. 34.

688. Desbordes, Jean.   LE   VRAI VISAGE DU MARQUIS DE  SADE.
Paris: Edition Nouvelle Revue Critique, 1939.   340 p.

Acknowledges a great debt to Maurice Heine, Paul
Bourdin, and Henri Chaubot, who gave advice and
documentation for this biography.   Includes several
unpublished manuscripts and illustrations.   Recounts
some hitherto unknown anecdotes, e.g., while traveling
in Italy under the name of Count de Mazan, Sade was
arrested for not paying homage, as was the custom, to
the king.   His difficulty was to give a logical
explanation for this behavior without revealing true
identity.   Also describes, in poetic terms, many
details pertinent to an understanding of Sade's life,
for instance, this description of the castle at La
Coste: "Aux charmes de la Provence, à ses oliveraies,
à sa temperature, à ses plantations odorantes, ajoutez
la noblesse d'un horizon depouillé.   Depuis Apt, la
route monte en lacets à travers une solitude qui
rappelle la Vieille-Castille.   Seul le dernier
tournant vous dévoile le sommet d'une colline de
roches décapées par le soleil.   Quant au village vous
ne le verrez qu'en dernier, tant la grisaille des tons
est uniforme.   Aucune fausse note dans l'apparence.
Aucune bâtisse neuve au toit de tuiles criardes; mais
des maisons d'époque Renaissance, comme les ruines
seigneuriales qui les dominent."

689.  Desmaze,   Charles.   LE  CHATELET  DE  PARIS.   Paris:
      Didier, 1863, p. 327.

      Deals  with  the  police report  on  the  Rose  Keller
      affair.

690.  Didier,   Béatrice.   "Le  journal  de  Charenton."   LA
      QUINZAINE LITTERAIRE 113 (1 March 1971):   11.

      Reviews  the  publication  by  Gallimard  Editions  of
      Sade's JOURNAL INEDIT, which consists of two notebooks
      written  at  Charenton,   the  first  dated  5 June 1807 to
      26  August 1808 and the second,   18 July  to  November
      1814.   Concludes:   "Cet  ensemble de textes prouve à
      quel point la 'folie' au XVIIIè siècle comme au XVIIè,
      est  encore  une  notion commode qui permet de constituer
      un ghetto pour les a-sociaux,  pour ceux qui  menacent
      l'ordre établi.  Tel fut bien, au premier chef, le cas
      du  marquis  de  Sade,  homme  on ne  peut  plus  sain
      d'esprit.   Non  pas fou,  mais génial demiurge de  la
      déraison."

691.  Dühren,  Eugen  (Dr.).   DER  MARQUIS DE SADE UND  SEINE
      ZEIT:   EIN  BEITRAG ZUR KULTUR UND SITTEN  GESCHICHTE
      DES 18.   JAHRHUNDERTS.   MIT BESONDERER BEZIEHUNG AUF
      DIE  LEHRE  VON DER  PSYCHOPATHIA  SEXUALIS.   Berlin:
      Verlag von H. Barsdorf, 1906.  538 p.

      See  annotation under LE MARQUIS DE SADE ET SON  TEMPS
      by Dr. Iwan Bloch, item 654.

692.  Dulaure,  Jacques  A.   LISTE  DES  NOMS  DES  CI-DEVANT
      NOBLES.  Paris: Garnery, 1790, pp. 89-96.

      Gives a brief biography of Sade.

693.  Eaubonne,  Françoise d' (pseudonym for Martine  Okapi).
      "Sade ou l'eros-vengeance."  In EROS NOIR.   Paris: Le
      Terrain vague, 1962, pp. 145-233.

      Criticizes the biography written by Marc Chadourne and
      recounts  in a fictional form the encounter with  Rose
      Keller and the Marseille prostitutes.  Concludes: "Si
      l'Eros de Sade est un ange noir,  un  cruel démon
      couronné   de   myrtes,   c'est   que   l'assassinat
      perpétré . . .  sur  les  corps  enfantins,  féminins,
      parfois,  males et adultes,  de n'importe quel âge  ou
      sexe pourvu qu'il soient innocents et  beaux,  cet

assassinat-là n'est autre que celui pratiqué par
l'écrivain Sade sur la bonne opinion, sur l'image
innocente et belle que le lecteur a de lui-même."

694. Eluard, Paul. "D.A.F. de Sade, écrivain fantastique et
révolutionnaire." LA REVOLUTION SURREALISTE 8, 1
December 1926, p.

Originated as response to articles written by Maurice
Talmeyer, published in LE FIGARO in which Eluard
states that there never existed a man as unhappy as
Sade. Article was later expanded and published as
"L'évidence poétique" in DONNER A VOIR.

695. Endore, S. Guy. SATAN'S SAINT. New York: Crown, 1965.
312 p.

Highly romanticized version of Sade's biography, or,
as the author states, "a novelized Ph.D. thesis."
Includes the following quotation from Jean Rostand:

Kill one--you're a murderer.
Kill millions--you're a conqueror.
Kill everyone--you're God.

696. Eulenberg, Albert (Dr.). "Der Marquis de Sade."
ZUKUNFT 26 (25 March 1899): 497-515.

One of the first and most remarkable studies on the
Marquis de Sade and sadism. Known to Maurice Heine
and mentioned by him in his article published in LE
PROGRESS MEDICAL but ignored by most scholars.

697. Fauville, Henri. LA COSTE, SADE EN PROVENCE. Aix-en-
Provence: Edisud, 1984. 250 p.

Gives historical background of La Coste, one of the
three castles owned by the Marquis de Sade and his
family. Built during the Middle Ages, that property
was ransacked and essentially destroyed after the
Revolution. It was acquired by André Bouër during the
1940's and partly restored. Presents many details on
Sade's stays at La Coste and includes numerous
diagrams and illustrations.

698. Feuillade, Lucien. "Dans notre courrier. . . ." LES
LETTRES NOUVELLES, October 1962, pp. 147-160.

Tongue-in-cheek review in epistolary form of Jacques
de Lacretelle's essay published in LE FIGARO
LITTERAIRE (10 February 1962). Takes this opportunity
to write a short biography of Sade, recounting "a sa
façon" the main events or--at least the most
sensational.

699.  Finas, Lucette.  "Voyage d'Italie par le marquis de
      Sade."  LES LETTRES NOUVELLES, November-December 1968,
      pp. 171-175.

      Reviews the publication of LE VOYAGE D'ITALIE, written
      by Sade during his travels in 1776.  Interesting text
      which lets the reader get a glimpse of the marquis
      enjoying a rare liberty:  "Sade fait participer le
      lecteur au tourisme studieux qui est le sien."  But
      already present is a trademark which will be
      accentuated in later projects:  the saturation of the
      literary space.

700.  Galtier, Charles.  "L'ARLESIENNE au château de Sade."
      LETTRES FRANCAISES 577 (1955): 10.

      Gives a brief history of La Coste, the castle which
      belonged to Sade's family since 1710.  Destroyed and
      vandalized during the Revolution, the castle was first
      purchased by a peasant in 1816, and sold again in 1952
      to André Bouër, who organized several theatrical
      representations including L'ARLESIENNE in order to
      raise funds and rehabilitate Lacoste.

701.  Gear, Norman.  SADE, LE DIVIN DEMON.  Paris: Buchet-
      Chastel, 1964.  225 p.

      Translated into French by C. Houzeau.  Admits the
      difficulty of writing a legitimate biography of Sade
      because numerous documents have been destroyed at the
      Bastille or at La Coste or even by Sade's own family.
      Acknowledges a big debt to Gilbert Lély, whose VIE DU
      MARQUIS DE SADE has exploited all the resources
      available to researchers.  Concludes: "Dans une
      société où les droits de l'homme étaient trop souvent
      niés, Sade a insisté pour que l'attention la plus
      soutenue soit accordée à l'ETRE qui, dans la condition
      humaine, se dissimule sous la chair.  La violence et
      la férocité de ses oeuvres sont d'essence
      métaphysique, les tortures et les extases de ses

personnages reflètent des explosions et des confluences universelles."

702. Gérard, W. "L'énigmatique marquis de Sade et sa décevante existence." AUX CARREFOURS (1958): 1236-1245.

Not available as listed.

703. Ginisty, Paul. "Le marquis de Sade était-il fou?" INTERMEDIAIRE 43 (1901): 263-266.

This article is incorrectly attributed by E. Pierre Chanover, item IL to Paul Ginisty, entry 215. It is in fact signed by Dr. V. D. Corput. See annotation item 677.

704. Ginisty, Paul. LA MARQUISE DE SADE. Paris: Fasquelle, 1901, pp. 1-134.

Contains seven short biographies, but only two relate to Sade. The first, "La Marquise de Sade," recounts in moving terms some of the main events in the life of the marquise, stressing the fact that she showed an enduring love and loyalty toward her husband, whom she protected against all comers, even her own mother. In the second essay, "Un amour platonique du Marquis de Sade," discusses the long friendship, mostly epistolary, of Sade with Melle de Rousset. (First published in LA GRANDE REVUE in 1900.)

705. Ginisty, Paul. "Les lettres inédites de la marquise de Sade." LA GRANDE REVUE 3 (1899): 1-31.

"Essential article and source for all modern biographers of Sade though not always fair to him. Kind of biographical sketch with quote from Marquise's letters for support; dates are unfortunately avoided. Conclusion has become a classic: 'elle mourut à Echauffour . . . le 17 juillet, 1810. Elle avait largement payé son tribut à la misère humaine.'" (Quoted from Cabeen, item 8.)

706. Giraud, Pierre. HISTOIRE GENERALE DES PRISONS. Paris: Alexis Eymery, 1814, p. 104. (Listed by E. P. Chanover in item 11, as written by Pierre Giraud.)

Gives a background of conditions in several well-known Parisian prisons--Vincennes, Bicêtre, Charenton, Sainte-Pélagie--and relates some anecdotes concerning some of the most famous inmates. About Sade states: "Malgré les glaces de l'âge, il sortait encore à travers les feux de cette imagination véritablement volcanique, des productions plus abominables encore que celles qui ont été livrées au public."

707.  Gorer, Geoffrey. "Department of Amplification." THE NEW YORKER, 10 January 1953, pp. 76-79.

A long letter of comments and refutation from the author of THE MARQUIS DE SADE: A SHORT ACCOUNT OF HIS LIFE AND WORK. An anthropologist who had published that book on Sade some seventeen years earlier, Gorer reiterates that "all the data, the numerous letters, the ascertainable facts seem to show that when Sade was not in one of his sexual rages, he was courtly, gentle, considerate, and even sentimental; the prolonged affections he inspired in nearly all the people with whom he had dealings are notable alike in duration and fervor. He was able to command loyalty in his many misfortunes to a quite remarkable extent."

708.  Gorer, Geoffrey. THE MARQUIS DE SADE. New York: Liveright, 1934. 250 p.

"Fairly scholarly study of life and works of Sade. One of the best in English, with ample quotes from Sade in support of all arguments, though certain biographical details such as an account of Sade's journey to Italy are inaccurate. Succeeds in main purpose of debunking monster legend and does well to establish Sade as serious reformer and philosopher. Remains, however, more excellent popularization than original study, and sources of information frequently not honored nor even mentioned in bibliography." (Quoted from Cabeen, item 8.) This book not available.

Reviewed by Albert Guérard, NEW YORK HERALD TRIBUNE BOOKS, 6 January 1935, p. 11; N. Maclaren, NEW STATESMAN AND NATION 7 (26 May 1934): 808-810; and anonymously in TIMES LITERARY SUPPLEMENT (London) , 10 May 1934, p. 346.

709.  Gorer, Geoffrey.  THE LIFE AND IDEAS OF THE MARQUIS DE
      SADE.  London:  Peter Owen,  1953;  New York: Norton,
      1963;  London:  Peter Owen, 1963.  250 p.

      This   is   a   revised   version   of   the   book   THE
      REVOLUTIONARY  IDEAS OF THE MARQUIS DE SADE,  published
      in  1934.   Author  states in introduction  that  most
      political  references have been omitted and quotations
      which had been edited in the first edition of the work
      are   now   unexpurgated.    A   few   psychological
      formulations have been removed and a new final chapter
      has  been added as well as a re-assessment of  sadism.
      Adds  "in whole or in part sixty hitherto  unpublished
      documents  of major importance in elucidating the life
      of the Marquis de Sade."  Last chapter,  "Thirty Years
      After"  was  also  published  in  shortened  form   in
      ENCOUNTER 103 (April 1962):  72-78.

710.  Gorer, Geoffrey.  THE REVOLUTIONARY IDEAS OF THE MARQUIS
      DE SADE.  London:  Wishart, 1934.  264 p.

      Very  readable  biography of Sade,  one of  the  first
      published  in English,  based in large part  on  three
      reference books:   DER MARQUIS DE SADE UND SEINE  ZEIT
      by  Iwan  Bloch;  L'OEUVRE DU MARQUIS DE  SADE  by
      Guillaume  Apollinaire;  and THE MARQUIS DE SADE by C.
      R. Dawes.  Includes an important chapter on sadism and
      algolagnia.   Reprinted  in 1963 under title THE  LIFE
      AND IDEAS OF THE MARQUIS DE SADE.

711.  Goulemot,   Jean-Marie.   "Divin   marquis   ou   objet
      d'études?"   REVUE DES SCIENCES HUMAINES  124  (1966):
      413-421.

      Comments  that in spite of the publication by  Gilbert
      Lély of Sade's biography,  much concerning the marquis
      remains  a mystery.   Suggests that it might become  a
      necessity  to  avoid  sadic hagiography  in  order  to
      search for a deeper truth.  As an example,  points  to
      new  readings of ALINE ET VALCOUR which would stress a
      conscious effort by the marquis at a revindication  of
      his class,  the aristocracy,  and states:  "La fidélité
      à  la  morale aristocratique qui se révèle  incapable
      d'assurer  la  satisfaction des  passions  libertines,
      apparaît socialement comme un leurre qui conduit  la
      noblesse  à sa perte. . . .  Nous substituerons peut-
      être  au mythe d'un Sade  'révolutionnaire  integral',

celui d'un Sade, aristocratique lucide, engageant un
pari impossible sur la Révolution et sur l'Histoire."

712.  Groffier, Jean.  "La Provence du marquis de Sade."
      MARSEILLE 118 (1979):  112-114.

      Attempts to reconstruct the setting in which Sade
      lived at Lacoste, the family castle now belonging to a
      Sadian  scholar,  André  Bouër,  who  is  slowly
      reconstructing the site as it was during Sade's
      lifetime.

713.  Guerre,  Pierre.  "Chroniques."  CAHIER  DU  SUD  320
      (1953):  177-179.

      Reviews VIE DU MARQUIS DE SADE, Vol. I, by Gilbert
      Lély, published by Gallimard.  Gives credit to Lély
      for the immense work of love done in the footsteps of
      Maurice Heine in order to bring to light a hitherto
      unknown  Sade.  A  very  meticulous  and  erudite
      researcher, Lély included a copy of original documents
      to back all his claims.  Wonders if at the bottom of
      Sade's sadism there is not an immense deception in
      love because Sade does not seem to know how to love
      with love.  His conception of love is inverted from
      the ancients' concept, that is, physical erotism was
      only a mechanism whereas feeling and the idea of love
      were exalted.

714.  Guicheney, Genevieve.  "Comment sortir du cercle de
      famille."  In SADE, J'ECRIS TON NOM LIBERTE.  Paris:
      Pygmalion, 1976, pp. 16-72.

      Brief biography of Sade's formative years.  Stresses
      the period preceding the writing of JUSTINE.

715.  Guiral, Pierre.  "Un noble Provençal contemporain de
      Sade, le marquis d'Antonelle."  In LE MARQUIS DE SADE.
      Paris:  Librairie Armand Colin, 1968, pp. 73-82.

      Proceedings of Colloquium on the Marquis de Sade, Aix-
      en-Provence, 19 and 20 February 1966.  Draws parallels
      between  the  Marquis  de  Sade  and  the  Marquis
      d'Antonelle, an infantry captain who, like Sade, spent
      a good deal of time in jail, participated during the
      Revolution as a member of the Revolutionary Tribunal
      and who also wrote a few books, now forgotten.

716.  Guy, Basil.  "Sur les traces du 'Divin Marquis'."  STUDI
      FRANCESI 14 (1970):  63-71.

      Recounts  a story presented by Fleury in his  MEMOIRES
      in  which  the  main  character might  have  been  the
      Marquis  de Sade.   While some facts seem to fit  well
      with what is known of the life of the Marquis de Sade,
      other  details do not belong in the same  frame.   The
      complete text of Fleury's story is included.

717.  Gysen,   R.   DE  SLECHT  BEFAAMDE  MARKIES  DE  SADE.
      Amsterdam: Heynis, 1961.  160 p.

      Outlines a short biography and a study which includes:

      1) De Banden tussen Rationalisme en Sadisme;
      2) Het Masker van het Niets;
      3) Schaduw van het Niets;
      4) De Weber geboorte van het Niets.

718.  Hardy,  Siméon Prosper.   "Mes loisirs,  ou journal d'un
      bourgeois  de Paris de 1766 à 1790."   NOUVELLE  REVUE
      ENCYCLOPEDIQUE, 4 (1912): 300-302.

      Discusses  the  events  that led to  the  Rose  Keller
      affair.

719.  Hayman, Ronald.  DE SADE: A CRITICAL BIOGRAPHY.  London:
      Constable, 1978.  252 p.

      Believes the corruption of someone  beautiful,  young,
      virtuous  is  one  of  the central  pleasures  of  LES
      LIAISONS  DANGEREUSES of Choderlos  de  Laclos.   That
      theme  appealed also to Sade who,  however,  gave more
      power  to his libertines over their victims "who seldom
      even  take  advantage of the little  opportunity  they
      have for resistance."  This highly readable  biography
      concludes that "with Sade, life and work could be said
      to  have  been conditioned by the same  fantasies  (as
      those  of  Genet) were it not for the fact  that  they
      were constantly developing, and it is important to see
      (as  clearly as we can) how he represented himself  to
      himself  in each successive phase of his  development.
      Even  the  books can be  regarded,  like  Genet's,  as
      efforts  to regain mastery over his life."   Includes  a
      bibliography.   Reviewed  by Derek Marlowe,  "Whipped
      In,"  SPECTATOR, 22 July 1978, pp. 21-28; and by Cecil

Jenkins, "The Cruel Marquis," TIMES LITERARY SUPPLEMENT (London), 28 July 1978, p. 844.

720. Hayman, Ronald. "The Birth of the Middle-Aged Writer." PARTISAN REVIEW 45 (1978): 192-205.

Believes that Sade "would probably never have become a writer if he had not had to spend so much time in prison" and proceeds to show how he lived and freed himself vicariously through the heroes he portrays in his novels.

721. Hayman, Ronald. "Hot Stuff." THE NEW REVIEW 37 (April 1977): 57-58.

Gives a poor review of THE MARQUIS DE SADE, by Donald Thomas: "Not only does he fail to understand Sade; I am left unconvinced that he genuinely wants to. The book cannot even serve as an introduction to the subject."

722. Heine, Maurice. "L'affaire des bonbons cantharidés du Marquis de Sade." HIPPOCRATE, REVUE D'HUMANISME MEDICAL 1 (1933): 95-133.

Retells in detail all the events that preceded and followed the affair of the "bonbons cantharidés" in July 1772. Gives the testimony of assorted witnesses and doctors. Also reports on the police search. Concludes from reading this report that there exists a great disparity between the facts and the fancy built around them.

723. Heine, Maurice. "Le marquis de Sade et Rose Keller, ou l'affaire d'Arcueil devant le parlement de Paris." ANNALES DE MEDECINE LEGALE 13 (July 1933): 309-366 and 434-437.

"Indispensable study publishing for first time all documents relative to Rose Keller affair. Letters of Mme Du Deffand and diary of Hardy tend to be borne out as reliable." (Quoted from Cabeen, item 8.)

724. Heinic, Lionel. "Le marquis de Sade." PROVENCE MAGAZINE 383 (February 1975): 74-78.

Biographical essay giving some interesting locations. Situates, for instance, the Marseille affair on the third floor a building at the corner of the Rue Longue and Rue d'Aubagne above a candy store! Claims there was a secret passage at the Château d'Echaufflour leading to the quarters of Sade's sister-in-law. Quotes a letter written to his wife in Provençal: "Adieou, poulide caro et meilleur couer; . . ." Concludes: "Certes, chez Sade, la peinture est sans concession du vice terrassant la vertu avant d'être récompensé. Or, il n'est que de tourner les yeux autour de soi pour constater combien la réalité peut souvent, dépasser la fiction."

725. Henriot, Emile. "La Vraie figure du marquis de Sade." COURRIER LITTERAIRE DU XVIIIe SIECLE. Paris: Michel, 1962, pp. 308-314. Reprinted from LE TEMPS, 25 February 1930, p. 12.

States that it is hazardous to speak of the marquis, since his name alone is offensive to many, and claims that Sade was bloodthirsty only in his writings: "Il n'était sanguinaire qu'en face de son écritoire; et, en matière d'atrocités, il en a certainement beaucoup moins fait qu'il n'en a écrit." Believes that Sade was probably not a "saint" but that, without the constant hostility of his family, his youthful tantrums would have gone unnoticed. Further states that in point of fact, Sade was far from being a terrorist: "Il s'exposa même aux foundres robespierristes, en refusant dit-on, de donner son adhésion au terrorisme."

726. Humbourg, Pierre. "Sade et moi." LE PROVENCAL, 22 November 1964, p. 5.

Like in Norman Gear, SADE: LE DIVIN DEMON, recounts some of the highlights of Sade's life, which he believes to be as dull as his works, but states: "Sans ce parti-pris de vice qui finira dans un verre d'O, il eût été Richardson ou Bernadin de Saint-Pierre avec moins de grâce, et il y a longtemps qu'on n'en parlerait plus. Mais le miracle fut bien plus tard que Laure de Sade, comtesse de Chevigné servit de modèle à Proust pour Mme. de Guermantes."

727. Izzo, Jean-Claude. "Sade, marquis de La Coste." EUROPE 522 (1972): 127-138.

Recounts once more the events of 27 June 1772, in
Marseille, which led to a charge of poisoning against
Sade and eventually to a death penalty. States that
Sade's way of life was that of a libertine: it is
clear that Sade never killed anyone except in his
books. As for the castle at La Coste, far from making
Sade a feudal lord, it barely provided for his
financial needs. Always short of funds, the marquis's
unbridled expenses hurried his downfall and
contributed to the ransacking of his ancestral home.

728. Janin, Jules. "Le Marquis de Sade." REVUE DE PARIS XI
     (1834): 321-360.

Begins with Sade's genealogy. Attests that Sade comes
from a very good aristocratic family and that he is a
direct descendant of Laure de Noves, the wife of
Hugues de Sade (and the woman who inspired Petrarch).
Adds a cursory biography. Then severely criticizes
Sade's writings: "le marquis de Sade a fait de ces
livres obscènes l'occupation de toute sa vie, mais de
ces obscénités qui n'étaient que cela dans la tête des
autres écrivains, le marquis de Sade a fait un code
entier d'ordures et de vices." Then describes an
apocryphal story of a young man gone mad after reading
the works of Sade.

Also published in LES CATACOMBES 1 (1839) and
summarized in LE LIVRE (Paris: Plon, 1870, pp. 279-
291). Includes Sade's last will, pp. 291-292.

729. Jannoud, Claude. "Une moment à la gloire du plus maudit
     des écrivains." LA VIGIE MAROCAINE, 2 February 1958,
     p. 6.

Gives a very favorable review of Lély's biography of
Sade. Exposes Lély's method thus: "Ne donner de la
naissance de son sujet à sa mort que des documents.
Ceux-ci sont quelquefois commentés, interprétés, mais
documents et interprétations sont toujours séparés
sans ambiguité." Makes the following comments about
Sade: "Véritable fondateur de la psychopathologic,
grand createur, Sade a été le plus maudit de tous les
écrivains parce qu'il a été le plus seul et le plus
libre d'entre eux." Insists that Sade cannot be
understood in terms of laws applicable to other men.

730. Jenkins, Cecil. "The Cruel Marquis." TIMES LITERARY SUPPLEMENT (London) 77 (1978): 844.

Reviews the book by Ronald Hayman, DE SADE: A CRITICAL BIOGRAPHY, published by Constable in 1978. Regrets that in "the rather flat staccato narrative itself is often perceptible the effect of straight summarizing of some of the principal secondary works especially the major biography of Lély" and laments that some of the "translations are often faulty, and on occasion convey the exact opposite of what was intended."

731. Jepsen, Hans Lyngby. MARQUIS DE SADE. Copenhagen: Stig Vendelkaers Forlag, 1963. 223 p.

Sade's biography written in Danish. Includes chapters on: "Vil vi kendes ved ham?"; "Den loerde abbed jesuiterskolen, krigen og den store koerlighed"; "Den store skandale og den smukke svigerinde"; "Det store hab, redningen gennem toilet vinduet og livet pa La Coste"; "En dydig veninde, jalousiens djoevel og revoluionens komme"; "Ensomhedens helvede, den dydige Justine, den lastefulde Juliette og sovekammerfilosofferne"; "Revolutionen, roedslen, kejser Napoleon og de sidste ar i Charenton"; and "Den historie, der ikke blev skrevet."

732. Jouffroy, A. "Un acte surréaliste: l'exécution du testament de Sade." ARTS, 29 December 1959, p. 16.

Calls the execution of Sade's last will, a surrealist action: his wishes were totally ignored.

733. Lacretelle, Jacques de. "Une épouse modèle: la marquise de Sade." FIGARO LITTERAIRE, 10 February 1962, pp. 1, 4.

Describes the tumultuous relationship of the marquise de Sade with her infamous husband: "la destinée pathetique de cette amoureuse aux prises avec des forces démentielles qui l'avaient subjuguée." Madame de Sade wrote her attorney on 13 June 1790 that, after long and difficult deliberation, she had decided to ask for a separation from her husband. After the separation, the Sades never saw one another again. The marquise died in 1810 at the Château d'Echauffour.

734.  Lacroix, Paul.  "La vérité sur les deux procès criminels
      du marquis de Sade."  REVUE DE PARIS 37 (1837):   135-
      144.

      "Inaccurate but first attempt to get at the truth
      behind the trials of Sade. Used by most later
      biographers, is often a source of their inaccuracies.
      However, reporting of judgments of Sade by his
      contemporaries is of real value, and statement that
      Sade was only 'un aimable mauvais sujet' often
      quoted."  (Quoted from Cabeen, item 8.)

735.  Laprade, J.  "Sur le Marquis de Sade de M. Heine."
      ARTS, 23 June 1950.

      Listed in E. Pierre Chanover's bibliography, item 11.

736.  Lély, Gilbert.  "Les ancêtres du marquis de Sade."
      MERCURE DE FRANCE 314 (1952):  81-90.

      Traces the genealogy of Sade's family back to the
      beginning of the twelfth century. Petrarch's
      inspiration, Laura, according to this article,
      belonged to Sade's family tree.

737.  Lély, Gilbert.  "Une maitresse du marquis de Sade:  Mlle
      Colet, de la Comédie italienne."  CAHIERS DE LA
      PLEIADE 12 (151):  137-147.

      Reports that Sade had an amorous intrigue with a shy
      young actress of the Comédie italienne.  He wrote her
      several letters which are reprinted in this article.
      The young woman died when she was only twenty-one
      years of age.

738.  Lély, Gilbert.  "Description du château du marquis de
      Sade à La Coste."  MERCURE DE FRANCE 311 (1951):  660-
      673.

      Gives a history and description of the Sade family's
      forty-two-room castle.  Also enumerates some of the
      furnishings known to have been in each of the rooms.
      However, concedes that total reconstruction of the
      castle's plan is not possible since the ruins still in
      existence do not give enough indications of each
      room's location.

739. Lély, Gilbert. "Une fiancée du marquis de Sade:   Mlle
     Laure-Victoire-Adeline de Lauris." TABLE RONDE 40
     (April 1951):  76-85.

     Discusses the Marquis de Sade's love for Laure-
     Victoire-Adeline de Lauris to whom he was briefly
     engaged, and publishes a letter addressed to her,
     dated 6 April 1763.   Includes a poem written by Sade,
     "Le Troubadour provençal," which could have been
     dedicated to her.   See also article   "L'Aigle,
     Mademoiselle. . . ." by Gilbert Lély.   Item 53.

740. Lély, Gilbert. "L'évasion du marquis de Sade à Valence
     d'après des documents inédits." TABLE RONDE 101 (May
     1956):  108-116.

     Recounts the events that led to Sade's escape from the
     prison of Vincennes where he had been incarcerated  on
     a  "lettre de cachet" sent by his  mother-in-law,  the
     subsequent stay he made at La Coste,  and his eventual
     arrest under ignoble conditions and reincarceration at
     Vincennes.

741. Lély,   Gilbert. "Un   laquais   du  marquis   de   Sade:
     Carteron, dit la Jeunesse." MERCURE DE  FRANCE  325
     (1955):  179-183.

     Publishes in its entirety a letter from Carteron  to
     Sade and  recounts some of the  transactions  between
     this valet and Sade and his family.

742. Lély, Gilbert. THE MARQUIS DE SADE: A BIOGRAPHY.
     London: Elek Book, 1961; Toronto: Ryerson Press, 1961.

     Translated by Alec Brown.   Also published by Grove
     Press (New York, 1962).

     See annotation to the French version:   VIE DU MARQUIS
     DE SADE, item 747.

743. Lély, Gilbert. "La mort du marquis de Sade d'après des
     documents inédits." BOTTEGHE OSCURE 18 (1956): 20-26.

     Describes Sade's last days at the Hospice of Charenton
     and mentions his peaceful death,  attended solely by a
     young intern,  L. J. Ramon. The marquis's son,
     Donatien-Claude-Armand,  disregarded his  father's

wishes and had him buried religiously in the cemetery of Charenton.

744. Lély, Gilbert. "La jalousie conjugale du marquis de Sade." LETTRES NOUVELLES 4 (1956): 674-682.

More than four years after his incarceration on 13 February 1777 at Vincennes, Sade was visited by his wife on 13 July 1781. From that day until the following October the marquis was assailed by fits of acute jealousy which he eventually translated into literary recitative in his JUSTINE of 1791 and also in the 1797 version in which one of the protagonists laments: "Rien ne m'amuse comme de travailler moi-même à mon déshonneur."

745. Lély, Gilbert. "Sade." In DICTIONNAIRE BIOGRAPHIQUE DES AUTEURS. Vol. II. Paris: Société d'édition de dictionnaires et encyclopédies, 1964, pp. 482-484.

Sketches Sade's life and gives an annotated bibliography of his works. States that a novel such as ALINE ET VALCOUR should rank among the great works of fiction, alongside the DECAMERON, DON QUIXOTE, and GULLIVER'S TRAVELS. Praises especially the HISTOIRE SECRETE D'ISABELLE DE BAVIERE, published only in 1952: "Par la richesse de ses matériaux et l'ampleur de sa vision, par la profondeur de ses réflexions touchant à la psychologie tant individuelle que collective, par les teintes noires et inquiétantes dont il a soutenu le tableau des crimes de la reine, l'auteur d'ISABELLE DE BAVIERE mérite de prendre place au nombre des meilleurs historiens qui ont précédé l'ère romantique."

746. Lély, Gilbert. "La belle-soeur du marquis de Sade: Mlle Anne-Prospère de Launay." TEMPS MODERNES 65 (March 1951): 1561-1581.

The correspondence between Mlle de Launay and her brother-in-law has apparently been destroyed, and not much is known about this young woman who inspired so much passion in Sade. She died of a sudden illness while still very young. (The date of her birth is not known.)

747. Lély, Gilbert. VIE DU MARQUIS DE SADE, ACCOMPAGNEE DE NOMBREUX DOCUMENTS INEDITS. Vol. I: DE LA NAISSANCE

A L'EVASION DE MOILLANS 1740-1773. Paris: Gallimard, 1952.

Donatien Alphonse François was born in Paris in 1740, to one of the most important families in Provence. Through his mother, the marquis was related to the royal family; his aunt and uncle occupied high posts in the Church. Sade studied in Paris at the College Louis Le Grand; afterward, in 1754, he was sent to military school. By 1759 he was an infantry captain. Four months after his marriage, to Mlle de Montreuil, he was incarcerated for two weeks because of excesses in a house of prostitution. On 3 April 1768, the marquis picked up a thirty-six year old woman, Rose Keller. He was later convicted of having beaten her and sentenced to pay a fine. It was about that time that his wife's sister, Mlle de Launay, became his mistress. On 27 June 1772, in Marseille, the marquis was accused of sodomy, poisoning and assault. He was tried in absentia and condemned to be executed but escaped to Italy. The king of Sardinia put out a warrant for the marquis's arrest. He was found in Savoy and detained at the Fort of Miolans where he stayed until April 1773, when he escaped.

748.  Lély, Gilbert.  VIE DU MARQUIS DE SADE, AVEC UN EXAMEN DE SES OUVRAGES.  Vol. II.  DES ANNEES LIBERTINES DE LA COSTE AU DERNIER HIVER DU CAPTIF, 1773-1814. Paris: Gallimard, 1957.

The marquis returned to his castle in 1773 and continued to anger his mother-in-law, who increased her pressure for his arrest. He fled to Italy but returned to Lacoste about a year later; he was then captured and sent to Vincennes. Was released in 1778, but because of a "lettre de cachet," he was sent back to Vincennes for five and a half years. Transferred to the Bastille in 1784, he remained there until the Revolution; and it was there that he started to write plays and novels. On 2 July 1789 he was transferred to an insane asylum, Charenton, but was liberated when all prisoners detained under lettres de cachet were freed. Between 1791 and 1801 he published numerous novels which were considered licentious; he was again arrested and sent to Charenton, where he died in 1814.

749.  Lenning, Walter.  "Sade."  SELBSTZEUGNISSEN UND BILDDOKUMENTEN. Hamburg: Rowohlt, 1965. 152 p.

Original version of this book is illustrated below and
has a certain flavor missing in the translation.

GERMAN VERSION

Als jedoch seine Leiche aus St. Helena nach Frankreich
zuruckgeführt wurde kniete das französische Volk
entlang der Landstrassen, uber die sein Sarg auf einer
die sein Sarg auf einer Lafette nach Paris gefahren
wurde, und jeder Seufzer lautete: Napoleon! (p. 96).

ENGLISH VERSION

However, when his body was brought from St. Helena to
France, the people knelt along the roadside to see his
coffin on the gun-carriage pass on its way to Paris
(p. 122).

750.  Lenning, Walter.  PORTRAIT OF SADE:  AN ILLUSTRATED
      BIOGRAPHY.  New York:  Herder and Herder.  1971,
      174 p.

      A translation by Sarah Twohig of MARQUIS DE SADE IN
      SELBSTZEUGNISSEN UND BIBDDOKUMENTEN.  Contains a
      section on Sade's theater and lists his interests in
      theatrical productions as early as 1769.  Mentions
      that his first play was performed at La Coste on 20
      January 1772 and that in 1790 his comedy SOPHIE ET
      DESFRANCS was accepted by the Comédie-française but
      was never produced; however, LE SUBORNEUR's first
      production in the Theatre Italien was staged on 5
      March 1792.

751.  Levêque, Jean-Jacques.  "Sade:  la figure de l'énigme
      absolue."  LES NOUVELLES LITTERAIRES 2869 (1983):  42.

      Comments on Gilbert Lély's book, LA VIE DU MARQUIS DE
      SADE, and laments that no authentic portrait of the
      "divine marquis" exists, except for the one concocted
      by Man Ray.

752.  Locard, E.  Review of LE MARQUIS DE SADE ET SON TEMPS.
      ARCHIVES D'ANTHROPOLOGIE CRIMINELLE, DE MEDECINE
      LEGALE ET DE PSYCHOLOGIE NORMALE ET PATHOLOGIQUE.  17
      (1902):  568-569.

Reviews book by Iwan Bloch, item 654.

753. Magne, Emile. "Revue de la quinzaine." MERCURE DE
FRANCE, 15 September 1928, pp. 654-655.

Laments that little tangible evidence is available up
to that date to document life and works of Sade.
Reviews briefly the biography written by Octave
Beliard. States: "L'auteur veut prendre toutes les
libertés du romancier et trouver en lui-même tel
détail que l'histoire lui refuse, qui lui semble
nécessaire pour animer d'une vie plausible et
humainement logique l'ombre maintenant inconsistante
du marquis."

754. Manganella, Diego. "Ombre nel tempo, la marchesa di
Sade." NUOVA ANTOLOGIA 302 (1 June 1922): 205-216.

Tells in moving terms of the relationship of the
Marquis de Sade with his wife, a gentle woman who was
passionately devoted to her husband: "La persistenza
della fedeltà e della devozione di questa donna verso
un tale uomo ha qualche cosa di sublime." She
eventually retired to a convent, but only death
relieved her of the sufferings that had been inflicted
upon her: "Solo la morte potette dare all'infelice
marchesa la pace."

755. Maréchal, Sylvain and Lalande, J. DICTIONNAIRE DES
ATHEES. Bruxelles: Grabit, An VIII.

Sade's name is not included in that edition and also
does not appear in the edition reviewed and enlarged
by J. Lalande (published in Brussels in 1833).
However, listed among the most illustrious atheists
are Marechal, d'Holbach, Spinoza, Fréret, Condorcet,
Buffon, Diderot, Frédérick the Great, d'Alembert, La
Mettrie.

756. McMahon, Joseph. Review of THE MARQUIS DE SADE by
Donald Thomas. In FRENCH REVIEW 52, no. 2 (1978):
351-352.

Gives a poor review of that book published in 1976 by
Weidenfeld and Nicolson. States: "Clearly this kind
of confusion and thinking will not do. . . ."

757.  Ménabréa, Léon.   In DES IRUGUBES FEODALES DANS LES ALPES
      OCCIDENTALES.  Turin: Imprimerie royale, 1865.

      Discusses  briefly  Sade's  stay  in  prison  at  Fort
      Miolans.

758.  Ménard,   Pierre   (Dr.).    "Portrait  graphologique  du
      marquis de Sade."  DOCUMENTS No. 7, December 1929.

      Listed in E. Pierre Chanover's bibliograpy, item 11.

759.  Michaud,  Louis-Gabriel.   "Article Sade."  In BIOGRAPHIE
      UNIVERSELLE ANCIENNE ET MODERNE.    Vol. 37.   Paris: C.
      Desplaces, 1863, pp. 219-222.

      Gives brief biography of Sade,  stressing that,  while
      the marquis led a rather dissolute life,  he never was
      guilty  of any barbarous or violent  actions.   Quotes
      Mme.  du Deffand,  who recounted the story  of  Rose
      Keller  in a letter to Horace Walpole.   Includes  an
      impressive listing of Sade's published and unpublished
      works.    Mentions a relatively little-known  fact:
      Louis-Marie  de Sade,  oldest son of the  marquis,  a
      gallant  and rather courageous infantry  captain,  was
      assassinated  on 9 June 1809 during a return  trip  to
      his regiment stationed at Corfou.   He had written and
      published  the first volume of a history of the French
      nation.

760.  Mitrani, Nora.   "Du  nouveau sur Madame de Montreuil."
      MEDIUM, February 1954.

      Presents another discussion of Sade's mother-in-law.

761.  Moreau de Tours.   "Affaire Keller."  In DES ABERRATIONS
      DU SENS GENESIQUE.  Paris: 1880.

      Listed in E. Pierre Chanover's bibliography, item 11.

762.  Nadeau, Maurice.   "Exploration de Sade, essai  pour
      précéder des TEXTES CHOISIS."  Paris: La jeune Parque,
      1947, pp. 4-27.

      In  this  introduction to Sade's COLLECTED TEXTS,
      attempts  to elucidate some of the paradoxical aspects
      of the Marquis de Sade's life and works.   In addition
      to confinement at Vincennes,  the  Bastille,  at
      Madelonnettes,  Carmes, Saint-Lazarre, Picpus, Sainte-

Pélagie, Bicetre, and Charenton during his lifetime,
Sade again became a prisoner after his death, this
time in the "enfer" of the Bibliothèque Nationale.
Reviewed by P. Klossowski, PARU, June 1948, pp. 60–63.

763. Naz, Chanoine R. "La captivité du marquis de Sade et
son évasion." SOCIETE SAVOISIENNE D'HISTOIRE ET
D'ARCHEOLOGIE 79 (1965): 69–96.

Recounts in detail the events that led to the arrest
and internment of Sade at the fort of Miolans (from 9
December 1772 to 30 April 1773), the conditions of his
detention, and daily life in prison. Also describes
Madame de Sade's devotion while her husband was in
jail; the fate of Sade's keepers, de Launay and
Duclos; Sade's escape; and the harsh punishment meted
out to de Launay and other guards at Miolans.

764. Neboit-Mombet, Janine. QUI ETAIT LE MARQUIS DE SADE?
Preface by Hubert Juin. Paris: Le Pavillon-Roger
Maria, 1972.

Presents a biography, an analysis of Sade's main works
and in appendix a choice of texts including the
DIALOGUE ENTRE UNE PRETRE ET UN MORIDOND, but cautions
(about giving resume of Sade's novels): "Les
'raconter' est une trahison; réduits à leur intrigue
les romans de Sade peuvent paraître puérils et
rocambolesques." Sees in Sade's literary production
not only a means of escape but a justification which
can be translated as a condemnation of the society in
which he lived. States: "L'irrationnel chez lui se
manifeste avec une puissance d'autant plus grande
qu'il se heurtait aux interdits de la société pour
parvenir à son accomplissement; l'amour de la raison
était en harmonie avec son esprit et son tempérament.
La seule synthèse possible était l'identification de
l'irrationnel au raisonnable, du Mal à la Logique.
Adopter une éthique du Mal lui permettait de créer un
système cohérent, de donner un but transcendant à ses
impulsions naturelles. Le Mal est la raison première;
la nature en donne la preuve, et la violence justifiée
sert à l'apologie exclusive de l'Individu."

Reviewed by Suzanne Rossat-Mignod in LA PENSEE 173
(January 1974): 146–147; Michel Delon in DIX-HUITIEME
SIECLE 6 (1974): 414–415.

765. Noailles, Marie-Laure de. "Sade." LE NOUVEL
     OBSERVATEUR, 28 September 1966, p. 37.

     Is quoted as saying: "Le Divin Marquis était un jeune
     homme très romantique et puis, on l'a forcé à épouser
     une femme qu'il n'aimait pas (c'est la soeur qu'il
     aimait). Ca lui a aigri le caractère. Il est devenu
     coureur."

766. Pappot, Gemma. DE MARKIES DE SADE, EEN RET MIT BRIEVEN
     EN DOCUMENTEN. Amsterdam: de Arbeider spers, 1967,
     213 p.

     Biographical details on Sade, based on letters and
     assorted papers. Concludes with a statement on the
     importance of Sade to numerous romantic writers:
     Hugo, Shelley, de Musset, D'Annunzio, Stendhal,
     Lautreamont, Baudelaire, Swinburne, Dostojevsky, and
     Flaubert.

767. Parrat, Marcel. "Sade; l'affaire de Marseille et la
     parlement d'Aix." In LE MARQUIS DE SADE. Paris:
     Armand Colin, 1968, pp. 51-57.

     Proceedings of the Colloquium on the Marquis de Sade,
     Aix-en-Provence, 19 and 20 February 1966. Recounts
     the Marseille events which resulted, for Sade, in a
     serious entanglement with the law. It would appear
     that in Sade's case punishment was disproportionate to
     the crime committed. Accused of having attempted to
     poison a prostitute (who survived), Sade was
     condemned--in absentia--to death. It was not until
     1778 that the death penalty was commuted to a simple
     reprimand. Gives this incident in the life of Sade as
     an example of injustice and the need for review of the
     penal code at the end of the Revolution in France.

768. Paulhan, Jean. "La déception de Sade." OBLIQUES 11-12
     (1977): 254-258.

     During the short time in 1791 that Sade enjoyed
     relative freedom he was plagued with all sorts of
     problems, financial and ideological. In his
     opposition to the death penalty, he showed early some
     communist tendencies, which he outlined in ALINE ET
     VALCOUR, but failed in most of his enterprises. By
     then he was mostly concerned with his writings: he
     wrote and rewrote LES INFORTUNES DE LA VERTU three

times.  Finally,  he again ended up in prison; no one
knows  for certain what the grounds were for that last
incarceration.

769. Pauvert,    Jean-Jacques.    "Introduction."    CHOIX
D'OEUVRES. Paris:  Club du Livre, 1953, pp. 3-63.

First-rate  biography stressing the facts rather  than
the myths  and legends connected with  the  marquis's
life.  Points out that Sade published his first novel,
JUSTINE,  at age 51.  Gives much credit to Guillaume
Apollinaire  for  Sade's rehabilitation  and  entrance
into the literary world.

770. Pia,  Pascal.  "Sade et les visiteurs de Charenton."  LA
QUINZAINE LITTERAIRE,  No. 6, 1 June 1966, pp. 18-19.

Recounts the visit at Charenton of two persons ignored
in Gilbert Lély's biography: M. de Rochefort, who sat
next  to Sade at a dinner table and  attended  FAUSSES
CONFIDENCES (a play performed at Charenton),  and Mlle
Flore,  who  gave  a long description of Sade  in  her
MEMOIRES DE MLLE FLORE,  ARTISTE DU THEATRE  DES
VARIETES,  published  in 1845.   "Cette chevelure  lui
appartenait,  quoiqu'il  fut  alors âgé de  soixante-
quatorze ans.  Sa taille était droite élevée, son port
noble était celui d'un homme de la haute société.   Il
avait   conservé  de  grandes  manières  et  beaucoup
d'esprit. . . ."

771. Piazzoli, Jacques.   Review of LE MARQUIS DE SADE.   LA
VERITE  SUR  LES DEUX PROCES CRIMINELS DE  MARQUIS  DE
SADE.  LE TOUT PRECEDE DE LA BIBLIOGRAPHIE DES OEUVRES
DU MARQUIS DE SADE by Jules Janin.  In CATALOGUE D'UNE
COLLECTION  DE  LIVRES ANCIENS ET MODERNES,  RARES  ET
CURIEUX. Milan:  Librairie Dumolard Frères, 1878, pp.
396.

Calls this a publication of little value, a study done
without  any worthwhile research,  attempted  only  to
please beautiful ladies who wanted a decent opinion of
the man and his works.

772. Pick,  Robert.  "The  Madman of  Charenton."  SATURDAY
REVIEW OF LITERATURE 19 (1954): 32-33.

Not  available as listed in E.  Pierre Chanover, item
11.

773.  Piva, Franco.  Review of SADE, by Ronald Hayman.  In
      STUDI FRANCESI 24 (1980):  169-170.

      Reviews Ronald Hayman's biography on Sade.  States
      that while the work is intended as a "critical
      biography," it is in fact, a reconstruction, not only
      of the "parties de plaisir" but also of the prevalent
      social climate of the Enlightenment.  Concludes that
      Hayman's work is one which can be read with interest
      but that should also be used and appraised with
      caution and checked for accuracy against other
      studies.

774.  Pomarède, Jean.  "Déposition de Jeanne Testars."  In LE
      PORTEFEUILLE DU MARQUIS DE SADE.  Paris:  Editions de
      la Différence, 1977, pp. 246-251.

      Brings to light the deposition of Jeanne Testars,
      sworn on 19 October 1763, who testified that she was
      the victim of an orgy organized by the marquis.  This
      accusation was only discovered in 1963 and is
      published with commentaries by Gilbert Lély, item 180.

775.  Pomeau, René.  "Sade (1740-1814)."  In LITTERATURE
      FRANCAISE.  Edited by Antoine Adam.  Paris: Larousse,
      1967, p. 383.

      Believes that prison made of Sade a writer who vented
      his furor in his writings.  States that much of his
      work has the "clinical" interest of a man obsessed.
      Concludes that much of what was good in the
      Enlightenment--"la bienfaisance, l'amour du bien
      public, l'idéal du bonheur social, l'enthousiasme
      encyclopédiste de la science"--have disappeared in
      Sade's works.  But still his work has the value of a
      testimony:  "Il a montré à l'homme un visage de
      l'homme qu'il n'est plus possible d'oublier."

776.  Ramon, L. J. (Dr.).  "Notes sur M. de Sade."  In CAHIERS
      PERSONNELS (1803-1804).  Paris: Corréa, 1953, pp. 41-
      47.

      Also published as a preface to Volume XV of OEUVRES
      COMPLETES DU MARQUIS DE SADE (Edition J. J. Pauvert,
      Cercle du livre précieux, 1964, pp. 41-47).  This is a
      medical report from the doctor who on 11 November
      1814, became officially the physician in charge, at

Charenton, where Sade died on 2 December of the same
year. Sade's family refused to allow him to perform
an autopsy on Sade; however, he was able to briefly
examine Sade's skull and he states: "Beau
developpement de la voûte du crane (bienveillance);
point de saillies exagérées dans les régions
temporales (point de férocité); point de saillies
exagérées derrière et au dessus des oreilles (point de
combativité, organes si developpés dans le crane de Du
Guesclin); cervelet de dimensions modérées, point de
distance exagérée d'une apophyse mastiode à l'autre
(point d'excès dans l'amour physique)." In other
words, nothing in the shape of Sade's skull suggests
that he is the author of JULIETTE or JUSTINE. Also
states that Sade was the organizer of many dances,
concerts, plays, and shows during his stay at
Charenton.

777. Reverzy, Jean-François. "Les journées de Charenton (ou
l'asile dévoilé). OBLIQUES 12-13 (1977): 177-187.

States that the second imprisonment of Sade was
arbitrary. His first stay at Charenton (from July
1788 to April 1790) was due to his disorderly conduct:
from the Bastille he incited prisoners to riot. His
second stay in Charenton (27 April 1803 to his death,
2 December 1814) was requested by his family, and he
was transferred from the prison at Pélagie to a mental
institution, not because he was declared insane but to
protect his family from embarrassment. Publishes a
letter from Royer-Collard to the Minister of Justice,
dated 2 August 1808. Royer-Collard was head of the
Hospice of Charenton when Sade was interned there.
The letter was addressed to "Son Excellence
Monseigneur le Senateur Ministre de la police générale
de l'Empire" and attacked the marquis violently. This
letter was also published in the introduction by
Guillaume Apollinaire to L'OEUVRE DE MARQUIS DE SADE,
Bibliothèque des curieux, 1909.

778. Richard, P. "Sade." In GRAND LAROUSSE ENCYCLOPEDIQUE.
Paris: Editions Larousse, 1964, pp. 484-485.

States that Sade was first incarcerated in 1768 at the
castle of Saumur, then at Pierre-Encise; next came the
imprisonments at the Fortress of Miolans and the
castle of Vincennes; from there he was transferred to
Aix; eventually he ended up back at Vincennes, then at

la Bastille, and finally at Charenton.  Concludes that
"la critique du XXe siècle a reconnu l'importance
d'une oeuvre au centre de laquelle il y a la révolte
d'un homme libre contre la société et le Créateur."

779.  Rossat-Mignod, Suzanne.  Review of QUI ETAIT LE MARQUIS
      DE SADE?, by Janine Neboit-Mombet.  LA PENSEE 173
      (January 1974):  146-147.

      Gives a positive review of Janine Neboit-Mombet's
      book:  "Tant par le choix des textes que par son
      étude, J. Neboit-Mombet aide à avoir une idée de Sade
      et à comprendre pourquoi il suscite aujourd'hui un tel
      intérêt et une si vive curiosité."

780.  Sade, Xavier de.  "Sade et sa famille."  MAGAZINE
      LITTERAIRE 114 (June 1976): 18.

      Says that Sade may not have been totally innocent, but
      he certainly was no hard-core criminal.  Only lately
      has he been partially rehabilitated and given back his
      place on the Sade family tree.

781.  Seaver, Richard.  "An Anniversary Unnoticed and a Note
      about JUSTINE."  EVERGREEN REVIEW 36 (June 1965):  53-
      60, 89-92.

      On the 150th anniversary (1964) of Sade's death, given
      the near total condemnation of Sade's works up to that
      date, asks how the marquis's production could have
      endured.  Suggests that Sade proclaimed the
      possibility of evil, of absolute evil, but that in
      order to profit from his vision, we do not have to
      agree to emulate him but "if we can accept to live
      with the daily specter of the absolute Bomb, we can
      accept to live with the works, inoffensive by
      comparison, of this possessed and extraordinary man."
      Gives an excerpt from JUSTINE (the visit to the
      Benedictine monastery) in English translation.

782.  Sereville, E. and F. de Saint-Simon.  DICTIONNAIRE DE LA
      NOBLESSE FRANCAISE.  Paris: Société française au XXe
      siècle, s.d., p. 944.

      Describes the Sade family coat of arms thus:

      "Deux gueules à l'étoile d'or de 8 rais chargée d'une
      aigle éployée de sable becquée diademée de sable.

Ancienne extraction. Président au Parlement d'Aix dès
le XVe siècle.   Obtint  en  1416,   de  l'empereur
Sigismond,  le  droit d'ajouter une aigle impériale  à
ses armoires.   Cette famille provoqua quelque tumulte
à  la  fin  du XVIIIe siècle  avec  Donatien Alphonse
François, (1740-1814) le divin marquis de Sade, auteur
libertin qui fait encore belle recette aujourd'hui."

783.  Sérieux,  Paul.  "L'internement  du marquis de  Sade  au
      Château  de Miolans."  HIPPOCRATE,  REVUE  D'HUMANISME
      MEDICAL 5 (January 1937): 385-401, 465-482.

      Discusses  a  fifty-one-year period during  which  the
      Marquis de Sade spent time in prison:    1) Donjon  de
      Vincennes,  29  October  1763  to  13  November  1763;
      2) Château  de Saumur et Pierre-Encize,  Conciergerie,
      April-June  1768;   3) Château de Miolans,   from  9
      December 1772 to 1 May 1773;  4) Donjon de  Vincennes,
      Bastille,  and  Charenton,  13 February 1777 to  March
      1790;  5) Les Madelonnettes,  les Carmes,  St. Lazare,
      Picpus,   December  1793  to  October  1794;   6) Ste-
      Pelagré,  Bicêtre,  Charenton,  from  March 1801 to  2
      December  1814  (his  death).   Concentrates  in  this
      report  on  his  stay at the Château  de  Miolans  in
      Savoie.

784.  Serra, Dante.  IL MARCHESE DI SADE, LA SUA VITA E I SUOI
      TEMPI.  Milan: Ceschina, 1950. 304 p.

      This book, subtitled L'AVENTUROSA VITA DEL MARCHESE DE
      SADE  is  a  biography  citing much  of  the  work  of
      Apollinaire,  Paul  Ginisty,  Eugene  Duehren,  Octave
      Beliard,   and  Otto  Flake.   It  stresses  the  most
      scandalous  events  in  Sade's  life  and  includes  a
      chapter,  entitled  "The  Angel and the Demon,"  which
      paints the Marquise de Sade as a most devoted,  loving
      wife.   Also gives an interesting discussion of sadism
      and masochism.

785.  Sieburg,  Friedrich.  "Freiheit zum Bösen."  FRANKFURTER
      ALLGEMEINE, 17 March 1962, p. 53.

      Reviews German translation of VIE DU MARQUIS DE  SADE,
      entitled  GILBERT LELY'S LEBEN UND WERK DES MARQUIS DES
      SADE:  MARQUIS  DE  SADE  (Dusseldorf:   Verlag  Karl
      Rauch,  1961,  462 p.).  The name of the translator is
      not  given.   States  that in Germany,  Sade  is
      essentially unknown except for the fact that his  name

is usually associated with abnormal psychology and sexual pathology but that, in France, Sade has a meaningful place as an eighteenth-century literary and philosophical figure. Notes also that, while Lély's book is obviously a research work, "gelobte und gewissenhafte Buch," not lacking in quality, it is difficult for a German reader to truly appreciate its worth since so many of Sade's works are not available in German bookstores or even libraries. Comments: "Was wir in unserer Unkenntnis brauchten ware eine elementare und müglichst schonende Angleichung des hüllischen und durchaus nicht willkèrlichen Rufes des Namens Sade an sein Schriftstellerisches Werk, das gross und machvoll ist, aber unter Gestrèpp einer wahnsinnigen Exentrik die mit dem bisweilen rokokohaften Zeitgeschmack so seltsam kontrastiert, fast unsichtbar geworden ist. Weniger Enthusiasmus und nor sanfter Elementarunterricht tate einer Leserschaft not, die von dieser schrecklichen, aber ergiebigen Figur nichts weiss und sich erst durch die Zweidentigheiten und Finsternisse dieses Lebens durchtasten muss, ehe es sich darauf einlassen kann, gemass dem Wunsche des Autors in dem M. de Sade'ein genie wie Shakespeare, Pascall oder Niershe' zu sehen. Es daarf nicht geschehen, daf der Name Sade morgen oder spétestens ubermorgen in jedem Feuilleton und jeden Nachprogramen mit Kennermiene vorgebracht wirde."

786. Siméon, Joseph-Jérome. "Précis des faits et extrait de la procédure contre laquelle le marquis de Sade et sa famille réclament destinés à ètre présentés au roi en son Conseil des Dépêches du 26 septembre 1777." In LE MARQUIS DE SADE. Paris: Libraire Armand Colin, 1968, pp. 55-57.

Proceedings of the Colloquium on the Marquis de Sade, Aix-en-Provence, 19 and 20 February 1966. Quotes a deposition made in favor of Sade for presentation to the king, attesting that Sade may have been a mad man but not a would-be murderer: "en admettant même comme recevables les dépositions de témoins récusables, on n'aperçoit dans leurs déclarations que les détails inconcevables de quelques faits de débauche dont la bizarrerie et la dépravation ne prouveroient que la démence de celui qui s'y seroit livré."

787. Swinburne, Algernon-Charles. "Charenton, en 1810." In
     MONCKTON MILNES. Edited by James Pope Hennessy. Vol.
     11. New York: Farrar, Straus and Cudahy, 1955.

     Describes the insane asylum where Sade was confined
     from 27 April 1803 until his death in 1814.

788. Talmeyr, Maurice. "La Marquise de Sade, un monstre dans
     un coton." LE FIGARO, 18 September 1926, p. 24.

     Discusses the unilateral devotion of the marquise de
     Sade for her husband, with emphasis on the domestic
     aspect of their relationship as illustrated in their
     correspondence.

789. Tauxe, Henri-Charles. "Le divin marquis et son siècle."
     GAZETTE DE LAUSANNE 70 (6 February 1965): 20.

790. Taxil, Léo (pseudonym of Gabriel-Antoine, Jogand-Pagès).
     LA PROSTITUTION CONTEMPORAINE, ETUDE D'UNE QUESTION
     SOCIALE. Paris: Librairie populaire, 1883, pp. 160-
     164.

     Relates Sade's way of life to prostitution in
     eighteenth-century France. Gives some totally
     inaccurate biographical details: "Se trouvant à
     Marseille en juin 1772, il se rendit avec son
     inseparable valet de chambre chez des filles
     publiques, leur fit prendre des pastilles dans
     lesquelles se trouvaient des mouches cantharides, et
     provoqua une orgie hideuse, à la suite de laquelle
     deux de ces filles moururent."

791. Thomas, Donald Serrell. THE MARQUIS DE SADE. Boston:
     Little, Brown: 1978. xi + 214 p.

     Very readable illustrated biography, undocumented for
     the most part. Recounts some interesting details
     about Sade's youth, his life in prison and during the
     Revolution. Discusses THE MISFORTUNES OF VIRTUE,
     ALINE ET VALCOUR, THE CRIMES OF LOVE, STORIES, TALES
     AND FABLES, JUSTINE and JULIETTE, THE PHILOSOPHY IN
     THE BOUDOIR, and THE 120 DAYS OF SODOM. Includes a
     chapter entitled "The Devil's Disciples" which gives a
     synopsis of Sade's influence.

     Reviewed by Arthur Calder-Marshall "The Fate of
     Fantasist," TIMES LITERARY SUPPLEMENT (London), 25

February 1977, p. 208; by Peter V. Conroy, EIGHTEENTH-CENTURY CURRENT BIBLIOGRAPHY (1976): 373; by Joseph McMahon, FRENCH REVIEW 52 (1978): 351-352; and by Michel Delon, DIX-HUITIEME SIECLE 11 (1979): 514.

792. Trouille, Clovis. "Portrait de Sade." In CAMPAGNE. Edited by Clovis Trouille. Paris: J. J. Pauvert, 1965.

There are no portraits of Sade though one by Van Loo is known to have existed; it is surmised that this painting has been destroyed along with some of Sade's writings.

793. Van Tieghem, Philippe. DICTIONNAIRE DES LITTERATURES. Vol. 3. Paris: Presses universitaires de France, 1968, pp. 3455-3456.

Presents a short biography and succinct bibliography. Sees the marquis as "materialiste integral et athée convaincu." His powerful analysis has opened the way to modern sexual psychology. While author does not believe that Sade invented the fundamental tendencies which are now called "sadism," the Marquis has the honor of having been the first to have elaborated them as a system. Powerful writer, Sade belongs to the eighteenth century in what it offered "de plus lumineux."

794. Vapereau, Georges. "Sade." In DICTIONNAIRE UNIVERSEL DES LITTERATURES. Paris: Librairie Hachette, 1884.

Not available.

795. Vicentiis, Gioacchino. "Vite in margine, il marchese de Sade." ELOQUENZA, September-October 1934, pp. 314-325.

Recounts some of the most notorious episodes in Sade's life, including the Rose Keller affair.

796. Villiot, Jean de. "Le marquis de Sade et Rose Keller." In LA FLAGELLATION A TRAVERS LE MONDE. Paris: Charles Carrington, 1900.

Brings nothing new to Sade's affair with the prostitute Rose Keller.

797. Voivenel, Paul (Dr.). "Les Allemands et le marquis de
     Sade." LE PROGRES MEDICAL 7 (February 1917): 7-14.

     Devastating review of Eugene Duhren's book, LE MARQUIS
     DE SADE ET SON TEMPS, more anti-German than anti-Sade.
     States: "Ce livre n'est qu'une occasion de fourrer un
     gros nez boche dans touts les ordures du XVIIIe. . . .
     Nos boches sentent la m. . . . partout en France."

798. Vovelle, Michel. "Sade et Lacoste suivi de Mirabeau et
     Mirabeau.   Réflexions sur le déclassement nobilitaire
     dans   la   Provence   du   XVIIIe   siècle."   PROVENCE
     HISTORIQUE 17 (1967): 160-171.

     Attempts to extract a typology of Provence's nobility
     under the Old Regime by comparing two well-known
     figures who were distantly related:  the Marquis de
     Sade and the Count de Mirabeau.  Both spent time in
     the donjon of Vincennes beginning in 1777.   Both men
     were from the region of Lubéron and encountered
     difficulties with the maintenance and care of their
     respective properties.  Both gave lavish parties they
     could   ill afford   and seem to have   enjoyed   a
     prodigality within  their domain that had no  reward.
     Concludes:  "Entre l'aggressivité nobilitaire du Sade
     antiparlementaire   et   l'ultime   et   volontaire
     déclassement de Mirabeau, l'apparente contradiction
     révèle un identique cheminement,  celui de cette
     moyenne noblesse provençale dont Sade et Mirabeau ne
     sont   peut-être pas à tout   prendre,   d'indignes
     representants."

799. Vovelle,   Michel.   "Sade,   seigneur de village."   LE
     MARQUIS DE SADE.   Paris:   Librairie Armand Colin,
     1968, pp. 23-50.

     Proceedings of the Colloquium of Aix-en-Provence, 19
     and 20 February 1968.  Proposes to study the relations
     existing between Sade and village of La Coste, nestled
     in Provence, a rural setting, made up of about 500
     people.   Sympathetic at first,   these uneducated
     farmers (only 23 percent could write) eventually
     vandalized the castle (17 September 1792),  perhaps an
     act warranted by an economic crisis.  Sade himself
     seems to have been totally uninterested in his family
     property.   La Coste does not appear in   Sade's
     writings.

800.  Weber,  W.   "Erbstècke.  L'affaire Sade."  In ZEIT OHNE
      ZEIT.  Zurich:  n.p., 1959.

801.  Wilson, Edmund.  "The Documents on the Marquis de Sade."
      THE BIT BETWEEN MY TEETH.   New York:  Farrar, Straus,
      and Giroux, 1965, pp. 174-227.

          Reviews several books on Sade:  VIE DU MARQUIS DE SADE
          (1952); L'AIGLE, MADEMOISELLE. . . (1949); LE CARILLON
          DE   VINCENNES   (1953);   MONSIEUR   LE   6   (1954);
          CORRESPONDANCE  INEDITE  DU MARQUIS DE  SADE,  DE  SES
          PROCHES ET DE SES FAMILIERS (1929),  and discusses the
          merit  of  each  of  these  publications.   Also  gives
          highlights  in  Sade's life which led the  marquis  to
          write  LES 120 JOURNEES DE SODOME.   Believes that  it
          was  Sade's intention to include,  in LES JOURNEES  DE
          FLORBELLE  OU LA NATURE DEVOILEE,  a series of "fetes"
          in which "children are blown up by rockets and bombs."
          Concludes:   "How gratified Sade would have been if he
          could  have foreseen the scale of which we were  later
          to indulge in this pastime!   Or would he perhaps have
          been appalled, as he was by the Terror?"

## C. COMIC STRIP AND FILM ADAPTATIONS

802. Accialini, F. EL, 1952.

Film directed by Luis Buñuel. Script by Luis Buñuel and Luis Alcoriza from a novel by Mercedes Pinto. Produced in Mexico.

803. Alex, Gabriel. "Il marchese sadico." CAHIERS DU CINEMA 209 (February 1969): 65.

Film produced in 1968, a satire of the erotomania mode.

804. Barrat, François. "Salo-Sadix, le signe de Sade." OBLIQUES 12-13 (1977): 189-192.

Comments briefly on a film by Pier Palo Pasolini, "Salo ou les 120 journées de Sodome," an adaptation (1975) of Sade's work; "Le film est vivant, frétillant même, humide de l'histoire de son temps, il ne se fige pas dans le contrat médiocre de l'adaptateur. . . ."

805. Benayoun, Robert. "Sadisme et cartoon." PRESENCE DU CINEMA 6/7 (1960): 54-55.

Considers all the variations of cruel treatments in cartoons such as TOM AND JERRY: the hot foot, cutting up in slices, etc. States: "Le standard n'est pas du registre en dessous, mais dans la surenchère du violent." All the fun consists in knowing who will do the most evil. Concludes that "(cette surenchère au hurlement de douleur) provoque, titille et satisfait en fin de compte le sadisme latent de chaque spectateur."

806. Benayoun, Robert. "Zaroff ou les prospérités du vice." PRESENCE DU CINEMA 6/7 (1960): 7-10.

States that Sade's name has been involved in situations which he would actually abhor. "Sadistic" does not mean either neurotic or inclined to torture, as with the Nazis: rather "le sadique est celui qui se crée de nouvelles sensations, qui égale Dieu et le bafoue en prouvant qu'il y a de l'ordre dans le mal."

807.  Breton, Emile.  "Pasolini, Sade et les communistes."  LA
      NOUVELLE CRITIQUE 94 (1976): 21.

      Reviews the film, SALO, OU LES 120 JOURNEES DE SODOME,
      by Pier Paoli Pasolini, who relentlessly confronts the
      spectators with unbearable sights:    horrors,  sodomy,
      coprophagy,  rape,  tortures,  and fascism:  "L'horreur
      du  fascisme--et pas que du fascisme,  celle aussi  du
      pouvoir  qui  fait de l'homme un  sujet--est  dicible.
      Mais il faut du courage à le dire,  et du courage pour
      la regarder."

808.  Brochier,   Jean-Jacques.   "Sade:   un   prisonnier
      exemplaire."   LE MAGAZINE LITTERAIRE   21   (September
      1968): 34-37.

      Reviews a short film by Maurice Frydland,  intended to
      be  largely  Sade's biography.   Prisoner  under  five
      different  regimes without ever being convicted of any
      crime,  Sade spent twenty-seven years  imprisoned  in
      thirteen different jails.   Sees in Sade a predecessor
      of  all  the  philosophers whose works  are  based  on
      negativity,  a  philosopher who led the way for Hegel,
      Freud,  and Marx.   Concludes:  "noble, enfermé par la
      noblesse,     révolutionnaire     attaquant     l'infâme
      Robespierre  parce qu'il avait inventé  le  culte  de
      l'être  Suprême et fait voter une loi garantissant  la
      propriété privée,  Sade minoritaire, persécuté, sûr de
      lui   nous  apparait  à  une  lumiere  récente   comme
      l'ancêtre  de nos gauchistes.   Gauchiste,  il l'était
      autant en politique qu'en érotisme."

809.  Brooks,  Peter.   "MARAT/SADE."   CAHIERS DU CINEMA  190
      (May 1967): 74.

      Reviews  the British film directed by Peter Brooks and
      starring  Clifford Rose,  Brenda Kempner,  and  Glenda
      Jackson,  THE  PERSECUTION AND ASSASSINATION OF  JEAN-
      PAUL  MARAT AS PERFORMED BY THE INMATES OF THE  ASYLUM
      OF  CHARENTON  UNDER THE DIRECTION OF THE  MARQUIS  DE
      SADE:   "Un  autre  film qu'il faut  ajouter  à  cette
      envahissante  série  des  films prétentieux  snobs  et
      chichiteux. . . ."

810.  Cavell,  Philippe.   LA  JULIETTE  DE  SADE.    Paris:
      Dominique Leroi, 1979.  2 vol. 120 p. and 56 p.

Comic strip with text adaptation by Francis Leroi.
Sold under the label "erotic" literature.

811.  Champarnaud, François.  "La JUSTINE de Sade vue par la
      bande dessinée."  CRITIQUE 38 (1982): 871-875.

      Discusses the adaptations of JUSTINE into two comic
      strips and states about the first by Gilbert Garnon:
      "Le sang, le sperme et la merde paraissent être au
      centre de son ouvrage. . . . L'humour de Garpon est
      court, faute d'avoir choisi un point de vue sur LA
      NOUVELLE JUSTINE de Sade. C'est un échec." About the
      second, by Guido Crépax:  "Il n'est pas la peine de
      rappeler la finesse du dessin de Crépax, son goût pour
      le détail juste, la notation historique et exacte, la
      mise en page variée et astucieuse.  Mais le talent de
      Crépax se révèle ici à plusieurs niveaux.  D'abord, il
      a su construire son récit en reprenant le double
      encadrement qu'avait donné Sade à son conte.  Un cadre
      philosophique. . . . Un cadre dramatique. . . . La
      bande dessinée de Crépax est rigoureusement
      construite.  Comparée à celle de Garnon, à chaque page
      sa supériorité éclate."

812.  Chaumeton, Etiènne.  "L'ombre de Sade sur l'écran,"
      CAHIERS DE LA CINEMATHEQUE, 7 (Summer 1972):  39-49.

      Discusses violence in the movies and views Sade's
      influence in films depicting horror mixed with
      eroticism.

813.  Cherasse, J. A. "Sade et le cinéma, ou les infortunes
      du divin marquis. . . ." OBLIQUES 12-13 (1977):  189-
      191.

      Lists numerous films influenced by Sade or relating to
      Sade.  Says he excluded all pornographic bric à brac.
      First is a film of Louis Feuillade, FANTOMAS,
      1913/1914; then Luis Buñel and Salvador Dali, UN CHIEN
      ANDALOU, 1928, and L'AGE D'OR, 1928; Abel Gance, LA
      FOLIE DU DOCTEUR TUBE, 1914; Erich Von Stroheim,
      FOLIES DE FEMMES, 1921, and LES RAPACES, 1923;
      Schoedsack and Pichel, LES CHASSES DU COMTE ZAROFF,
      1932; Erle C. Kenton, L'ILE DU DOCTEUR MOREAU, 1932;
      Charles Brabin, LE MASQUE D'OR, 1932; Edgar G. Ulmer,
      THE BLACK CAT, 1934; Louis Friedlander, THE RAVEN,
      1934; William Neill, THE BLACK ROOM, 1934; Terence
      Fisher, THE CAUHEMAR DE DRACULA.  Also listed as

influenced by Sade are LEAVE HER TO HEAVEN; JOHNY
ALLEGRO; KILL OR BE KILLED; BLOOD OF THE VAMPIRE;
HORRORS OF THE BLACK MUSEUM; JACK THE RIPPER; THE
FLESH AND THE FIENDS; THE PIT AND THE PENDULUM; BLOOD
LUST; WHATEVER HAPPENED TO BABY JANE?; LADY IN A CAGE;
TWO THOUSAND MANIACS; THE COLLECTOR; LA DECIMA
VITTIMA; THE BOSTON STRANGLER; and three films
directly connected to the life of Sade: THE SKULL;
THE MARQUIS SADIQUE; and DE SADE; SALO OU LES 120
JOURNEES DE SODOME.

814.  Cornand, André. "Sade sadisme." REVUE DU CINEMA:
      IMAGE ET SON 272 (May 1973): 16-24.

      States that there exist essentially no Sadian films:
      "Pour respecter Sade, il faut le libérer du récit, lui
      être fidèle en le trahissant . . . et jusqu à ce jour,
      personne n'a su trahir Donatien pour lui être fidèle."
      However, states that there are sadistic films which
      may not have any relationship to Sade but which
      exploit latent sadism of audience.

815.  Coulteray, G. de. LE SADISME AU CINEMA. Paris: Le
      Terrain vague, 1964.

      See annotation under the English version, item 876.

816.  Coulteray, George de. "Buñuel Meets de Sade." SADISM
      IN THE MOVIES. New York: Medical Press, 1965, pp.
      177-184.

      Translated by Steve Hult from the French LE SADISME AU
      CINEMA. Reproduces an excerpt from the script of
      L'AGE D'OR because the work of Luis Buñuel "offers the
      unique example of awareness and perfect understanding
      of Sade."

817.  Coulteray, G. de. "Petit dictionnaire de la mort."
      PRESENCE DU CINEMA, 7 (December 1960): 41-55.

      Gives a list of the movies gruesome ways death is
      inflicted in the movies i.e., asphyxiation, cremation,
      decapitation. Includes a long list of films in which
      these types of death occur.

818.  Crépax, Guido. LA NOUVELLE JUSTINE. Paris: Albin
      Michel, 1981. 160 p.

Comic strip based on the story of JUSTINE. Does not include any word. Drawings, in fairly good taste, emphasize the role of victim chosen by Justine. Highly entertaining.

819. Curelin, Jean. "Avant propos." PRESENCE DU CINEMA 6/7 (1960): 1.

Describes this special issue of PRESENCE DU CINEMA as an anthology of Sadian films rather than a study on sadism.

820. Debord, Guy E. "Hurlements en faveur de Sade." ION. CENTRE DE CREATION, 1 April 1952, pp. 219-230.

Another film "avant garde" which is supposed to deal with the "lettriste" period of Sade.

821. Enfield, Cyril. LE DIVIN MARQUIS. Film, 1971.

Film directed by Cyril Enfield, script by M. Matheson, and starring Keir Dullea. Deals mostly with Sade's biography--ingeniously produced but mostly apocryphal.

822. Foucault, Michel. "Rien de plus allergique au cinéma que l'oeuvre de Sade." CINEMATOGRAPHE 16 (December 1975-January 1976): 1-22.

Argues against the feasibility of presenting Sade's works in the movies. Impediments revolves around the constraints imposed by the media.

823. Garnon, Gilbert. LA NOUVELLE JUSTINE. Paris: n.p., n.d. 73 p.

Comic strip in fairly pornographic form. Sold under the label of "erotic" literature. Not recommended.

824. Heine, Maurice. "Lettre ouverte à Luis Buñuel." LE SURREALISME AU SERVICE DE LA REVOLUTION, 4 December 1931, pp. 12-13.

Writes an open letter to Luis Buñel after the showing of his film, L'AGE D'OR, and comments on the exclusively sadistic inspiration of the last part. Would have preferred an interpretation which would include not only Christ, but also Mohammed, Moses, and Confucius.

825.  Hoda, F.  "Sadisme au midi-minuit."  PRESENCE DU CINEMA 6/7 (1960):  26-30.

Discusses second-rate movies which specialize in films made up of cruelty and sensuality.  Gives numerous examples:  LE MONSTRE,  THE BLACK CASTLE,  THE STRANGE DOOR,  BLOOD OF THE VAMPIRE,  GRIP OF THE  STRANGLER, etc.  Concludes that these films constitute "the sadism of the poor."

826.  Iimura, Takahito.  DE SADE.  Film.

This short film (nine minutes),  very avant-garde, has an obscene overtone and a background setting of pop music.

827.  Joubert, Alain.   "Les forces vives du cinéma japonais: notes cruelles sur le Japon des soupirs."  PRESENCE DU CINEMA 6/7 (1960): 32-40.

Gives several examples of sadistic encounters in Japanese movies and concludes:  "Le défi que Sade lança à la société restera, bien sûr, incomparable jusqu'à la fin des temps.  La fascination du sacrifice érotique qu'il imposa à la face du monde est par trop subversive pour être acceptée sans reaction violente. Néanmoins, lorsqu'un peuple sait écarter les tabous moraux et religieux, ou les menaces biologiques dispensées par les gardiens d'un ordre rétrograde, afin que cesse la limitation du comportement naturel de l'homme, alors tout espoir est permis."

828.  Lefèvre, Raymond.   "Après Sade:  Pédagogie et travaux expérimentaux."   REVUE DU CINEMA:   IMAGE ET SON  272 (May 1973):62-63.

Reviews the British film directed by Michael Winner, THE NIGHTCOMERS, 1971 (French title LE CORRUPTEUR), starring Marlon Brando and Stephanie Beacham.  The sado-masochistic relationship of the two adults is converted into a game by two admiring children. Concludes that the film is beautifully interpreted by Marlon Brando but lacks good taste in the production.

829. Lefèvre, Raymond. "Filmer l'impossible." REVUE DU
     CINEMA: IMAGE ET SON 272 (May 1973): 64-70.

     Sees in Sade's writing "le plus beau cri
     libérateur de notre littérature," though Sade's text
     presents many difficulties of interpretation in the
     movies, so many in fact that filming Sade has become
     an impossiblity: "Filmer Sade revient donc à filmer
     l'impossible. . . . Le beau texte libérateur est
     encore en avance sur son temps. Sade, à l'époque
     avait su aller trop loin. Le cinéma ne nous le permet
     pas encore, malgré quelques étincelles de génie."

830. Lefèvre, Raymond. "Justine." LA REVUE DU CINEMA:
     IMAGE ET SON 276/277 (1973): 217-218.

     Claude Pierson's production, introduced in France in
     1972, starring Alice Arno as Justine and France
     Vardier as Juliette. States: "Dans un extrême souci
     de fidélité, les auteurs ont tenu à conserver le
     merveilleux texte de Sade, mais si la phrase de Sade
     s'accommode fort bien de la voix off [sic], elle passe
     difficilement lorsqu'elle est dite en dialogues. D'où
     une sorte de distance par rapport au spectateur que
     certains interprète comme un ridicule ratage et que
     d'autres apprécient comme une démarche intéressante."

831. Marchand, Jacqueline. "Filming the Enlightenment."
     ANNALS OF SCHOLARSHIP 3 (1984): 1-14.

     Discusses several film adaptations of eighteenth-
     century novels, including Buñuel's LA NOUVELLE
     JUSTINE. Stresses the importance of Sade as a link
     between Voltaire and Buñuel and concludes that great
     literary masterpieces do not necessarily become great
     films but states that filming of eighteenth-century
     novels is only at the dawn of its full development.

832. Morin, Edgar. "Le Tabour de la mort et le meurtre au
     cinéma." PRESENCE DU CINEMA 6/7 (1960): 13-22.

     Discusses the role played by the representation of
     death in the movies and states that most often death
     is pictured as an extreme case of aggression, i.e.,
     murder which may lead to an analysis of culpability.

833.   REVUE DU CINEMA:  IMAGE ET SON 272  (May 1972):   3-70.

Special issue dealing with Sade and sadism.   Includes:

Jacques Zimmer, "Portraits de l'homme";
Andre Cornand, "Sade sadisme";
Jacques  Zimmer and Daniel Sauvaget,  "Entretien  avec
    Claude Pierson";
Daniel Sauvaget, "Points de repère pour JUSTINE";
Jacques Scandelari, "LA PHILOSOPHIE DANS LE BOUDOIR";
Daniel Sauvaget, "Sado masochisme sur les boulevards";
Jacques Zimmer, "Sadiricon";
Raymond  Lefèvre,  "Après Sade:   pédagogie et travaux
    experimentaux";
Raymond Lefèvre, "Filmer l'impossible."

834.   "Le  sadisme au cinéma."  PRESENCE DU CINEMA 6/7   (1969):
       1-56.

Special  issue of PRESENCE DU CINEMA devoted to sadism
in the movies.   Includes the following articles:  Jean
Curtelin,   "Avant-propos"; Robert Benayoun, "Zaroff ou
les prospérités du vice"; Edgar Morin, "Le tabou de la
mort et le meurtre au cinéma"; F. Hoda, "Sadisme   au
Midi-Minuit"; Alain  Joubert,  "Les forces  vives   du
cinéma   japonais"; Georges  de   Coulteray,   "Petit
dictionnaire  de la mort";  Robert Benayoun,  "Sadisme
et . . . cartoon."

835.   Sauvaget, Daniel.  "Le divin marquis de Sade."  LA REVUE
       DU CINEMA:  IMAGE ET SON 276/277 (October 1973):   115-
       116.

Reviews  a film begun by Roger Corman and completed by
Cy Edfield.   Despite some inaccuracies,  states  that
the  film  is  worthy  of  interest:   "Jusqu'ici  Sade
n'avait guère été gâté par les arts de masse,  il  est
heureux  que  grâce à ce film il soit devenu le  héros
d'une  méditation baroque sur l'ambiguité du  souvenir
et  de  l'histoire  individuelle  plutôt  que   d'une
'réhabilitation' sacrifiant au romanesque."

836.   Sauvaget, Daniel.   "Points  de  repère pour  JUSTINE."
       REVUE DU CINEMA:  IMAGE ET SON 272 (May 1973):  31-33.

Gives  a  brief history of Pierson's film SADE OU  LES
MALHEURS DE JUSTINE, produced in 1971 but forbidden to

be presented for 18 months.  Yet "le film de 1971  ne peut être aussi subversif que le livre de 1791."

837. Sauvaget, Daniel.  "Sado-masochisme sur les boulevards." REVUE DU CINEMA:  IMAGE ET SON 272 (May 1973):  38-48.

Presents  an  interesting discussion on aggression  in the movies,  which has accustomed us to view women as objects:  "La femme est l'objet du cinéma érotique. Elle est l'objet du plaisir sadique dans la majorité des cas."  Concludes,  however,  that these  are expressions of existing tastes rather than  a  trend toward something new.

838. Sauvaget,  Daniel and Zimmer,  Jacques.  "Entretien avec Claude Pierson."  REVUE DU CINEMA:  IMAGE ET SON  272 (May 1973):  25-30.

Discusses JUSTINE,  a film directed by Claude Pierson and Huguette Boisvert.  States that an audience interested only in erotic films would be bored by the cinematographic  production  of  JUSTINE:  "[Ils] s'ennuient  encore  plus que s'ils lisent Sade en  n'y cherchant que les descriptions osées."

839. Scandelari,  Jacques.  "LA PHILOSOPHIE DANS LE BOUDOIR." REVUE DU CINEMA:  IMAGE ET SON 272 (May 1973):  31-33.

Discusses a film which has some relationship to Sade's book but  only to the level of an idea or a state  of mind:  "mon livre n'a aucun rapport avec le livre  de Sade si  ce n'est au niveau d'une idée et  d'un  état d'esprit."  This film's title was eventually  changed to TRIOMPHE DE L'EROTISME and received  favorable reviews only in PLEXUS (January 1970).

840. Weigend,  Friedrich.  "Und der Rauch ihrer Qual. . .Das Hölenzeugnis  des  Marquis de Sade und  der  Film Pasolonis,  'DIE  120 TAGE VON SODEM.'"  In CHRIST  IN DER GEGENWART 28 (1976):  83-84.

Reviews the film by Pasolini,  THE 120 DAYS OF  SODOM, and discusses torture and the infernal marquis.

841. Zimmer,  Jacques.  "Portraits de  l'homme."  REVUE  DU CINEMA:  IMAGE ET SON 272 (May 1973):  4-15.

Notes some of the "transpositions" done in the movies not only on Sade's biography but on his physical appearance as well. Believes that intentions are to transform the marquis into "un être rêveur, doux et passablement désarmé, victime de l'influence pernicieuse de son oncle l'abbé."

## D. CORRESPONDENCE

842. Adam, Antoine. Préface aux LETTRES DE VINCENNES. In OEUVRES COMPLETES, Vol. XXX. Paris: J.J. Pauvert, 1966, pp. i-xxi.

Begins his preface with one of the most negative comments on Sade's sanity: "En lui la recherche du plaisir sous des formes anormales atteint une violence qui, vers la fin surtout, prend l'aspect d'une vraie folie." Also sees in Sade a man whose mental equilibrium was badly damaged by imprisonment and who suffered greatly because of the living conditions enforced in the different jails he occupied. Interprets all of Sade's extravagant cruelty not as a product of a powerful genius but rather as that of "une imagination surexcitée." Believes that Sade's revolt was addressed against all the values usually most admired, such as goodness and virtue. Sade had only one god: the god of destruction.

843. Anonymous. "Wicked Mister Six--A Portrait of the Marquis de Sade." THE TIMES (London), 87 (4 March 1966): 108, 111.

Writes a lengthy tongue-in-cheek essay following the publication by October House of the MARQUIS DE SADE: SELECTED LETTERS (Ed. G. Lély). About the marquis, "what he could not do, he dreamed, and what he dreamed, he wrote."

844. Baccolo, Luigi. "Le lettere del detenuto Sade." TEMPO PRESENTE, March-April 1968, pp. 61-67.

Reviews the publication of Sade's correspondence, L'AIGLE, MADEMOISELLE, LE CARILLON DE VINCENNES, and MONSIEUR LE 6, which represent volumes 29 and 30 of THE COMPLETE WORKS, published by J. J. Pauvert. Sade's letters seem to show 1) that the marquis was always in need of money; 2) that his sons were indifferent and ungrateful; 3) that his health was not excellent. He seems to have suffered often from ear aches and stomach trouble.

845. Bataille, Georges. "La valeur d'usage de D.A.F. de Sade." L'ARC 32 (1967): 88-90.

Writes an open letter to his "camarades" not because
the propositions contained in it are of special
concern to them but simply because of the need for
listeners, possibly nonexistent. Then proceeds to
classify some of his propositions in the field of
gratuitous impertinence. Also published in OEUVRES
COMPLETES: ECRITS POSTHUMES 1922-1940 (Gallimard).

846.  Bourdin, Paul. Introduction to CORRESPONDANCE INEDITE
      DU MARQUIS DE SADE, DE SES PROCHES, ET DE SES
      FAMILIERS. Paris: Librairie de France, 1929; Geneva:
      Slatkine, 1970. 450 p.

Presents the most complete collection to date of
Sade's correspondence, an indispensable tool for his
biographers. States that Sade was far less interested
in discovering truth than in justifying himself; in
the process his method was not always acceptable:
"Peu lui chaut de saccager la maison d'autrui pour
faire lever son gibier. Il laisse divaguer sa pensée
et s'amuse des conclusions auxquelles il parvient
derrière elle. Il ne choisit ni ne médite; il flaire
plus qu'il n'invente. M. de Sade n'est jamais plus
plaisant que lorsqu'il court à s'imprimer les talons
au cul, mais c'est une grâce communément attachée à la
quête du paradoxe: elle vient du détachement des
idées moyennes et fleurit au premier palier de la
supériorité intellectuelle." Concludes that Sade's
vices are too similar to a skin rash--the marquis has
no self-control. It is, therefore, difficult to take
him seriously.

Reviewed by Maurice Heine, NOUVELLE REVUE FRANCAISE 35
(August 1930): 269-271.

847.  Brochier, Jean-Jacques. "Sade à notre horizon."
      MAGAZINE LITTERAIRE 114 (June 1976): 8-17.

Publishes two letters with biographical and historical
interest and precedes them with another account of
Sade's life. Nothing new added to what has already
been said by Paul Bourdin, Jean Desbordes, and Gilbert
Lély.

848.  Celce-Murcia, Daniel. "Une Lettre inédite de Sade."
      CHIMERES, Spring 1974, pp. 69-77.

849. Coulmier, M. "Lettre du 23 mai 1810, écrite à Madame Cochelet du directeur Coulmier sur les spectacles par Sade à Charenton." REVUE ANECDOTIQUE 10 (1860): 101-106.

Reproduces a letter dated 23 May 1810 addressed to Madame Cochelet, a lady-in-waiting to the Queen of Holland, concerning the reservation of theater tickets to a production of Sade's play at Charenton.

850. Daumas, Georges. "A propos d'une lettre inédite du Marquis de Sade à Maître Gaspard Gaufridi, 16 Frimaire An VII (7 Décembre 1799)." OBLIQUES 12-13 (1977): 84-87.

Discusses one of the last letters written by Sade to his lawyer and longtime friend, Gaspard Gaufridi, who, for twenty-five years, took care of the marquis's legal affairs and administered his estate. In this hysterical letter, Sade requests urgently to be sent money: "Je meurs de faim, oui mon ami, toutes mes ressources sont usées et je meurs exactement de faim, je suis prêt à me bruler la cervelle si vous ne m'envoyés [sic] pas de l'argent à la minute."

851. Daumas, Georges, editor. MONSIEUR LE 6. LETTRES INEDITES 1778-1784. Paris: Julliard Sequana, 1954, pp. 261-284.

Presents a valuable collection of Sade's letters, courtesy of Xavier de Sade, and includes 23 pages of notes and explanations. Sade occupied the room No. 6 at the prison of Vincennes. Preface by Gilbert Lély.

852. Droguet, Robert. Review of MONSIEUR LE 6. LETTRES INEDITES. In NOUVELLE REVUE FRANCAISE 4 (1954): 909.

Reviews MONSIEUR LE 6, a collection of Sade's correspondence. To his wife he wrote: "As-tu bien voulu mettre PAPILLONS? Si c'est "papillons," tu sais que papillons sont des choses absolument entre toi et moi. . . ."

853. Ginisty, Paul. "Un amour platonique du marquise de Sade." GRANDE REVUE 3 (1900): 128-147.

This essay was reprinted as chapter II of the book published by Fasquelle in 1901. Discusses the

friendship of Melle de Rousset first with Madame de
Sade, then with the marquis. Shows that Sade had
quite a talent as an epistolary lover. He wrote poems
in provençal to Melle de Rousset: "Per aio, te cresi
sourciere M'as encanta Samblas dou diou d'amour la
maire. . . ." The lady was quite flattered and was
soon herself adopting a very amorous tone: "Mon cher
de Sade, délice de mon âme, je meurs de ne pas te
voir. . . . That relationship was doomed, however, to
remain platonic.

854. Hallier, Jean-Edern. "Sadisme et souffrance." TABLE
RONDE 80 (1954): 148-153.

Reviews the volume of Sade's correspondence MONSIEUR
LE 6. Stresses the modern outlook of Sade's thoughts.
Comments--very briefly--on the publication of Sade's
letters, which renders the approach to "sadism" more
accessible. But, in the final analysis, feels that
none of Sade's writings are great works, because their
extreme singularity detracts from their universality,
which is the first condition of genius. At best, Sade
"est un génie de la masturbation."

855. Heine, Maurice. Review of CORRESPONDANCE INEDITE DU
MARQUIS DE SADE. Edited by Paul Bourdin. NOUVELLE
REVUE FRANCAISE 35 (1 August 1930): 269-271.

Reviews the CORRESPONDANCE published by Paul Bourdin
(Librairie de France) who, unfortunately, took it upon
himself to make running commentaries. Heine states:
"Un tel livre doit être abordé sans guide. . . ."

856. Huysmans, Joris-Karl. LETTRE INEDITE A JULES DESTREE.
Genèva: Droz, 1967, p. 53.

Brief references to Sade in a letter dated 27
September 1885 and attributing to the Count of
Lautréamont "des enragements sanglants du Marquis de
Sade."

857. Lély, Gilbert. "Deux lettres du marquis de Sade." LES
CAHIERS DE LA PLEIADE, Autumn, Winter, 1949, pp. 167-
184.

Letter to Madame de Sade dated 17 February 1779 (?)
and a letter to Monsieur Carteron (Martin Quiros), not
dated but probably written at the end of December 1779

or in January 1780. These two leters are published in
a collection of twenty-six letters under the title
L'AIGLE, MADEMOISELLE (Editions Georges Artigues).

858.  Lély, Gilbert.  Foreword to MONSIEUR LE 6, LETTRES
      INEDITES (1778-1784).  Paris: Julliard Sequana, 1954,
      pp. 9-46.

      In this long foreword, explains that forty-two letters
      of this collection were written at Vincennes between
      February 1777 and June 1778;  one hundred and one were
      written shortly thereafter, between September 1778 and
      February 1784;  and the last batch was written at the
      Bastille between February 1784 and September 1785.
      About Sade's style, writes:  "Personne avant le
      romantisme, n'a écrit avec une liberté aussi totale,
      ni Montaigne, ni Saint-Simon, ni Diderot. . . ."

859.  Lély, Gilbert.  MARQUIS DE SADE, L'AIGLE, MADEMOISELLE.
      . . . Paris:  Georges Artigues, 1949.

      Important publication of some of Sade's letters.
      Contains an interesting introduction and commentaries.

      Reviewed by C. Mauriac in TEMPS MODERNES, March 1950,
      pp. 139-147;  Maurice Nadeau in MERCURE DE FRANCE,  1
      February 1950,  pp. 304-308;  L.  Pierre-Quint in
      L'OBSERVATEUR, 25 May 1950.

860.  Lély, Gilbert, ed. LETTRES CHOISIES. Paris: Union des
      Grandes Ecoles, 1969.

      Discovered in the Château de Condé-en-Brie,  179
      letters,  several notes and requests written between
      1777 and 1785.  Most are addressed to Madame de Sade
      and show again the true feelings of the marquis for
      her and prove that "the only person whose profound
      attachment,  and even heroic devotion Sade had been
      able to appreciate in many circumstances [was] namely,
      his wife."  Describes these letters, written with
      total freedom, in elogious terms quoted from Carteron:
      "the erotic boldness of its opening,  the tone of
      exquisite lightheartedness which distinguishes it, the
      finesse and firmness of its language,  and its
      continuously enchanting grace can make such a letter
      comparable to the music of Mozart who knows well how
      to make us aware of human dignity."

861. Lély, Gilbert. "Lettre à madame de Sade." LA NEF, March 1950, pp. 33-38.

Reproduces a letter written by Sade to his wife from the prison of Vincennes on July 1783. Shows the talent of the marquis as an epistolary writer.

862. Mauriac, Claude. "L'aigle, Mlle." TABLE RONDE, March 1950, pp. 139-147.

Reviews the publication under the title "L'aigle, Mademoiselle . . ." of Sade's correspondence. Attacks with virulence Gilbert Lély's devotion to Sade; yet concedes that there is some grandeur in Sade's work, grandeur which explains "la merveilleuse délicatesse de certaines de ses lettres à sa femme, d'autant plus émouvante qu'elle succède à des accès d'une obscénité exacerbée. Elle explique la dignité qu'il conserve en dépit des outrages dont il est abreuvé."

863. Nadeau, Maurice. "Lettres du marquis de Sade." MERCURE DE FRANCE 308 (1950): 304-308.

Reviews the publication by Gilbert Lély of L'AIGLE, MADEMOISELLE in 1949. States that in these twenty-four letters Sade admits to being a libertine but not a criminal. He was a person forced by his imprisonment to "realize his fantasms." It is prison that molded him into what he became, and it was through his writings that he organized both his vengeance and his deliverance.

864. Pidanzat de Mairobert, A. L'OBSERVATEUR ANGLOIS OU CORRESPONDANCE SECRETE ENTRE MILOR ALL'EYE ET MILORD ALL'EAR. London: John Adamson, 1764. 23 p.

This publication, signed in the introduction with only the initials A. P.-M., attributes the letter which follows it to Charles Villers who, after reading JUSTINE, had felt he wanted to set the record straight. JUSTINE would be the work of a pervert, "a monument mystérieux d'aliénation et d'infamie." Also denies in a post script that JUSTINE could have been written by Choderlos de Laclos.

865. Sade, Madame de. "Lettre au marquis de Sade." LES CAHIERS OBLIQUES 1 (1980): 9-10.

Unpublished letter from the marquise de Sade to her husband, who was then a prisoner at Vincennes, because of a "lettre de cachet" sent by Madame de Montreuil, his mother-in-law. Includes commentaries by G. Lély, who states that the marquise's spelling was somewhat whimsical: "he crin point que lon entre dan ton cabinet il non point les clef et noserai [sic] . . ." but her love and concern for the marquis seems genuine: "mon bon ami est bon courage et patience et surtout ne te laisse point aller à des accès de désespoir qui me font trembler. . . ."

866. Sade, Xavier de. "Deux lettres inédites de Sade." LE MAGAZINE LITTERAIRE 114 (June 1976): 26-27.

Two letters written by the Marquis de Sade, 3 November 1777 and 5 November 1777, courtesy of Count Xavier de Sade. Presents much of interest, since between the original lines in black ink there are several complaints against the system, scribbled with lemon juice. Parts of the letters were, of course, censored.

867. Schorr, James L. "Deux lettres inédites du marquis de Sade à Gaufridi." DIX-HUITIEME SIECLE 12 (1980): 247-249.

Publishes two letters belonging to the Carlton Lake Collection in the Humanities Research Center of the University of Texas, Austin. The first is dated 9 November 1790 and is addressed to Gaufridi; the second, with the same addressee, is dated 7 November 1793. In both Sade complains to his "friend" Gaufridi.

868. Soboul, Albert. "Le Marquis de Sade et la liberté retrouvée après le 9 thermidor." ANNALES HISTORIQUES DE LA REVOLUTION FRANCAISE, July-September 1977, p. 483.

In 1975 the Librairie Morssen published a catalog of autograph manuscripts which included a letter from Sade dated 29 November 1794 and addressed to his attorney Gaufridi (seven pages in quarto). A. Soboul gives excerpts of that letter, which ended with a postscript: "N'oubliés [sic] pas le mot homme de lettres dans mon adresse."

869.  Sollers, Philippe.    "Lettre de Sade."  TEL QUEL 61
      (1975):   14-20.

          Quotes a short sentence written by Sade in a letter to
          his  wife (1783):    "Vous savez que personne n'analyse
          les  choses  comme  moi."   With  this  passage  as  a
          starting point, discusses Sade's idealism, philosophy,
          and style of writing.  Criticizes  Lacan, who, in KANT
          AVEC  SADE,  failed to recognize Sade's sense  of  the
          comical.    Concludes   "Tout  ce  qu'écrit  Sade  est
          humour."

870.  Sollers, Philippe.    "Lettre de Sade."  OBLIQUES  12-13
      (1977):   213-217.

          Originally  published in TEL QUEL 61  (1975):   14-20.
          See annotation,  item 869 under the same title in that
          journal.

871.  Swinburne, Algernon-Charles.    THE  SWINBURNE  LETTERS.
      Edited  by  Cecil Lang.   New Haven:  Yale  University
      Press, 1960.

          Lists  several dozen references to the Marquis de Sade
          in letters of Swinburne who had obviously read all the
          published works of Sade.    Mentioned in particular are
          ALINE ET VALCOUR;   IDEE SUR LES ROMANS;   JULIETTE,  OU
          LES PROSPERITES DU VICE; JUSTINE OU LES MALHEURS DE LA
          VERTU;  LA  NOUVELLE JUSTINE;  LA PHILOSOPHIE DANS  LE
          BOUDOIR; and ZOLOE ET SES DEUX ACOLYTES.

872.  Thierry, Augustin.    "Lettres  sur Sade, notamment  du
      sieur  Thierry qui le connut à Charenton."   L'AMATEUR
      D'AUTOGRAPHES,  1863, p. 279; idem, 1864, pp. 105-106;
      idem, 1865, p. 235.

E. DISSERTATIONS

873. Berman, Lorna. AN APPRAISAL OF THE WORKS OF THE MARQUIS DE SADE AND OF HIS PORTRAYAL OF MAN. (Ph.D., University of Toronto, 1961).

Abstract not available. See annotation under THE THOUGHT AND THEMES OF THE MARQUIS DE SADE, item 1745.

874. Blair, Thomas Edward. "Le Roman de Sade: La Nature comme volcan." DISSERTATION ABSTRACTS INTERNATIONAL 36 (1976): 7459A. (Ph.D., University of Wisconsin, Madison.)

States that Sade's technique is "to take the data, examples and axioms of earlier materialists and, denying all limits, to draw the most extreme conclusions. Thus his materialism does not propose as a goal a Garden of Eden governed by reason, but rather a world ruled by nature, that is the constructive and destructive force exemplified by the volcano. Man, Sade argues, would do well to accept the reality of nature and imitate it by following the direction and dictates of his own bodily organization. This philosophy is reflected in Sade's aesthetics and his conception of the novel: the novel must be realistic and must carefully avoid the artificial happy ending with its triumph of virtue." Concludes that "the analysis of the three versions of JUSTINE AND JULIETTE demonstrates that, as for Diderot, Sade's basic philosophy and its elaboration condition the modification of other elements of the novels. Aesthetic concerns are superseded by didactic intentions; the traditional form disguises a radical philosophical content based upon Sade's concept of the dynamic, creative and destructive power of nature." (Quoted from DAI.)

875. Blamire, R. S. "The Notion of Project in the Works of Sade." (Thesis from the University of Manchester, 1976).

Unpublished dissertation mentioned in Otto Klapp publication on Sade.

876.  Cha, Michel.  LEGENDE DE SADE.  HISTOIRE D'UN MYTHE DE
      L'EROTISME.  (Thèse de 3ème cycle, Université de Paris
      VII, 1976, 162 p.)

      Unpublished dissertation from the University of Paris.

877.  Durin, Jacques.  LA PENSEE MATERIALISTE DU MARQUIS  DE
      SADE:  GENESE D'UNE PHILOSOPHIE DU MAL.  (Thèse de 3è
      cycle, Université d'Aix-en-Provence, 1976, 392 p.)

      Unpublished thesis  dealing with the  materialism  of
      Sade and his approach to a philosophy of evil.

878.  Foster, Annetta.  "The Place of Theater and Drama in the
      Life  of  the  Marquis  de  Sade,  'homme  de  lettres
      extraordinaire.'"  DISSERTATION ABSTRACTS INTERNATIONAL
      36 (1975):  4860.   (Ph.D.,  University of California,
      Los Angeles.)

      "The 'missing link' to an understanding of the strange
      and  complicated psyche of  Donatien-Alphonse-François
      de Sade was discovered during this study in the corpus
      of  his dramatic writing published for the first  time
      in 1970. . . .   Sade is a much discussed,  but little
      understood figure.   From an aristocrat with a private
      theater   in  his  chateau,   he  became  during   the
      Revolution a hungry citizen peddling plays,  a walk-on
      and  prompter at the public theaters,  and he finished
      his  career as a writer,  director,  and  producer  of
      plays  at the Charenton Insane Asylum. . . . Sade  was
      not  a  monster,  nor was he  insane.   All  reports--
      medical,  civil,  legal--have  exonerated him of  such
      charges.   He was, instead, a playwright whose mentors
      were Aristotle,  Molière,  Aretino, and Voltaire.  His
      plays  are  Sadean,   not  sadistic.   He   espoused
      knowledge,   not  ignorance;  virtue,   not  innocence.
      Behind  his facade of written violence is a thoughtful
      Sade  who  favors woman's liberation and  a  place  of
      dignity for her in this world.

      "Cell, stage, brothel, château, convent, study, petite
      maison,  Charenton--all  symbolize an enclosed  space,
      the world of Sade where the real and the unreal merge.
      Sade  distilled the essence of his age,  and also  its
      dregs.   They are in the plays and the novels which he
      wrote  in  his  cell--the  womb and the  tomb  of  his
      existence. . . ."  (Quoted from DAI.)

879.  Foucault, Gérard.  LIBERTE  INDIVIDUELLE ET ALIENATION
      SOCIALE CHEZ SADE.  (Thèses,  Université de Toulouse,
      1980.)

      Unpublished doctoral dissertation ($3^e$ cycle).

880.  Gallop,  Jane.  "Intersexions:   A Reading of Sade with
      Bataille,  Blanchot,  and  Klossowski."   DISSERTATION
      ABSTRACTS  INTERNATIONAL  38  (1977):      1434A-14335A.
      (Ph.D., Cornell University, 1976.)

      Approaches  the works of Sade through "the  filter  of
      three readers of Sade,"  G. Bataille, M. Blanchot, and
      P. Klossowski.   Concludes  that  "Sade's scandal  is
      based, not on some nonhuman, unthinkable violence, but
      upon  an  inextricable mixture of violence  with  that
      which is most comfortably familiar.  Sade's characters
      are  capable  of  a relationship that  is  undeniably
      friendship,  and  yet capable of murdering  a  friend.
      Sade's work is frightening and disgusting, because the
      greatest  violence  is inscribed into the most  normal
      human relations.   No part of existence remains a safe
      asylum. . . .  Sade's work continues to simultaneously
      arouse,  disgust, and unsettle, and thus it exerts its
      fascination  upon seekers of a universal  prostitution
      of beings."  (Quoted from DAI.)

881.  Gibbons,  Raymond  Wood.   "DANTONS TOD and  MARAT/SADE:
      Social Confrontation or Existential Dilemma?"  MASTERS
      ABSTRACTS  16  (1975):    16  (M.A.,  Pacific  Lutheran
      University.)

882.  Habert,  Gabriel.  INNOCENCE  POLITIQUE DU  MARQUIS  DE
      SADE.  (Thèses,  Université Aix-Marseille,  1956, 136
      p.)

      Unpublished  dissertation  under  the  direction  of
      Michel-Henry Fabre.

883.  Harari, Josué V.  "Les Métamorphoses du  désir  dans
      l'oeuvre de Sade." DISSERTATION ABSTRACTS INTERNAIONAL
      35 (1975):   4429-A.   (Ph.D., State University of New
      York at Buffalo.)

      Attempts  to demonstrate that Sade "is not mad in  the
      ordinary  sense  of  the word and he  does  not  equal
      sadism, nor does he even approximate the stereotypical
      sadist or pervert with whom his name has,  more  often

than not, been associated by traditional criticism."
Then "shows how Sade has systematically pitted desire
in conflict against cultural customs." Then proceeds
"to study how Sade expounds his theory of desire from
a philosophical standpoint. First, showing how Sade's
characters must of necessity always demonstrate a
truth (a philosophical truth) which is indissolubly
linked to the activation of desire; second, explaining
the multiple and complex relationships which underpin
libertinage and philosophy in the Sadian system of
thought." (Quoted from DAI.)

884. Harris, Kim Bradford. "Marat/Sade: The Play's
Ambiguities as a Result of Weiss's Struggle with
Political Commitment." DISSERTATION ABSTRACT
INTERNATIONAL 36-A (1975): 4848. (Ph.D., Southern
Illinois University.)

"Peter Weiss's THE PERSECUTION AND ASSASSINATION OF
JEAN-PAUL MARAT AS PERFORMED by the INMATES OF THE
ASYLUM OF CHARENTON (or MARAT/SADE) is a play
frequently produced in the modern theater. A probable
reason for its popularity is the multiplexity of
meaning present in the play: the richness of quality
present in MARAT/SADE is not evident in the
playwright's other dramatic works. The play's high
artistic quality is probably, to some extent, a
consequence of Weiss's internal struggle whether or
not to commit himself to the communist cause. . . .
Weiss's indecision over committing himself to
communism and the parallel decision to leave his
revolutionary play ambiguous cause Weiss to choose
historical data that have contradictory elements and
motivate him to arrange the data in such a way that
obvious political slant is not present. Four general
sources in this study of MARAT/SADE serve to
demonstrate the ambiguities and how they result from
the playwright's struggle with himself over political
commitment: 1) Wiess's personal philosophical
struggles as he ages; 2) the historical data which
cause levels of meaning in the play; 3) the convergent
but contradictory political and theatrical traditions
that come to light when the play's various
interpretations are described; and 4) three of the
various stage interpretations of the play." (Quoted
from DAI.)

885. Hass, Robert Louis. "REASON'S CHILDREN: Economic Ideology and the Themes of Fiction, 1720-1880." DISSERTATION ABSTRACTS INTERNATIONAL 36 (1976): 8033-A. (Ph.D., Stanford University.)

States: "Reason's Children is a study of economic and psychological themes in the novel related to the rise of capitalism. It contains discussions of the following works: Hobbes, LEVIATHAN; Defoe, ROXANNA and MOLL FLANDERS; Laclos, LES LIAISONS DANGEREUSES; Sade, LA PHILOSOPHIE DANS LE BOUDOIR; Balzac, LE PERE GORIOT; Dickens, HARD TIMES and OUR MUTUAL FRIEND; George Eliot, ADAM BEDE; Tolstoy, WAR AND PEACE; Dostoevsky, CRIME AND PUNISHMENT; Freud, THE INTERPRETATION OF DREAMS. . . . The study concludes by observing that the novel itself, as an art form provided to its readers the experience of nurture, dependence and interconnectedness which the economic ideology of their culture denied." (Quoted from DAI.)

886. Heine, Maurice. "Une thèse de doctorat sur le marquis de Sade." LE PROGRES MEDICAL 2 (1932): 9-13.

Another scholarly article by this Sadian authority. Reviews the doctoral dissertation written by Salvator Sarfati under the title ESSAI MEDICO-PSYCHOLOGIQUE SUR LE MARQUIS DE SADE. Declares: "On ne peut que s'incliner devant la loyauté scientifique d'une telle étude. Entreprise sans prévention et conduite avec impartialité, elle contribuera fortement à achever de détruire 'des légendes d'autant plus immorales qu'elles sont fausses.'"

This essay was also included as a chapter in the book LE MARQUIS DE SADE, by the same author, published by Gallimard in 1950, pp. 104-110. Excerpted in OBLIQUES 12-13 (1977): 197-200.

887. Hocke, T. "Artaud und Weiss: Untersuchung zur theoretischen Konzeption des 'Theaters der Grausamkeit' und ihrer praktischen Wirksamkeit in Peter Weiss' Marat/Sade." DISSERTATION ABSTRACTS INTERNATIONAL 40 (1979): 56-C.

Not available.

888. Horowitz, Marilyn L. "The Attitude of Cruelty in Late Eighteenth-Century French Fiction." DISSERTATION

ABSTRACTS INTERNATIONAL 39 (1978): 1620-A. (Ph.D., City University of New York.)

"This study is concerned with cruelty, not as a subject matter of the works examined, but as a literary attitude that steadily developed in the second half of the eighteenth century. We have restricted our inquiry to the attitude of cruelty seen in the aristocratic libertine hero, a constant figure in the literature of the time. Among those writers whose works show the attitude of cruelty, Crébillon fils, Laclos, and Sade are the most important. . . . What particularly interests us is the way in which libertinism, imitating philosophy, combines two strong currents of eighteenth-century thought—rationalism and eroticism. The essential, but at first glance unexpected, connection between these two elements is one of the most important aspects of the works of the writers to be examined. It is the blending of rationalism and eroticism that produces the philosophy of cruel libertinism and constitutes the link between earlier writers and the Marquis de Sade, for whom, however, cruelty poses philosophical and social problems not dreamed of by his more conservative predecessors." (Quoted from DAI.)

889. Ibrahim, Annie. "Kant et Sade, ou l'affectivité persécutée." (Thèse, 3e cycle, Université de Paris I, 1972, 312 p.)

This is an unpublished dissertation from the University of Paris I.

890. Ivker, Barry. "Sexual Perversion in Eighteenth-Century English and French Fiction." DISSERTATION ABSTRACTS INTERNATIONAL 29 (1968): 1512-A. (Ph.D., Indiana University.)

States that "a large amount of erotic literature was produced in the eighteenth century, ranging from bawdy songs to transcripts of sensational trials, pseudo-scientific tracts on primitive sexual rites and scandalous accounts of court life and the activities of secret societies. Among this material can be found literary traditions or genres cultivated by both major and minor authors and essentially perverse or sadistic in character. . . . In France, the libertine movement, under way since the early part of the

seventeenth century, had combined a critique of
traditional religion and philosophy based on Natural
Law with a portrayal of promiscuous and often aberrant
sexual behavior. . . . The height of the libertine
movement is reached in the works of Sade, where the
libertine hero tries to justify his conduct with an
appeal to nature and to transcend nature through the
perpetration of horrible acts, committed without
passion or motive. The libertine movement as such,
ends with Sade. . . ." (Quoted from DAI).

891. Javelier, André Eugène-François Paul. LE MARQUIS DE
SADE ET LES CENT-VINGT JOURNEES DE SODOME DEVANT LA
PSYCHOLOGIE ET LA MEDICINE LEGALE. (Doctoral
dissertation, Paris Le François, 1937, 81 p.)

This dissertation from the Faculté de médecine of
Paris, sees in Sade a precursor of our modern
sexologists. This aspect of Sade's works was first
understood by nineteenth-century scholars: Dr.
Marciat, Krafft-Ebbing, Dr. Cabanes, etc. Includes a
twelve-page bibliography.

892. Kernstock, Wiltrud. DIE SEXUALANTHROPOLOGIE DES MARQUIS
DE SADE, DARGESTELLT IN ANTITHESE ZU DEN THEORIEN J. J.
ROUSSEAU. (Ph.D., Univ. Munchen, Medizinische
Fakultät, 1971, 156 p.)

This is an unpublished dissertation from the
University of Munich.

893. Leduc, Jean. LES IDEES RELIGIEUSES ET MORALES DU
MARQUIS DE SADE ET LEURS SOURCES. (Thèses, Paris,
1965.)

Unavailable at this writing.

894. Longhi, Gilbert. PROBLEMES DE L'AUTOBIOGRAPHIE DANS
L'ECRITURE DE SADE. (Doctoral dissertation
Université Toulouse II, 1978.)

Doctoral dissertation ($3^e$ cycle) written in French, in
typed manuscript form.

895. Mabiala, Marcel. "La femme chez Sade." (Thèses
Université de Grenoble III, 1975, 211 p.)

Unpublished dissertation in typed manuscript form,
with an appendix and a "Dictionary of the Women in
Sade."

896. Marsaud, Marie-Isoline Françoise. "The Notion of the
Monster in the Works of de Sade and Flaubert."
DISSERTATION ABSTRACTS INTERNATIONAL 37 (1977):
4401A. (Thesis, University of Michigan, Ann Arbor.)

"Illustrates the study of the Monster in the works of
Sade and Flaubert. Starting with the notion of
sacrifice as it has been studied by R. Girard in LA
VIOLENCE ET LE SACRE, and applying that model to texts
of Sade and Flaubert, the dissertation will show the
diverse aspects of the sacrificial ritual. The
sacrifice introduces other points of consideration
such as the Feast. . . . The conclusion parallels the
ritualized sacrifice as well as "murder" to our modern
"terrorism"--unpredictable death not computerized by
doctors and hospitals. With de Sade and Flaubert,
death is restored in its function of a sacred and
criminal act. Death is Law, is what Kafka teaches us
in his Penal Colony, and what de Sade's and Flaubert's
monsters continually repeat." (Quoted from DAI.)

897. Marshall, Russell Eugene. "The Role of the Family in
the Works of the Marquis de Sade." DISSERTATION
ABSTRACTS INTERNATIONAL 38 (1977): 3544. (Ph.D.,
University of New Mexico.)

"Despite the Marquis de Sade's rejection of the
traditional family, the family plays an important but
largely unrecognized role in his works. A careful
examination of Sade's OEUVRES COMPLETES in relation to
five authors contemporary to him and an account of his
own family experiences establishes a social and
personal background that reveals the family's
importance to Sade and the ways in which his attitudes
toward the family are unique. . . . The family plays
a more important part in Sade's works than has been
previously acknowledged. Sade is not unique in
rejecting the traditional family, but his rejection is
more violent and complete than that of any
contemporary author and reflects his denial of the
validity of any institution that might try to limit
the total freedom of the individual. (Quoted from
DAI.)

898.  McAllister, Harold S.  "Apology for Bad Dreams:  A Study
      of  Characterization  and  the  Use  of  Fantasy  in
      CLARISSA, and JUSTINE, and THE MONK."  DISSERTATION
      ABSTRACTS  INTERNATIONAL 32  (1972):   6383-A  (Ph.D.,
      University of New Mexico.)

      "The  purpose  of this dissertation is to analyze  the
      roles  of characterization and fantasy in three  major
      eighteenth    century    novels--Samuel    Richardson's
      CLARISSA,  and  the  Marquis de Sade's JUSTINE,  and
      Matthew   G.   Lewis's  THE   MONK.   Such   analysis
      demonstrates   the interrelatedness of the three  works
      and  illustrates  a continuum of influence  among  the
      three   authors.   In   more   general   terms,   the
      dissertation  deals  with the problems of fantasy  and
      reality  in the novel and the psychological appeal  of
      the novel . . .  and is an attempt to demonstrate that
      in  each  novel  the author is working out his  anti-
      social  fantasies,  with  varying degrees of  psychic
      safety and artistic success."

899.  Redalie,  Isabelle  Tatiana.   "L'internement de Sade  à
      Charenton, considérations sur les deux internements de
      Sade  à  l'hospice de  Charenton,  leur  signification
      historique  et   médico-légale."    (Thèse
      médecine, Paris, 1969 no. 898.)

      Unpublished dissertation.

900.  Rocca,  Marthe Tirelli.  "Sade:  Le Problème du Mal dans
      ALINE    ET    VALCOUR."    DISSERTATION    ABSTRACTS
      INTERNATIONAL 41 (1981):  5121-A.  (Ph.D., University
      of California, Los Angeles.)

      Attempts  to  study  the problem of  evil,  with  its
      politico-social, religious, and sexual connotations in
      the novel ALINE ET VALCOUR.   States: "Nous analysons
      le  texte sadien en montrant les rapports étroits  qui
      existent  entre  la  forme et le fond.   Aux  fins  de
      mettre  en  lumiére  le probléme du mal,  Sade  fait
      éclater  les  structures  trop rigides  du  langage
      conventionnel et le façonne sur les actions démesurées
      de  ses  libertins.   Cette libération du mot et  de
      l'acte est peut-être la plus grande originalité de son
      style.   Cependant  l'auteur a  toujours  recours  au
      langage  traditionnel et s'il choisit parfois des mots
      crus pour décrire des situationa à la fois cruelles et
      grossières,  jamais le mot chez Sade ne renonce à  ses

prérogatives historiques.  Il ne fait que le libérer de la censure.  Dans le chapitre II, le mal est present comme la loi souveraine des peuplades primitives parmi lesquelles les faibles sont soumis aux plus forts et les scélérats même, s'inclinent devant le caractère suprême de la Nature.  L'auteur emploie une technique très répandue au 18e siècle, celle de la réduction par l'absurde, pour mettre en valeur le mal. . . .  La quête sadienne du plaisir . . . a pour bût essential de montrer la puissance créatrice de l'homme et, en dernier ressort, sa libération complète.  Sade, en effet, reconnait à l'homme un potentiel de destruction identique à celui de la nature, faisant de ce potentiel une qualité intrinsèque de l'espèce humaine.

"Nous insistons sur le fait que jamais dans sa description de la formation du libertin-scélèrat, Sade ne dévoile les subtilités psychologiques qui feraient de ses héros des êtres réels; il s'attache, au contraire, à ne réveler que des signes de l'homme, ce qui ôte à son oeuvre tout sens éthique.  Cette approche fournit la base éthique idéale au texte sadien dont l'intensité n'a pas son égale parmi les oeuvres du 18e siècle, qu'il s'agisse de la peinture des scélérats et des sophismes de leurs discours, ou de la définition de la liberté qui est toujours exaltée dans ses romans."  (Quoted from DAI.)

901.  Rosenberg, Steven L.  "A Holonic Interpretation of Aggression, Hostility, and Sadism."  DISSERTATION ABSTRACTS INTERNATIONAL 39 (1978):  2841.  (Ph.D., Kent State University.)

"The purpose of this dissertation was to define aggression, hostility, and sadism, and to detail their implications for mental health.  An alternative model is developed in which these terms are used to represent three different aspects of human motivation which are often collapsed under the single rubric of aggression.  The thesis of this study is that these phenomena must be distinguished from one another since the efficiency of treatment may depend upon the accuracy of the diagnosis.  The holonic model of behavior developed clearly defines aggressive, hostile, and sadistic behavior, and discriminates among these important motivational processes.

"Hostility differs from aggression in several important ways. It occurs when aggressive behavior is blocked by an interference which is perceived as deliberate. Anger is the affect associated with hostile behavior. It is relieved when the obstacle blocking the aggresive behavior is overcome or accepted as legitimate. Hostility, therefore, is negative only insofar as its concomitant affect is anger. It is essentially a positive motivational process since it provides the individual with the theoretical opportunity to overcome obstacles and ultimately satisfy desires. It is, therefore, described as a legitimate, natural, and positive process.

"Sadism differs from both of these behavior patterns as the goal of the sadistic individual is neither to satisfy desires nor gain relief from anger. Rather, the purpose of pure sadistic behavior is solely to inflict injury upon an object.

"Finally, the relationship among hostility, aggression, and mental health is detailed in terms of both psychotherapeutic procedures and educational practices. Implications for the educator implementing primary preventive programs in institutions and/or the clinician involved in psychotherapy are drawn." (Quoted from DAI.)

902. Sarfati, Salvator. ESSAI MEDICO-PSYCHOLOGIQUE SUR LE MARQUIS DE SADE. Lyon: Bosc & Riou, 1930. 187 p.

First doctoral dissertation conducted under the guidance of Etienne Martin, professor at the School of Lyon. Studies Sade, the man and his works, from the point of view of a medical doctor. Three-part study includes about sixty pages of biographical data. In his introduction states: "Que son nom se prête donc à jamais pour désigner le sadisme, cela est non seulement naturel, mais aussi l'acquittement d'un devoir qu'a le monde scientifique de rendre hommage à la mémoire de Sade."

Reviewed by Maurice Heine, LE PROGRES MEDICAL 9 (1932): 9-13.

903. Senelick, Laurence Philip. "The Prestige of Evil: The Murderer as Romantic hero from Sade to Lacenaire."

(Ph.D., 1972, Harvard University--not available from University Microfilms International).

904. Sichère, Bernard. "Sade ou le discours du désir." (Thèse complémentaire, Paris, Nanterre 1969.)

Unpublished dissertation.

905. Taylor, Robert Edward. "The Marquis de Sade and the Enlightenment." MICROFILM ABSTRACTS XI, 1 (1951): 493-494. (Thesis, Columbia University.)

"Justly one of the most colorful figures of the eighteenth century, Sade has long been one of its most maligned and legendized characters. In recent years, largely because of the surrealists, the marquis has emerged for many as a kind of symbol of freedom from all restraints as well as from tyranny. Not until this present study, however, has anyone attempted to put his thoughts and convictions side by side with those of the other writers and thinkers of his age. This study does that systematically in the various realms of his activity: atheism, social reform, political theory, and sexology. An attempt is made to evaluate Sade in each of these fields and to contrast his contribution to each one with others of the Enlightenment. It is most clearly demonstrated perhaps that he went farther than his contempories in the field of atheistic materialism and that he created out of his own imagination wrought to a turbulent peak from years of enforced abstinence, a new set of values that would later make up the science of sexology.

"A sketch of Sade's life opens the book. There the myths are disposed of by reference to established facts, in many cases to court room records. The truth that is left, however, is even more interesting than the legends. In conclusion, there is a discussion of the man and the writer in which Sade's personal letters, some of them brought to light only in 1949, are used to help show why he wrote as he did." (Quoted from MICROFILM ABSTRACTS.)

906. Taylor-William, Diane. "Directing Shadows: Drama and Psychodrama in Shaffer's EQUUS, Arrabal's L'ARCHITECTE ET L'EMPEREUR D'ASSYRIE," and Weiss' MARAT/SADE." DISSERTATION ABSTRACTS INTERNATIONAL 42 (1981): 1627. (Ph.D., University of Washington.)

"Psychodrama is a modern term for a dramatic form as old as drama itself. The word refers specifically to a therapeutic theater originated by Jacob L. Moreno in Vienna in the early 1920's. Psychodrama is a form of psychotherapy that helps a patient solve problems by dramatic means. Psychodrama and drama are related, not because drama necessarily is or should be therapeutic, but because drama, like psychodrama, seems to have the power to transform, change or heal. Psychodramatic material and methods have been incorporated as internal theater in some modern plays for their artistic, rather than therapeutic, quality. Psychodramatic techniques, originally borrowed from drama and modified to enhance their purgative objectives, are borrowed back in turn by playwrights who understand their theatrical value. The emphasis of my dissertation is on the re-assimilation of psychodramatic techniques in Peter Shaffer's EQUUS, Fernando Arrabal's L'ARCHITECTE ET L'EMPEREUR D'ASSYRIE and Peter Weiss' MARAT/SADE."

"These three plays are, in different ways, plays about psychodrama." (Quoted from DAI.)

907. Thiher, Roberta J. "The Quantitative Moral Universe in Six Tales by the Marquis de Sade." DISSERTATION ABSTRACTS INTERNATIONAL 31 (1971): 4136-A (Ph.D., University of North Carolina, Chapel Hill.)

"The Quantitative Moral Universe in Six Tales by M. de Sade" is a study of the moral vocabulary in six out of eleven tales that compose LES CRIMES DE L'AMOUR. The moral terminology in the six tales is classified and then analyzed from the point of view of recurrent vocabulary patterns, grammatical discrimination and certain stylistic devices. The stable and unstable elements which emerge from the verbal data show what constructs Sade has put into play, how they are used and to what purpose. Certain phenomena which result such as the transfer of certain virtue vocabulary to the vicious protagonist and vice vocabulary to the virtuous protagonist help to illustrate Sade's rhetorical manipulation. The result is the creation of a mythology of morality where the overworked moral clichés do no more than to occupy verbal space. Sade's moral concepts become at least one more level of primarily decorative elements. Moral words are

used to sustain a moral universe as much as they are
used for any specific didactic intent." (Quoted from
DAI.)

908.  Webb, Shawncey Jay. "Aspects of Fidelity and Infidelity
      in the Eighteenth-Century French Novel from Chasles to
      Laclos." DISSERTATION ABSTRACTS INTERNATIONAL 38
      (1977): 2165-A. (Ph.D., Indiana University.)

      Examines the importance of fidelity in five types of
      novels: ROMANS DE MOEURS, novels by women, ROMANS
      LIBERTINS, ROMANS MORAUX ET SENTIMENTAUX, and ROMANS
      PHILOSOPHIQUES. "Fidelity is presented as a dual
      concept. In order to portray reality in their works,
      the majority of authors limit their consideration of
      faithfulness to either FIDELITE DU CORPS or FIDELITE
      DU COEUR. Within the novels depicting sexual
      fidelity, it is primarily female fidelity that is
      discussed. The hero of the eighteenth-century novel
      is, in general, a flagrantly unfaithful individual but
      experiences little condemnation. The heroines fare
      less well. The novels, like the century, tend to
      define woman in terms of her sexuality. With the
      exception of Manon Lescaut and Julie de Wolmar, the
      heroines are either faithful or unfaithful, and
      consequently, either virtuous or immoral. . . ."
      (Quoted from DAI.)

909.  Wood, W. T. LA PLACE D'ALINE ET VALCOUR DANS L'OEUVRE DE
      SADE. 1968, (Thesis, Monash University.)

      Unpublished dissertation from Monash University,
      Australia. 68 p.

910.  Zacot, Fernand. "Essai à partir des grands romans
      sadiques du XVIII$^e$ siècle: Sade, Voltaire, Laclos, B.
      de St. Pierre, Diderot, l'abbé Prévost." (Thèses,
      Université Paris VIII, Vincennes, 1974.)

      Thesis (3$^e$ cycle) in French in typewritten manuscript
      form.

# F.  ETHICS

911.  Adorno,  Theodor  W.  and Max Horkheimer.  "Juliette or
Enlightenment  and  Morality."  In  DIALEKTIK  DER
AUFKLARUNG:  PHILOSOPHISCHE  FRAGMENTE.  Amsterdam:
Querido, 1947, pp. 88-121.

In  this long critique of American  commercialism  and
industrial  culture,  present  two  excursions  into
related topics.  See the ODYSSEY of Homer as an early
example of reason winning over violence, and the works
of the Marquis de Sade,  a rationalist destruction  of
all  categories of bourgeois morality.  Sade's  works
reveal  "the mythological character of the  principles
on  which  civilization rests after religion  [becomes
outmoded].  The principles of the Decalog of paternal
authority, . . .  each  of  the  ten  commandments  is
proven  to  be  invalid by  the  authority  of  formal
reason.  They  are  proven to be nothing  but  simple
ideology."  In this manner,  the enlightenment attacks
the  principle  of  virtue  and  human  kindness  the
bourgeoisie  still believed in and it does so  because
of its own principles of criticisms until these maxims
were  destroyed by capitalism and fascism.  Concludes
that decay was the product of capitalism.

912.  Almási,  Miklós.  "Sade  márki:  A  racionalizmus
szatirjátéka."  In AZ ERTELEM  KALANDJAI.  Budapest:
Szepirodalmi K, 1980, pp. 335-439.

Long  article,  "The Marquis de Sade:  A  Satiricical
Game of Rationalism," published in Hungarian.

913.  André,  Arlette.  "Sade et l'éthique de l'apathie."  In
MELANGES  LITTERAIRES  FRANCOIS  GERMAIN.  Dijon:
Section  de  Littérature  française de la  Faculté  de
lettres et philosophie de Dijon, 1979, pp. 95-104.

Invokes  the  epicurian ideal of  "ataraxia"  and  the
stoic  notion of "apatheia" to explain the eighteenth-
century concept of "apathie" which is much in evidence
in the works of Sade,  especially in JULIETTE:  "Chez
Sade l'éthique de l'apathie discrédite la  sensibilité
pour  mobiliser  l'énergie  au  service  de  la
transgression,  et l'agressivité subsiste au terme  de
cette  aventure  spirituelle.  Le constat final  sera
celui d'une impossible conquête de la sérénité."

914.  Anonymous.  "Evil  Man--A  Portrait of the  Marquis  de
      Sade."  TIME, 31 December 1956, pp. 22-23.

      Reports  on a question debated in the French  Judicial
      courts  after the publication by Jean-Jacques  Pauvert
      of  Sade's complete works:   "Was Sade a  pornographer
      whose works should be banned or a serious  contributor
      to  the wisdom of mankind?"  Findings of the Court not
      reported in the article.

915.  Audouin,  Philippe.  "Une  hypermorale."  LE  NOUVEL
      OBSERVATEUR, 16 March 1966, pp. 38-39.

      Assesses Sade's ethical theory,  a hypermorality which
      does  not  deny man's original bestiality but  on  the
      contrary  lets him assume his own "divinity":  "Sade
      est  exemplaire:  il  est en tout homme.  Il tend  à
      chacun le miroir où s'inscrit l'image terrifiante mais
      inoubliable de sa propre liberté."

916.  Aulagne,  Louis-Jean.  "Sade,  ou  l'apologétique  à
      l'envers."  PSYCHE 25 (1948):  1245-1264.

      "Worthwhile  comments  on Sade  as  atheist,  lyric
      stylist,  educational theorist,  and early sexologist.
      Well  documented  with pertinent and  interesting
      footnotes."  (Quoted from Cabeen, item 8.)

917.  Barruzzi,  Arno.  "Die Apathie des Denkens (Sade)."  In
      MENSCH UND MASCHINE:  DAS DENKEN SUB SPECIE MACHINAE.
      Munich:  Fink, 1973, pp. 117-172.

      In  the fourth chapter of this philosophical  treatise
      discusses:  1.  Das System der  Akzidentien:  a) Von
      Hobbes  und Holbach zu Sade,  b) Natur als  Produktion
      von  Negation,  c) Die  Negationstranszendenz  des
      Menschen;  2.  Vomsystem  der Notwendigkeit zum System
      der Freiheit oder di Libertinage des  Denkens,  a) Die
      libertine  Gesellschaft,  b) Die  Gesellschaft  der
      Freunde  des Verbrechens,  c) Die Gesellschaft  der
      Freunde  der Vernunft--die Polis,  d) Die Gesellschaft
      der  Freunde  der  Leidenschaft--der  Leviathan,
      e) Vernunft  und Gesellschaft;  3.  Libertinage  und
      Phantasie;  4.  Sades Grundsatz;  5.  Das Vorstellen.
      In  a most interesting conclusion states:  "Sade  als
      Denker  der  Libertinage  ist  kein  Denker  der
      Sexualitä."

918. Barthes, Roland. "L'Arbre du crime," TEL QUEL 28 (Winter 1967): 23-37.

Also published in OBLIQUES 12-13 (1977): 219-226, and in SADE, FOURIER, LOYOLA (Paris: Editions du Seuil, 1971), pp. 15-37.

919. Barthes, Roland. SADE, FOURIER, LOYOLA. Paris: Editions du Seuil, 1971, 192 pp. Translated by Richard Miller. New York: Hill & Wang, 1976. London: J. Cape, 1977, pp. 15-37.

States that in the Sadian enclosure, which has a dual purpose—to shelter vice from the world's punitive attempts and to form the basis of a social autarchy— the impossibilities of the referent are turned into the possibilities of the discourse: "constraints are shifted: the referent is totally at the discretion of Sade, who can like any narrator, give it fabulous dimensions, but the sign, belonging to the order of the discourse, is untractable, it makes the laws." In other words, what Sade represented was purposely misrepresented because it is "constantly being deformed by the meaning." This essay was also published as "L'Arbre du crime," TEL QUEL 28 (Winter 1967): 23-37. Reviewed by Jacques-Pierre Amette, "Apprendre à litre," LA QUINZAINE LITTERAIRE 132 (January 1972): 15-16; Claude Jannoud, "Roland Barthes réunit dans une même lecture Sade le maudit, Fourier, l'utopiste et Loyola le jésuite," LE FIGARO LITTERAIRE, 3 December 1971, p. 24; Jean d'Ormesson, "Logothètes et littérature," NOUVELLES LITTERAIRES 2309 (24 December 1971): 8; and by Michel Riffaterre, "Sade, or Text as Fantasy," DIACRITICS 2 (1972): 2-9.

920. Bartolommei, Sergio. "ALINE ET VALCOUR: Pornoutopia e 'silenzio delle leggi' nel pensiero del marchese di Sade." PENSIERO POLITICO: RIVISTA DI STORIA DELLE IDEE POLITICHE E SOCIALI 9 (1976): 461-471.

States that in Sade's system one of the fundamental dogmas of eighteenth century thought—the belief in the goodness of human nature—is overturned and nature is shown instead to be a disjointing, amoral and irrational power, and concludes that Sade uses the political message of the French Revolution to invoke private vices rather than improbable virtues.

Also published in STUDI SULL'UTOPIA.    Ed. Luigi Firpo
(Florence, Italy: Olschki, 1977, pp. 87-106).

921.  Bataille, Georges.    "Dali hurle avec Sade."    OEUVRES
      COMPLETES.    Tome II. Paris: Gallimard, 1970, pp. 113-
      115.

      Superficial essay on dreams.  Suggests that scandalous
      claims  in Sade are as natural as fever  when  animals
      are thirsty.

922.  Bataille, Georges.    "Le mal dans le platonicisme et dans
      le sadisme."  In OEUVRES COMPLETES.    Tome VII.    Paris:
      Gallimard, 1976.

      This  is a report on a conference presented on 12  May
      1947    at    the  "College  Philosophique"  and    first
      appeared--shorter version--under the title "Sade et la
      morale"  in  LA  PROFONDEUR ET  LE  RYTHME  (Vol.   III
      CAHIERS DU COLLEGE PHILOSOPHIQUE.   Grenoble:   Arthaud,
      1948).  Discusses the contradiction inherent in Sade's
      philosophy.  Opposed to the death penalty, Sade in his
      works presented death as, so to speak, a "good thing,"
      "un  bien."  This he justified by a  principle:    one
      cannot,  in  cold  blood,  exercise a  sanction  which
      demands the unleashing of passion.   Sade connects the
      passions    with    the   sacred   and,    in    opposition,
      identifies the profane with "la transcendance."   This
      excellent  presentation  is  followed  by  interesting
      questions from Jean Wahl.

923.  Bataille, Georges.    "Sade et la morale."  LA PROFOUNDEUR
      ET LE RYTHME.    Grenoble:  Editions Arthaud, 1948, pp.
      333-344.

      Opposes platonic morality to Sadian morality.    In the
      former,  evil  occurs when reason is controlled by the
      passions;  in  the latter,  the opposite seems  to  be
      true.  At the basis of all this reasonable morality is
      God.   But if we assume that God is dead, what becomes
      of these God-given rules?   If God is dead, then, "le
      déchaînement  des passions est le seul bien,--c'est là
      ce  que j'avais à dire.   Dès le moment oç la  raison
      n'est plus divine, il n'y a plus de Dieu."

924.  Beauvoir, Simone de. "Faut-il brûler Sade?" LES TEMPS
      MODERNES 74 (1951): 1002-1033; 75 (1952): 1197-1230.

      Published in English as "Must We Burn Sade?" (London:
      Peter Nevill, 1953). Appeared also in French in
      PRIVILEGES 76 (1955). Also as Preface to THE MARQUIS
      DE SADE: THE 120 DAYS OF SODOM AND OTHER WRITINGS.
      Translated by Annette Michelson (New York: Grove
      Press, Inc., 1966), pp. 3-64.

      Begins with an appraisal of Sade's relevance in the
      conflict between man as an individual and man as a
      member of society, and states that it is neither as a
      sexual pervert nor as an author that Sade made his
      mark but rather by describing the relationship which
      existed between those two sides of himself. Believes
      in Sade's total perversity to such an extent as to
      peevishly suggest that Sade's fatherhood has never
      been proven. Includes some astute statements
      regarding the functions of writing for Sade who was
      able to unleash some of his nightmares and who
      "exhibits criminal visions in an aggressive way."
      Also to be admired are Sade's "epic vehemence and his
      irony" and probably his talent as a real innovator in
      psychology. Concludes this first-rate essay with some
      telling appraisal: "To sympathize with Sade too
      readily is to betray him." Sade was a moralist who
      stood against the mores of his century and showed in
      his own way his disappointment with the Terror.

925.  Berman, Lorna. "The Marquis de Sade and Religion."
      REVUE DE L'UNIVERSITE D'OTTOWA 39 (1969): 627-640.

      "Analyzes in detail the justification of the various
      religious beliefs expressed in Sade's works since it
      is with justifications that Sade is concerned. For
      the most part, in his discussions of religion, the
      author illustrates that all Sade's characters, whether
      believers or non-believers, justify their beliefs with
      the same three fundamental arguments, and that Sade
      was aware of the inadequacy of these arguments. These
      arguments are based on 1) perception or awareness
      2) idealism 3) concern for the preservation and/or
      well-being of the human individual or of society."
      (Quoted from PHILOSOPHER'S INDEX, item 15.)

926.  Brochier, Jean-Jacques. SADE. Paris: Editions
      Universitaires, 1966. 124 p.

Gives a short biography and discussion of Sade's main
works (THE 120 DAYS, the three versions of JUSTINE,
JULIETTE, the CORRESPONDENCE). Then tackles the
different themes found in Sade's production: atheism,
death, refusal of all determinism in spite of an
avowed materialism, total loneliness, uniqueness of
man, moral relativism. Concludes: "Sade met en jeu,
à son époque, toute la pensée occidentale, la détruit
frénétiquement, pour laisser libre la naissance d'une
autre pensée, qui n'apparaitra qu'après la
Révolution."

Reviewed by J. Vercruysse, DIX-HUITIEME SIECLE 2
(1979): 360.

927.  Brochier, Jean-Jacques. LE MARQUIS DE SADE ET LA
      CONQUETE DE L'UNIQUE. Paris: Le Terrain vague,
      1962. 277 p.

      Sees in Sade a man who was excluded from "social
      universality" because he wanted to assume his
      particularity as an individual and who asserted in his
      writings--in spirit--the liberty he was denied in
      kind--physically. While it is generally assumed that
      he was incarcerated because of his writings, it seems
      more likely that his imprisonment helped him produce
      his writings. His thoughts revolved around some
      definite categories: negativity, totality,
      universality and, of course, individuality--which are
      so much a part of contemporary thinking. Concludes
      with some of the contibutions made by Sade: "La
      compréhension de cette contradiction qu'est l'homme,
      la lente montée vers une totale libération,
      l'affrontement sans merci de la négation et
      l'acceptation de ses résultats, voilà quelques-unes de
      ses trouvailles . . . en fait Sade a accompli plus que
      ce travail négatif, il a fait jair une evidence; celle
      du désir, et montre qu'on ne pouvait parvenir à
      l'Universalité qu'en assumant le plus complètement la
      Particularité de soi-Même."

928.  Cain, Jacques. "Le fantasme sadique et la réalité." LE
      MARQUIS DE SADE. Paris: Librairie Armand Colin,
      1968, pp. 279-288.

      Proceedings of colloquium on the Marquis de Sade, Aix-
      en-Provence, 19 and 20 February 1966. Explains that
      sadistic behavior existed long before Sade but that

sadistic behavior existed long before Sade but that the marquis was the first to let himself be known as having mixed fantasy and reality to such a cruel extent. While it is relatively easy to find in one person the genius of invention--that is, great imagination--it is usually rare to find someone who will couple this inventive mind with the desire and the power to turn theories into actions. Sade is one of the few to have possessed both. "L'originalité de Sade, ce qui en fait un cas particulier peut se résumer en ceci: chez lui se sont alliés ces deux mécanismes d'une recherche d'un objet réel à posséder dans la douleur de l'autre, pour que la pulsion s'apaise; et, conjointement, d'une complaisance à faire souffrir, dans un imaginaire débordant, un autre objet qui n'est là qu'en tant que leurre."

929. Cavailles, Roger. "Le matérialisme électrique et la Métaphysique du crime: une lecture épistémologique de Sade." L'Unversité de Toulouse-Le Mirail, tome IX, fasc. 6. PHILOSOPHIE II (1973): 33-49.

930. Châtelet, Noelle. SYSTEME DE L'AGRESSION: CHOIX DE TEXTES PHILOSOPHIQUES. Paris: Aubier-Montaigne, 1972.

Attempts, by reprinting assorted essays from Sade's writings, to isolate the philosophical themes explicitly or implicitly contained in Sade's writings. Excerpts emphasize Sade's views on 1) atheism; 2) natural order; 3) social order; and 4) moral problems. In a thirty-page introduction, author shows that all these themes are interwoven. Even philosophical texts cannot be separated from the so-called erotic texts. Includes a short bibliography.

Reviewed by Michel Delon, EUROPE 522 (1972): 64-70.

931. Cirio, Rita and Favari, Pietro. UTOPIA RIVISITATA. Milano: Arti Grafiche Luigi Granata, 1973. 283 p.

Includes original and representative essays and illustrations. Included are A. Huxley, Da Vinci, Marquis de Sade, Boccaccio, K. Marx, J. Verne, and R. Barthes, among others.

932. Corey, Lewis. "Marquis de Sade--The Cult of Despotism." ANTIOCH REVIEW 26 (1966): 17-31.

This essay was written by Lewis Corey shortly before
his death in 1953 but was only published fourteen
years later. Depicts Sade as a libertine who indulged
in virtually all kinds of sexual perversion, insisting
that nothing should hamper the sexual pleasure of man.
Also discusses attitudes toward women of several
prominent writers: Rousseau, Byron, Barbey
d'Aurevilly, Baudelaire, Paul Eluard. Criticizes
Geoffrey Gorer's sympathetic portrayal of Sade.
Concludes: "The 'revolutionary' apology for the
practices and philosophy of the Marquis de Sade is an
apology for despotism. Sadism and despotism are
interlocked as defilers of humanity."

933. Crocker, Lester G. "Au coeur de la pensée de Sade." In
THEMES ET FIGURES DU SIECLE DES LUMIERES. MELANGES
OFFERTS A ROLAND MORTIER. Edited by Raymond Trousson.
Geneva: Droz, 1980, pp. 59-71.

Believes that Sade postulated two questions in his
writings: First, to satisfy a certain universality,
must man renounce his individuality? And in order to
be properly integrated in his society, must he
sacrifice his liberty? Attempts to show that Sade
answers the first question in the affirmative and
eliminates the second. Concludes: "Si Sade n'est pas
un grand artiste ni un grand philosophe, il n'en est
pas moins un grand moraliste, dans la mesure oç il
nous oblige à réfléchir sur le sens profound
d'importants phénomènes de notre vie consciente et
inconsciente."

934. Cronk, George Francis. "Vicissitudes." KINESIS 2
(Spring 1970): 106-124.

"Approaches the metaphysical and ethical dimensions of
the fact of mutability. The analysis is focused upon
three novels: Samuel Beckett's MURPHY, Hermann
Hesse's SIDDHARTHA, and the Marquis de Sade's JUSTINE.
Each of these novels is highly philosophical in
character and explicitly concerned with the problem of
change. The hermeneutic moves from Beckett's
absurdism, through Hesse's quietism, to Sade's raging
activism. It is suggested that while the positions of
Beckett and Hesse are not unintelligent nor without
force, sadism offers something rather more
exhilarating. All three of these writers are
extremists, and extremism is always preferable to

extremists, and extremism is always preferable to
moderation; but Sade's extremism is of particular
value to those of us who are interested in a politics
for the end of the world." (Quoted from PHILOSOPHER'S
INDEX.)

935. Dawes, C. R. THE MARQUIS DE SADE, HIS LIFE AND WORKS.
     London: R. Holden, 1927. 240 p.

     Gives credit to Summers for biographical data and
     includes a long section (p. II, pp. 85-176) on an
     analysis of Sade's works. Discusses the chief factors
     that helped mold Sade's outlook: the influence of his
     times, and the influence of his personal
     circumstances. In the bibliography of primary and
     secondary sources (pp. 223-238), claims that LA
     MARQUISE DE GANGE, L'ETOURDI, LA FRANCE FOUTUE, and
     PAULINE ET BELVAL were not written by Sade.

     Reviewed by S. M. Ellis in FORTNIGHTLY REVIEW 128
     (1927): 572-573 (old series).

936. Delon, Michel. "Sade, maître d'agression." EUROPE 522
     (1972): 64-70.

     Reviews Noelle Châtelet's book, SYSTEME DE
     L'AGRESSION. Interprets "agression" as a "philosophie
     de combat." Has some negative comments but concludes
     that "le livre de Noelle Châtelet possède le grand
     mérite de prendre Sade au sérieux et nous présente des
     matériaux nécessaires à la réflexion. Il constitue
     une fort bonne introduction à la lecture de Sade."

937. Delon, Michel. Review of SADE ET SES MASQUES by Roger
     Lacombe. LE DIX-HUITEME SIECLE 8 (1976): 504-505.

     Criticizes Lacombe for attempting, as had been done
     before, to reconstruct a synthetic explanation of Sade
     in order find the real Sade behind the mask. The
     first part of the book is therefore built around
     several hypotheses. As for the last two, states that
     they add little and concludes: "Quant aux hypothèses
     du début, elles méritent attention, mais demandent à
     être nuancée."

938. Delon, Michel. "Sade comme révélateur idéologique."
     ROMANISTISCHE ZEITSCHRIFT FUR LITERATURGESCHICHTE 5
     (1981): 103-102.

This is a longer article of an abstract in STUDIES ON
VOLTAIRE AND THE EIGHTEENTH CENTURY 190 (1980): 241-
243, item 15.

939.  Delormes, Alain. "As for Sade and Hegel." PENSEE 169,
(June 1973): 30-48.

Studies "the two parallel attitudes of the Marquis de
Sade (1740-1814) and Georg Hegel (1770-1831) on the
philosophy of man's alienation and nonfulfillment,
reflecting Sade's materialism and Hegel's idealism ca.
1750-1850." (Quoted from HISTORICAL ABSTRACTS.)

940.  Delormes, Alain. "Quant à Sade et Hégel." LA PENSEE,
June 1973, pp. 30-48.

Gives a synopsis of a master's thesis in comparative
literature written under the supervision of Jacques
Body, President of Tours University. Thesis
investigates the relationship of man's daily life to
his death and his ensuing alienation. Includes a most
interesting section on Sadian discourse: "C'est
erreur de croire (que l'impossible se manifeste dans
le texte sadien) et pour deux raisons. La première,
que nous avons dite, vient de la clôture de
l'inventaire des possibilités dont le tortionnaire
dispose. La seconde vient de ce qu'une fois cette
fermeture exprimée, la scène est le discours et l'être
impossibles. Autrement dit, non pas l'Impossible,
mais des impossibilités. Manque à l'homme sadien
comme à l'homme hégélien la conscience de son
aliénation. C'est faute ici de la présence dans le
texte d'un équivalent du lecteur."

941.  Deprun, Jean. "La Mettrie et l'immoralisme sadien."
ANNALES DE BRETAGNE 83 (1976): 745-750.

Assuming that the Enlightenment pushed people to
adulate crime, wonders whether Sade himself was
influenced in that direction by La Mettrie.
Concludes: "Si notre hypothése est exacte, Sade n'a
pas seulement soumis la philosophie de La Mettrie à
une majoration psychologique et morale: majoration et
gauchissement s'élevèrent jusqu'au plan
cosmologique. . . . Un fait, en tous cas, demeure:
soucieux de se trouver des ancêtres spirituels et de

cautionner philosophiquement ses fantasmes, Sade s'est

cautionner philosophiquement ses fantasmes, Sade s'est
construit un La Mettrie à sa propre image."

942.  Deprun, Jean.  "Sade et le rationalisme des lumières."
      RAISON PRESENTE 3 (May-July 1967):  75-90.

      Asks whether the philosophy of the Enlightenment leads
      to  crime.  The Enlightenment is defined both  as  an
      intellectual  method  and  an attitude which  has  its
      beginning with a concern with logical coherence.  Sade
      opposed  the rationalism of the eighteenth century  in
      three areas:  "insentivisme, isolisme, antiphysisme."
      In Sade, conflicts and antagonism take on a primordial
      importance  but  cannot  be  resolved.   In  the  last
      analysis, contradictions remain.

943.  Didier, Béatrice.  "Le  château  intérieur  de  Sade."
      EUROPE 522 (1972):  54-64.

      Makes a structural analysis of the role of the castles
      in the works of Sade.  Their first characteristic  is
      that  they are inaccessible except to the  libertines,
      who  have  to  lead a life of crime in order to  gain
      admittance.  The castle, then, becomes a sort of state
      within  a  state,  with  its  own  laws:   judicial,
      legislative,  and executive.  Concludes: "Le  château
      dissipe   le   vertige  devant  l'espace,  par  une
      architecture  à la fois resserrée, et qui se  ramifie
      dans  d'infinies profondeurs.  Le temps y  est  aussi
      vaincu:   il  n'existe  plus  dans  cette  forteresse
      retranchée du monde.  Enfin le libertin y vient à bout
      de  son angoisse de la mort,  en la donnant justement,
      cette mort,  à d'innombrables victimes et en associant
      la mort à l'image du plaisir."

      This  article was reprinted as chapter II in the  book
      SADE, published in 1976 by Gonthier.

944.  Didier, Béatrice.  "Sade et le dialogue philosophique."
      CAHIERS  DE  L'ASSOCIATION  INTERNATIONALE  DES  ETUDES
      FRANCAISES 24 (1972): 59-74.

      Considers  the  philosophical  dialogues  in  only  two
      works  of  Sade, LE DIALOGUE D'UN PRETRE ET D'UN
      MORIBOND and LA PHILOSOPHIE DANS LE BOUDOIR,  in order
      to  appraise what might be a manifestation of a will to
      power.  In  the  first,  Sade expresses  a  form  of
      masochist  transfer,  purposely imagining himself  in

second, there is a convergence of languages: that of
the libertines, that of the victims, and lastly that
of the lampoonist who wrote FRANCAIS, ENCORE UN
EFFORT. Concludes: "Ainsi dans la PHILOSOPHIE éclate
de facon manifeste à la fois la force de destruction,
de déconstruction du dialogue philosophique, et aussi
sa véritable fonction qui est d'instaurer un autre
langage. Ce texte de Sade est exemplaire, et unique
dans son oeuvre, parce que centré exclusivement sur
cette acquisition du langage libertin."

945. Ducloux, Léopold. "Sade, ambiguités d'une apothéose."
     LA NOUVELLE CRITIQUE 181 (1966/1967): 57-76.

     Attempts to elucidate Sade's philosophy. Sees in the
     text of LES INFORTUNES DE LA VERTU the most
     representative of Sade's works. "Sa lecture rend bien
     vite évident qu'à travers les raisonnements des héros
     qui justifient le crime et le mal comme servant les
     fins de la nature destructrice, Sade exprime avec
     force sa propre pensée morale." Because Justine does
     not justify feelings of pity and because she is never
     rewarded for being so virtuous, the implication is
     that Sade was betting on vice. Concludes with a
     sobering comparison between nazism and sadism and
     states: "ce que les accusateurs du marquis n'ont pas
     voulu voir, c'est que la philosophie sadienne est
     porteuse de liberté et que les phantasmes qui lui
     permettent de s'incarner au travers de créations
     romanesques sont de peu d'importance. L'essentiel
     demeure cette volonté sans defaillance qui pousse Sade
     à liberer les hommes de leurs tabous et de leurs
     idoles." In other words, sees in Sade an aristocrat,
     who went beyong the contradictions presented by his
     social milieu, and a man caught up in the machinery of
     his thoughts, which led him to a philosophy of
     liberty.

946. Dumas, François Ribadeau. LE MARQUIS DE SADE ET LA
     LIBERATION DES SEXES. Paris: Jean Dullis Editeur,
     1974. 332 p.

     Summarizes Sade's theories thus: "Sex is king.
     Nature which gave birth to man wants it that way. Sex
     has all the rights. It is appropriate to obey its
     demands in order to liberate oneself. It is through
     sex that man finds human bliss and the possibility of
     happiness enunciated in the Declaration of Human

happiness enunciated in the Declaration of Human
Rights. The burdensome inheritance of oppression,
legislation, "lettres de cachet," religion, family
tradition, society's mores, not only constitutes
prejudices which must be rejected without scruples but
are often the causes in the best of people of the
worst mistakes. Anomalies, vices, sexual follies stem
not from a mental aberration but from overactive
sexual glands. Sex is not solely a reproductive need.
It is a powerful instinct, capable of influencing your
mind in a positive as well as a negative fashion.
Pleasure and suffering are closely tied together and
are often confused in exacerbation. It is the
wealthy, the corrupt government leaders who in high
places give examples of the most atrocious depravity."

947. Duncan, Catherine and Peraldi, François. "Discourse of
the Erotic—The Erotic in the Discourse." MEANJIN
QUARTERLY 33 (1974): 62-71.

Discussion between Catherine Duncan and François
Peraldi on the topic of "erotic" discourse. For
Peraldi there is no such thing as an erotic discourse;
instead he suggests the substitution of a notion of
text and intextuality which allows for "partial
reading." For Duncan this means that "as a libertine
reader, what [she] asks is to be ravished by the text,
and any text may serve to provoke that moment of
swooning voluptuary which obliges [her] to close [her]
eyes and put the book aside for an instant."

948. Fink, Béatrice. "Lecture alimentaire de l'utopie
sadienne." In SADE: ECRIRE LA CRISE. Paris: Pierre
Belfond, 1983, pp. 175-191.

Stresses the importance of nourishment in the Sadian
utopias: Tamoé, Butua, and the castle at Silling.
Foods can be classified as a function of their type:
cooked or uncooked, allowed by or infringing on the
laws; or in conjunction with their use: to drug,
poison, etc. Concludes that there are ties between
food and the figurative usage of dietary vocabulary:
"Le lecteur complice auquel on s'adresse constatera
donc que le château peuplé d'une société de
consommation est en fait une phagotopie, que la fuite
à l'infini qu'est le récit le plus impur qui ait été
fait depuis que le monde existe est alimentée par une
infinité de contre-nourritures. Que Sade ait voulu

sont sublimés ses désirs, où se réalisent ses pulsions
d'émancipation, de transgression et de dépassement ne
doit pas nous surprendre."

949.   Fink, Béatrice C.   "Sade and Cannibalism."   L'ESPRIT
       CREATEUR 15 (1975): 403-412.

Explores the metonymic character of cannibalism
(defined as "the ingestion, partial or whole, of one
human being or its derivatives by another"). Gives
four excerpts to illustrate how cannibalism in Sade's
works turns into imaginary projection, thus depicting
a whole range of human activities as crime. Suggests
that "by adopting and adapting current philosophical
arguments and literary techniques, by implementing
them in an antiarchy slanted toward the excessive and
grotesque, [Sade] makes cannibalism assume the role of
his entire writing: absorb, yet distort the
Enlightenment. It therefore functions as metonymy."

950.   Fink, Béatrice C.   "Sade's Libertine:   A Pluralistic
       Approach."  EIGHTEENTH-CENTURY LIFE 2 (1975): 34-37.

Argues that too rigid a definition of the word
"libertine" has falsified the real issues in Sade's
fiction. Traditionally, Sade's libertine has been
examined as spokesman for the author's ideas or as the
expression of an eighteenth-century writer influenced
by and/or acknowledging some definite sources--e.g.,
D'Holbach, Montesquieu. Rather, what is investigated
here is how Sade "transforms reflection [of
contemporary works] into diffraction, gross distortion
or, perhaps, hypertrophia of the Enlightenment's
latent nihilism." Gives to the Sadian libertine a
certain autonomy with its own characteristics, which
differentiate him from other libertines. Concludes
that the cases discussed underline "the inadequacy of
critical readings relying exclusively on conventional,
or implicitly formulated, conceptions of the
libertine."

951.   Fleuret, Victor.   Review  of SYSTEME DE L'AGRESSION by
       Noëlle Châtelet.   DIX-HUITIEME-SIECLE 6 (1974):  365-
       366.

Observes that the main part of this book is a choice
of texts by Sade situated under several headings:
atheism, natural order, social order, etc., and

atheism, natural order, social order, etc., and remarks that Châtelet has assumed, quite justifiably, that the works of Sade, without being the product of a systematic philosopher, contain nevertheless a philosophical doctrine. About the second part of the book, declares: "Au niveau de l'analyse, souvent riche, on pourrait peut-être reprocher à N. Châtelet de ne pas toujours permettre à son lecteur de faire le départ, dans son rapport à l'auteur étudié, entre ce qui chez elle serait simple exposition et ce qui serait complicité."

952. Foucault, Michel. HISTOIRE DE LA FOLIE A L'AGE CLASSIQUE. Paris: Plon, 1961, pp. 634-643.

Includes numerous references to Sade in this well-researched book. Reassesses the relationship of a totally free man to nature; states that there is nothing in men's madness which was not, at one time or another, already in nature: "La nuit de la folie est alors sans limite; ce qu'on pouvait prendre pour la violente nature de l'homme n'était que l'infini de la non'nature."

953. Gallop, Jane. "The Immoral Teachers." YALE FRENCH STUDIES 63 (1982): 117-128.

Shares Sade's fascination with numbers and attempts to deduce a meaning from the number 14. Concludes that "it does not seem inappropriate that an arithmetic perversion should arise in a discussion of pedagogy."

954. Glass, James N. "Rousseau's Emile and Sade's Eugénie: Action, Nature, and the Presence of Moral Structure." PHILOSOPHICAL FORUM 7 (1975): 38-55.

Discusses Rousseau's Emile and Sade's Eugénie, "two irreconcilable philosophical symbols." For Rousseau, nature becomes the ally of the Tutor and Emile is "more than just good; he is an ideal representation of what a good boy might be under the supervision of a highly moral and demanding super-ego." Sade's teachings are of a different mettle: "Sade reveals human nature and action as a sordid descent into cruelty, as an egoistic compendium of pursuits lacking any morally uplifting consequence or aim. In that sense he is saying that the world gives little that is morally worth salvaging and that individuals might

awareness and a very sober sense of what to expect
from others. It is a cynical message. . . . Sade,
however, is useful to look at as a philosopher."

955. Gorer, Geoffrey. "The marquis de Sade." ENCOUNTER:
LITERATURE, ARTS, POLITICS 103 (April 1962): 72-78.

Reduces Sade's philosophy to a series of axioms which,
briefly stated, are derived from the following:
1) "Pleasure is the sign that we are acting in
accordance with Nature and with our own nature.
2) Consequently, all acts which give pleasure must be
natural and right." Follows six corollaries to the
above statements. Also comments on the scholarly
works of Maurice Heine and Gilbert Lély. The latter,
he feels, did not adequately emphasize the major role
played in Sade's life by the theater and
theatricality; nor did he assert that there is a
relationship between sadism and theatricality.
Concludes: "If I am right in thinking that some sort
of theatricality or dramatic ritual was a constant
component in Sade's sexual sado-masochism, then it
perhaps becomes understandable why he could never
admit his incapacity as a professional dramatist. If
he could have been a successful playwright then he
would have been able to achieve in a socially
acceptable way many of the pleasures which he could
otherwise only obtain from dangerously unsocial acts."

956. Goulemot, Jean Marie and Michel Launay. "Prince, O très
haut marquis de Sade." In LE SIECLE DES LUMIERES.
Paris: Editions du Seuil, 1968, pp. 234-242.

In spite of interdictions and condemnations, believes
that Sade--a moralist and philosopher--is still very
much alive today and states: "la quéte du plaisir
dont il se fait l'apôtre repose sur une éthique, et
une philosophie la justifie." Concludes that Sade
leads his readers to the justification of a limitless
sexuality. According to the logic of Sadian
philosophy, it would follow that one must choose evil.

957. Hampshire, Stuart. "Absolute license." THE NEW
STATESMAN, 26 January 1962, pp. 124-125.

This article is an excerpt from the "Sade" chapter of Hampshire's book, MODERN WRITERS AND OTHER ESSAYS. See annotation to item 958.

958. Hampshire, Stuart. "Sade." In MODERN WRITERS AND OTHER ESSAYS. London: Chatto and Windus, 1969, pp. 56-62.

Sees two starting points in Sade's philosophy. He was an angry atheist, a thoroughgoing determinist. He studied the varieties of sexual perversion. His method was analytical, and he took three steps beyond any of his contemporaries: "First, he assumed that the sexual impulses and emotions are the foundations of individual temperament and character. Secondly, he noticed that in human beings the sexual impulses are originally polymorphous, and that socially recognized normality is only one specialization of sexual desire among many others. Thirdly, he believed that the primary impulses are ambivalent, and that the emotions of love and hatred, in any pure, unmixed form, are an artificial and precarious development of them."

959. Han, Jean-Pierre and Valla, Jean-Pierre. "A propos du système philosophique de Sade." EUROPE 522 (1972): 105-123.

Attempts to set down the main points of Sade's philosophy. Purposely omits the marquis's view on religion and his social outlook, but admits the task is difficult: "Que Sade ait eu la passion des systèmes, que son oeuvre soit la démonstration d'un système unique, nous ne pouvons le nier. Mais par oç le saisir? Son articulation joue à tous les niveaux; synchronique et diachronique." Concludes: "philosopher c'est PLUS-JOUIR. Ce que n'implique aucun dédoublement de la fonction philosophique. . . . Puisque le savoir est corrélatif au jouir, imaginons toutes les jouissances, alors nous sera tenu ce qu'il nous a été promis, entendre ce qu'elle veut nous dire."

960. Harari, Josué V. "De Sade's Narrative: Ill-logical or Illogical?" GENRE 7 (1974): 112-131.

States that in order to give an appraisal of Sade's work and philosophy, we should recognize the marquis's true adversaries: God, religion, law, nature, death, and reason. In his avowed atheism, Sade is typical of his century, but he applies the logic which proved God's inexistence to repudiate other "so-called cultural realities or verities." Concludes: "Sade, by repudiating everything culture holds true-- especially God, conscience, laws, and nature--affirms that desire is the only real truth. Therefore, Sadian narrative refutes, point by point, every tenet of Western philosophical discourse. Whereas Western metaphysics is affirmative on the ontological level (God, conscience, and laws all exist) and negative on the prescriptive level (everything is not permitted; desire must be bridled), Sadian discourse displaces the negation by one degree and declares itself negative with regard to assertion (nothing exists) and positive with regard to prescriptiveness (everything is permitted; desire desires). . . . Libertine and philosopher all in one, the Sadian character is always able to demonstrate a philosophical truth indissolubly linked to the exercise of his libertine desires." This article was translated into English by Héline Pellegrin.

961.  Hector, Josette. "Sade ou la négation de la négation." QUINZAINE LITTERAIRE 113 (March 1971): 8-9.

States that Sade's dialectic is founded on excess--it is thus that reason and unreason are cosmogonically tied. And that this dialectic is normative, but without reciprocity for the libertine who is both a skeptic and a stoic and "finit par douter du plaisir et par ne plus pouvoir en prendre la mesure que par la cruauté envers soi et envers les autres. Nous retrouvons l'équation du sado-masochisme sous les noms de Juliette et de Justine. Justine, c'est Sade, dit Paulhan. Juliette, c'est Sade, semble dire Béatrice Didier." This article was published on the occasion of the Editions Livre de Poche publication of a version of LES INFORTUNES DE LA VERTU annotated by Béatrice Didier and prefaced by Jean Paulhan.

962.  Heine, Maurice. "Actualités de Sade III. Pensée inédite de D.A.F. de Sade." LE SURREALISME AU SERVICE DE LA REVOLUTION, 4 December 1931, pp. 1-3.

Transcribes pages 31-34 of the manuscript, which includes LE DIALOGUE ENTRE UN PRETRE ET UN MORIBOND. Presents an assortment of Sade's ideas on God and religion such as: "La religion est la chose du monde

qu'il faut le moins consulter en matière de
philosophie, par ce quelle [sic] est celle qui en
obscurcit le plus tous les principes, et qui courbe le
plus honteusement l'homme sous ce joug ridicule de la
foi destructeur de toutes les vérités."

963. Heine, Maurice. LE MARQUIS DE SADE. Paris: Gallimard,
1950.

Includes several essays and prefaces published
elsewhere. Avant-propos au DIALOGUE ENTRE UN PRETRE
ET UN MORIBOND (Stendhal & Cie, 1926); Avant-propos
aux CONTES, HISTORIETTES ET FABLIAUX (Simon Kra,
1927); Introduction aux INFORTUNES DE LA VERTU
(Fourcade, 1930); Avant-propos aux 120 JOURNEES DE
SODOME (aux dépens des Bibliophiles souscripteurs,
1930); "Une thèse de doctorat sur le marquis de Sade";
"Dramaturgie de Sade"; "Promenade à travers le roman
noir"; "Chronique sadiste"; "La conception romanesque
chez le marquis de Sade."

Reviewed by C. Bo, MILANO SERA, 11 June 1950;
J. Brenner, PARIS NORMANDIE, 6 June 1950;
L'OBSERVATEUR, 15 June 1950; and J. Laprade in ARTS,
23 June 1950, p. 2.

964. Hood, Robin. "Le marquis de Sade, libre penseur et non
conformiste." In LES UTOPISTES ET LA QUESTION
SEXUELLE. Edited by E. Armand, H. Treni, and R. Hood.
Paris: L'en-dehors, 1936, pp. 49-74.

"Essay not without merit even if poorly documented and
rather sensationally presented. Treats Sade
successively as free thinker, his life and works, his
philosophic and political conceptions." (Quoted from
Cabeen, item 8.)

965. Huxley, Aldous. "Note on Sade." In ENDS AND MEANS.
London: Chatto and Windus, 1947, pp. 269-272.

Sees the works of Sade as theoretical justifications
of the marquis's erotic practices. But states that
"his books indeed contain more philosophy than
pornography. The hungry smut-hound must plough
through long chapters of abstract speculation in order
to find the cruelties and obscenities for which he
hungers. De Sade's philosophy was the philosophy of
meaninglessness carried to its logical

conclusion. . . . He was enthusiastically a
revolutionary--at any rate in theory; for, as we have
seen, he was too gentle in practice to satisfy his
fellow-Jacobins. His books are of permanent interest
and value because they contain a kind of REDUCTIO AD
ABSURDIUM of revolutionary theory."

966. Ivker, Barry. "Sources of Contradiction in Sade's
     Philosophy." RESEARCH STUDIES 40 (1972): 285-290.

     "Difficulties in determining a consistent, coherent
     philosophy in the works of Sade are due in large
     measure to his literary techniques and his
     indebtedness to libertine philosophy. Sade's
     borrowing of popular narrative genres, such as the
     epistolary novel and the sentimental-moral tale, leads
     to a jarring contrast between his own radical ideas
     and those implicit in the borrowed forms. His
     incorporation of several genres in a given work often
     leads to juxtaposition of contrasting ideas, all of
     which seem to represent the author's viewpoint. Even
     in works like JUSTINE and JULIETTE, however, where the
     above problems are minimal, Sade's philosophy is
     inherently paradoxical. On the one hand, his endless
     documentation of 'perverse' behavior among savage
     tribes, ancient civilizations, and contemporary
     individuals serves to 'prove' the naturalness and
     hence the goodness of such behavior. On the other
     hand, Sade's libertines ultimately wish to perform
     motiveless, passionless acts in order to demonstrate
     their separateness from the tyranny of Nature and
     their desire to affect the natural order. Nowhere
     does Sade even attempt to resolve this basic
     philosophical inconsistency, and critical attempts to
     make of him a consistent thinker must therefore fail."
     (Quoted from the 1972 MLA ABSTRACTS, p. 13.)

967. Jones, Gary E. "On the Permissibility of Torture."
     JOURNAL OF MEDICAL ETHICS 6 (1980): 11-13.

     "Shows through both counter-example and hypothesis
     that there may be a case for permitting torture on
     utilitarian grounds. The arguments of Jonsen and
     Sagan in their essay "Torture and the Ethics of
     Medicine" fail to prove conclusively that torture is
     impermissible." (Quoted from the PHILOSOPHER'S
     INDEX, item 15.)

968. Juin, Hubert. "Les torts de l'esprit," LES LIBERTINAGES
     DE LA RAISON. Paris: Belfond, 1968, pp. 211-246.

     Discusses the many-faceted aspects of Sade's works.
     The logical arguments perfectly well engendered
     contradict each other, making the totality of the
     product a challenge to reason itself: "A une thèse
     succède l'exposé d'un thèse contraire. Dire qu'il est
     double serait plus que risqué: ce serait
     simpliste. . . . Le discours est composé de détours,
     d'avancées, de reculs: c'est l'image du cercle, plus
     exactement de la spirale. Ainsi vont la pensée et la
     main de Sade: dans un labyrinthe tournant."

969. Klossowski, Pierre. "De l'opportunité à étudier
     l'oeuvre du marquis de Sade." CAHIERS DU SUD 285
     (1947): 717-721.

     In a short article contends that the study of profane
     literature can open new vistas on Holy Scriptures as
     well as on the human heart and creation.
     "Aujourd'hui, dans notre monde de l'incroyance, il n'y
     a plus de scandale au sens propre. Dans ce monde, le
     scandale est dans l'absence de scandale et à lui seul
     le monde de l'incroyance se conçoit comme le sacrilège
     par absence de sacrilège."

970. Klossowski, Pierre. "Le mal et la négation d'autrui
     dans la philosophie de D. A. F. Sade." RECHERCHES
     PHILOSOPHIQUES 4 (1936): 268-293.

     Investigates the problem of evil as it relates to the
     negation of the Other in Sade's philosophy and defines
     it precisely as it is outlined in JULIETTE: "the
     misfortune of being virtuous in crime and criminal in
     virtue." Suggests a formula--or a commandment--as a
     solution to the dialectical drama of the Sadian
     conscience: "Par vertu même, tu ne concevras plus le
     repentir, car tu auras pris l'habitude de faire mal
     dès qu'elle se montre et pour ne plus faire mal tu
     l'empêcheras de paraître. . . ." First-rate essay.

971. Klossowski, Pierre. "Esquisse du système de Sade."
     Preface to CENT VINGT JOURNEES DE SODOME. In OEUVRES
     COMPLETES DU MARQUIS DE SADE. Vol. XIII. Paris:
     Cercle du livre précieux, 1964 and 1967, pp. xliii-
     lxxxi.

Suggests that it is in his capacity to imagine ad
infinitum some monstruous reflex that man, deprived of
liberty, can regain some kind of liberty. Materialist
or mechanistic systems are no more than the expression
of an interiorized mind which intends to compensate
for this kind of restriction by advocating an external
freedom on a social plane. Considers especially the
main characteristics of Sade's materialist atheism.
Makes an unexpected development: "Pour Sade, la
substitution à Dieu de la Nature à l'état de mouvement
perpetuel signifie non pas l'avèvement d'une ère plus
heureuse de l'humanité, mais seulment la commencement
de la tragédie, son acceptation consciente et
volontaire! On pressent le motif nietzschéen qui
oppose aux souffrances de l'innocent une conscience
qui accepte de souffrir sa culpabilité parce qu'elle
ne se sent exister qu'à ce prix. Tel est le sens
caché de son athéisme qui le distingue si nettement de
ses contemporains. Admettre la matière à l'état de
mouvement perpétuel comme individu dans un état de
mouvement perpetuel." With such inclinations, Sade
will go forward with his materialist atheism to the
point of giving it the shape of a fatalism truly
transcendental, such as that postulated by the pope in
the SYSTEME DE LA NATURE and presented to Juliette.
Concludes that the dosage of cruelty in all of us
would then only be thwarted impulses of desire, to
which each of us would identify himself in a primary
egocentrism when these impulses tend to destroy us as
much as they tend toward the destruction of others.

972.   Klossowski, Pierre.    SADE, MON PROCHAIN.    Paris:
       Editions du Seuil, 1947.

       Winner of the PRIX SAINTE-BEUVE in 1947, this
       publication includes three essays: "Sade et la
       Révolution," "Esquisse du système de Sade," and "Sous
       le masque de l'athéisme." The third was also
       published as a preface to LES CRIMES DE L'AMOUR (Vol.
       X of the complete works, Cercle du Livre Précieux,
       1967). Author attempts to trace the evolution of the
       Sadian spirit beginning with the first version of
       JUSTINE and progressing in a clearly outlined quasi-
       theological format to the anarchical philosophy of the
       later works.

       Reviewed by G. Bataille in CRITIQUE 15-16 (1947): 147-
       160; and in CRITIQUE 17 (1947): 304-312; by M.

Blanchot in TEMPS MODERNES 25, October 1947, pp. 597–598; by Gaeton Picon in FONTAINE 62 (1947): 646-654.

973. Klossowski, Pierre. "Sade ou le philosophe scélérat." TEL QUEL 28 (1967): 3-22.

Excerpt of this article was published in OBLIQUES 12-13 (1977): 245-247. Also published in OEUVRES COMPLETES DU MARQUIS DE SADE. Vol. XVI, pp. 477-505. Paris: Cercle du livre précieux, 1967.

States that, according to Sade, atheism is an act of normative reasoning since the notion of God, in order to maintain its own autonomy, must also include along with norms, arbitrary, deviant, behavior. This leads to illogicality because such behavior would include phenomenon detrimental to species conservation. Also opposes perversion to libertinage since perversion manifests itself as a mania--idée fixe. Perverts usually pursue the execution of a unique gesture. Sees the transgression of norms as best exemplified by the sodomite act practiced by men. Gives interesting answers to the question: "Qu'en est-il de l'actualisation par l'écriture du sensible dans un acte aberrant et du rapport de cette actualisation avec l'exécution de l'acte indépendamment de sa description?"

974. Kristol, Irving. "The Shadow of the Marquis: Notes on Some Possible Related Matters." ENCOUNTER, February 1957, pp. 3-5.

Asserts that Sade is admired today for reasons that have nothing to do with literature, and quotes Klossowski, who pointed out that the basic ideas and the general movement of Sade's thought "have affinities with the various gnostic-manichean heresies that have continually undermined and infiltrated the official 'Christian' civilisation of the West. Despite his militant atheism and the crude materialism of his rhetoric, Sade believes, along with them, that Nature, in imposing her harsh necessities and painful limitations on human existence, must be the work of Satan, not of God; that the only possible resistance to the demonic creator of this world is a form of non-resistance; that sin must be 'used-up' by the practice of all the crimes; that only in the very depths of sin, and particularly in those rites that are at once blasphemous and orgiastic, can one have a perception of the original purity which preceded creation."

975. Laborde, Alice M. "La Notion d'isolisme et ses implications lyriques dans l'oeuvre du marquis de Sade." STUDIES ON VOLTAIRE AND THE EIGHTEENTH CENTURY 88 (1972): 871-880.

Comments that "isolisme" is the most likely authentic human sentiment in which one can acknowledge the sadistic libertines as normal beings. Continues by discussing the notion of isolisme in the writings of Sade. Discusses the origin of the complex notion of isolisme and discerns its different degrees. Sade undeniably suffered in his heart and soul a certain form of this sentiment. Cites as examples Sade's writings to his wife. States that Sade's heroes refuse love and tenderness, a form of suicide termed aggressive isolisme. The characters Sade created were unusual and abnormal, according to the norms set by society. The notion of isolisme can also be explained in that it is necessary to commit crimes in order to be isolated from the rest of the world. Concludes by stating that Sade suggests the handicaps and limits of libertinism while at the same time revealing the potential of creativity in the victims of isolisme. First-rate article. This is Chapter VI of SADE ROMANCIER.

976. Leduc, Jean. "Les Sources de l'athéisme et de l'immoralisme du marquis de Sade." STUDIES ON VOLTAIRE AND THE EIGHTEENTH CENTURY 68 (1969): 7-66.

Attempts to make a census of sources for Sade's philosophical ideas. Encounters two main difficulties: 1) not all the works of Sade present the same philosophical concepts, 2) most of Sade's output is not in philosophical treatises but in erotico-philosophic novels. Studies these sources only in connection with the authors cited in Sade's works. Most important single influence seems to be Holbach, especially in the SYSTEME DE LA NATURE. Also prominent as an influence is the materialism of La Mettrie and Helvetius. Sade had read La Mettrie's L'HOMME-MACHINE, DISCOURS SUR LE BONHEUR, and L'ART DE JOUIR and Helvetius's DE L'ESPRIT. Sade was also very well acquainted with the erotic literature of the times. Found in the inventory of his library are

VENUS DANS LA CLOITRE, MARGOT LA RAVAUDEUSE, L'ACADEMIE DES DAMES, LE PORTIER DES CHARTREUX, L'EDUCATION DE LAURE, and THERESE PHILOSOPHE. Suggests that Sade may have been influenced not only by the ideas contained in these works but also by their audacity. Also, while the marquis mentions several ancient writers, he seems to have been influenced the most by Aristippe, even though the latter is mentioned only once in Sade's works. The name which appears most frequently is that of Nero, and many of Sade's heroes emulate the Roman emperor. While only one English philosopher, Hobbes, is mentioned in Sade's works, the marquis is representative of his times. Concludes: "Cette dette de Sade envers la pensée de son époque montre bien qu'il n'est pas ce phénomène aberrant que certaines voudraient voir en lui. Il est le produit de l'esprit philosophique auquel il apporte une conclusion dans cette entreprise de démolition amorcée vers 1670."

977.  Landolt, Katherine.   "The Attempt and Failure to Break Out of Materialist Framework as Performed by the Characters of the HISTOIRE DE JULIETTE under the Direction of the Marquis de Sade." PAPERS IN ROMANCE 2 (1980): 182-193.

Deals with "the relationship of Sade's novel, the HISTOIRE DE JULIETTE, to eighteenth-century philosophical thought, especially materialism." In conclusion offers several speculations. Sade might be "using his characters to explore the trap of humanity's position in the universe and to search for the avenues of escape." Or Sade's libertines might be "acting out for him man's inability to reach the absolute and in this context Sade seems to be laughing at his characters, and at humanity in general, and at himself."

978.  Lopez, Eduardo. "Introducción a Sade." PAPELES DE SON ARMADANS 64 (1971): 241-255.

After briefly reviewing Gilbert Lély's biography on Sade, published in 1967 by Gallimard, attempts to analyze the marquis's thought system. With this objective, Lopez examines Sade's conception of Nature, of God and of Evil, and the specific "option" which man has in his "tragic universe."

979.  Lotringer, Sylvère.  "Sade incesticide."  LITTERATURE 30
      (1978): 67-78.

      Discusses incest in Sade's novels as a conception
      stemming from a totally different outlook on the
      relationship of nature to culture:  philosophy without
      conscience, passion without spontaneity.  Yet it has a
      function within the Sadian text:  "tout dire de la
      sexualité afin de donner à chacun sa place parmi la
      grande famille des pervers, dans le grand tableau de
      la vérité à constituer."

980.  Luckow, Marion.  "Sade." In DIE HOMOSEXUALITÄT IN DER
      LITERARISCHEN TRADITION; STUDIEN ZU DEN ROMANEN VON
      JEAN GENET.  Stuttgart: Enke, 1962, pp. 6-11.

      Considers Sade as a precursor of the romantic movement
      because the marquis intepreted the expression of all
      men's desires--or even crimes such as homosexuality--
      as belonging in, existing as, acts of nature.  Such
      tendencies as lust and cruelty which are so prevalent
      in twentieth century literature were already well
      known and described by Sade:  "Die gemeinsame Tendenz
      von Wollust, Religion, und Grausamkeit die in der
      romantischen Literatur so oft dargestellt,
      wissenschaftlich jedoch erst im 20 Jahrhundert erklärt
      wurde, hat Sade als erster erkannt."

981.  Magny, Claude-Edmonde.  "Sade martyr de l'athéisme."
      CALIBAN, October 1947, pp. 41-44.

      Claims that the real significance of Sade's work goes
      beyond the suggestive erotic power it contains.  The
      most lurid descriptions make sense only if one
      understands their subjacent metaphysics: "Erotisme et
      cruauté sont seulement pour Sade des moyens, une
      manière de reculer, au besoin au delà du possible, les
      frontières de l'être humain . . . son originalité est
      d'être un manichéiste évolutionniste, oç le drame se
      joue non plus entre Ormuz et Ahrimane, entre Mal et
      Bien, mais entre la Nature et l'une de ses créatures,
      l'homme, qu'elle a engendré bien involontairement et
      comme malgré elle et qui a fini par catalyser
      artificieusement et coupablement à son profil la
      puissance évolutrice de l'univers, devenant ainsi pour
      la nature, sa mère une sorte de concurrent d'autant
      plus dangereux qu'il est inconscient . . . le divin
      marquis est sacrilège et blasphémateur bien plus

qu'athée: il croit à l'existence de ce qu'il nie, profane et veut détruire plus fortement que ceux qui l'affirment et pensent le servir." In this system the main doctrine is the incontestable presence of human vice, in the midst of a godless world where no redemption is possible.

982. Margolin, Jean-Claude. "Sade démythifié." REVUE DE SYNTHESE 97 (1976): 403-404.

Reviews briefly the book SYSTEME DE L'AGRESSION by Noëlle Châtelet, published by Aubier-Montaigne in 1972: "Cette anthologie philosophique a le mérite, quelle que soit notre opinion--ou notre prétention-- sur Sade, de montrer à la fois l'originalité de sa pensée et son rattachement au courant matérialiste et athéiste du XVIIIe siècle."

983. Massey, Irving. THE OBJECTS. Bloomington: Indiana University Press, 1970, pp. 76-79.

Considers several conceptions of innocence and states that Sade provides a crucial illustration. There could not be any evil unless there was an acknowledgment of virtue: "The innocence available in that world may ultimately be referred to the positive category with which we began."

984. Maulnier, Thierry. "L'actualité du marquis de Sade." HOMMES ET MONDES 10 (1947): 502-508.

Sees in Sade a slave of an obsession which had its beginning in a physiological determinism and which only expressed itself in literary output because of Sade's long confinement. Because Sade was expelled and repelled by society, there is in him a spirit of fascination and vengeance. Concludes: "La délectation blasphématoire, la délectation érotique et la délectation cruelle, étroitement associées, sont chez Sade des actes d'obédience aux valeurs de la foi, de la pudeur et de la pitié, parce qu'elles sont des exorcismes."

985. Milner, Max. "Sade." In LE DIABLE DANS LA LITTERATURE FRANCAISE DE CAZOTTE A BAUDELAIRE. Paris: Corti, 1960, pp. 186-191.

States that the religious problem is constantly and
explicitly present in all the works of Sade, who gives
examples of satanism in the use of the supernatural.
In his closed universe of the "roman noir" he treats
perversity and vice not as moral or immoral
ingredients but as sources of poetry and factors of
bewilderment.

986.  Molino, Jean.  "Sade devant la beauté." LE MARQUIS DE
      SADE.  Paris:  Armand Colin, 1968, pp. 141-170.

Proceedings of the Colloquium of Aix-en-Provence which
took place on 19 and 20 February 1966.  Analyzes
several eighteenth-century concepts of beauty, such as
those of Shaftesbury, Hutchinson and Burke, all of
whom were influential in displacing the classical
notions.  States that for Sade beauty is in the
effects produced on the person viewing it:  "Le beau
n'est plus déduit d'une règle, il est expliqué par la
physiologie." The heroes in Sade's novels are judged
according to the means to an end, a unique orientation
toward erotic pleasures.  Discusses the role of excess
and of imagination in Sade's scheme as well as the
inherent contradiction in the stand taken by the
libertine hero:  "On comprend ainsi l'importance de la
beauté dans l'oeuvre de Sade, dont elle est la
condition de possibilité, présence essentielle mais
sourde et jamais explicitée.  Elle est la marque de
l'impossibilité de vivre avec conséquence le stoïcisme
solipsiste qui se manifeste dans le discours des
héros."  First-rate essay.

987.  Moreau, Marcel.  "Le Devoir de monstruosité." OBLIQUES
      12-13 (1977): 15-18.

Sees in Sade a constant, never fulfilled, quest toward
desire.  To submit to that quest is the "devoir de
monstruosité," an expression without a moral or
immoral overtone but one which does have a didactic
connotation:  "assumer courageusement la part
dangereuse, voire inadmissible et anti-social e de
nous-mêmes . . . en souscrivant au devoir de
monstruosité, nous ne faisons qu'époumoner quelques
réponses à la question centrale de notre plénitude."

988.  Nadeau, Maurice.  MARQUIS DE SADE, OEUVRES.  Paris:  La
      jeune Parque, 1947.

"Perhaps best selection of Sade's writings, preceded by excellent 58-page introduction. Outline of life as established by M. Heine also given. Selections, all with accurate indications of source, are chosen to illustrate Sade as philosopher, sadist, moralist, man of politics, poet and visionary. Very important pamphlet, FRANCAIS ENCORE UN EFFORT SI VOUS VOULEZ ETRE REPUBLICAIN, given in entirety. Bibliography only of editions of Sade used; no index. Supersedes selections by Balkis and Apollinaire and is not superseded by Lély." (Quoted from Cabeen, item 8).

Reviewed: M. Faure in GAVROCHE, 7 April 1948; R. Stephane in NEF 43 (1948) 121-23; P. Klossowski in PARU, June 1948, pp. 60-63; A. Patri in TABLE RONDE 5 (1948): 824-833.

989. Namer, Emile. Review of SADE, by Vincenzo Barba. REVUE PHILOSOPHIQUE, April-June 1979, pp. 226-227.

Review of SADE: LA LIBERAZIONE IMPOSSIBILE, published in 1978 by Nuova Italia. States that author attempts to delineate Sade's thoughts and interprets his works in terms of the totality of his production.

990. Naville, Pierre. "Sade et les principes de la morale." In PAUL THIRY D'HOLBACH ET LA PHILOSOPHIE SCIENTIFIQUE DE XVIIIe SIECLE. Paris: Gallimard, 1943, pp. 366-369.

Briefly mentions Sade in the chapter entitled "Principes de la morale" and advances that "les moeurs PEUVENT, chez la Mettrie, assurer le bonheur des hommes, chez d'Holbach, elles le DOIVENT. Chez Sade, elles NE PEUVENT QUE LE DETRUIRE." For Sade, only individual passions have a right to exist: that is the main tenet of his philosophy.

991. Naville, Pierre. "Sade et la philosophie." In OEUVRES COMPLETES DU MARQUIS DE SADE. Vol. XI. Paris: Cercle du livre précieux, 1964, pp. 11-23.

Notes that Sade cannot be considered a philosopher, as the term was defined in his time, but that he followed closely the philosophy of d'Holbach in the SYSTEME DE LA NATURE (1770). However, Sade utilizes the SYSTEME in a way which differs from that of d'Holbach: he projected some frightening lights in a field of human behavior that everything had hitherto conspired to render obscure because of taboos. That philosophy let him freely investigate a realm that was as much scientific as philosophical. For him, the individual's desires and passions are the center of the world: "Le Moi de Sade affirme: Je jouis, donc je suis." But if one looks closely at the philosophical discourses of Sade's extraordinary "puppets," each attempts incessantly to justify himself: "Chaque personnage éprouve un besoin irrésistible de légitimer chacun de ses actes, chacune de ses impulsions, tous ses goûts, et ses penchants, par un raisonnement, une décision rationnelle." Concludes that in the words of Sade the apparent disorders in nature and in men are only misunderstood linkages. In nature there can only be order.

992. Neboit-Mombet, Janine. "Un logicien de la déraison." EUROPE 522 (1972): 48-53.

Attempts to situate Sade within his century. A materialistic atheist, Sade belonged to the Enlightenment; yet he was also an aristocrat who tried to give rational explanations of sexual aberrations, regarding them as a combination of environmental influences and physiological misfunctions.

993. Parrot, Louis. "Sade blanc, Sade noir." CAHIERS DU SUD 285 (1947): 707-714.

Traces this century's resurgence of interest in Sade's work to the revolutionary era. The initial footwork on Sade was done by Maurice Heine, whose research triggered interest on the part of subversive writers of the 1920's who related to Sade as an unrestrained free thinker and a revolutionary of the purest form. Views Sade as personifying the collective degeneration of the pre-revolutionary aristocrat. His egoism, his disdain for universal laws of human conduct, and his twisted, self-serving philosophy are seen as representative of his class. Sade's conduct, and that of his contemporaries, precipitated the revolution by legitimizing the philosophy of the subversives. Views Sade as a victim of a hypocritical society, condemned for flagrant, imprudent non-conformism. As a philosopher, Parrot considers him weak: his system is based on and justified by his disdain for humankind. Interprets Sade's morbid reverie as the product of the solitude of incarceration, which left him to explore the darkest recesses of his troubled soul and to recount his discoveries with vivid, delirious imagination. Labels Sade "obsessed" with this morose, self-debasing research, concludes that he is the pitiful object of unjust hatred.

994. Patri, Aimé. "Sur la pensée philosophique de Sade. Compte rendu d'ouvrages sur Sade." TABLE RONDE 5, (1948): 824-832.

Calls Sade a "moralist" but defines the word as "someone who contributes to the knowledge of man." States that the extraordinary works of Sade should not be studied from a falsified point of view; rather, it is appropriate to study him not with a moralist apology but with the spirit of exegesis. If interpreted in this fashion, Sade appears as a literary Christopher Columbus, discovering by accident a new world: consciously or unconsciously, he destroyed everything that was thought by the men of the Enlightenment, stressing not what is logical and human, but, on the contrary, the part in men which is inhuman.

995. Paulhan, Jean. "Le marquis de Sade et sa complice, ou les revanches de la pudeur." TABLE RONDE 3, (July 1945): 97-136.

Also published as a preface to LES INFORTUNES DE LA VERTU (Gallimard, 1970). In this very readable essay, states that Sade who wrote a gospel for evil doings had at least one secret: he was Justine. Believes that the XVIIIth century which gives us the most cynical writers also produced two worthy defenders of virtue, Marivaux and Sade. Also suggests that Sade was not sadistic but probably masochist: ". . . il s'est refusé à être sadique, alors que tout l'y invitait--ses rancunes, les passions du moment et la Section des Piques comme un seul homme. Encore faudrait-il discuter là-dessus: le vrai sadique est celuiqui repousse les facilités du sadisme, et n'admet que personne l'invite à exercer sa manie."

Reviewed by Georges Bataille in CRITIQUE 15-16 (1947): 147-160 and 17 (1947): 304-312.

996.  Paulhan,  Jean.  "Sade, ou le pire est l'ennemi du mal."
      LABYRINTHE 11 (August 1945):  11.

      "Keen  remarks on value of Sade in light of world  war
      and catastrophe.  Biographical and critical  comments
      on  Sade  also of value.  Idea advanced that Sade  is
      valuable counter-irritant or antidote who has made  no
      one  crueler and has even made some,  Lamartine by his
      own  confession, more tender."  (Quoted from  Cabeen,
      item 8).

997.  Peret,  Benjamin.  "Le noyau de la comète."  ANTHOLOGIE
      DE L'AMOUR SUBLIME.  Paris: Albin-Michel,  1956, pp.
      54-56.

      Explains  that  it is not love that Sade described  in
      all its details but physical pleasure, going so far as
      to  list a complete catalog of sexual anomalies.  But
      suggests that Sade may have been "tempted" by  sublime
      love for the young actress Marie Quesnet, who remained
      faithful to him to the end of his days.

998.  Peyrebonne,  Micheline.  LE  MARQUIS  DE  SADE  OU  LES
      MALHEURS  DU VICE.  Montrouge: Europe notre  patrie,
      1970.  46 p.

      This diatribe states that Sade, this "brutal misogyne"
      conceives of love as semite, or more follows precisely
      a rule of conduct contrary to the general mentality of
      the European male.  Contrasts the term with  "semite"
      the term "aryan" and explains that,  for the latter, a
      woman  is  a being worthy of  consideration;  however,
      this is not the case for the former.  Concludes:  "Le
      sinistre  marquis  avait  donc  l'âme  d'un  potentat
      oriental.  Pour être vraiment heureux, le marquis eut
      dû vivre dans un harem d'Arabie Séoudite ou du Yémen."

999.  Pia,  Pascal.  "Le marquis en poche."  CARREFOUR,  30
      December 1970, pp. 16-17.

      Comments  on the recent edition (Collection  livre  de
      Poche) of the INFORTUNES DE LA VERTU,  with preface by
      Béatrice Didier, and of the JOURNAL INEDIT (Gallimard,
      Collection  Idées).  Discusses  the  different
      interpretations  given to the character of Justine  by
      Jean  Paulhan and Béatrice Didier.  For Jean Paulhan,
      Justine is Sade.  This assimilation of Sade to Justine
      is rejected by Béatrice Didier, who claims:  "Justine

est aussi la victime de Sade." Also states that the numerous letters written by Sade are opposed to J. Paulhan's thesis and refutes the notion that Sade wished to be incarcerated. States that the fragments published from Sade's JOURNAL were written between 5 June 1807 and 26 August 1808 and from 18 July to 30 November 1814. These fragments also corroborate facts which are fairly well known. "En fait, les plus grands forfaits du monstre étaient d'avoir fouetté une prostituée et d'avoir offert à trois ou quatre autres filles des pastilles qu'il croyait aphrodisiaques et qui les avaient précipitées à la garde-robe. De nos jours et dans la plus sévère des chambres correctionnelles, cela lui aurait valu mille francs d'amende et quinze jours, avec sursis, sa belle-mère eut-elle intrigué pour lui donner une belle leçon."

1000. Picon, Gaetan. "Sade et l'indifférence." FONTAINE 62 (1947): 646-654.

Disagrees with P. Klossowski and G. Apollinaire on the interpretation of Sade's philosophy. Believes that the marquis identified himself with Justine, refusing on several occasions to join the ranks of the tormentors and remaining in the camp of the tortured, yet totally indifferent to religious and legal morality. First-rate article showing Sade in a totally new light. Sade was not sadistic but masochistic.

Also published in MERCURE DE FRANCE 1 (1960): 55-64; in Volume XI, OEUVRES COMPLETES DU MARQUIS DE SADE (Paris: Cercle du livre précieux, 1964, 1967); and in L'USAGE DE LA LECTURE MERCURE DE FRANCE 1 (1960): 55-64.

1001. Planhol, René de. LES UTOPISTES DE L'AMOUR. . . . RESTIF DE LA BRETONNE, LE MARQUIS DE SADE. Paris: Garnier frères, 1921.

1002. Pleynet, Marcelin. "Sade lisible." TEL QUEL 34 (Fall 1969): 75-85.

Suggests that when reading Sade we are conditioned by the fact that his work has been time and again censored. The reader who claims Sade is illegible becomes a censor's accomplice, refusing to acknowledge the cultural referent, a materialistic and scientific eighteenth-century philosophy. To read only a fictional text of Sade is to make him illegible; to read only a didactic text renders him equally illegible. Concludes: "La lecture de Sade passe de l'un à l'autre sans jamais se laisser prendre au piège culturel qui consiste à réduire chaque texte à une unité et à additionner les points. Sade n'est lisible que pour une lecture qui pense l'articulation multiplicative des contradictions textuelles et qui se pense dans l'orde de ces contradictions. . . . Dire de Sade qu'il est lisible, c'est dire qu'il est encore à lire, et par tous."

1003. Ribadeau Dumas, François. LE MARQUIS DE SADE ET LA LIBERATION DES SEXES. Paris: Dullis, 1974. 332 p.

See item 946 under Dumas.

1004. Rickword, Edgell. "Notes for a Study of Sade." CALENDAR OF MODERN LETTERS 2 (1926): 421-431.

Investigates the selfish roots of men's apparently disinterested actions, showing that morality is dependent on both physiology and environment, a premise carried to "its logical extreme" by Sade. In the phantasmal world of his romances, the marquis illustrated "with the audacity and inventiveness of the dream-power the futility of virtue, its fatal contradiction by the actual workings of the world of matter which makes it a source of pain and disappointment to those who try to carry out its ludicrous code. . . ." Concludes that there is abundant evidence "in literature and in experience, for the view that the impulse which in him was developed to the degree of mania, is an essential component of the most commonplace, as well as the most exceptional expressions of vitality."

1005. Roger, Philippe. SADE: LA PHILOSOPHIE DANS LE PRESSOIR. Paris: Grasset, 1976. 232 p.

Considers Sade as a man led to a belligerent stand by fifty nine months under pressure at the prison of Vincennes. Prevented from making laws for the aristocracy to which he belonged, Sade avenged himself by drafting laws as a writer: "D'une inclination au libertinage, la prison va faire une conviction philosophique; et la Révolution transformer des

dispositions littéraires en une condition sociale."
In this first-rate book, includes a chapter
"Consideration simples" which deals brilliantly with
Sade's humor: "Cet humour de Sade a mis plus d'un
siècle à se faire entendre. Janin et ses successeurs
l'ignorent. C'est qu'ils ont décidé de prendre la
pédagogie du libertinage au sérieux, puisque avec
elle, ils tiennent leur fantasme directeur, leur
texte-programme. Sade leur fournit même le mot de sa
fin, celui du 'meurtre moral.'"

Reviewed by Claude Mauriac in LE FIGARO LITTERAIRE
1559 (3 April 1976): 14.

1006. Roy, Claude. "Marat, intellectuel de gauche." LE
NOUVEL OBSERVATEUR 98 (28 September 1966): 28-29.

Believes that what is most obvious in some writers--
for example, Gorki, Zola, Sartre--is that, like
Marat, they are intellectuals, "engagés," but they
have no other power than that of language. Compares
Sade's ideology with that of other writers, especially
Marat. "Pour Sade un fouet est l'instrument de son
plaisir, pour Marat une arme afin de chasser les
marchands du temple et de libérer les infortunés.
L'un sera scélérat par volupté, l'autre méchant sans
plaisir, et contre les méchants. . . . L'idée de Peter
Weiss d'incarner le dialogue entre le yogi de la
volupté et le commissaire de la Raison en faisant
s'affronter le Moi absolu de Marat est une belle idée.
Il est vrai que Marat et Sade partent du même
postulat."

1007. Sauvaget, Daniel. "Sado-masochisme sur les boulevards."
REVUE DU CINEMA: IMAGE ET SON 272 (May 1973): 38-48.

Presents an interesting discussion on aggression in
the movies which has accustomed us to view women as
objects: "La femme est l'objet du cinéma érotique.
Elle est l'objet du plaisir sadique dans la majorité
des cas." Concludes, however, that these are
expressions of existing tastes rather than a trend
toward something new.

1008. Schuwer, Camille. "Sade et les moralistes." In OEUVRES
COMPLETES DU MARQUIS DE SADE. Paris: Cercle du livre
précieux, 1964, pp. 25-51.

Situates Sade within eighteenth-century tradition and mores and relates his hedonism and epicurism, which are based on an ethical stand without compromises, to other philosophers: Hobbes, La Mettrie, d'Holbach, and Helvetius. Hedonism for Sade is worthy of the appellation if and only if pleasure is total; he annexes and justifies even pain as pleasure. In today's definition of sadism, only part of the meaning of hedonism has been retained, that meaning connected with pain. Concludes that Sade deserves top ranking as an eighteenth-century writer.

1009.  Seldon, E. S. "A New Writer: The Marquis de Sade." HUDSON REVIEW 6 (1953): 300-308.

Reviews THE MARQUIS DE SADE, an essay by Simone de Beauvoir, with SELECTIONS FROM HIS WRITINGS, chosen by Paul Dinnage, published by Grove Press. The essay by Beauvoir was entitled "Must We Burn Sade?" Seldon interprets the meaning of Sade's revolt as an affirmation of the human potential to be bad and the need to value freedom more than moral conformity. What Beauvoir does is "acknowledge the philosophical justice of Sade's critique of ethical 'immanence' in eighteenth-century naturalism, and thereby makes a valuable contribution to our understanding of Sade and his age."

1010.  Summers, Montague. "The Marquis de Sade, a Study in Algolagnia." In ESSAYS IN PETTO. London: Fortune Press, 1928, pp. 77-99.

Attempts to correct errors connected with Sade, who "has been uniformly covered with excess of obloquy and abuse by those who neither knew nor could communicate knowledge, who never read a word of his writings nor troubled to comprehend the smallest fragment of his philosophy." Sees in Sade a writer, a critic, a philosopher of "no mean order," and a pioneer who "considerably furthered the progress of knowledge in the field of sex by his serious and precise attitude toward sexual aberrations." States that today the line of arguments used by Sade in reference to homosexuality are commonplace, but points out that it has become so only in the last twenty years. Discusses algolagnia, or the relationship of the sex impulse to pain, recognized as one of the most difficult yet one of the most fundamental problems in the whole range of sexual psychology. This essay also published as No. 6 of the publications of the British Society of Sex Psychology.

1011. Thody, Philip. "The Case of the Marquis de Sade." TWENTIETH CENTURY 162 (1957): 41-52.

Repeats the view, held in some French intellectual circles, that Sade is "an objective and pessimistic moralist who describes scenes of lust and violence in order to show how wicked men really are." Yet maintains that Sade cannot be totally praised as a moralist since he offers no constructive solution as a counterpart to the destructive criticism of systems he attacks. While there is no doubt that Sade did not commit all the crimes he has been accused of, he certainly had an imagination capable not only of understanding all possible sexual perversions but also of inventing them. Concludes that "it is more interesting to read about Sade than actually to read his works, and a deception awaits those who go from his commentators to his works."

1012. Thomson, Ann. "L'Art de jouir de La Mettrie à Sade." In AIMER EN FRANCE, 1760-1860. Clermont-Ferrand: Association des Publications de la Faculté des Lettres et Sciences humaines, 1980, pp. 315-22.

Proceeding of the Colloquium held in Clermont-Ferrand.

1013. Tortel, Jean. "Le philosophe en prison." CAHIERS DU SUD 285 (1947): 729-746.

Comments on Sade's opinions on crime as interpreted from the reading of LA PHILOSOPHIE DANS LE BOUDOIR. Does not take into account other important works and is therefore somewhat slanted.

1014. Traz, Robert de. "Sade l'inhumain." REVUE DE PARIS, July 1948, pp. 124-128.

Comments on the rather astonishing popularity the Marquis de Sade achieved in the twentieth century and presents an interesting analysis of his doctrine, which the author sees as "un illuminisme macabre et libidineux, une suite de vues de l'esprit, arbitraire et sinistre. Dans sa ferveur exaspérée Sade apparaît alors non plus comme un érotomane sanguinaire mais

comme un idéaliste à rebours, un mystique noir, un
théoricien délirant, combinant des schémas et
s'excitant sur des concepts."

1015. Vené, Gian Franco. "La crisi della raggione nell'opera
di De Sade." LA FIERA LETTERIA, 23 December 1962, p.
4.

Reviews Gian Piero Brega's introduction to Sade's
complete works, published in Italian. Brega's thesis,
suggests author, is that Sade represents an extreme
aspect of eighteenth-century rationalism which is now
very much a part of our modern world: "Il marchese de
Sade rappresenta l'aspetto estremo del rationalismo
settecentesco, una esaperazione voluta di quel modo di
pensare e di essere dal quale è nato il mondo
moderno."

1016. Verdonk, Wessel Eliza. PEUT ETRE. DE BETEKENIS VAN
SADE'S ANTHROPOLOGIE VOOR DE ETHIEK: EEN HOFFSTUK UIT
DE PROBLEMATIEK VAN DE VERLICHTING. Amsterdam:
Rodopi, 1977. 254 p.

Divides book into four chapters with French titles:
Chap. I, "L'homme . . . tel qu'il peut être"; chap.
II, "Humain, sans crainte et sans espérance"; chap.
III, "L'isolisme m'effraye"; and chapter IV, "La
conscience n'est pas l'organe de la nature." Among
the conclusions, presents some of the social, ethical
aspects of Sade's works. Some comparisons between his
political works. Deals also with individual ethics
and shows some interest in cultural anthropology.

Includes a four-page résumé of the book in French and
a bibliography pp. 251-24.

1017. Vier, Jacques. "Le Marquis de Sade." ITINERAIRES 124
(June 1968): 56-71.

In a superb article attacks Sade: "opiniâtre et
enfermé en sa propre manie comme en un donjon
intérieur"; his defenders (Maurice Heine and Gilbert
Lély); his art: "entre différentes formes possibles,
Sade tâtonne sans jamais se fixer"; his philosophy:
"Ce n'est pas l'une des moindres aberrations de notre
temps que de faire sourdre une poétique d'aussi
obscènes pierrailles"; and the totality of his works:
"Qu'on cesse une bonne fois de voir un artiste, un

poète  dans l'écrivain qui commence par soustraire ses
héros  au monde et qui prétend leur tenir de  société,
de nature ou de Dieu."

1018.  Vyverberg,  Henry.    HISTORICAL PESSIMISM IN THE  FRENCH
ENLIGHTENMENT.    Cambridge:  Harvard University Press,
1958.

"The  presence of concepts of decadence and historical
flux  in  the thought of eighteenth-century France  is
pointed out by this study.  Antecedents of eighteenth-
century optimism and pessimism are indicated in  brief
sketches  on  seventeenth-century  thinkers;  the
eighteenth-century  doctrine  of  optimism  is
characterized by accounts of the principal forms
optimism took; and pessimistic views are related  to
various  intellectual  elements  of  the  time.
Examination of the social,  historical,  and scientfic
theories of leading writers, from Montesquieu to Sade,
are  offered as evidence of the intermixture of
pessimism with the more characteristic optimism of the
era."  (Quoted from PHILOSOPHER'S INDEX, item 15.)

1019.  Walter,  Eric.  "Le Complexe d'Abélard ou le célibat des
gens de lettres."  DIX-HUITIEME SIECLE 12 (1980): 127-
152.

Attempts to reconstruct, in the myths of the classical
era,  the genealogy of the writer-bachelor and relates
the Abélard complex to Sadian libertinism, which
denies the propagation instinct.  Sparse references to
Sade.

1020.  Wilson,  Jason.  OCTAVIO PAZ:  A STUDY OF HIS POETICS.
New York: Cambridge University Press, 1979, pp. 34-43.

Discusses  Paz's poem "El prisionero," subtitled
"Homage  to D. A. F. de Sade," as it relates to
surrealism.  Contrasts Sade's views with those of
Octavio  Paz.  Concludes:  "Sade laid bare the
mechanism that prevented the true man from discovering
himself;  on that level he is admirable like a rock
crystal  or diamond,  and there he still remains  (his
work),  indestructible and absolute (no one can replace
his excess).  But Sade himself found no way out; his
philosophy  was a 'callejon sin salida' (blind alley);
he was trapped in his own magnificence,  a prisoner in
his own splendour.  But because the world has not

changed or has not incorporated his discoveries,   Sade
is still explosive,   destroying and re-making   himself
in each generation."

## G. FEMINISM

1021. Abraham, Pierre. "Le lecteur de Sade." EUROPE 522 (1972): 3-9.

In a badly slanted masculine pen, reviews several articles. States about Béatrice Didier's presentation of LES INFORTUNES DE LA VERTU: "Les exemples qu'elle donne [de la littote], les commentaires dont elle les accompagne, sont à la fois précis, savoureux et délicatement inattendus sous une plume féminine". [sic]

1022. Carter, Angela. THE SADEIAN WOMAN. New York: Pantheon, 1979. 152 p.

In a polemical preface, assesses women's relationship to pornography, defined as "basically propaganda for fucking, an activity, one would think, that did not need much advertising in itself, because most people want to do it as soon as they know how." The second chapter, devoted to JUSTINE, compares "a gratuitous victim" to a Blessed Virgin, a Christ-figure, to reinforce the glamour of blasphemy which can occur only in the world of the true believer. The dialectical relationship of Juliette's life to that of her sister is the subject of the third chapter. Juliette is the perfect whore living in an earthly brothel, "a model of the world, in its cash-sale structure; and also it is a place of exile from the world, a place of imaginary liberty where the ritual perversions of the libertines contain no element of a taboo freely broken but which come to dominate their lives." Interprets PHILOSOPHY IN THE BOUDOIR as a detailed account of the erotic education of a Sadeian heroine, describing rage and despair of such quality as to give it a heroic monumentality. Concludes: "Sade's eroticism, with its tragic style, its displays, its corteges, its sacrifices, its masks and costumes, preserves something of the demonology of primitive men. The libertines are indeed like men possessed by demons."

1023. Claude, Catherine. "Une lecture de femme." EUROPE 522 (1972): 64-70.

States that this article is a deliberate partisan
reduction of a reading of Sade by a woman. "Disons
donc que ma lecture de Sade est celle d'un lecteur
trop concerné, parce que femme, pour que je ne sois
pas agacée par une 'bévue,' un non-vu symptomatique
dans la lecture critique qui en est faite."

1024. Dworkin, Andrea. "Le marquis de Sade (1740-1814)." In
PORNOGRAPHY: MEN POSSESSING WOMEN. New York: Putnam
Books, 1981, pp. 70-100.

Attacks Sade in a violent diatribe claiming that "in
him, one finds rapist and writer twisted into one
scurvy knot. His life and writing were a piece, a
whole cloth soaked in the blood of women imagined and
real. In his life he tortured and raped women. He
was a batterer, rapist, kidnapper, and child
abuser. . . . His ethic—the absolute right of men to
rape and brutalize any 'object of desire' at will—
resonates in every sphere." For the most part
undocumented.

1025. Fauchery, Pierre. LA DESTINEE FEMININE DANS LE ROMAN
EUROPEEN DU DIX-HUITIEME SIECLE. Paris: Armand
Colin, 1972. 890 p.

Refers to Sade throughout this enormous and well-
documented book. Quotes from several of Sade's works,
claiming that Sade was a feminist of sorts: "Et Sade
lui-même, à sa manière, vient à leur secours: 'Sexe
charmant, s'écrit-il, vous serez libre; vous jouirez
comme les hommes de tous les plaisirs dont la nature
vous a fait un devoir.'" Concludes, however, that
Sade was indeed very much an eighteenth-century person
who described his era better than most: "Complice des
noirceurs de ce siècle et sans doute aussi de
quelques-unes de ses candeurs, en mimant pieusement
les rêves, lors même que, du haut de son cachot-
mirador, il semble en surveiller l'agonie."

1026. Finas, Lucette. "L'increvable féminin dans FAXELANGE,
ou les torts de l'ambition." SADE, ECRIRE LA CRISE.
Paris: Ed. Belfond, 1983, pp. 15-30.

Analyzes the notion of femininity in FAXELANGE. As
interpreted by Sade, the notion lends itself to some
contradictions. In a way, to be feminine is to be
weak and gentle, "an angel" (as in Faxelange, false

angel). But it is also to endure, because of that
weakness, much abuse: "Endurante, certes, Faxelange
l'est, mais à son corps défendant. Son endurance est
tissée par la faiblesse." But this weakness is also
woven with the determination to survive, no matter
what hell is to be endured. Just like Justine,
Faxelange "almost" succumbs but time and again bounces
back with amazing resilience. She is also the last to
die--after her tormentor, who dies first, after her
defender. Therefore "on peut se demander quelle
relation existe entre cette répartition du récit
(entre extrême force et extrême faiblesse) et la
rencontre de la faiblesse-force dans un personnage
féminin, interrogation d'autant plus légitime que,
dans telle autre nouvelle, la faiblesse-force est
l'apanage d'un personnage masculin." Concludes that
the synthesis of that dialectic is the marquis's
desire to write.

1027.   Fink, Béatrice C.  "Ambivalence in the Gynogram: Sade's
        Utopian Woman."  WOMEN & LITERATURE 7 (1979): 24-37.

        States that "deciphering Sade is particularly
        challenging when the text is read as a female-encoded
        cryptogram, which we call a gynogram. The challenge
        lies in the very centricity of the female, and in the
        emergence of ambivalent patterns within the gynogram
        when female signs are plotted against a thought system
        founded on the dynamics of transgression." Explains
        the problem in terms of the needs of a master as well
        as a slave in a master-slave relationship, or as need
        of "a divinity for a professed atheist." But, more to
        the point, women in Sade's works are also the "prime
        movers in terms of plot lines," for men are from
        beginning to end masterful, whereas the female
        personality changes: women live and learn--but do not
        necessarily know how to handle equal rights.
        Concludes that "equality is not attainable in any
        meaningful sense. In the last resort, such equality
        is either contingent upon some form of power or
        becomes a dead letter pursuant to psychological
        manipulation by a father figure." This essay has been
        reprinted in Janet Todd, ed., BE GOOD, SWEET MAID (New
        York: Holmes and Meier, 1981), pp. 41-52.

1028.   Goncourt, Edmond and Jules. In LA FEMME AU XVIII ème
        SIECLE. Paris: Eugene Fasquelle, 1882, pp. 185-224.

States that love eighteenth-century style hides much
bitterness and poison. It is mostly a deadly and
cruel game, "jeux sans pitié, où se révèlent, dans une
sorte de grâce qui fait peur, la cruauté d'esprit de
l'époque et la profondeur de son libertinage moral."
And toward the end of the century both men and women
competed in wickedness and villainy: "Il se glisse
dans les relations d'hommes à femmes quelque chose
comme une politique impitoyable, comme un système
reglé de perdition. La corruption devient un art égal
en cruautés, en manque de foi, en trahisons, à l'art
des tyrannies."

1029.  Irigaray, Luce. "Françaises ne faites plus un
       effort. . . ." LA QUINZAINE LITTERAIRE 238 (August
       1976): 12.

       Also published in LE SEXE QUI N'EN EST PAS UN (Ed. de
       Minuit, 1977).

1030.  Izzo, Galuppi Clotilde. "Tra Rousseau e Sade: i tre
       saggi L'EDUCATION DES FEMMES Choderlos de Laclos."
       ANNALI ISTITUTO UNIVERSITARIO ORIENTALE 17 (1975):
       125-140.

       Discusses Laclos's three essays on the education of
       women, the first stating that there can be no
       education if slavery exists and that in every society
       women are slaves; the second advocating an education
       which would bring out the "natural" qualities of women
       and denouncing the effects of society on free beings;
       and the third, outlining a program of reading.

1031.  Josephs, Herbert. "Sade and Women: Exorcising the Awe
       of the Sacred." STUDIES IN BURKE AND HIS TIME 18
       (1977): 99-113.

       "The Marquis de Sade, fearing and hating women, viewed
       them as either fascinating libertine adventuresses or
       as the passive and devoted feminine ideal. This
       confusion grew out of his iconoclastic desire to
       destroy inherited values. Based on primary sources;
       40 notes." (Quoted from H. T. Blethen, HISTORICAL
       ABSTRACTS, item 15.)

       "Examines--in a fustian manner--the paradox of Sade's
       libertine hedonism. 'Pleasure . . . depends for Sade

upon the possibility of evil, to which, however, he
denies any existence. It is to the restoration of the
sacred and its taboo, therefore, all destroyed by the
rationalism that he professed, that his energies must
frequently be directed.'" Quoted from THE EIGHTEENTH
CENTURY: A CURRENT BIBLIOGRAPHY (1977).

1032. Lee, Hermione. "Unfair Shares." NEW STATESMAN, 6 April
1979, pp. 487-488.

Reviews of THE SADEIAN WOMAN by Angela Carter, who is
the author of several works of fiction, including THE
PASSION OF NEW EVE and FIREWORKS, two novels which
betray Sade's influence. Criticizes some of Carter's
stands and her conclusion: "This abrupt ending is in
keeping with the rather irritating high-handedness of
the text, which is prone to brash formulations like
'kitschification' and which, though authoritative, has
lapsed into careless repetition and unfocused changes
of direction."

1033. Nahas, H. "La femme dans la littérature existentielle."
Paris: 1957. TIMES (London), 24 December 1961.

1034. Suleiman, Susan. "Reading Robbe-Grillet: Sadism and
Text in PROJET POUR UNE REVOLUTION A NEW YORK."
ROMANIC REVIEW 68 (1977): 43-62.

Explores the relationship between "the reader and the
fantasies enacted in the text; the significance of the
intertextual relations between sadic fantasy and the
theory of the 'self-engendered' text." Observes that
"in Sade both victims and aggressors can be either
male or female (even though female victims and male
aggressors are by far the more numerous), whereas in
PROJET the victims are always female and the
aggressors always male. The difference, however, is
only apparent, and it can be shown that in Sade and in
Robbe-Grillet, the male-female opposition operates as
the opposition between aggressor and victim." Also
asserts that "viewed in the light of the sadic
intertext, PROJET POUR UNE REVOLUTION A NEW YORK takes
on a curiously nonsubversive aspect. Far from de-
constructing male fantasies of omnipotence and total
control over passive female bodies, PROJET repeats
them with astonishing fidelity. Indeed . . . to the
fantasy of total domination is added the fantasy that

'if it's done right, she will enjoy it.'" An
outstanding article.

1035.  Thomas, Chantal. "Juliette, O Juliette!" TEL QUEL 74
       (Winter 1977): 58-67.

       Studies the "sadist" female libertine as typified by
       Juliette and describes her in these terms: "Ce que
       nous rejoignons à travers la figure sans modèle de la
       libertine sadienne, et sous prétexte de la complète
       'gratuité' de ce choix c'est le prodige de ce savoir
       en creux qui nous fait nous rencontrer et nous
       éteindre dans le non-lieu d'une communication perdue,
       sans nostalgie et sans projet, dans l'instant
       renversant d'un continent atteint c'est le théatre
       d'un discours dont nous jouons étourdiment, dans
       l'ignorance superbe de sa maitrise mais non de sa
       pratique, abandonnant à d'autres l'illusion de s'y
       reconnaitre et nous en tenant quant à nous au droit
       définitivement non fondé de nous trahir c'est l'envie
       de rire qui nous saisit à nous voir ainsi évoluer avec
       les allures les plus convaincantes dans l'assurance
       d'une parole manquée que nous nous modulons de l'une à
       l'autre selon la régulation de nos ivresses. Car
       l'athéisme bien compris ne doit pas nous priver des
       enfantillages de la profanation sinon à se révéler
       aussi chiant qu'une religion. . . ."

1036.  Tourné, Maurice. "Pénéope et Circé, ou les mythes de la
       femme dans l'oeuvre de Sade." EUROPE 522 (1972): 71-
       88.

       Quotes Apollinaire, who had said that Sade, besides
       having some specific ideas about women, advocated for
       them just as many liberties as for men. Proceeds then
       to show how Sade's enterprise is a systematic attempt
       to emancipate women. Shows how women themselves have
       accepted with the passivity of slaves the abiding
       prejudices that reinforce their own alienation. The
       freedom obtained by Juliette or Leonore is that of a
       Don Juan, which demands the denial of the established
       order and its oppressive mores and the replacement of
       unfair values with new ideologies. Concludes with a
       very important appraisal of the works of Sade: "Alors
       qu'une tradition, née de l'absence de lecture ou d'une
       lecture incomplète sinon hative, fait du sens de
       l'oeuvre une exaltation du male, dont la toute-
       puissance naitrait de l'asservissement de la femme ou

de  la négation du couple,  il faut lire cette  oeuvre
comme la première tentative systématique de libération
de la femme, faite sans hypocrisie pour l'élever, sans
reniement de sa nature,  au rang d'être humain,  digne
d'assumer et de vivre une philosophie."

1037.  Williams,  David.   "Another Look at the Sadean Heroine:
       The  Prospects  for  Femininity."   ESSAYS  IN  FRENCH
       LITERATURE 13 (1976): 28-43.

In  this  first-rate article,  attempts  a  structural
analysis  of  the  Sadian feminine heroines  in  works
other than the polarized stories of  Justine/Juliette.
Contends  that neither of them possesses "real freedom
or  authenticity."   On the other  hand,  "the  contes
illuminate dimensions to the sadean heroine that  tend
to  displace  the accepted centers of gravity  in  the
more familiar scenarios.  If anywhere in Sade's work,
it  is  in  this  area  of  his  fiction that  the
characteristic  themes  of the Enlightenment  myth  of
femity spring into relief."  Points,  in particular,
in ALINE ET VALCOUR, to Leonore, who "does not seek to
deflect responsibility for her destiny onto  God,  nor
does  she  strive to transcend the limitations  placed
upon  her by Nature and by her own  femity.   Rather
she  seeks  to  understand  the  implications  and
potentialities of the feminine condition in the  light
of  an  educative  encounter. . . ."   Concludes  that
"Leonore  can  thus be seen as one of the  truly  free
figures of Sade's fiction."

## H.  FOREIGN CRITICISM

### Arabic

1038.  Bakari, Salih al.  "Fi-al-Dhikra al-Sadisah Liwafal Taha Hussayn."  AL-FIKR 25 (1979): 30-40.

1039.  Marzabadi, Gholam Hoseyn.  "Ruydadha-ye Siyasi-ye Sade(h) ha-ye Chaharom va Panjom-e Hejri va Ta'sir-e An dar Farhang va Adab-e Iran."  NASHRIYYE(H)-YE DANESHKADE(H)-YE ADABIYYAT VA OLUM-E ENSANI-YE TABRIZ 23 (1971-1972): 254-260.

### Danish

1040.  Jepsen, Hans Lyngby.  MARQUIS DE SADE.  Copenhagen: Stig Vendelkaers Forlag.  1963, 223 p.

1041.  Tang, Jesper.  DEN OPRORSKI ELSKER: KRITIK AF VORES KAERLIGHEDSPRAKSIS GENNEM ANALYSE AF KLASISKE KAERLIGHEDROMANER.  Copenhagen: Borgen, 1977.  207 p.

### Dutch

1042.  Andries, Marc.  "De Sade van de Galg Gehaald."  DIE NIEUWE STEM 20 (1965): 702-704.

1043.  Bakker, Rodolf.  "De heer Venus en mervouw de Sade of: Het dubbelleven van Rachilde (1860-1953)."  MAATSTAF 26 (1978): 23-75.

1044.  Beauvoir, Simone de.  "Moeten wij Sade Verbranden?" Amsterdam: Van Ditmar, 1963-1964.

1045.  Flam, L.  "Het Satanisme." NIEUW VLAAMS TIJDSCHRIFT 11 (1957): 1076-1088.

1046.  Gysen, R.  DE SLECHT BEFAAMDE MARKIES DE SADE.  Amsterdam: Heynis, 1961.  160 p.

1047.  Pappot, Gemma.  DE MARKIES DE SADE, EEN RET MIT BRIEVEN EN DOCUMENTEN.  Amsterdam:  de Arbeider spers, 1967, 213 p.

1048. Verdonk, Wessel Eliza.   PEUT ETRE.   DE BETEKENIS  VAN
      SADE'S ANTHROPOLOGIE VOOR DE ETHIEK:   EEN HOFFSTUK UIT
      DE   PROBLEMATIEK  VAN   DE   VERLICHTING.   Amsterdam:
      Rodopi, 1977.   254 p.

## German

1049. Adorno,  Theodor  W. and Max Horkheimer.    DIALEKTIK DER
      AUFKLARUNG:   PHILOSOPHISCHE  FRAGMENTE.   Amsterdam:
      Querido, 1947, pp. 88-127.

1050. Barruzzi,  Arno.   "Die Apathie des Denkens (Sade)."   In
      MENSCH UND MASCHINE:   DAS DENKEN SUB SPECIE MACHINAE.
      Munich:  Fink, 1973, pp. 117-172.

1051. Barthes,   Roland.    "Der   Baum   des   Verbrechens.
      Reflexionen   über   das   Werk  Sade's."   DIE   NEUE
      RUNDSCHAU, 80 (1969):   32-49.

1052. Bessmertny, Alexander.   DER  MARQUIS DE SADE.   Berlin:
      Querschnitt, 1925.

1053. Blanchot,  Maurice.   "Sade."  In WOLLUSTIGE  PHANTASIE,
      SEXUALASTHETIK  IN  DER LITERATUR.   Edited by  Albert
      Glaser.  Munich:  Hanser, 1974, pp. 25-61.

1054. Bloch,  Iwan  (Dr.) (pseudonym for Eugen  Dühren).   DER
      MARQUIS  DE  SADE  UND SEINE ZEIT.   EIN  BEITRAG  ZUR
      KULTUR  UND SITTENGESCHICHTE DES  XVIII  JAHRHUNDERTS.
      Berlin: Bardsdorf, 1900.

1055. Bloch, Iwan (Dr.)   (pseudonym for Eugen Dühren).   "Neue
      Forschungen  über den Marquis de Sade und seine  Zeite
      mit  besonderer Berücksichtung der  Sexual-philosophie
      de  Sade's  auf  Grund  des  Neueendeckten  original-
      manuskriptes  seines Hauptwerkes."  In DIE EIN HUNDERT
      UND ZWANZIG TAGE VON SODOM. Berlin: Harrowitz, 1904.

1056. Bürger,  Peter.  "Moral und Gesellschaft bei Diderot und
      Sade."   In   AKTUALITAT   UND   GESCHICHTLICHKEIT.
      Frankfort:  Suhrkamp, 1977, pp. 48-79.

1057. Carter,  Angela.  SEXUALITAT  IST MACHT:   DIE FRAU BEI
      SADE.  Aus  dem Englischen von  Leiselotte  Mietzner.
      Reinbek:  Rowahlt, 1981.  200 p.

1058. Drach, Albert. IN SACHEN DE SADE. Dusseldorf: Claassen, 1974. 354 p.

1059. Dühren, Eugen (Dr.). DER MARQUIS DE SADE UND SEINE ZEIT: EIN BEITRAG ZUR KULTUR UND SITTEN GESCHICHTE DES 18. JAHRHUNDERTS. MIT BESONDERER BEZIEHUNG AUF DIE LEHRE VON DER PSYCHOPATHIA SEXUALIS. Berlin: Verlag von H. Barsdorf, 1906, 538 p.

1060. Epting, Karl. "Neo-Sadimus." ZEITWENDE 39 (1968): 542-547.

1061. Eulenburg, Albert (Dr.). SADISMUS UND MASOCHISMUS. Wiesbaden: J. F. Bergmann, 1902.

1062. Eulenberg, Albert (Dr.). "Der Marquis de Sade." ZUKUNFT 26 (25 March 1899): 497-515.

1063. Fingerhut, K. H. Review of AUF DER SUCHE NACH DER REALITAT by Marianne Kesting. In GERMANISTIK XIII (1972): 483.

1064. Flake, Otto. MARQUIS DE SADE. MIT EINEM ANHANG ÜBER RESTIF DE LA BRETONNE. Berlin: S. Fisher, 1930.

Translated from the German by Pierre Klossowski and published as LE MARQUIS DE SADE. Paris: Bernard Grasset, 1923.

1065. Glaser, Horst A. "Literarischer Anarchismus bei de Sade und Burroughs: Zur methodologie seiner Erkenntnis." In LITERATURWISSENSCHAFT UND SOZIALWISSENSCHAFTEN: GRUNDLAGEN UND MODELLANALYSEB. Edited by Thomas W. Metscher et al. Stuttgart: Metzler, 1971, pp. 341-356.

1066. Goldschmidt, Georges-Arthur. "Sade einmal anders." MERKUR 35 (1981): 440-443.

1067. Grossel, Hans. "Das Denken von Sade." NEUE DEUTSCHE HEFTE 20 (1973): 176-180.

1068. Haas, J. "Uber die JUSTINE und die JULIETTE des Marquis de Sade." ZEITSCHRIFT FUR FRANZOSISCHE SPRACHE UND LITERATUR 22 (1900): 282-296.

1069. Hartung, Rudolf. "Die Lust an der Form. Roland Barthes über Sade." FRANKFURTER ALLGEMEINE ZEITUNG FUR DEUTSCHLAND, 14 September 1974.

1070. Hayn, Hugo. BIBLIOTHCA GERMANORUM EROTICA. Leipzig: Verlag von Albert, Unflad, 1885, p. 267.

1071. Heckroth, Hein. THEATRUM SADICUM DER MARQUIS DE SADE UND DAS THEATER. Emsdetten: Lecte, 1963. 341 p.

1072. Henniger, Gerd. MARQUIS DE SADE WERKE. Ausgewählt ubersetzt, mit Dokumentation und Nachwort. Augsburg: Verlag Kurt Desch, 1965. 398 p.

1073. Hetner, Edgar. PORNOTOPIA. DAS OBSZONE UND DIE PORNOGRAPHIE IN DER LITERARISCHEN LANDSCHAFT. Bonn: Athenäum Verlag, 1970.

1074. Hocke, T. "Artaud und Weiss: Untersuchung zue theoretischen Konzeption des 'Theaters der Grausamkeit' und ihrer praktischen Wirksamkeit in Peter Weiss' Marat/Sade." DISSERTATION ABSTRACTS INTERNATIONAL 40 (1979): 56-C.

1075. Keller-Schumacher, Brigitte. DIALOG UND MORD: EINE INTERPRETATION DES MARAT/SADE VON PETER WEISSS. Frankfurt: Athenum, 1973. 434 p.

1076. Kernstock, Wiltrud. DIE SEXUALANTHROPOLOGIE DES MARQUIS DE SADE, DARGESTELLT IN ANTITHESE ZU DEN THEORIEN J. J. ROUSSEAU. (These, Univ. Munchen, Medizinische Fakultät, 1971, 156 p.)

1077. Kesting, Marianne. "Die Planung der irdischen Gluck seligkeit. Sade, ein Vodenker des totalitaren Staates." In AUF DER SUCHE NACH DER REALITAT. KRITISCHE SCHRIFTEN ZUR MODERNEN LITERATUR. Munich: Piper, 1972, pp. 231-236.

1078. Kesting, Marianne. "Sade und die Literatur. Eine franzosische Essaysammlung." In AUF DES SUCHE NACH DER REALITAT. KRITISCHE SCHRIFTEN ZUR MODERNEN LITERATUR. Munich: Piper, 1972, pp. 237-240.

1079. Knapp-Tepperberg, Eva-Marie. "Warum ist der Marquis de Sade kein 'feministicher' Autor?" LENDEMAINS. ZEITSCHRIFT FUR FRANKREICHFORSCHUNG UND FRANZOSISCHSTUDIUM V, 17-18 (June 1980): 125-137.

Written in German with a résumé in French.

1080. Krafft-Ebing, R. V. NEUE FORSCHUNGEN AUF DE GEBIETE DER
      PSYCHOPATHIA SEXUALIS. Stuttgart: S.n., 1891.

1081. Lély, Gilbert. LEBEN UND WERK DES MARQUIS DE SADE.
      Dusseldorf: Karl Rauch Verlag, 1961.

1082. Lemmi, D. A. "Il trionfo di Sade." ABC (Milan), 10
      July 1966.

1083. Lenning, Walter. "Sade." SELBSTZEUGNISSEN UND
      BILDDOKUMENTEN. Hamburg: Rowohlt, 1965. 152 p.

      Original version of that book is amply illustrated and
      has a certain flavor missing in the translation.

1084. Leyser, H. "Sade, oder der andere Florestan. Eine
      Skizze zur tragikomùdie der Intelligenz." ANTAIOS 2
      (1960-1961): 515-526.

1085. Luckow, Marion. "Sade." In DIE HOMOSEXUALITAT IN DER
      LITERARISCHEN TRADITION; STUDIEN ZU DEN ROMANEN VON
      JEAN GENET. Stuttgart: Enke, 1962, pp. 6-11.

1086. Luka. MARQUIS DE SADE, UND SEINE VOLK. DER HISTORISCHE
      FRANZMANN IM SPIEGEL SEINER KULTUR UND SEINER
      GRAUSAMKEIT, UNTER BRONUTZUNG AMTLICHER UND
      HISTORISCHER QUELLEN ZUSAMMENGESTELT UND BEARBEITET.
      Bremer: 1921.

1087. Mainusch, Herbert. "Sade und die Geschichte der O."
      In PORNOTOPIA. DAS OBSZONE UND DIE PORNOGRAPHIE IN
      DER LITERARISCHEN LANDSCHAFT. Bonn: Athenäum Verlag,
      1970, pp. 200-229.

1088. Nagele, Rainier. "Zum Gleichgewicht der Positionen:
      Reflexionen zu Marat/Sade von Peter Weiss." BASIS:
      JAHRBUCH FUR DEUTSCHE GEGENWARTSLITERATUR 5 (1975):
      150-165.

1089. Petriconi, Hellmuth. "Laclos und Sade." DIE VERFUHRTE
      UNSCHULD. Hamburg: n.p., 1953, pp. 72-98.

1090. Petriconi, Hellmuth. "Laclos und Sade." In
      FRANZOSISCHE LITERATUR VON BEAU-MARCHAIS BIS CAMUS--
      INTERPRETATIONEM H.G. VON DIETER STELAND. Hamburg:
      Fischer Bücherei, 1969.

1091. Rabenalt, Arthur Maria. THEATRICUM SADICUM: DER
      MARQUIS DE SADE UND DAS THEATER. Mit Illustrationen
      von Hein Keckrotch. Emsdetten: Verlag Lechte, 1963,
      341 p.

1092. Seelman-Eggebert, Ulrich. "Das Theater des marquis de
      Sade." NEUE ZURCHER ZEITSCHRIFT, n° 53, 1 October
      1972.

1093. Sieburg, Friedrich. "Freiheit zum Bösen." FRANKFURTER
      ALLGEMEINE, 17 March 1962, p. 53.

1094. Siegert, Michael. DE SADE UND WIR: ZUR
      SEXUALOKONOMISCHEN PATHOLOGIE DES IMPERIALISMUS.
      Frankfurt-am-Main: Makol-Verlag, 1971. 263 p.

1095. Starke, Manfred. Marquis de Sade. BEITRAGE ZUR
      ROMANISCHEN PHILOLOGIE 8 (1969): 108-114.

1096. Steinhagen, Harald. "Der junge Schiller swischen
      Marquis de Sade und Kant. Aufklärung und idealismus."
      DEUTSCHE VIERTELJAHRSSCHRIFT 56 (1982): 135-157.

1097. Taberner-Prat, Josemaria. UBER DEN MARAT/SADE VON PETER
      WEISS: ARTISTICHE KREATION UND REZEPTIVE MISSVER-
      STANDISSE. Stuttgart: Heinz, 1976. 419 p.

1098. Tarnowsky, B. DIE KRANKHAFTEN ESCHEINUNGEN DES
      GESCHLECHTSSINESS. Berlin: Hirschfeld, 1886.

1099. Thody, Philip. "Der Marquis de Sade im Urte der
      Literaturkritik und der Justiz." DER MONAT, February
      1957, pp. 22-33.

1100. Waldemar, Austryn. HOLLENFAHRT DES MARQUIS DE SADE:
      ROMAN AUS DEM LEBEN EINES EROTOMANER. Schmiden:
      F. Decker, 1963.

1101. Weber, W. "Erbstücke. L'affaire Sade." In ZEIT OHNE
      ZEIT (1959): 8.

1102. Weigend, Friedrich. "Und der Rauch ihrer Qual. . .Das
      Höllenzeugnis des Marquis de Sade und der Film
      Pasolonis, 'DIE 120 TAGE VON SODEM.'" In CHRIST IN
      DER GEGENWART 28 (1976): 83-84.

1103. Weinhold, Ulrike. "Das Universum in Kopf: De Sade und
      der junge Hofmannsthal." NEOPHILOGUS 63 (1979): 108-
      119.

1104. Weiss, Peter.   DIE  VERFOLGUNG UND ERMORDUNG JEAN-PAUL
      MARATS  DARGESTELLT  DURCH  DIE  SCHAUSPIELGRUPPE  DES
      HOSPIZES  ZU  CHARENTON UNTER ANLEITUNG DES  HERRN  DE
      SADE. Frankfurt: Suhrkamp, 1964.

1105. Wolf, Oskar Ludwig Berhardt. "Analyse de Justine."  In
      ALLGEMEINE GESCHICHTE DES ROMANS.  Iena: 1850.

## Hungarian

1106. Almási, Miklós.   "Sade  márki:   A  racionalizmus
      szatirjátéka."  In AZ ERTELEM KALANDJAI.  Budapest:
      Szepirodalmi K, 1980, pp. 335-439.

## Italian

1107. Accialini, F.  "La passion selon Sade."   CINEMA  E
      CINEMA 7-8 (April 1976): 21-28.

1108. Alex, Gabriel.  "Il marchese sadico."  CAHIERS DU CINEMA
      209 (February 1969): 65.

1109. Baccolo, Luigi.   "Sadiana."  TEMPO PRESENTE, November-
      December 1968, pp. 60-69.

1110. Baccolo, Luigi.  "Le lettere del detenuto Sade."  TEMPO
      PRESENTE, March-April 1968, pp. 61-67.

1111. Baccolo, Luigi.   "Sade  e  la  Rivoluzione."   TEMPO
      PRESENTE,  June 1968, pp. 21-30.

1112. Baccolo, Luigi.  CHE  COSA HA VERAMENTE DETTO DE SADE.
      Rome:  Ubaldini, 1970.  136 p.

1113. Baccolo, Luigi.  "Rileggendo  Sade." PONTE 21  (1965):
      828-833.

1114. Baccolo, Luigi.  "Un Turista di nome Sade."  NUOVA
      ANTOLOGIA 506 (1968): 245-254.

1115. Barba, Vincenzo.  INTERPRETAZIONI DE SADE.  Rome:
      Savelli, 1979.  224 p.

1116. Barba, Vincenzo. SADE: LA LIBERAZIONE IMPOSSIBLE. Florence: Nuova Italia, 1978. 317 p.

1117. Barthes, Roland. SADE, FOURIER, LOYOLA. Turin: Einaudi, 1977.

This is a translation by L. Lonzi of the publication with same title by Editions du Seuil, 1971. For annotation, see item 919.

1118. Bartolommei, Sergio. "ALINE ET VALCOUR: Pornoutopia e 'silenzio delle leggi' nel pensiero del marchese di Sade." PENSIERO POLITICO: RIVISTA DI STORIA DELLE IDEE POLITICHE E SOCIALI 9 (1976): 461-471.

1119. Bausola, Adriano. "Sade: l'uomo 'subi commissus.'" RIVISTA DEL CLERO ITALIANO (February 1980), pp. 124-137.

1120. Benelli, Graziano. "Il marchese rivisto." CANONI (1) LETTERARI STORIA E DINAMICA. Pref. di Giuseppe Petronio e Ulrich Schulz-Buschlaus. Trieste: Istituto di Filologia Moderna, 1981, pp. 221-233.

1121. Betti, P. "Sade, o la forma naturale." PER LA CRITICA 2 (April 1973): 11-16.

1122. Boatto, A. CERIMONIALE DI MESSA A MORTE ININTERROTTA. Rome: Cooperativa Scrittori, 1977, pp. 42-48.

1123. Boatto, A. "Sull'erotismo: Sade, Bataille, Breton." In STUDI SUL SURREALISMO. Rome: Officina Edizioni, 1976, pp. 97-103.

1124. Bona, G. "Sade." In ARCANA. IL MERAVIGLIOSI, L'EROTICA, IL SURREALE, IL NERO, l'INSOLITO NELLE LETTERATURE DI TUTTI I TEMPI. Milan: Sugar, 1969, pp. 593-596.

1125. Brega, Gian Pietro. "Justine-Juliette." In ARCANA. IL MERAVIGLIOSO, L'EROTICA, IL SURREALE, IL NERA, L'INSOLITO NELLE LETTERATURE DI TUTTI I TEMPI. Milan: Sugar, 1969, pp. 387-392.

1126. Brega, Gian Pietro. "L'anticipazione del téatro di Sade." SIPARIO, June 1965, pp. 2-4.

1127. C. P.   "I personnaggi minori della storia.   De Sade."
        STORIA ILLUSTRATA, November 1964, pp. 53-57.

1128. Castoldi, Alberto.   "Le aventure della ragione." In IL
        REALISMO BORGHESE.  Rome:  Bulzoni, 1976, pp. 104-112.

1129. Ceronetti, G.   "Sade à Charenton."   LA CARTE E STANCA.
        Milan:  Adelphi, 1976, pp. 84-89.

1130. Cerruti, Giorgio.   "Il Marchese di Sade:  La sua recente
        fortuna e gli ultimi studi critici (1958-1968)."
        STUDI FRANCESI 13 (1969): 420-441.

1131. Cerruti, G.   Review of SADE ET SES MASQUES, by Roger
        Lacombe.  STUDI FRANCESI 19 (1975):  363.

1132. Cirio, Rita and Favari, Pietro.  UTOPIA RIVISITATA.
        Milano: Arti Grafiche Luigi Granata, 1973.  283 p.

1133. Cordero, F.  TRATTATO DI DECOMPOSIZIONE.   Bari:  De
        Donato, n.d., pp. 162-165.

1134. Costa,   Corrado.     INFERNO   PROVVISORIO.     Milan:
        Feltrinelli, 1970, pp. 31-36; 58-64; 100-107.

1135. Costa, Corrado.  "Sextrapolazioni."   QUINDICI 11 (15
        June 1968): viii.

1136. Costa, Corrado.  "L'Economia di Sade."  QUINDICI, 17 May
        1969, p. 11.

1137. Costa, Corrado.  "Neosade."  QUINDICI 4 (1967):  32-34.

1138. Dalmasso, Gianfranco.  LA POLITICA DELL'IMAGINARIO:
        ROUSSEAU-SADE.  Milan: Jaca Book, 1977, pp. 105-151.

1139. Dandolo, Comte Tullio.  REMINISENCE FANTASIE, SCHERZI
        LITTERATURE.  Turin: n.p., 1840.

1140. Drain, G. A. (pseudonym of Couperyn).   LE BORDEL DE
        VENISE.  Venice: n.p., 1921.

1141. Fallia, Alfredo.  "Lo spirito più libero del manicomio
        di Charenton."  GIORNALE DI SICILIA, 26 May 1961, pp.

1142. Fé, Franco.  Review of LAUTREAMONT E SADE, by Maurice
        Blanchot.  IL PONTE 31 (1975):  296-297.

143. Finzi Ghisi, V.  "Sade o della separazione."  UTOPIA, January 1972, pp. 29-30.

144. Fiorioli, Elena.  "La fortuna di Sade in Italia." CULTURE FRANCAISE (BARI) 24 (1977): 3-10.

145. Galuppi, Clotilde Izzo.

    See item 1150.

146. Ghisi, V. F.  "Sade o delle separazione."  UTOPIA, January 1972, p. 29-30.

147. Giannessi, F.  "Storia secreta di Isabella di Baviera." LA STAMPA, 28 October 1964, p. 11.

148. Guaraldo, Enrico.  Review of SADE/ARTAUD, by Carlo Pasi. RIVISTA DI LETTERATURE MODERNE E COMPARATE 33 (1980): 157-159.

149. Ippolito.  "La persecuzione e l'assassinio de Jean-Paul Marat."  SIPARIO, 232-233 (1965):  61-64.

150. Izzo Galuppi, Clotilde.  "Tra Rousseau e Sade:  I tre saggi su L'EDUCATION DES FEMMES di Choderlos de Laclos."  ANNALI ISTITUTO UNIVERSITARIO ORIENTALE 17 (1975):  125-140.

151. Jesi, F. MITOLAGIE INTORNO ALL'ILLUMINISMO.  Milan: Edizione di Comunità, 1972, pp. 123-133, 134-136, 140-148.

152. Klossowski, Pierre.  "Sade e Fourier."  ADELPHIANA 1971. Milan: Adelphi, 1970, pp. 109-131.

    This is a translation by E. Turolla of the article with same title originally published in TOPIQUE.  See item 1646.

153. Knight, G. Wilson.  "Sadism and the Seraphic."  In ITALIA LINGUISTICA NOUVA ED ANTICA:  STUDI LINGUISTICI IN MEMORIA DI ORONZO PARLANGELI.  Edited by Vittore & Ciro Santoro.  Galatina: Congedo, 1976, pp. 226-237.

154. Lély, Gilbert.  SADE PREFETA DELL'EROTISMO.  Milan: Feltrinelli, 1960.

1155. Livio, G. "Manzoni e Sade ou 'Les Prospérités de la vertu.'" UTOPIA, April 1973, pp. 20-24.

1156. Macchia, Giovanni. "Il diavolo in biblioteca." IL MITO DI PARIGI: SAGGI ET MOTIVI FRANCESI. Turin: Giulio Einaudi Editore, 1965, pp. 257-262.

1157. Macchia, Giovanni. "Sade alla follia." PANORAMA, 10 August 1976, pp. 68-75.

      Interview conducted by M. L. Pace.

1158. Macchia, Giovanni. "Un sogno di Sade." In IL MITO DI PARIGI. Turin: Einaudi, 1965, pp. 181-186.

1159. Manganella, Diego. "Ombre nel tempo, la marchesa di Sade." NUOVA ANTOLOGIA 302 (1 June 1922): 205-216.

1160. Montagna, Bonatti G. Review of L'ANTICIPAZIONE DEL TEATRO DI SADE by G. P. Brega. STUDI FRANCESI 11 (1967): 559.

1161. Moravia, Alberto. "Sade per Pasolini: Un sasso contro la societa." CORRIERE DELLA SERA, 6 December 1975, p. 3.

1162. Nardis, L. de. "Il castello di Sade." LA LETTERATURA FRANCESE: DALL'ILLUMINISMO AL ROMANTICISMO. Edited by G. Macchia, L. de Nardis, M. Colesanti. Florence Sansoni Accademia, 1974, pp. 376-389.

1163. Nicoletti, Gianni. "Antropologia aristocratica: tra Laclos e Sade." In INTRODUZIONE ALLO STUDIO DELL ROMANZO FRANCESE NEL SETTECENTO. Bari, Italy Adriatica Editrice, 1967, pp. 169-194.

1164. Nicoletti, Gianni. "Due castelli per Sade." L'ALBERO 27, 58 (1977): 105-111.

1165. Pasi, Carlo. "Sotto il segno della crudeltà: Sade e Artaud." MICROMEGAS 1 (September-December 1947): 23-40.

1166. Pasi, Carlo. "Justine e il suo doppio." SAGGI E RICERCHE DI LETTERATURA FRANCESE 15 (1976): 183-207.

1167. Pasi, Carlo. SADE E ARTAUD. Rome: Bulzoni, 1979. 191 pp.

1168. Paulhan, Jean. "Il marchese di Sade e la sua complice ovvero la rivincita del pudore." VERRI 32 (1971): 20-46.

1169. Paz, Octavio. "Corriente alterna." SUR 274 (1962): 34-46.

1170. Perrelli, Franco. "Tre voci per un dizionario sadiano." ANNALI DELLA FACOLTA DI LETTERE E FILOSOFIA DELL'UNIVERSITA DEGLI STUDI (Bari) 19-20 (1976-1977): 487-496.

1171. Petrucci, Antonio. "Quasi un diario." L'OSSERVATORE ROMANO, 22 October 1966, p. 3.

1172. Pleynet, Marcel. "Sade." IL PENSIERO DI SADE. Naples: Guida, 1973, pp. 126-150.

       This article was originally published in TEL QUEL in 1968.

1173. Praz, Mario. "All'insegna del divin marchese." In LA CARNE, LA MORTE E IL DIAVOLO NELLA LETTERATURA ROMANTICA. Milan: Società editrice La cultura, 1930, pp. 91-184.

1174. Serra, Dante. IL MARCHESE DI SADE, LA SUA VITA E I SUOI TEMPI. Milan: Ceschina, 1950. 304 p.

1175. Servadio, E. "Il diavolo in terra: il marchese de Sade. Il carnefice vittima." STORIA ILLUSTRATA, August 1961, pp. 225-229.

1176. Sgard, Jean. "Le voyage à Naples du marquis de Sade (1775-1776)." ANNALI DELL'ISTITUTO UNIVERSITARIO ORIENTALE, SEZIONE ROMANZA 24 (1982): 23-35.

1177. Sollers, Philippe. "Lettera di Sade." VEL (1975): 124-132.

       Issue dedicated to MATERIA E PULSIONE DI MORTE.

1178. Solmi, S. "All'ombra del divin Marchese." In LA SALUTE DI MONTAIGNE. Milan: s.n., 1952, pp. 155-159.

1179. Tessari, R. "Sade: 'mostro' e regista a Charenton." DISMISURA 20-26 (November 1975-December 1976): 51-66.

1180. Testa, A. "La cosa sadica." ES. 7 (April 1978): 3-25.

1181. Torchia, Francesco. "Per una lettura testuale della PHILOSOPHIE DANS LE BOUDOIR di D.A.F. de Sade." NUOVA CORRENTE: RIVISTA DI LETTERATURA 75 (1978): 42-68.

1182. Toscano, Rita. "De Sade e la natura. Filosofia e scienza oltre l'illuminismo." BOLLETTINO DE STORIA DELLA FILOSOFIA DELL'UNIVERSITA DEGLI STUDI DI LECCE 4 (1976): 407-419.

1183. Valluri, Luigi Lombardi. "Il Soggeto assoluto e i suoi diritti nell'universo sadista." RIV. INT. FILOSOF DIRITTO 56 (1979): 21-42.

1184. Vené, Gian Franco. "La crisi della raggione nell'opera di De Sade." LA FIERA LETTERIA 23 (1962): 4.

1185. Vicentiis, Gioacchino. "Vite in margine, il marchese de Sade." ELOQUENZA, September-October 1934, pp. 314-325.

1186. Weise, G. L'IDEALE EROICO DEL RINASCIMIENTO DIFFUSIONE EUROPEA E THAMONTANO. Naples: Esi, 1965.

## Japanese

1187. Iimura, Takahito. DE SADE. Film.

1188. Mishima, Yukio, pseud. MADAME DE SADE. Tokyo: C. E. Tuttle Co., 1971.

1189. Shimpachiro, Miyata. "The Marquis on Trial." JAPAN QUARTERLY 8 (1961): 494-496.

## Norwegian

1190. Fauskevag, Svein Eirik. SADE I SURREALISMEN. Oslo: Univ. Inst. for idehist., 1977. 518 p.

## Polish

1191.  Lojek, Jerzy.  WIEK MARKIZA DE SADE;  SZICE Z HISTORII
       OBYCZAJOS   I  LITERATURY  WE  FRANCJI  XVIII   WIEDU.
       Lublin: Wydawnictwo Lubelskie, 1972, pp. 227-430.

       Includes  four  sections entitled The Century  of  the
       Marquis  de Sade:   Studies on Mores and  Civilization
       during the Eighteenth-Century;  Crébillon fils and His
       Contemporaries  or Smiling Libertinage;  Restif de  la
       Bretonne or Condemned Libertinage; The Marquis de Sade
       or Human Nature Unveiled.

## Portuguese

1192.  Alvarenga,  (O.-M.).   "O  papel  de Sade  na  revoluçao
       francesa," REVISTA DO LIVRO, March 1959.

1193.  Duran,  Manuel.   "Del Marqués de Sade a Valle--Inclan."
       ASOMANTE 10 (1954): 40-47.

## Russian

1194.  Erofeev,  V.  "Metamorfoza odnoj literaturnoj reputacii:
       Markiz  de Sad,  sadizm i XXvek."  VOPROSY  LITERATURY
       17, 6 (1973): 135-168.

1195.  Molcanov,  V.   "La  poétique de la violence."   VOPROSY
       LITERATURY 1 (1974): 146-170.

## Spanish

1196.  Arias  de  la Canal,  Fredo.   "El complejo de  Edipo."
       NORTE:  REVISTA HISPANO AMERICANO 257 (1977): 46-55.

1197.  Duran,  Manuel.   "Del Marqués de Sade a Valle--Inclan."
       ASOMANTE 10 (1954): 40-47.

1198.  Lebrun,  A.   "Sade et la roman noir:  les dessous d'une
       mode."  EL TECHO DE LA BALENA, April 1966, p. 14.

1199.  Lipschutz, [Frank].  Noticias sobre el marquese de Sade.
       N.p: n.p., n.d.

1200.  Lopez,  Eduardo.  "Introducción a Sade."  PAPELES DE SON
       ARMADANS 64 (1971): 241-255.

1201.  Marchant,  Patricio.   "Socrates  o  Sade:   Una  Apuesta
       Filosofica."  DIALOGOS 8 (1972):  107-137.

1202.  Revol,  Enrique-Luis.  CAMINOS DEL EXCESO, WILLIAM BLAKE
       Y EL MARQUIS DE SADE.   Córdoba:  Republica argentina,
       1964.

1203.  Rumazo,  Lupe.   "La  presencia del sadismo en  Sabato."
       CUADERNOS  HISPANOAMERICANOS:    REVISTA  MENSUAL   DE
       CULTURA HISPANICA 270 (1972):  551-558.

1204.  Sanchez-Paredes,  P.  EL MARQUES DE SADE, UN PROFETA DEL
       INFIERNO.  Barcelona: Ediciones Guadarrama, 1974.

1205.  Young,  George J.  "Sade, los decadentistas y Bradomin."
       CUARERNOS HISPANOAMERICANOS 298 (1975): 112-131.

## Swedish

1206.  Meurling,  P.  DEN  GÄFULLE MARKIS DE SADE.   Stockholm:
       1956.

# I. MASOCHISM AND SADISM

1207. Alexandrian, Sarane. "Le marquis de Sade et la tragédie du plaisir." In LES LIBERATEURS DE L'AMOUR. Paris: Editions du Seuil, 1977, pp. 75-106.

Attempts to demonstrate that Sade was not "sadique" but "taquiniste"; and defines the "taquinisme" (or teasing) as a very subdued form of sadism. Believes that Sade described a universe of absolute liberty, incarnated in principles by the Sadian heroes who discarded all prejudices, all conventions in order to give first priorities to man's instincts: "Si cet univers est horrible, c'est à cause du pessimisme extraordinaire de Sade: entièrement persuadé que ce qui prédomine en la plupart des êtres, c'est l'instinct de la destruction." Concludes that while the picture painted by Sade is frightening, it is necessary for the knowledge of mankind: each individual after reading him must reconstruct for himself with more insight all the values that Sade has so radically destroyed.

1208. Arias de la Canal, Fredo. "El complejo de Edipo." NORTE: REVISTA HISPANO AMERICANO 257 (1977): 46-55.

Investigates the different forms of Oedipal complexes as described from the time of antiquity by Sophocles, in OEDIPUS REX, to Shakespeare, Freud, Lope de Vega, and others, including Sade in FLORVILLE ET COURVAL.

1209. Armand, E. "Interdit à tous les âges." DEFENSE DE L'HOMME 105 (July 1957): 20-21.

Insists that there is no connection between true criminals and readers of Sade's CRIMES DE L'AMOUR. In fact, it might be proved that the works of Sade interest only a minority of the curious and sexologists. There might even be something to be said for putting these books within the reach of anyone knowing how, and wanting to, read them.

1210. Arrivé, Michel. "Un Aspect de l'isotopie sexuelle dans le texte de Jarry: Sadisme et masochisme." ROMANIC REVIEW 66 (1975): 57-75.

Intends to relate some semiotic concepts (isotopy and
that of a text) to concepts used in psychoanalysis
(sadism and masochism) in order to examine Jarry's
intertext    CESAR-ANTECHRIST-UBUROI-UBU    ENCHAINE.
Describes     the     contents     of     these     texts     in
psychoanalytic terms, using the definition given by
Laplanche and Pontalis of the term "sado-masochism."

1211. Astruc, P.  "Maurice Heine et le marquis de Sade."
      PROGRES MEDICAL, 24 June 1950, p. 366.

      Honors Maurice Heine, a distinguished scholar who
      devoted his life to the study of Sade's works. States
      that Heine had a strong medical background and an
      intellectual portfolio that made him well qualified to
      study Sade.

1212. Bachellier, Jean-Louis.  Review of L'INVENTION DU CORPS
      LIBERTIN, by Marcel Hénaff.  MAGAZINE LITTERAIRE 151-
      152 (September 1979): 109.

1213. Baker, Robert and Elliston, Frederick, eds.  PHILOSOPHY
      AND SEX.  Buffalo, N.Y.: Prometheus Books, 1975.

      "PHILOSOPHY AND SEX is an anthology of twenty-two
      contemporary philosophical essays on sexual morality,
      sexual perversion, sexual language, marriage, feminism
      and abortion. The articles were selected (and in some
      cases, commissioned) to aid, abet, as well as to
      document the recent rebirth of interest in sexual
      philosophy."  (Quoted from PHILOSOPHER'S INDEX, item
      15.)

1214. Balkis.  Preface to PAGES CURIEUSES DU MARQUIS DE SADE.
      Paris:  Editions  de  la  Grille,  Collection  Les
      Bibliophiles Libertins, 1926.

      Collected an odd assortment of fragments written by
      Sade. Examples of some of the titles:  "Sur la
      necessité du libertinage pour les jeunes filles," "Sur
      le goût du scandale," "Sur la sodomie," "Sur la
      félicité de la corruption," "Sur le devoir de
      détruire," "Sur l'infanticide," "Sur l'inceste," etc.

1215. Bataille, Georges.  "Le Bonheur, l'érotisme, et la
      littérature."  CRITIQUE V (1949):  401-411.

Discusses the essay written by Maurice Blanchot on
Sade (Editions de Minuit, 1949) and begins his review
with an analysis of words like BONHEUR, PLAISIR,
VOLUPTE, EROTIQUE, SEXUEL, in order to arrive at his
first conclusion: sexual behavior and ordinary
behavior are mutually exclusive. The erotic world of
Sade is doubly negative since normal sexual activity
usually unites beings whereas, for Sade, it is
interpreted in his works solely as the negation of the
partners and the negation of ordinary behavior: "la
négation de Sade a laissé l'esprit devant une vérité
qui n'est ni la nature ni l'univers, ni rien, mais la
négation même de la nature et de l'univers, comme s'il
était dans la nature--et dans l'univers--une ultime
possibilité, à la limite, une transcendance possible,
dans l'insatisfaction d'être, dans l'obsession d'un
passage de l'être au non-être."

1216.  Bataille, Georges. "De Sade's Sovereign Man." In
       EROTICISM. Translated by Mary Dalwood. London: John
       Calder, 1962, pp. 164-176. Originally published as
       L'EROTISME. Paris: Editions de Minuit, 1957.

       States: "De Sade's sovereign individual is no longer
       a man encouraged to his extravagance by the crowd.
       The kind of sexual satisfaction that suits everyone is
       not for de Sade's fantastic characters. The kind of
       sexuality he has in mind runs counter to the desires
       of other people; they are to be victims, not partners.
       De Sade makes his heroes uniquely self-centered; the
       partners are denied any rights at all; this is the key
       to his system."

1217.  Bataille, Georges. "L'érotisme: projet d'une
       conclusion." L'ARC 32 (1967): 81-84.

       Begins with a description of a dream and projects a
       conclusion which is not forthcoming: "Si j'avais visé
       un changement pratique . . . je pourrais à la fin
       reprendre utilement les résultats de mes efforts, j'en
       enconcerais clairement la somme. Au contraire, je
       dois m'éloigner de ces possibités reassurantes. Je ne
       puis plus parler."

1218.  Bataille, Georges. "Sade et l'homme normal." In
       L'EROTISME. Paris: Ed. de Minuit, 1957, pp. 209-214.

This essay was also published as a preface to LA
NOUVELLE JUSTINE Vol. VI. (OEUVRES COMPLETES DU
MARQUIS DE SADE. Paris: Cercle du livre précieux,
1963, pp. 58-65) and translated into English by Mary
Dalwood. See item 1220.

1219. Bataille, Georges.    "Si nous admirons Sade, nous
édulcorons sa pensée." OBLIQUES 12-12 (1977):   201-
206.

This is an excerpt from "Sade et l'homme normal,"
originally published in L'EROTISME (Paris:   Editions
de Minuit, 1957).

1220. Bataille, Georges.    "De Sade and the Normal Man."  In
EROTICISM. London:  John Calder, 1962, pp. 177-196.

Also published in 1957 by Editions de Minuit and
translated from the French by Mary Dalwood, this
stresses the fact that the criticisms that Sade
defined were all well founded but that "Sade expounded
his doctrine of irregularity in such a way, mingled
with such horrors, that no one paid any heed to it.
He wanted to revolt our conscious minds; he would also
have liked to enlighten them, but he could not do
both at the same time.  It is only today we realise
that without de Sade's cruelty we should never have
penetrated with such ease the once inaccessible domain
where the most painful truths lay hidden. . . .  And
if today the average man has a profound insight into
what transgression means for him, de Sade was the one
who made ready the path." See longer version
published as preface to JUSTINE, item 87.

1221. Beausobre de, Julia.  "Creative Suffering." THEOR THEOR
12 (1978): 111-121.

1222. Beauvoir, Simone de.   "Moeten wij Sade Verbranden?"
Amsterdam : Van Ditmar, 1963-1964.

Translation into Dutch by C. Veerman and Jenny Tuin of
"Must we Burn Sade?"

See item 924.

1223. Belaval, Yvon.  Review of SADE:   L'INVENTION DU CORPS
LIBERTINE, by Marcel Hénaff. ROMANIC REVIEW 16
(1981):  184-190.

1224. Bettinotti, Jula. "La Segmentation masculine dans LA PHILOSOPHIE DANS LE BOUDOIR." DEGREES: REVUE DE SYNTHESE A ORIENTATION SEMIOLOGIQUE. 14 (1978): g/1-g/12.

Analyzes the segmentation in LA PHILOSOPHIE DANS LE BOUDOIR, where a special semiotic field, that of sexual relationship is presented. Concludes that neither Sade nor any sexual revolutionary seems to have overthrown an act as institutionalized as the sexual act: "Aucune segmentation nouvelle ne vient enrichir le code et le Marquis lui-même suit, dans LA PHILOSOPHIE DANS LE BOUDOIR les chemins les plus frustes. . . . A ce propos accuser le Marquis de monotonie sans s'apercevoir que cette monotonie frappe d'abord et avant tout la structuration figée de l'acte sexuel."

1225. Blanchot, Maurice. "A la rencontre de Sade." TEMPS MODERNES 25 (1947): 577-612.

Attempts to show that for the "integral man" there exists no possibility of doing evil and that for Sade's libertines, pain inflicted on others is voluptuous while pain inflicted on the self can be made pleasurable. This total negation of man's humanity is, in a sense, a negation of God, and at the same time the construction of man as God. Concludes that, in spite of all the contradictions, there may be in Sade some views with more meaning that had been hitherto conceived: "Nous ne disons pas que cette pensée soit viable. Mais elle nous montre qu'entre l'homme normal qui enferme l'homme sadique dans une impasse et le sadique qui fait de cette impasse une issue, c'est celui-ci qui en sait le plus long sur la vérité et la logique de sa situation et qui en a l'intelligence la plus profonde, au point de pouvoir aider l'homme normal à se comprendre lui-même, en l'aidant à modifier les conditions de toute compréhension."

1226. Bloch, Iwan (Dr.) (pseudonym for Eugen Dühren). MARQUIS DE SADE'S ONE HUNDRED AND TWENTY DAYS OF SODOM AND THE SEX LIFE IN THE FRENCH AGE OF DEBAUCHERY. Translated by Raymond Sabatier. New York: Falstaff Press, 1934.

See also item 1249 under Dühren.

1227.   Bloch, Iwan (Dr.) (pseudonym for Eugen Dühren). THE
        SEXUAL EXTREMITIES OF THE WORLD. New York: Book
        Awards, 1964.

        Deals with one chapter on sadism and masochism.
        Relates brutality in boxing to a "strong sadistic
        streak among the English people." Describes the
        "uncanny fascination" of great masses of people for
        public executions, especially during the eighteenth
        century. Mentions that Samuel Johnson, the famous
        biographer, was such an execution habitué. Describes
        books which deal with the "apotheosis of the joy which
        springs from inflicting physical or psychological
        cruelty."

1228.   Bonneau, Alcide. "Liber sadicus." CURIOSA. ESSAIS
        CRITIQUES DE LITTERATURE ANCIENNE IGNOREE OU MAL
        CONNUE. Paris: Isidore Liseux, 1887, pp. 284-286.

        Gives a good review of the first JUSTINE, which, he
        feels, is by far the best of the several editions.
        Later expansions of the work were detrimental: "Il
        nous suffira de dire que cette JUSTINE primitive, au
        rebours de la longue divagation qui en a été
        postérieurement tirée, non seulement est lisible, mais
        se laisse lire avec intérêt. C'est un document."

1229.   Bourbon, Jacques de Busset. "La négation érotique."
        TABLE RONDE 182 (1963): 109-112.

        Attempts to explain Sade's nihilism as it relates to
        love and interprets the special qualities of sadistic
        eroticism to a will to power especially attractive to
        intellectuals incapable of showing true tenderness.
        Concludes that "la négation du sadique est, au fond,
        un aveu d'impuissance, le signe de l'incapacité de
        sortir de sa propre citadelle."

1230.   Breton, André. LA LAMPE DANS L'HORLOGE. Paris: Ed. R.
        Morin, 1948, p. 56.

        Sees in Sade one of the eighteenth-century's writers
        most eager to shake the yoke of hypocrisy concerning
        sensual pleasure. Includes a full size photograph of
        André Breton in the Castle at La Coste.

1231.  Brunet, Pierre Gustave.   "Sade." LES FOUS LITTERAIRES.
       Brussels:  Gay et Doucé, 1880, p. 177.

       Reports  only two facts on this famous  "erotomaniac":
       First,  discloses that IDEE SUR LE MODE DE LA SANCTION
       DES  LOIS may well have been written by Sade (it  is);
       then  reports  that the  INDEX  LIBRORUM  PROHIBITORUM
       lists an unpublished, unnamed work by Sade.

1232.  Buisson, Françoise.   "Les  bougres,  ou  les  derniers
       archanthropes." OBLIQUES 12-13 (1977):  19-22.

       Believes that Sade's work has gained a new status:  it
       is  supposed  to  represent  some  reality,  lending
       strength  to  the figure of Sade himself as a  symbol,
       begun  on  paper,  of a  social  revolutionary.   Sade
       dehumanized man,  took away his thoughts and  emotion.
       He was master of form and substance.   But his art was
       in   the   manner   in  which  he  went   about   this
       dehumanization.   In  contemporary  mores,   men  are
       dehumanized  with the efficiency of  the  factory,  no
       longer  cutting  off  a  person's  head  but  simply
       destroying his mind.   Sade would dissect a body on an
       anatomy table; now it is done on an autopsy table.

1233.  Cabanes,  Auguste  (Dr.).    "Sur Sade."   CHRONIQUE
       MEDICALE, 15 December 1902, pp. 802-803.

1234.  Camus, Michel.  "L'impasse mystique du libertin."   In
       SADE,  ECRIRE LA CRISE:  COLLOQUE DE CERISY.   Paris:
       Belfond, 1983, pp. 259-276.

       Formulates  several hypotheses concerning the mystical
       impasse  created  by  Sadian-style  libertinage.   The
       first deals with Sade's attempt,  while in prison,  to
       free  himself  mentally through the natural medium  of
       sex expressed as an intellectual transgression of  all
       cultural  and social human taboos.   Conjectures  that
       all  of  it  was talk,  never becoming a  real  action
       except  as  the action of writing.   But  then  Sade's
       language  is as murderous as the "verbe de Yahveh"  in
       the   Old  Testament.   This  leads  to  the   second
       hypothesis:  "il  y a chez Sade une  structure  sado-
       masochiste  dans laquelle son esprit sadique opère  sa
       sensibilité masochiste, son écriture la sensibilité du
       lecteur." The offense on the reader is perpetrated to
       such  an extent of saturation that apathy sets in:   a
       state  of non-suffering without compassion."  Au  sens

rhétorique du terme, l'effet Sade est un effet d'ithos sans pathos." Concludes that the reader is led into a linguistic impasse.

1235. Chasseguet-Smirgel, Janine. "Le corps chez Sade." In CORPS CREATION ENTRE LETTRES ET PSYCHANALYSE. Directed by Jean Guillaumin. Lyon: Presses Universitaires de Lyon, 1980, pp. 169-182.

1236. Châtelet, Noëlle. "Le Libertin à table." In SADE, ECRIRE LA CRISE. Paris: Belfond, 1983, pp. 67-83.

Investigates the role played by culinary pleasures in a Sadian universe. Stresses especially a French play on words. "Se mettre a table" is both to sit for a meal and denounce or confess. Sees a relationship between gastronomical excesses and sexual ones: both are orgies. But contrary to Pantagruel, who pays with his physical appearance for his over-indulgence, the Sadian heroes devour with impunity, thus creating a kind of scandal. "L'ogrerie sadienne, contrairement à celle de Rabelais--même si elle se concrétise par des actes physiques--demeure profondément psychique, pour ne pas dire morale. Celle de Rabelais fondamentalement extravertie au travers de ventres qui gonflent, de bouches qui s'ouvrent comme des gouffres, des langues lagunaires, des culottes qui éclatent pour être trop remplies. La deuxième est saine, festoyante, la première est pervertie, déroutante." Concludes that in culinary matters we could have been accomplices of Sade and indulged in similar excesses, but there, too, we somehow are relegated through a process of distancing to our own "normality," strangely barren in front of the inconceivable talent of Sade for isolating perversion.

1237. Cleugh, James. THE MARQUIS AND THE CHEVALIER. New York: Duell, Sloan and Pearce, 1952, pp. 10-145.

Presents a study on the psychology of sex as illustrated by the works of the Marquis de Sade and the Chevalier de Masoch. Includes sections on "Stars and Eagles"; "Frustration"; "The Eddying Stream"; "The Marquis de Sade and the Detectives"; "The Mind Alone"; "Citizen Sade"; and "Danse Macabre." Outdated on Sade.

1238.  Clouard, Henri.  "Le siècle sadique."  TABLE RONDE,
       March 1953, pp. 147-149.

       While admitting that Sade may be a "dominating" figure
       in the twentieth century because of his revolt, his
       demand for total liberty, his black humor, and his
       absolute subjectivism of inspiration, still contends
       that Sade should not be "canonized" and "s'inquiète du
       dérèglement de cervelle dont [cette canonisation]
       semble être les symptômes."

1239.  Connolly, Cyril.  "The Original Sadist."  SUNDAY TIMES
       (London), 19 February 1961, p. 17.

1240.  Cornand, André.  "Sade sadisme."  REVUE DU CINEMA:
       IMAGE ET SON 272 (May 1973): 16-24.

       States that there exists essentially no Sadian films:
       "Pour respecter Sade, il faut le libérer du récit, lui
       être fidèle en le trahissant . . . et jusqu'à à ce
       jour, personne n'a su trahir Donatien pour lui être
       fidèle."  However, states that there are sadistic
       films which may not have any relationship to Sade but
       which exploit latent sadism of audience.

1241.  Crocker, Lester G.  "Sade and the FLEURS DU MAL."  In
       NATURE AND CULTURE:  ETHICAL THOUGHT IN THE FRENCH
       ENLIGHTENMENT.  Baltimore:  Johns Hopkins University
       Press, 1963, pp. 398-429.

       Sketches Sade's system of nihilism, which he traces to
       Sade's discovery of the sexual libido with its
       connection to aggression. As we are "natural" beings,
       perversion is not in us but in the society; and
       cruelty is only a part of our natural inclinations or
       needs.  From the rights of the strongest it follows
       that it is natural to take advantage of the weak and
       anything that is pleasurable is defensible, including
       systematic cruelty performed on the most defenseless
       creatures.  Concludes that "while Sade's man, as we
       now know, is indeed what men could be 'naturally' if
       'artificial' pressures were not exerted to restrain
       them, that is, if men could live outside of culture,"
       yet "the philosophy of nihilism is a nonviable one,
       and it annuls itself. Although Sade showed courage in
       uncovering truths about human nature, the
       philosophical system he draws from those truths is

false and untenable, as well as dangerous to human life."

1242. Deleuze, Gilles. PRESENTATION DE SACHER-MASOCH. Paris: Editions de Minuit, 1967; and Paris: U.G.E., 1971.

See annotation of English translation under the title SACHER-MASOCH: AN INTERPRETATION item 1242.

1243. Deleuze, Gilles. SACHER-MASOCH: AN INTERPRETATION. Translated by Jean McNeil. London: Faber and Faber, 1971. 248 p.

Contains four chapters especially relevant to the study of Sade. In the first chapter, "The Language of Sade and Masoch," says, "In Sade the imperative and descriptive function of language transcends itself towards a pure demonstrative institutive function, and in Masoch towards a dialectical, mythical and persuasive function." In Chapter II, "The Role of Descriptions": "Of Masoch it can be said, as it cannot be of Sade, that no one has ever been so far with so little offence to decency." In Chapter III, "Are Sade and Masoch Complementary?" states that "The concurrence of sadism and masochism is fundamentally one of analogy only; their processes and their formation are entirely different." And in Chapter XI, "Sadistic Superego and Masochistic Ego," gives eleven propositions which account for the differences between sadism and masochism, namely:

1) Sadism is speculative-demonstrative; masochism, dialectical-imaginative.
2) Sadism operates with the negative and pure negation; masochism with disavowal and suspension.
3) Sadism operates by means of quantitative reiteration, masochism by means of qualitative suspense.
4) There is a masochism specific to the sadist and equally a sadism specific to the masochist, the one never combining with the other.
5) Sadism negates the mother and inflates the father; masochism disavows the mother and abolishes the father.
6) The role and significance of the fetish and the function of the fantasy are totally different in each case.

7) There is an aestheticism in masochism, while sadism is hostile to the aesthetic attitude.
8) Sadism is institutional, masochism contractual.
9) In sadism the superego and the process of identification play the primary role; masochism gives primacy to the ego and the process of idealization.
10) Sadism and masochism exhibit totally different forms of desexualization and resexualization.

1244.   Delon, Michel. Review of L'INVENTION DU CORPS LIBERTIN, by Marcel Hénaff. In DIX-HUITIEME SIECLE XI (1979): 514-515.

Reviews Hénaff's book, remarking that in this rich study Hénaff has been able to mix a precise explication of texte with theory: "C'est le mérite de Sade de soulever des questions essentielles, le mérite de M. H. de l'avoir montré avec une vigueur inaccoutumée."

1245.   Deprun, Jean. "Sade et la philosophie biologique de son temps." LE MARQUIS DE SADE. Paris: Librairie Armand Colin, 1968, pp. 189-205.

Proceedings of the colloquium on the marquis de Sade which took place in Aix-en-Provence on 19 and 20 February 1966. Compares Sade's thesis with that of the naturalists of his time. Sade divided the world into two types of people: victims and executioners, but with an added dimension; even in victims there is a tendency to wish to be the executioner, and violent deaths are necessary evils. "L'action prédatrice de l'homme et des animaux carnassiers borne donc utilement l'exubérance de la nature. . . . L'homme et les carnassiers servent les desseins de la nature en prévenant des ruptures d'équilibre nuisibles en fin de compte aux dévoreurs comme aux dévorés." Concludes that the diachronic theory of crime was not a direct expression of Sade's personal vision but an outcome of the scientific and philosophic views of eighteenth-century biology. "Sade l'a accentuée, radicalisée, éclairée à l'ardent foyer de ses passions. Il ne l'a pas crée."

1246.   Desnos, Robert. "Sade." In DE L'EROTISME CONSIDERE DANS SES MANIFESTATIONS ECRITES ET DU POINT DE VUE DE

L'ESPRIT MODERNE.     Paris:      Editions Cercle des Arts,
n.d. 113 p.

Passes  in review some of the authors who have written
erotic novels.     Mentions,  in  particular,  Guillaume
Apollinaire,  Pierre  Louys,  Joris Huysmans,  Charles
Baudelaire,  Théophile  Gautier,  Andréa  de  Nerciat,
Giovanni  Casanova,  Faublas,  Crébillon fils,  et al.
About Sade, states that all of our present aspirations
have  been  formulated  by him when he  first  saw  in
sexual life the basis to well-adjusted  living.    Also
believes that the works of Sade had a great influence.
"Cette influence ne se borne d'ailleurs pas à l'esprit
mais encore à la forme.  Nulle n'est plus actuelle que
la  prose  de Sade. . . .    Du point de vue  érotique,
l'oeuvre  de  Sade  est  une  oeuvre  supérieurement
intellectuelle.  Quelles que soient les raisons qui la
provoquèrent,  érotomanie ou impossibilité  matérielle
[prison]  de  vie active,  elle est une création  d'un
universe absolument nouveau."

1247.   Didier, Béatrice.    "Sade dramaturge de ses 'carceri.'"
        NOUVELLE REVUE FRANCAISE 36 (December 1970): 72-86.

        Connects  the  sufferings of some of  Sade's  literary
        victims  to  Sade  himself,  who  spoke  of  "chains,"
        "wounds," "blood."  But Sade is better off  than  the
        heroes  he describes,  for he can be superior to  them
        through  his  writings.    Justine does not  have  this
        liberating  means;  nor do many of Sade's  characters.
        Concludes:    "L'oeuvre  de  Sade  portait en  elle  la
        prison et le théâtre comme une nécessité.  Il est bien
        vraisemblable que,  n'eut-il jamais connu Vincennes ni
        la Bastille, le marquis aurait enfermé ses personnages
        dans la pierre des prisons,  des maisons fortes ou des
        châteaux . . . or la prison de pierre, comme la prison
        du verbe,  est ambiguë chez Sade:   l'une et  l'autre
        l'enferment  et le libèrent.    Et les trois 'mystères'
        de  cette existence--au sens ou l'on parle  des  trois
        mysteres du Rosaire:   joyeux,  douloureux,  glorieux--
        sont  bien  inscrits en ces trois temps:   libertinage,
        prison,  écriture.    Le libertinage a  certainement
        permis  cette  seconde  naissance--en attendant  la
        troisième par l'écriture,  cette seconde naissance qui
        est  à  la fois joie sensorielle d'être,  mais  aussi
        prise  de  conscience de soi  et  finalement  révolte
        contre  tous  les  interdits  sociaux  ou  moraux  qui
        empêchent l'homme d'être.   De tous ces interdits,  le

plus terrible est finalment celui que l'homme s'impose
à lui-même, en s'interdisant, par peur, par lâcheté,
d'être soi jusqu'au bout."

This was reprinted as Chapter I of SADE, published in
1976 by Gonthier.

1248. Dominique, Pierre. "L'Erotisme dans la littérature et
sa répression." Le CRAPOUILLOT, October 1963, pp. 2-
21.

Well-documented essay on eroticism in literature.
Presents an account of Sade's stay in the Bastille,
discusses the relationship of the Marquis with
Bonaparte and reports on the Editions J. J. Pauvert's
trial following the publication of several of Sade's
works. Concludes with a quote from the presentation
made by the defense attorney, Maître Maurice Garçon:
"Dans le même temps où le Parquet poursuit la JUSTINE,
on a jugé les passages que je viens de lire, dignes de
recevoir le prix Nobel. Ni l'une ni l'autre oeuvre ne
méritent cet excès de sévérité et cet excès de gloire.
Tirons seulement de ces lectures qu'il faut être
prudent avant de vouloir s'offusquer au nom de la
moralité publique."

1249. Dühren, Eugen (Dr.). "Notre däfinition du sadisme."
OBLIQUES 12-13 (1977): 269-275.

Subtitled "La prostitution et la vie sexuelle au
XVIIIè siècle; Les Aphrodisiaques, les cosmétiques,
les abortifs et les arcanes au XVIIIè siècle."
Believes that Sade made thorough investigation of
houses of prostitution in order to get some of his
information, especially in connection with
aphrodisiacs and birth control which, he claims,
already existed in some primitive form in the
eighteenth century. Investigates the whole matter
from the medical point of view and concludes with a
definition of sadism which he feels is valid in all
cases, a definition which can be applied to all forms
of algolagnia: "Le sadisme est la relation recherchée
à dessein, ou s'offrant par hasard, entre l'excitation
et la jouissance sexuelles et la réalisation véritable
ou seulement symbolique d'évènements terribles, de
faites épouvantables, et d'actions destructives qui
menacent la vie, la santé et la propriété de l'homme
et des autres êtres animés, et qui mettent en danger

ou annulent la continuité de choses inanimées; dans
toutes ces occurrences, l'homme qui en extrait un
plaisir sexuel peut en être l'auteur direct lui-même,
ou les fait produire par autrui, ou bien il n'en est
que le spectateur, ou enfin il est de gré ou de force
l'objet d'attaque de la part de ces agents."

1250. Duncan, Catherine. "First Steps in Eroticism." THE
MEANJIN QUARTERLY 21 (1972): 270-281.

Investigates the meanings of eroticism and discovers
at the end of her journey that Sade "incites in us a
Passion of Revolt, a desire—as imperative as any
erotic drive—to overthrow the tyranny of 'law and
order.'" Concludes that eroticism is "always a
transgression of the normal, an anarchist's plot to
arrive at the abnormal where, if only for one brief
May, the Master/slave complicity is broken, splintered
into the individualities of new relationships."

1251. Evola, Julius. "Le Marquis de Sade et la voie de la
main gauche." OBLIQUES 12-13 (1977): 255-258.

Excerpt from METAPHYSIQUE DU SEXE (Ed. Payot, 1959).
Claims that Sade's "sadism" is essentially cerebral.
Sade never took advantage of any situation during the
Terror of the French Revolution and was in fact on the
side of moderation, yet in his writings he recognizes
the power of evil forces. Nature seems to be bent on
destruction, and destruction is the first of its laws.
Once this is accepted, an inversion of all our values
becomes mandatory: "l'élèment négatif et destructeur
doit y être reconnu comme l'élément positif, comme
étant celui conforme non seulement à la nature, mais
aussi à la volonté divine, à l'ordre universel."

First published in METAPHYSIQUE DU SEXE. Paris:
Payot, 1959.

1252. Faye, Jean-Pierre. "Folie de la répression, répression
de la folie." CHANGE 32-33 (1977): 28-35.

At the International Congress of Psychoanalysis held
in Milan in December 1976, presented this article
which suggests, after new interpretative readings of
JULIETTE and JUSTINE, innovative exploratory methods
in the diagnosis of repressive madness.

1253. Faye, Jean-Pierre. "Juliette et la Père Duchesne, Foutre." In SADE, ECRIRE LA CRISE: COLLOQUE DE CERISY. Paris: Belfond, 1983, pp. 289-302.

Attempts to go beyond the text, to a parallel investigation of two words distinguished by two letters: BOUGRE and FOUTRE. Relates the FOUTRE to PERE DUCHESNE, not a father at all but a well known revolutionary review published during the French Revolution by Georges Hebert, who was guillotined by Robespierre. The title of the review LE PERE DUCHESNE implies "un bon bougre" whereas the writings found in it were very inflammatory and comparable to the philosophy advocated by Sade's Juliette.

1254. Flake, Otto. LE MARQUIS DE SADE. London: Davies, 1931. 230 p.

Presents the marquis de Sade as an unpleasant individual, "a negative phenomenon" deserving to be singled out for examination as an example of the seedy side of human nature. Suggests that many incidents written about in Sade's novels were not products of his wild imagination but events, perhaps magnified, that really took place and were parts of the "manners of the time." And in the first chapter, on sadism, writes: "Had Sade been a mere pornographist there would be nothing more tasteless than an attempt to attach any significance to him. Had he been mad, there would be no need to dwell on his life. But he was more than a pornographist, and he was not a lunatic. He was one of the great abnormal phenomena which are so much more valuable in the quest for knowledge of human nature than any normal man can be. Hopelessly ensnared in the web of sexuality, he is a subject for the investigators of this monstrous complex, and thus takes his place in the history of the mind."

Translated from the German by Edward Crankshaw.

1255. Flam, L. "Het Satanisme." NIEUW VLAAMS TIJDSCHRIFT 11 (1957): 1076-1088.

Cites passages from JUSTINE to defend thesis that Sade's atheism is nihilistic. Also states that satanisme in the moral sense takes on a different form in William Blake and Charles Baudelaire than in Sade or Jean Genet. Also sees difference in the existentialism of Sartre and that of Sade. Concludes: "Tegenover de ene oneigenlykleid, die van een hol klinkende moraal, plaast hij een andere, die van de nithollendre wreedheid, maar zonder het christendom is markies de Sade ondenkbaar."

1256.   Fletcher, John. "Sade and His Progeny." NEW DIRECTIONS IN LITERATURE. New York: Humanities Press, 1969, pp. 53-65.

States that Sade "was not only the forerunner of the modern sexologists, he also anticipated much that Freud was to systematize in psychological theory, and the visions of his remarkable poetic imagination have permanently enlarged and enriched the domain of the creative writer . . . it is hardly surprising, therefore, that the Surrealists idolized him, or that writers as diverse as Baudelaire, Flaubert, Swinburne, Apollinaire, Camus, Simone de Beauvoir, George Bataille, Maurice Blanchot, Pierre Klossowski, Pauline Reage, Giancarlo Marmori, Peter Weiss and Lawrence Durrell should have pondered on his works or followed his example."

1257.   Freedman, William. "Oral Passivity and Oral Sadism in Norris's MCTEAGUE." LITERATURE AND PSYCHOLOGY 30 (1980): 52-61.

Discusses McTeague's sadistic instinct as described in Frank Norris's MCTEAGUE, which dwells on degenerate transformations. States that McTeague is "more than the story of its principal characters. It is the story of a society whose tendencies, as Norris advised, are expressed through character." Very little connection with Sade.

1258.   Gallop, Jane. "The Critics' Exchange: Review of Exogamy and Incest." MODERN LANGUAGE NOTES 89 (1974): 1041-1045.

States that Josué Harari, in his article "Exogamy and Incest: De Sade's Structures of Kinship," attempts the worthwhile task of "talking seriously about Sade, of treating Sade as more than an anomaly, of lifting the restriction of interest in Sade to the sexual register as if that were a closed field of specialization. . . . Yet his attempt turns to

confusion as he doesn't seem ready to choose between
the view of Sade pointed to in his derivations from
structural anthropology, and a view of Sade that
glorifies the marquis as a tragic hero is doomed to
failure in his struggle to free egotistical primal man
from the bonds of culture."

1259. Garai, J. "L'Invasion du sadisme." LE NOUVEAU CANDIDE,
9 October 1966, pp. 4-8.

Stresses Sade's influence in the history of ideas
because he catalogued perversions at a time when most
writers were still collecting herbarium: "(Sade) se
dresse au carrefour de deux siècles comme un énorme
défi aux moeurs et au bon sens." Deplores the fact
that sadophilia and sadology occupy such a large place
in our lives.

1260. Garai, J. "Sade au Prisunic." LE NOUVEAU CANDIDE, 16
October 1966, pp. 47-50.

Contends that during the sixties sadomasochism invaded
every aspect of our daily lives; these tendencies
toward violence are reflected not only in books and
films but also in fashion--(includes fashion models
with chains and dog collars), and Sade's biography (by
Gilbert Lély) is now on sale in dime stores: "Qu'on
le déplore ou qu'on s'y résigne, notre demi-siècle
porte à la boutonnière l'oeillet noir du sadisme."

1261. Garbouj, Bechir. "L'Infraction didactique: Notes sur
la PHILOSOPHIE DANS LE BOUDOIR." DIX-HUITIEME SIECLE
12 (1980): 218-229.

Gives lessons on infraction centering on the
experimental theme stated in LA PHILOSOPHIE DANS LE
BOUDOIR: "Faire circuler le venin d'immoralité pour
déraciner les semences de la vertu." First lesson:
"L'inceste est la forme de sexualité la plus
naturelle." Second lesson: "La sexualité, impliquant
le contact avec d'autres corps, impose la necessité
que ceux-ci soient neutralisée." Concludes with an
extra dividend: "L'historien de la pensée de Sade
aura donc à penser le boudoir comme avancée théorico-
pratique. Le projet libertin s'enrichit de son propre
pervertissement avec, en prime, la possibilité d'un
ancrage effectif dans l'histoire qui se fait."

1262.   Gateau, Jean-Charles.   Review of SADE:  L'INVENTION DU
        CORPS LIBERTIN,  by Marcel Hénaff.   JOURNAL DE GENEVE
        (August 1980):  19-20.

1263.   Gauthier, Xavière.   "Sa perversion et son rapport et son
        rapport de destruction à la societé."   In  SURREALISME
        ET SEXUALITE.  Paris:  Gallimard, 1971, pp. 48-57.

        States  that  the  question  of  perversion  and  its
        relationship  to  society's destruction is  especially
        pertinent  to  Sade.    Perversions  can  only  have  a
        transgressive  value within a society which refuses   a
        certain type of behavior.   Moreover, it is not so much
        for  society that certain perversions are a danger   as
        for   the   human   species,   because   they   prevent
        propagation of the individual.   Also suggests that the
        stereotyped  woman,  object  of desire,  is  much  less
        interesting than the possibility of women who consider
        men  as both objects of contemplation and  possession.
        "Les  révolutionnaires  marxistes,   pour  leur  part,
        tendent  à  réduire la différenciation sexuelle  et  à
        éliminer  une  des 'vocations' attribuées à la  femme:
        celle   d'être   un  objet  de   désir.    Il   serait
        certainement plus intéressant qu'au contraire   l'homme
        puisse l'être, lui aussi, regardé comme tel."

1264.   George, André.   "Sade et le sadisme."   LES  NOUVELLES
        LITTERAIRES 1469 (27 October 1955):  1, 4.

        Gives a short report on Sade's literary fortune in the
        nineteenth  century  and calls Sade  "un  écrivain  du
        troisième ordre et ennuyeux quoique immoral."

1265.   Gillibert, Jean.   "L'emprise sadienne."   In SADE, ECRIRE
        LA  CRISE:   COLLOQUE DE CERISY.   Paris:   Belfond, 1983,
        pp. 277-287.

        Argues  that  violent crimes are necessary  to  insure
        cosmic equilibrium; this material necessity is imposed
        by  a  relationship of ascendancy between  nature  and
        "individuation."    Destruction must occur as a natural
        occurrence.    It  is taught to human beings by nature.
        Concludes:    "Le  sadien  se  soumet  à  la   volonté
        d'emprise  pour  nier.   Ce qu'il sent de  son  'être-
        mourir'--l'auto-destruction--demande      pourtant  une
        extrême  sensibilité à autrui.   Il  faut  encore  et
        surtout l'effacement narcissique,  et la démonstration
        nette de l'inutilité 'perditrice' de toute   inflation

subjective.   Du sensible à l'avènement de la présence
insensible,  l'humain  se déprend de lui-même.   C'est
certainement là qu'il est une figure  anthropophagique
de l'humain."

1266.  Goulemot,   Jean-Marie.    "Beau   marquis   parlez-nous
d'amour."   In  SADE,  ECRIRE LA CRISE:   COLLOQUE  DE
CERISY.  Paris:  Pierre Belfond, 1983, pp. 119-132.

Examines Sade's text as a type of aphrodisiac designed
to   incite  or  disturb  the   reader's   sensuality.
Suggests  that there are as many answers as there  are
readers,  each  of  whom  assents to  different  moral
infractions  on  the  basis  of  his  own  code.   Yet
concludes there are limits to these infractions in and
out of the sexual:  reading does not lead to incest or
murder.

First-rate article.  See also essay by J. M. Goulemot,
"Et  tout  le reste n'est que sadisme," in  NOUVELLES
LITTERAIRES 2527 (8 April 1976):  5.  (Not annotated.)

1267.  Gourmont,   Rémy   de.   "Le   sadisme."   PROMENADES
PHILOSOPHIQUES.   Paris:  Mercure de France, 1908, pp.
269-275.

Begins  with  the  notion that human  beings  have  an
abnormal type of animality and gives examples of love-
making  considered "normal" among  insects--e.g.,  the
female praying mantle eats the male  after mating,  as
a habit,  not as an act of cruelty--and concludes that
these standards cannot be applied to humans!

1268.  Guillemain,   Bernard.   "Sade était masochiste."  PSYCHE
83 (September 1953):  1124-1129.

Explains  Sade's  behavior  in terms  of  his  need to
suffer mingled with his fear/hatred of his  torturers.
Gives examples to support this contention.

1269.  Heine,  Maurice.   Foreword  to CENT VINGT JOURNEES  DE
SODOME OU L'ECOLE DU LIBERTINAGE.   Paris:  S.  and C.
aux dépens des bibliophiles souscripteurs,  1931,  pp.
Also  published as "Préface de l'édition de  1931"  in
the OEUVRES COMPLETES du marquis de Sade.  Vol.  XIII.

Stresses  the  importance of Sade on research done  on
man's sexual life.  Underscores the works done on this

subject in 1895 by Dr. R. Krafft-Ebing, in
PSYCHOPATHIA SEXUALIS and in 1904 by Iwan Bloch, a
Berlin psychiatrist pseudonym for Eugen Dühren. Then,
maps out his own plans for the publication of Sade's
works. Concludes: "Toute pensée sincère mérite le
respect, n'eut-elle d'autre tenant au monde que son
propre auteur. Celle tu marquis de Sade s'exprime ici
avec tant de force et d'autorité que la plupart de ses
ouvrages peuvent être assimilé à des paraphrases de
cette somme antérieure. . . ."

1270.  Heine, Maurice. "Regards sur l'enfer anthropoclassique."
       LE MINOTAURE, 15 June 1936.

1271.  Helpey. "Le marquis de Sade et le sadisme." Préface.
       LA PHILOSOPHIE DANS LE BOUDOIR. Sadopolis: Edition
       privée, aux dépens de la société des études sadiques,
       1975, pp. 5-40.

       Believes that while LA PHILOSOPHIE DANS LE BOUDOIR
       might not be Sade's main work, it is indubitably the
       one that outlines most clearly what is known as
       "sadism." States first that the marquis is far from
       being the madman imagined by Jules Janin, who wrote in
       1834 in the REVUE DE PARIS some fanciful details
       concerning the marquis's life. Reviews other
       inaccuracies and attempts to straighten out the facts.
       Confirms the story of the deep attachment Sade
       professed for his sister-in-law. Gives a detailed
       description of the assorted publications of JUSTINE,
       LA NOUVELLE JUSTINE, JULIETTE, LA PHILOSOPHIE DANS LE
       BOUDOIR and ZOLOE ET SES DEUX ACOLYTES.

1272.  Hénaff, Marcel. SADE, L'INVENTION DU CORPS LIBERTIN.
       Paris: Presses Universitaires de France, 1978. 336 p.

       Studies the highly delineated universe of excesses
       which is Sade's and questions the prodigious
       provocation it engenders. Indeed, the facts suggested
       in that fiction are never given, either as unshakable
       truths or as objects of emulation. In rather an
       incongruous way, Sade follows in the footsteps of
       Aristotle and Boileau and enunciates a limitless
       mimesis of nature. He takes Reason as a weapon and
       uses it to betray the esthetic canons: "En jouant
       l'hyper-rationalisme, Sade réintégre dans la raison ce
       dont elle ne veut rien savoir, ce dont le sacrifice
       garantit son officielle innocence et lui fait admettre

que l'horreur n'est pas son autre mais son effet le
plus constant. . . . Ce qui s'annonçait dans son texte
se réalise dans notre histoire.  Il fut en quelque
sorte l'archiviste de notre avenir.  Nous sommes
entrés dans l'exactitude et l'effectivité du corps
sadien:  du marché du sexe à l'ecrasement
concentrationnaire des corps, les modalités des
jouissances et des souffrances ont pris depuis leurs
formes ordinaires jusqu'aux paroxystiques, la figure
de son univers. . . .  Pourtant, si Sade nous étonne
d'avoir eu si TERRIBLEMENT raison, la question qui
inéluctablement revient à son sujet c'est de
déterminer en quoi il souhaitait ce monde fou. . . .
Un énoncé théorique enchassé dans une fiction est lui-
même une fiction, quels que soient ses effects de
persuasion. . . . Le dicible est toujours reversé dans
l'ordre de la loi (esthétique).  On peut représenter
la tyrannie le crime, le vol, le désir sous réserve de
sanction ou de rachat.  C'est là que Sade fait la
mauvaise tête, qu'il fait semblant de ne pas avoir
compris.  Il s'empare du droit formel de tout dire,
l'arrache au pacte qui en restreint l'exercice et
tente l'aventure inouie, en énonçant favorablement le
crime, le vice, l'injustice, de prospecter les limites
du supportable, de voir jusqu'où peut parler la
littérature."  See annotations of chapters II and IV
under titles "Tout dire ou l'encyclopédie de l'excès"
and "L'Espace du tableau et l'imaginable."

Reviewed by Philippe Roger in LA QUINZAINE LITTERAIRE
282 (1 July 1978):  18; and Jean-Charles Gateau in
JOURNAL DE GENEVE, 19-20 August 1978; and by Jean-
Marie Goulemot, LES NOUVELLES LITTERAIRES, 3 November
1977, p. 7.

1273. Herron, M.  "Meanings of Sadism and Masochism."
PSYCHOLOGICAL REPORTS 50 1 (1982): 199-202.

Gives a clinical definition of sadism and masochism
based on the readings (among others) of Sade's
JUSTINE; Freud's ESSAYS ON THE THEORY OF SEXUALITY
(1905); S. Reik's MASOCHISM IN MODERN MAN (1941);
Krafft-Ebing's PSYCHOPATHIS SEXUALIS (1900); Sacher-
Masoch's VENUS FURS (1965).

1274. Hesnard, André (Dr.).  "Rechercher le semblable
découvrir l'homme dans Sade." OEUVRES COMPLETES DU

MARQUIS DE SADE.   Vol. III.   Paris: Cercle du livre
précieux, 1963 and 1966, pp. 13-25.

(Hesnard is the former president of the French Society
of Psychoanalysis).   Describes some of the main tenets
of sadomasochism.   Sadism would only be an   excessive
development  of  an aggressive element in  the  sexual
instinct,  probably  related to an infantile phase  or
experience.   Does  not  diagnose a mental illness  in
Sade, only sees in him the wild imagination of a truly
unhappy man.  "Son être profond adhérait absolument et
autant  qu'à  son  genre d'érotisme,  à  sa  passion
existentielle   de  vérité  humaine.    Sa   sincérité
profonde,  inaltérable n'avait que la ressource de  la
démesure imaginaire et verbale pour affirmer,  dans le
comble de l'affranchissement éthique, son droit humain
à être lui-même et rien que lui."

1275.   Hesnard, André (Dr.).   "Réflexions sexologiques à propos
des  120  JOURNEES."  OEUVRES COMPLETES DU MARQUIS  DE
SADE.   Vol. XIII.   Paris: Cercle du livre précieux,
1964 and 1967, pp. xvii-xxiii.

Defines  in  medical  terms the  most  commonly  known
sexual  deviation:   sadomasochism.    Gives  several
typical  examples  but  stresses  the  fact  that
sexologists  have  not  only collected data of  the
numerous possibilities of sadism or masochism but have
also  tried  to  analyze  in  depth  such  perversion,
leading   to  the  conclusions  that  sadism  can  be
integrated  as  a masculine trait and masochism  as  a
feminine  element  and  that both can  be  tied  to  a
domination-submission duality.   And  both  types  of
aberration  are  allied to a kind of narcissism  which
leads to a moral sadism.   It is in this moral problem
that  Sade saw an individual's opposition to  society.
In filigrain, it is also Sade's inspiration for all of
his works.

1276.   Holland,  M. B.   Review of INTERSECTIONS by Jane Gallop.
FRENCH STUDIES  36 (1982):   360.

Review  of  INTERSECTIONS:   A  READING OF SADE  WITH
BATAILLE,  BLANCHOT,  AND  KLOSSOWSKI by Jane  Gallop,
published by the University of Nebraska  Press,  1981.
Observes   that   "Gallop's  work  will   satisfy   no
one. . . .  Nevertheless, in her lively exploration of
the ins and outs of whoring and sodomy,  she intimates

a fundamental pattern of textual behavior which no
theory of fiction has yet defined or even truly
recognized. Gallop has written a daringly original
book, and one which, having blazed its trail, may well
remain as a landmark."

1277. Hyde, Montgomery H. "The Pornography of Perversion." A
HISTORY OF PORNOGRAPHY. New York: Farrar, Straus and
Giroux, 1965, pp. 122-123.

Discusses the notion of perversion as illustrated in
Sade and others. States that "although his wife was
devoted to him he [Sade] much preferred the company of
her sister, with whom he lived and whom he idealized
in his novel JULIETTE. After her death he gave
himself up completely to a life of dissipation,
although his actual exploits were by no means as
terrible as those he liked to imagine and which he was
to describe in his books."

1278. Jacobus, (Dr.). LE MARQUIS DE SADE ET SON OEUVRE
DEVANT LA SCIENCE MEDICALE ET LA LITTERATURE MODERNE.
Paris: Charles Carrington, 1901. 480 p.

Attempts a study of Sade from four points of view:
literary, medical, philosophical, and social; analyzes
the main works in last half of the book. Warns
against the consequences of reading the "bloody"
novels of the marquis: "Je me contente de les
signaler et de faire toucher du doigt au lecteur, que
si ces ouvrages monstreux tombent entre les mains d'un
dégénéré inverti, ayant des gouts érotico-
sanguinaires, chez un sadiste né, la lecture de cet
ouvrage peut le conduire à des actes épouvantables
pour peu que le sujet en ait les moyens. C'est ce qui
rend la publication de ces ouvrages si redoutable et
l'on conçoit que n'importe quel pays ne puisse les
laisser circuler à l'air, car ils constituent un
danger public. . . ."

Gives "full description of Sade's novels and stories
'qu'on peut lire' and makes no mention of his more
important clandestine works." (Quoted from Cabeen,
item 8).

Reviewed by A. Cabanes, CHRONIQUE MEDICALE (1902):
802-803.

1279. Klossowski, Pierre. "Eléments d'une étude psychanalytique sur le Marquis de Sade." REVUE FRANCAISE DE PSYCHANALYSE 6 (1933): 458-474.

Attempts a psychoanalytic study of the marquis de Sade. First discusses the role of the father and the mother in Sade's works. States that in JUSTINE, JULIETTE, and THE PHILOSOPHIE DANS LE BOUDOIR, the mother always appears as a tyrannical idol and is reduced to a pleasurable object. As for the father, his attributes and privileges are sodomy and incest. Then discusses the meaning of evil (for Sade) but warns that it would be very risky to confuse--as it has often been done--the "sadistic" thinking of the marquis with the sadism of the characters depicted in his writings. Defines the Good as a static notion whereas evil is in essence dynamic, part of a Nature perpetually in motion and in the process of being transformed. Concludes that "si l'union amoureuse avec la mère a échoué, l'union avec le père a permis l'établissement d'une communion de l'individu et de la Nature au sein de l'ingratitude universelle."

1280. Klossowski, Pierre. "A Destructive Philosophy." YALE FRENCH STUDIES, 35 (December 1965): 61-79.

States: "In Sade's work the uneasy conscience of the debauched libertine represents a transitional state of mind between the conscience of the philosopher and of Nature. It offers at one and the same time those negative elements which Sadian thought, in its dialectical movement, makes great efforts to eliminate, and the positive elements which will make it possible to move beyond this intermediary state of mind in order to get to the atheistic and asocial philosophy of Nature and a moral system based on the idea of Nature as perpetual motion."

Also published as a preface to THE MARQUIS DE SADE: THE 120 DAYS OF SODOM (New York: Grove Press, 1966), pp. 65-86.

1281. Klossowski, Pierre. "Sous le masque de l'athéisme." Preface to LES CRIMES DE L'AMOUR. In OEUVRES COMPLETES DU MARQUIS DE SADE. Vol. X. Paris: Cercle du livre precieux, 1967.

Also published as Part III of SADE MON PROCHAIN. First-rate, very provocative essay. Stresses the special meaning of "virtue" for Sade who speaks "le langage d'un jansenisme larvé." States: "Toute l'oeuvre de Sade paraît bien n'être qu'un seul cri désespéré, lancé à l'image de la virginité inaccéssible, cri enveloppé et comme enchâssé dans un cantique de blasphèmes."

1282. Knight, G. Wilson. "Sadism and the Seraphic." In ITALIA LINGUISTICA NOUVA ED ANTICA: STUDI LINGUISTICI IN MEMORIA DI ORONZO PARLANGELI. Edited by Vittore & Ciro Santoro. Galatina: Congedo, 1976, pp. 226-237.

1283. Kreis, Bernard. "Le Marquis." L'ALSACE, 1 April 1964, pp. 5-6.

Stresses that from time immemorial man has been perverse if the occasion presented itself with immunity. This was the case of the Spaniards who according to a reputable historian, Bartholemy de las Cases, annihilated 20 million native Americans; the Hitlerian Holocaust and other such atrocities would be examples as well. In the eighteenth century, the prevalent optimism defending the goodness of man and faith in progress was labeled insane by Sade; the entire production of the marquis is nothing less than a gigantic refutation of his century's thinking: "A l'homme 'dialoguant' de Diderot, à celui 'herborisant' de Rousseau, Sade oppose le sien: brutal, cruel, jouissant de sa brutalité et de sa cruauté."

1284. Kulcsar, S. "De Sade and Eichmann." MENTAL HEALTH AND SOCIETY 3, nos. 1-2 (1976): 102-113.

Reports published in Tel Aviv University, from the Chaim Sheba Medical Center Department of Psychiatry. Quotes from Sade's JULIETTE; Simone de Beauvoir's "Faut-il brûler Sade?" and other selected writings; and numerous references to Sigmund Freud's COLLECTED WORKS.

1285. Laborde, Alice. "Etude du rituel sadique dans ses rapports avec les rituels des sociétés primitives." STUDIES IN EIGHTEENTH-CENTURY CULTURE. Vol. 4. Edited by Harold E. Pagliaro. Madison, Wis.: University of Wisconsin Press, 1975, pp. 109-117.

Compares the Sadian rituals to archaic rituals.
Interprets them as a technique to help man discover
some once known but now forgotten truths. "Le
romancier invite le lecteur à faire une sorte
d'exploration des possibles jusqu'à là limite non plus
seulement de son imagination mais de l'infini
mathématique." Concludes that Sade borrows from
ethnology, mathematics, some of the framework for his
writings; yet he frees himself by adding some of the
rigid details imposed by archaic rituals. This essay
is also part of a chapter entitled "Le Rituel Sadique"
from a book entitled SADE ROMANCIER published in Fall
1974 by Les Editions de la Baconnière (Neuchâtel-
Suisse) in the Collection Languages.

1286.  Laborde, Alice M. "Sade: L'Erotisme démystifié."
       L'ESPRIT CREATEUR 15 (1975): 438-448.

Discusses the place of eroticism in Sade's work.
Whereas in literature the norm is to write only what
can be read by the general reader, leaving to the
imagination the task of filling in the missing
details, Sade does the opposite. Skipping over the
"accepted," he dwells at length on what had been left
unsaid before. States that Sade uses erotic
situations as a narrative structure much as
conventional playwrights borrow conventional
scenarios. By contrast, Sade only uses one structure,
that of the erotic confrontation, which is endlessly
multiplied, allowing a total demystification of erotic
excesses. "Cet emploi de l'érotisme est de toutes les
subversions qu'il [Sade] s'est permises l'une des plus
efficaces. Le tour de force est d'avoir pu l'exposer
intellectuellement au fil de tant de pages et d'avoir
su garder une forme de cohérence entre le message
cognitif et la morphologie de message."

1287.  Laws, Dr.; Meyer, J.; Holmen, M. "Reduction of Sadistic
       Sexual Arousal by Olfactory Aversion--Case-study."
       BEHAVIOR RESEARCH AND THERAPY 16, no. 4 (1978): 281-
       285.

Reports from Atascadero (California) State Hospital
Sexual Behavior Laboratory. Contains fifteen
references to clinical psychiatrists, psychologists,
and behavior therapists.

1288.  Lély,  Gilbert.  "L'Almanach illusoire de M.  de  Sade."
       TEL QUEL 78 (1978):  58-62.

       Makes  some  comments on the covers requested by  Sade
       from  his wife.   States that there is little doubt on
       the  intended  use of these "étuis" which were  listed
       with   dates   in  an  annotated   document   entitled
       "Recapitulations."  This article is followed  by  the
       list written by Sade himself.

1289.  Levimakarius, L.  "Sade et Pasolini dans le cercle de la
       transgression."   HOMME ET SOCIETE 41-4 (1976):    273-
       275.

       Analyses the work of the film director Pasolini in the
       same  light  as  that of Sade;  both  were  intent  on
       transgression.

1290.  Lynch,  Lawrence  W.   THE  MARQUIS  DE  SADE.   Boston:
       Twayne Publishers, 1984.  150 p.

       Intends to show a rebellious Sade bent on  challenging
       the established order by fostering blasphemy, robbery,
       and  rape.   Believes  that the repeated additions  to
       JUSTINE  gave  this novel an epic  dimension  with  an
       "acutely  pornographic  nature."  Concludes with  more
       questions  than answers:   "Sade's revolt goes  beyond
       the usual paradoxes and questioning of values by other
       writers of his time.  Yet he leaves us with unanswered
       questions and contradictions.   If revolt is to be the
       new order of things,  what follows? His closed sphere
       of  operations can succeed for only a small  number  of
       oppressors.   The earliest lesson from the boudoir was
       the  defilement  of  all  that  is  sacred,   and  the
       rejection of that which was previously valued.   If it
       is natural to pursue limitless pleasure,  what is  the
       nature of those who are supposed to  participate?   If
       feminine  beauty  is  of  any value,  how  can  it  be
       continually  destroyed?   Sade does not answer all  of
       these questions."

1291.  Marchand,  Max.   DU MARQUIS DE SADE A ANDRE GIDE; ESSAI
       DE   CRITIQUE   PSYCHOPATHOLOGIQUE  ET  PSYCHOSEXUELLE.
       Oran:  Fouque, 1956.  145 p.

       Attempts  to explain the works of André Gide in  terms
       of Sade's and Rousseau's influences.  Deals especially
       with onanism and erotic  fetishism.   Concludes:   "La

méthode psychopathologie appliquée à Gide nous semble
aboutir a une compréhension de son oeuvre plus
parfaite que celle dont se réclament des admirateurs
trop indulgents."

1292. Marchand, Max. "Actualité du marquis de Sade." DU
MARQUIS DE SADE A ANDRE GIDE; ESSAI DE CRITIQUE
PSYCHOPATHOLOGIQUE ET PSYCHOSEXUELLE. Oran: Fouque,
1956, pp. 55-59.

In order to understand what is meant by "sadism,"
considers the life of the marquis de Sade. Advances
the thesis that sadists are found among passionate or
nervous people who express an abnormal "avidity" which
goes hand in hand with the vindication of a total
liberty. Considers sadism as sickness of intelligence
rather than a disorder of bodily oranization and
states that "dans l'oeuvre de Sade, nous trouvons
fréquemment des personnages qui témoignent de cette
déviation intellectuelle." Then applies many of the
traits of the sadistic person to André Gide.

1293. Marcuse, Herbert. "The Transformation of Sexuality into
Eros." EROS AND CIVILIZATION. A PHILOSOPHICAL INQUIRY
INTO FREUD. Boston: Beacon Press: 1966, pp. 197-221.

Investigates the transformation of the libido "from
sexuality constrained under genital supremacy to
erotization of the entire personality." Links
suppressed sexuality with sadistic and masochistic
orgies of concentration camp guards.

1294. Masson, André. "Note sur l'imagination sadique."
CAHIERS DU SUD 285 (1947): 715-716.

Indicates that there is nothing in Sade's books to
suggest the marquis was irrational. Stresses that
Sade was working solely on research on the laws of
eroticism and that this search took him to "the
franges de la poésie." See also annotation of
publication in CAHIERS DU SUD, item 42.

Two paragraphs on Sade's imagination where "domine
l'hyperbole d'une exigeante et saine sensualité."

1295. Mauriac, Claude. "En finir avec la sacralisation de
Sade?" FIGARO LITTERAIRE 1559 (3 April 1976): 14.

Reviews two publications, UNE ECRITURE DU DESIR, by Béatrice Didier, and LA PHILOSOPHIE DANS LE PRESSOIR, Philippe Roger. Suggests an end to the "sacralization" of Sade: "Il s'agit de sortir de cela et de l'érotisme de Sade. . . il nous ennuie, c'est un disciplinaire, un sergent du sexe, un agent-comptable des culs et de leurs équivalents."

1296.   May, Charles E. "Explorers in the Realm of Sex." In PROCEEDINGS OF THE FIFTH NATIONAL CONVENTION OF THE POPULAR CULTURAL ASSOCIATION, SAINT LOUIS, MISSOURI, March 20-22, 1975. Edited by Michael T. Marsden. Bowling Green, Ky.: Bowling Green State University Popular Press, 1975, pp. 1156-1174.

1297.   Moreau, Marcel. "Le Devoir de monstruosité." OBLIQUES 12-13 (1977): 15-18.

Sees in Sade a constant, never fulfilled, quest toward desire. To submit to that quest is the "devoir de monstruosité," an expression without any moral or immoral overtone but one which does have a didactic connotation: "assumer courageusement la part dangereuse, voire inadmissible et anti-social de nous-mêmes . . . en souscrivant au devoir de monstruosité, nous ne faisons qu'époumoner quelques réponses à la question centrale de notre plénitude."

1298.   Naville, Pierre. "Sade et l'érotisme d'aujourd'hui." LE MARQUIS DE SADE. Paris: Colin, 1968, pp. 289-305.

Proceedings of the Colloque of Aix-en-Provence of 19 and 20 February 1968. Sees in the multiple paths taken by Sade's thoughts one common source, which he calls "erotism" and defines as "une escalade permanente du désir qui s'assouvit à peine pour renaître aussitôt, qui n'est jamais trop compliqué, trop exagéré, trop libre, que rien ne saurait trop exciter, qui se perd et se retrouve dans une fantastique mathématique." However, contemporary eroticism is something else, with all its dependence on culpability and accepted frustrations; therefore far removed from the type of eroticism described--advocated--by Sade, who totally negated the notion of sin and defended the appeasement of desire with virtually no restrictions. Biological and social sciences are still in the process of evaluating the debt due to Sade.

1299. Norris, Margot. "Sadism and Masochism in two Kafka
      Stories: In DER STRAFKOLONIE and EIN HUNGERKUNSTLER."
      MODERN LANGUAGE NOTES 93 (1978): 430-447.

      Discusses "the symptoms of the psychological
      conditions known as sadism and masochism" in two of
      Kafka's short stories: IN DER STRAFKOLONIE and EIN
      HUNGERKUNSTLER. Does not specifically make a contrast
      with Sade's approach to the same topic.

1300. Pastoureau, Henri. "Du sado-masochisme aux philosophies
      de l'ambivalence." In OEUVRES COMPLETES DE MARQUIS DE
      SADE. Vol. XIII. Paris: Cercle du livre précieux,
      1964, pp. xxv-xli.

      First published as a preface to LES 120 JOURNEES DE
      SODOME OU L'ECOLE DU LIBERTINAGE. See annotation to
      the same article, published in translation in YALE
      FRENCH STUDIES 35 (1965): 48-60, item 50.

1301. Pastoureau, Henri. "Sado-Masochism and the Philosophies
      of Ambivalence." YALE FRENCH STUDIES 35 (December
      1965): 48-60.

      Deals with Sadian-psycho-sexology and gives many
      examples of the type of information psychologists,
      philosophers, and moralists have drawn from Sade's
      works. "Sadism," as it has been coined, means "the
      instinctive tendency to inflict pain, a tendency which
      may or may not bring about morbid manifestations."
      Whereas "masochism" is the acceptance of pain done to
      oneself (coined by Sacher-Masoch). Another term
      discussed in that article is "ambivalence," a term
      created by Eugen Bleuler in 1911 in a book called
      DEMENTIA PRAECOX ODER GRUPPE DER SCHIZOPHRENIA.
      Ambivalence is defined as "a disposition within the
      mind of the schizophrenic which allows him to express
      simultaneously two opposite psychic states."

1302. Paz, Octavio. THE BOW AND THE LYRE. Austin, Tex.:
      University of Texas Press, 1973, pp. 110 and 193.

      (Translated from the Italian by Ruth C. Simms; Italian
      title is EL ARCO Y LA LIRA.) States that in the
      marquis de Sade's world "the relation between victims
      and executioner is nonexistent; nothing destroys the
      libertine's loneliness because his victims turn into

objects. The pleasure of his executioners is pure and solitary. It is not really pleasure, but cold fury."

1303. Perceau, Louis. "Le marquis de Sade et le sadisme." Preface LA PHILOSOPHIE DANS LE BOUDOIR. Sadopolis [sic]: aux dépens de la Société des études sadiques, n.d.

1304. Peter, Colette C. "Maurrassisme, sadisme et nazisme." ESPRIT 411 (1972): 184-192.

Also published in CHARLES MAURRAS ET L'IDEOLOGIE D'ACTION FRANCAISE. Paris: Editions du Seuil, 1972, 220 p.

Compares Charles Maurras's political views with those of Sade. For both men, laws are an abuse of power against men and against nature; contrasts both writers' ideologies with that of the Nazi doctrine which advocated a confiscation of individual rights in the name of a social concept of liberty.

1305. Pizzorusso, Arnoldo. Review of LAUTREAMONT ET SADE, by Maurice Blanchot. REVUE DES LETTRES MODERNES 1 (1950): 157-160.

1306. Pompidou, Georges. "Interview." LE FIGARO LITTERAIRE, 1ᵉʳ septembre 1966, p. 9.

Brief allusion to Sade in an interview conducted by J. J. Pauvert. Question: "Que pensez-vous du sort fait aujourd'hui à l'érotisme après tant de savants commentaires sur la littérature et le mal, Sade ou Gilles de Rais?" Answer: "L'érotisme m'ennuie. Il a sa signification, bien sûr, et des sectateurs de grand talent. Il est peu d'artistes qui ne lui aient fait sa part. Mais, à dose répétée, ou élevé à la hauteur d'une philosophie de l'art ou de la vie, il a bien du mal à se frayer une voie entre la pornographie et la démence. Et la littérature érotique est d'une intolérable monotonie. Voyez Sade, précisement, malgré son indiscutable génie. J'ajoute que la place prise par l'érotisme dans l'art, la pensée et la littérature aujourd'hui, comme dans la vie d'ailleurs ne présage rien de bon, pour parler comme le docteur Knock. Les sociétés où l'érotisme s'étalait ont toutes mal fini."

1307. Revel, Jean-François. "Les succès du moi: Variations autour de la tentation de parler de Sade." PREUVES 208 (1968): 45-50.

> In this tongue-in-cheek article, compares the works of a critic to that of a sadistic libertine: both take enjoyment from someone who has no part in the pleasurable act. In a postscript and almost as an afterthought states: "Le jouisseur sadiste est avide d'un solipsisme toujours plus complet. Sade tourne donc complètement le dos à la sexualité moderne, dont il est lénifiant mais bête de la présenter comme un précurseur. Il est grand précisément à cause du contraire. . . . Le génie de Sade est d'avoir mis au service d'une sexualité en fait archaïque des moyens littéraires, une habileté dialectique et des ressources philosophiques secrétées par une époque de grande civilisation."

> Also published as a preface to THE 120 DAYS OF SODOM in THE COMPLETE WORKS, J. J. Pauvert edition, item 282.

1308. Ribon, J. F. "Le marquis de Sade: malade ou précurseur." NOUVELLE PRESSE MEDICALE, 6 April 1974.

> Discusses the work of the marquis as that of a man with a vision who foresaw some of the applications and methodology of contemporary sexual psychology.

1309. Robbe-Grillet, Alain. Preface to LA NOUVELLE JUSTINE. In OEUVRES COMPLETES DE SADE. Vol. XV. Paris: Cercle du livre précieux, 1967,

> Ask the questions "What is eroticism?" and "What is literature?" and concludes with the remarks that in literature "l'érotisme ne fait pas d'enfants, c'est un pur mouvement de l'esprit, un pur mouvement créateur qui, tel le séducteur de Kierkegaard, traverse le monde--c'est-à-dire le néant--sans y laisser de trace."

1310. Roger, Philippe. "Au nom de Sade." OBLIQUES 12-13 (1977): 23-27.

> Traces the etymology of the word "sadist" and breaks down the development into three stages: 1) the invention of the term "sadism" and its counterpart

"masochism"; 2) the extension of the word as a medical term into a myriad of contexts; and 3) the breaking away of "sadism" from its origins into a multitude of different meanings, the "hard core" of which is the image of the violent killer. States that the word "sadism" was coined by Krafft-Ebing in his work, PSYCHOPATHIA SEXUALIS (1865), for a category of perversion involving the derivation of pleasure through the infliction of pain. The term later became associated with "masochism," which serves as its antonym. Sigmund Freud also contributed to the term's ambiguity by assigning to it contradictory meanings. "Sadism" broke out of the purely clinical context and into literary usage via the work of Marcel Proust, who used it to describe the various objectionable traits of one of his characters, Charlus. "Sadism" has since evolved into a more nebulous term, whose multiplicity of applications seems to include the description of just about anything with a twinge of violence or ill-will.

1311. Roger, Philippe. "La pédagogie du libertinage chez Sade." BULLETIN DE LA SOCIETE DES PROFESSEURS FRANCAIS EN AMERIQUE, 1973.

1312. Rosolato, Guy. "Etude des perversions sexuelles à partir du fétichisme." In LE DESERT DE LA PERVERSION. Paris: Le Seuil, 1967.

1313. Rosolato, Guy. "Généalogie des perversions." L'INCONSCIENT 2; also in ESSAIS SUR LE SYMBOLISME. Paris: Gallimard, 1970.

1314. Rougemont, D. "Don Juan et Sade." L'AMOUR ET L'OCCIDENT. Paris: Plon, 1939, pp. 177-181.

States that the tactics of a Don Juan are based on rape and escape, whereas for Sade the existence of desire turns that "object" into the key to pleasure and liberty. Only murder of the love-object can thus give back this stolen liberty: "Le meurtre seul peut rétablir la liberté, mais le meurtre de ce qu'on aime, puisque c'est cela qui nous enchaîne."

1315. Rousseaux, André. "Littérature Sadiste." LE FIGARO LITTERAIRE 13 (8 February 1958): 2.

1316.  Ruff, Marcel. "Le fond de l'abime." L'ESPRIT DU MAL ET
       L'ESTHETIQUE BAUDELAIRIENNE. Paris:   Armand Colin,
       1955, pp. 47-62.

       Discusses the "spirit of evil" in some well-known
       eighteenth-century writers:  Crébillon fils, Marivaux,
       Prévost, Rousseau, Laclos, Cazotte, Restif de la
       Bretonne, Diderot, and Sade.   Defines algolagnia as
       the  desire to associate sensuous pleasure with
       suffering inflicted or received, at least in its
       symbolic or fictional representation. This perversion
       existed long before Sade wrote about it;  the author
       gives a list of works depicting acts of cruelty.
       Well-documented essay, giving numerous sources.

1317.  Sardou, V. "Lettre sur le marquis de Sade." CHRONIQUE
       MEDICALE, 15 December 1902, pp. 802-803, 807-808.

       Discusses in medical terms Sade's perplexing and
       probably apocryphal gesture:  demanding to have the
       most beautiful roses brought to him so that he could
       tear out the petals and scatter them in the slime of a
       latrine.

1318.  Sartre, Jean-Paul. "L'indifférence, le désir, la haine,
       le  sadisme." In L'ETRE ET LE  NEANT.   Paris:
       Gallimard, 1943, pp. 447-503.

       Presents a long discourse on sadism, which is defined
       as an engagement without the knowledge or precise
       notion of what is the consistency of that engagement.
       Also sees in sadism "un effort pour incarner Autrui
       par la violence et cette incarnation 'de force' doit
       être déjà appropriation et utilisation de l'autre."
       No mentions of specific works of Sade.

1319.  Serstevens, Albert.  "Le marquis de Sade." In ESCALES
       PARMI LES LIVRES.  Paris: Nouvelles éditions latines,
       1969, pp. 142-145.

       Devotes a few paragraphs to "ce pretendu novateur
       (qui) n'a rien inventé." Names several writers who
       wrote, before Sade, on sadism--Brantome, Saint-Simon,
       Tallemant des Reaux. Concedes that Sade was the first
       "à avoir délayé à l'infini ce sujet scabreux, à
       l'avoir poussé jusqu'au paroxysme, à avoir fait une
       théorie de ce qui n'est qu'un phénomène pathologique."
       Also  mentions  as  "erotic  novels"  Aretin's

RAGIONAMENTI, Andrea de Nerciat's APHRODITES, and John
Cleland's MEMOIRS OF FANNY HILL.

1320.  Sichère, Bernard.   "Pour en finir avec le 'Sadisme' et
       sa haine."  OBLIQUES 12-13 (1977):  69-78.

       States that Sade is the first modern writer to
       appreciate the tragedy of the individual as subject of
       desire and the first to write about desire in the
       Freudian sense, whereas previous materialists had only
       investigated the mechanisms of sensations or the
       empirical ethics of happiness. Suggests a
       rapprochement with Hegel:  "La vérité du maître, c'est
       l'esclave qui la détient."

1321.  Siegert, Michael.   DE SADE UND WIR: ZUR
       SEXUALOKONOMISCHEN.   PATHOLOGIE DES IMPERIALISMUS.
       Frankfurt-am-Main:  Makol-Verlag, 1971.  263 p.

       The author, a Marxist scholar, sees Sade as a radical
       satirist of his society's mores, a kind of prosecutor
       who unmasked former colonialism and capitalism.
       Writing about sexual aberrations, Sade was also a
       precursor of Freud in his analytical description of
       perversions and a forerunner of Nietzche in his
       proclamation of the rights of the strongest. Makes
       interesting comparison between Sade and Marx, going as
       far as seeing a congruence between some of Sade's
       texts and that of Marx and also between Hitler and
       Sade:  "Das, was die Faschismustheoretiker an Hitler
       nicht verstehen, der irrationale Rest, ist der
       undewusste Regress auf Sade. Wenn wir die
       massenpsychische Mechanik der grossen Gewaltmaschinen
       des Imperialismus begreifen wollen, mussen wir uns dem
       Werk Sades aussetzen."

1322.  Siomopoulos, V. and Goldsmith, J.  "Sadism Revisited."
       AMERICAN JOURNAL OF PSYCHOTHERAPY 30, no. 4 (1976):
       631-640.

       Discusses the program of forensic medicine at Illinois
       State Psychiatric Institute. Mentions many literary
       figures and works as well as medical ones: Sartre's
       INTIMACY; Dostoyevski's THE POSSESSED; Sade; Freud; E.
       Fromm; H. Ellis; Krafft-Ebing.

1323.  Smirnoff, Victor N.   "Pouvoir sexuel."  NOUVELLE REVUE
       DE PSYCHANALYSE, 8 Autumn 1973.

1324.  Soulié, Frédéric.  LES MEMOIRES DU DIABLE.  Paris:
       Ambroise Dupont, 1838.

       This six-volume memoir recounts in fictional form
       sadistic encounters but does not relate directly to
       Sade.  Of little interest.

1325.  Spang-Hanssen, Ebbe.  Review of SADE:  L'INVENTION DU
       CORPS LIBERTINE, by Marcel Hénaff.  ROMANTIC REVIEW 16
       (1981): 193-195.

1326.  Starke, Manfred.  "Sade."  BEITRAGE ZUR ROMANISCHEN
       PHILOLOGIE 8 (1969):  108-114.

       Writes a short autobiography of the marquis and tries
       to show that his life and works were a product of his
       time; yet claims that there was something new and
       original in his writings which were of interest to a
       blasé society in search of sensationalism:  what was
       new was sadism.  States:  "Sade bietet erstmals eine
       breite und unfassende Darstellung der Perversitaten,
       vomit, hundert Jahre vor Krafft-Ebing, die
       Sexualpsychopathie angebahnt wird."  Concludes with
       unanswered questions:  What were Sade's intentions
       when he wrote such unusual literature?  Did he intend
       to free men from some of their taboos or bring them a
       new kind of freedom?

1327.  Stéphane, Nelly.  "Morale et nature."  EUROPE 522 (1972):
       23-42.

       Sees in Sade a very moral man and in Juliette a
       virtuous character.  Juliette is terrified by the
       death of her sister and repents, renouncing all her
       possessions and entering a convent.  Sade, who
       suffered untold indignities from his mother-in-law,
       never took any steps toward revenge.  Concludes:  "Si
       notre époque qui favorise l'érotisme et tolère la
       pornographie interdit l'oeuvre de Sade, ce ne peut
       être à cause de son caractère licencieux.  Celui-ci
       n'est que le prétexte qui permet de proscrire des
       ouvrages jugés dangereux par la virulence de la
       critique qu'ils enferment."

1328.  Stockinger, Jacob.  "Homosexuality and the French
       Enlightenment."  In HOMOSEXUALITIES AND FRENCH
       LITERATURE:  CULTURAL CONTEXTS/CRITICAL TEXTS.  Edited

by George Stambolian and Elaine Marks.     Ithaca:
Cornell University Press, 1979, pp. 161-85.

Believes that no assessment of the status of
homosexuality in the Enlightenment can be made without
taking account of Sade's work and views.    Only in the
twentieth century has its importance and significance
begun to be understood.    Sade passed "from
incomprehension as the infamous marquis through
culthood as the 'divine marquis' and can finally be
viewed as a writer and thinker.    Even today, however,
he inspires paradox. . . .    It would be
erroneous . . . to see the homosexual legacy of the
age solely in terms of liberation."

1329.  Taxil, Léo.  "Le Sadisme."  In LA CORRUPTION FIN-DE-
       SIECLE.  Paris:  Georges Carre, 1894, pp. 213-245.

Deals at length with corruption, eighteenth-century
style, and in particular, discusses prostitution as it
was practiced by the marquis de Sade, "célèbre par ses
passions effrayantes."    Denounces many of the
practices of the day and concludes with a request for
the abolition of such customs.

1330.  Taylor, Robert E.  "The Marquis de Sade and the First
       Psycopathia Sexualis."  In AN ANALYSIS OF THE KINSEY
       REPORTS ON SEXUAL BEHVIOR IN THE HUMAN MALE AND
       FEMALE.  New York:  E. P. Dutton, 1954, pp. 193-210.

Gives much credit to Sade for his work on psychopathia
sexualis and as a precursor to both Richard von
Krafft-Ebing and Havelock Ellis.    States that Sade
"not only described in detail every sexual aberration
that modern science has since observed," but he also
attempted analyses and explanations: "Recognizes that
'sadism' has existed for thousands of years but that
Sade was the first to 'stress the total passion of
algolagnia.'"    Deplores contemporary mores: "our
officialdom, so warped by the puritanical aspect of
our culture as to believe that anything connected with
love and the human body must be 'dirty,' carefully
cuts away anything 'normal' from before our
eyes. . . ."    And concludes with a nod of gratitude
toward the scientists of today who advocate a
healthier attitude, including Sade, who "helped
greatly to pave the way when he had nothing but
daring, insight, and vision for his tools."

1331.   Taylor, Robert E. "The Sexpressive S in Sade and
        Sartre." YALE FRENCH STUDIES 11 (1953): 18-24.

        Stresses the fact that both Sade and Sartre wrote
        profusely on algolagnia: "Faire souffrir, c'est
        posséder et créer tout autant que détruire," wrote
        Sartre in BAUDELAIRE; in LA NOUVELLE JUSTINE Sade
        states: "Si la jouissance de la nature est la
        création, celle de l'homme qui détruit doit infiniment
        flatter la nature; or, elle ne réussit à ses créations
        que par des destructions. Il faut donc étonnamment
        détruire des hommes pour lui composer la voluptueuse
        jouissance d'en créer." But author concludes that
        even if sexual satisfaction and liberty are really
        synonymous (for Sade and Sartre) still "sexual
        satisfaction cannot of itself give a man personal
        liberty. Sartre's voice is more tired than that of
        [Sade] but it may be wiser."

1332.   Vannoy, Russelle. SEX WITHOUT LOVE: A PHILOSOPHICAL
        EXPLORATION. Buffalo: Prometheus, 1980.

        "The thesis of this book is that a sexual relationship
        between individuals who are not in love can be
        meaningful and fulfilling. Truly fulfilling sex
        occurs, so the author claims, when the act is pursued
        for its own sake and is not wedded to the commonly
        accepted form of love. In fact, erotic love is an
        impossibility, a contradiction. Some points of
        interest touched on in the discussion are
        masturbation, perversion, the orgasm, and privacy; and
        a chapter on four 'philosophers of love' (Singer,
        Schopenhauer, Freud, and Sartre). Connects the
        argument to some main lines of philosophical thought."
        (Quoted from PHILOSOPHER'S INDEX, item 15.)

1333.   Villeterque. "Article sur LES CRIMES DE L'AMOUR."
        JOURNAL DES SCIENCES ET DE LITTERATURE, No. 90, 22
        October 1800, pp. 281-284.

        Very short but negative review essay of LES CRIMES DE
        L'AMOUR. Sade wrote an answer which was published in
        a twenty-page pamphlet by Massé in 1800.

1334.   Villiers de l'Isle Adam, August. "Le sadisme anglais."
        In HISTOIRE INSOLITES. Paris: Librairie moderne, p.
        18.

1335.  Voivenel, Paul (Dr.).  "A propos de Sacher-Masoch." LE
       PROGRES MEDICAL, 1 (January 1917): 1-6

       Little essay containing some peremptory statements
       attacking mainly the German type of mind:  "Les
       Allemands sont à la fois et d'excellents soldats et
       facilement des pervertis sexuels. . . . On dirait que
       le boche n'est satisfait que quand il est flagellé et
       battu par ses dirigeants."  Describe Sade as an
       "adorable adolescent."

1336.  Weddington, William and Leventhal, B.  "Sadistic Abuse
       of Haloperidal." AMERICAN JOURNAL OF PSYCHIATRY 139,
       no. 1 (1982): 132-133.

       Comments on the overuse and abuse of some
       hallucinogenic drugs.

1337.  Weightman, John.  "King Phallus."  NEW YORK REVIEW OF
       BOOKS, 26 August 1965, pp. 5-6.

       Declares that it is easy to see why Sade, "after one
       hundred fifty years of clandestinity, has finally been
       brought out in the open again.  With the recent
       development of sexual frankness . . . in [Sade's]
       particular line, there is no one to touch him; he
       ranks as King Phallus. . . .  Sade seemed to write
       with his penis as Renoir said he painted with his."
       Concludes that Sade should be discounted as a writer.
       States:  "Sade's transcendent obscenity is an
       atheist's maniacal tribute to sexual energy conceived
       as an immanent divine or diabolical force.  This is,
       no doubt, why he has excited so many eminent writers
       whom one would have expected to be put off by the all
       pervading stench of blood, excrement, and sperm."

1338.  Weinberg, Ts.; Falk G.  "The Social Organization of
       Sadism and Masochism." DEVIANT BEHAVIOR 1, nos. 3-4
       (1980): 379-393.

       Reports on investigation of sexual aberrations.
       Contains sixteen references, to books including HAPPY
       HOOKER, GROUP SEX, GAY MEN, etc.

1339.  Willard, Nedd.  "Le génie et la folie à travers les
       oeuvres du marquis de Sade."  In LE GENIE ET LA FOLIE

AU XVIIIe SIECLE.  Paris:  Presses universitaires de
France, 1963, pp. 131-164.

Presents a literary schizophrenic Sade.  On the one
hand, mirror of his own century, his thinking
parallels that of Diderot and Mercier; on the other,
Sade presents the image of a very original artist, a
man tortured in an unfriendly universe who thought
human beings are vicious because they are a product of
nature and in its image.  Sade is the destroyer, par
excellence, of everything his contemporaries hold
dear.  Long before Nietzsche, he holds a theory of a
superman (who is not considered a madman):  "Il crée
une aristocratie de puissance:  puissance de
caractère, de pouvoir, de sensibilité, d'intelligence.
Le surhomme se fait une loi à lui-même, qui n'est pas
celle des autres.  C'est un homme qui ne se repose
jamais, qui est toujours en lutte contre la société et
contre ses semblables.  Cet homme a une conception de
la vie et même de la sensualité qui diffère de celle
de ses concitoyens."

1340.  X. (Dr. Jacobus).  LE MARQUIS DE SADE ET SON OEUVRE
DEVANT LA SCIENCE MEDICALE ET LA LITTERATURE MODERNE.
Paris: Carrington, 1901.

See annotation for item 1278, under Jacobus.

1341. André, Arlette. "Recherches sur l'épicurisme de Sade: Florville et Courval." TRANSACTIONS OF THE FOURTH INTERNATIONAL CONGRESS ON THE ENLIGHTENMENT. STUDIES ON VOLTAIRE AND THE EIGHTEENTH-CENTURY 151 (1976): 119-129.

Examines in detail Sade's romantic creation in FLORVILLE ET COURVAL, a work labelled as a chef d'oeuvre, and shows how the author's epicurism differs from that of his predecessors, especially Lucretius in DE RERUM NATURA, and that of his contemporaries, in particular Holbach in LE SYSTEME DE LA NATURE. Concludes: "FLORVILLE ET COURVAL montre comment l'histoire d'une femme frivole et voluptueuse peut aboutir à une méditation essentielle. Par-delà les complaisances équivoques, par-delà le scandale et le défi, l'érotisme littéraire peut comporter un message philsophique." In other words, in this short story, Sade attempts to present an applied version of his own brand of epicurism.

1342. Apollinaire, Guillaume. "Le divin Marquis." LES DIABLES AMOUREUX. Paris: Gallimard, 1964, pp. 179-232.

Much publicized essay written before World War I. Includes some scholarly data on Sade, analysis of his main works, and states: "Le marquis de Sade, cet esprit le plus libre qui ait encore existé, avait sur la femme des idées particulières et la voulait aussi libre que l'homme. Ces idées, que l'on dégagera quelque jour, ont donné naissance à un double roman: JUSTINE ET JULIETTE. Ce n'est pas au hasard que le marquis a choisi des héroïnes et non des héros. Justine, c'est l'ancienne femme, asservie, misérable et moins qu'humaine; Juliette, au contraire, représente la femme nouvelle qui l'entrevoyait, un être dont on n'a pas encore idée, qui se dégage de l'humanité, qui aura des ailes et qui renouvellera l'univers." Ends this first-rate essay with a quote from Sade: "Je ne m'adresse qu'à des gens capables de m'entendre, et ceux-là me liront sans danger."

1343. Baccolo, Luigi. CHE COSA HA VERAMENTE DETTO DE SADE. Roma: Ubaldini, 1970. 136 p.

Another first-rate publication from Italy on Sade.
Presents a comparative analysis of four versions of
JUSTINE (the first three by Sade and the fourth by
Restif de la Bretonne). Also discusses the theater,
Sade's passion at Charenton, and concludes with a
chapter appraising Sade's influence and fortune with a
quote from Benedetto Croce: "Il marchese de Sade
asserì dure e coraggiose verità, di quelle verità da
cui si suol torcere il viso, quasi che in tal modo si
riesca ad annullarle." See annotations of chapters I
and II under the titles "Un turista du nome Sade"
item 638 and "Le lettre del detenuto" item 844.

Reviewed by G. Cerruti, STUDI FRANCESI 15 (1971): 362.

1344. Bartolommei, Sergio. "ALINE ET VALCOUR: Pornoutopia e
'silenzio delle leggi' nel pensiero del marchese di
Sade." PENSIERO POLITICO: RIVISTA DI STORIA DELLE
IDEE POLITICHE E SOCIALI 9 (1976): 461-471.

States that in Sade's system one of the fundamental
dogmas of eighteenth century thought--the belief in
the goodness of human nature--is overturned and nature
is shown instead to be a disjointing, amoral and
irrational power. Concludes that Sade uses the
political message of the French Revolution to invoke
the silence of the laws, which do not guarantee the
practice of virtues but make more likely the exercise
of private vices.

Also published in STUDI SULL'UTOPIA. Ed. Luigi Firpo
(Florence, Italy: Olschki, 1977, pp. 87-106).

1345. Bataille, Georges. "Le secret de Sade, (II)." CRITIQUE
17 (1947): 304-312.

Suggests that by going beyond the boredom created by
the monotonous repetitions in the works of Sade in
general, and in LES 120 JOURNEES DE SODOME in
particular, one might have access to one of Sade's
most important secrets: "Il connut des états d'extase
et de déchaînement qui lui parurent pleins de sens à
l'égard des possibilités communes. . . . Chacun de
nous est visé personnellement; s'il n'a pas rompu avec
l'humanité, ce livre souille comme un blasphème et
comme une maladie du visage ce qu'il a de plus cher,
de plus saint. Mais s'il passe outre, il accède par

lui à une invivable région où l'être nu, sans espoir, se mesure seul à seul avec la lumière. C'est qu'en vérité ce livre est le seul où l'homme est égal à CE QUI EST. . . . Telle est la vérité fondamentale implicite dans l'oeuvre de Sade. . . . Mais cette vérité ne nous est donnée que nous mêlant. Il y a dans l'ENVERS qu'est le fond des choses tant d'horreur, de loudeur, que nous ne pouvons y accéder, en tous les sens des mots, que chassé à coups de fouet. Tel est le secret maudit de Sade. . . ."

1346. Bataille, Georges. Preface to JUSTINE, OU LES MALHEURS DE LA VERTU. Paris: Jean-Jacques Pauvert, 1955, pp. viii-xli.

Long preface to the second version of JUSTINE. Insists first on the paradoxical aspect of Sade's enterprise, which was doomed to fail from the start since Sade's apparent only request was to be rejected. Also analyzes the "divine," which is interpreted to be just as paradoxical as the vice which is inherent in mankind. Then observes that there is an aspect of human existence which tends toward duplicity: on the one hand, a fundamental worry about an honest living with concerns for children and principles of loyalty and, on the other, violence without pity; given the right conditions, the same men kill, rape, torture. But whereas civilized people talk, the barbarous are silent, which, translated, means that violence is without voice and common language cannot express violence. This leads to still another paradox, the language of Sade: "un langage désavouant la relation de celui qui parle avec les hommes auxquels il parle, en conséquence désavouant le langage même." First-rate preface.

1347. Bernard, Paul R. "Structure et composition dans LES INFORTUNES DE LA VERTU." LES BONNES FEUILLES 2, no. 2 (1973): 28-35.

From a close chronological analysis of events in LES INFORTUNES DE LA VERTU deduces a plan for the novel, a unified structure which begins with an introduction from an omniscient narrator and ends also with a recitative from the same omniscient narrator.

1348. Bloch, Iwan (Dr.) (pseudonym for Eugen Dühren). MARQUIS DE SADE'S ONE HUNDRED AND TWENTY DAYS OF SODOM

AND THE SEX LIFE IN THE FRENCH AGE OF DEBAUCHERY. Translated by Raymond Sabatier. New York: Falstaff Press, 1934.

1349. Bonneau, Alcide. "Juliette ou les prospérités du vice par le Marquis de Sade. In LA CURIOSITE LITTERAIRE ET BIBLIOGRAPHIQUE. Paris: Isidore Liseux, 1882, pp. 131-176.

Reviews JULIETTE and gives long quotation from the novel. Also includes an interesting comparison of Sade with P. J. Proudhon and comments: "Bien fin qui découvrirait quelque différence entre les théories du marquis de Sade et celles de P. J. Proudhon." Also publishes a poem, "Le fauve," which he calls an apology for Sade, in a book entitled VIRILITES (by Emile Chevé).

1350. Brissenden, R. F. "La Philosophie dans le boudoir; or A Young Lady's Entrance into the World." STUDIES IN EIGHTEENTH-CENTURY CULTURE 2 (1972): 113-141.

Compares Sade's JUSTINE, OU LES MALHEURS DE LA VERTU with Jane Austen's SENSE AND SENSIBILITY and finds the points of resemblance of some interest and significance. The implications of what those two authors wrote are disturbing. To Austen's excessive indulgence in sensibility, one must juxtapose the more ferocious and self-centered elements of Sade's inhumanity, "and any balanced view of mankind must somehow take them both into account. The Marquis de Sade, limited and horribly distorted though his own image of man may be, forces us as few other writers do to acknowledge this. But if we must return to Sade, we should also return to Jane Austen, for even in the slightest and most inconsequential of her works she offers us the reassurance that with wit, intelligence, and a sense of humour, it is possible, at least for most of the time, to contemplate and even bear the condition of being human."

1351. Brissenden, R. F. "LA PHILOSOPHIE DANS LE BOUDOIR; or A Young Lady's Entrance into the World." In VIRTUE IN DISTRESS: STUDIES IN THE NOVEL OF SENTIMENT FROM RICHARDSON TO SADE. New York: MacMillan Press, 1974, pp. 268-293.

Originally published in 1972 in STUDIES IN EIGHTEENTH-CENTURY CULTURE and incorporated in this book as Chapter 5.

Reviewed by John A. Dussinger, EIGHTEENTH-CENTURY STUDIES 9 (1976): 623-625.

1352.  Châtelet, Noëlle. "Juline." OBLIQUES 12-13 (1977): 61-63.

Investigates the different aspects of the twin characters of Justine and Juliette. Justine is humiliated not as a woman but because destiny (her credulity toward men and God) puts her in a position of weakness which facilitates the excess of others. Yet as soon as she speaks, Justine is heard; she conquers as long as she talks. As for Juliette, men are her victims, proving that power is not sexist but depends on personality. Describes the world in which the sisters live as a jungle of debauchery, a place filled with passions and perversions but finds no proof that both sisters are walking different paths. Both types of lives are cruel and torturous. Simply, they do not stumble upon the same places and they feel differently about them. Juliette experiences a voluptuous zeal while Justine emits a painful resistance.

1353.  Cottez, Henri. "Le livre du jour: JUSTINE OU LE MALHEUR DE LA VERTU." MERCURE DE FRANCE 1043 (JULY 1950): 567-572.

Gives a poor review of another edition of JUSTINE OU LES MALHEURS DE LA VERTU published in 1950: "JUSTINE est un roman d'une structure commune, devidant dans leur ordre les aventures du personnage principal, en une série d'épisodes liés de la manière la plus lâche. L'auteur ne se soucie pas d'une technique nouvelle: l'effort d'imagination est ailleurs." And states that the reader finds himself in the same position as Justine, cut off from any possible enjoyment or pleasurable participation: "Le plus dur, dans le destin de Justine, c'est moins les sévices, les blessures, la mort incessamment menacante, que l'humiliation, le ravalement de la condition féminine à l'état d'objet ou d'instrument de la mécanique des hommes."

1354.  Coulet, Henri. "La vie intérieure dans JUSTINE." In LE
       MARQUIS DE SADE. Paris: Colin, 1968, pp. 85-101.

       Proceedings of colloquium on the marquis de Sade, Aix-
       en-Provence, 19 and 20 February 1966. With a long
       analysis, reminds us that "sadism" is not a simple
       matter and that an author does not necessarily have to
       assume the characteristics of the heroes he created.
       They are products of his imagination, not of his
       experience. In fact, there are changes in the
       portrayal of some of his characters. This is
       especially true of the three versions of JUSTINE, in
       which one notes an evolution in the successive
       expressions of sadism. In the first version there is
       always the moral dilemma of how to behave when
       confronted by evil; the third version tends toward
       pornography. Obscenities are explicit. Sade inflicts
       on his readers a sort of degradation which is similar
       to the one a sadist inflicts on his victims. "Le
       récit à la première personne dans la première version,
       permettait une oeuvre bien équilibrée, le roman de la
       victime; le récit à la première personne dans la
       seconde version était, au contraire, une source
       d'invraisemblance, précisément parce que la victime
       parlait; le récit à la troisième personne, dans la
       troisième version, restitue au sadisme sa véritable
       portée philosophique et lui confère une puissante
       qualité romanesque . . . qui oblige le lecteur à
       prendre au sérieux l'âme délirante."

1355.  Didier, Béatrice. "L'Exotisme et la mise en question du
       système familial et moral dans le roman à la fin du
       XVIIIe siècle: Beckford, Sade, Potocki." In
       TRANSACTIONS OF THE FOURTH INTERNATIONAL CONGRESS ON
       THE ENGLIGHTENMENT. STUDIES ON VOLTAIRE AND THE
       EIGHTEENTH CENTURY, 152 (1976): 571-586.

       Examines several works, ALINE ET VALCOUR and LA
       PHILOSOPHIE DANS LE BOUDOIR by Sade, VATHEK by
       Beckford, and LE MANUSCRIPT TROUVE A SARAGOSSE by
       Potocki in order to show how exotism in eighteenth
       century literary production was used to combat
       prevalent prejudices concerning traditional moral
       systems. States that these three writers practiced
       writing as a revolt, a transgression, not as a genre.
       Concludes: "L'exotisme n'est pas constitué en genre
       comme la fantastique; le discours exotique est une
       écriture en liberté; au moment même où le colonialisme

naissant précisément tue cette liberté chez les
indigènes que décrit la littérature, la fantaisie
permet une certaine bonne conscience intemporelle."

1356.  Didier, Béatrice.  "Un roman baroque."  Preface to ALINE
ET VALCOUR.  Paris:  Livre de Poche, 1976, pp. 5-19.

Comments    on    the    crisscrossing    of    several
correspondences   in   this epistolary novel which   owes
its   sustained   interest   to   its   baroque   esthetic.
Complex,  diversified,  but never boring, "le roman le
plus varié, le plus romanesque de Sade."

1357.  Dussinger,  John A.   Review of VIRTUE  IN  DISTRESS:
STUDIES  IN THE NOVEL OF SENTIMENT FROM RICHARDSON  TO
SADE by R.  F. Brissenden.  EIGHTEENTH-CENTURY STUDIES
9,4 (1976):  623-625.

States  that  "if VIRTUE IN DISTRESS does  not  alter
substantially  the  specialist's familiarity with  the
subject,  it  does very well as a guide for  beginning
students.   But for fresh critical inquiry one  should
turn to Leo Braudy's essay in NOVEL 7 (1973) pp.  5-13
which    argues    effectively    against    Brissenden's
ideological method."

1358.  Ehrard,  Jean.   "Pour une lecture non sadienne de Sade:
mariage et demographie dans ALINE ET VALCOUR."   SADE,
ECRIRE   LA   CRISE:   COLLOQUE   DE   CERISY.    Paris:
Belfond, 1983, pp. 241-257.

Presents an in-depth analysis of ALINE ET  VALCOUR,  a
"manichean" and "polyphonic" novel.  Believes that the
worth  of  the  text  is to be found  in  the  complex
narrative    structure    which    eludes    simplistic
interpretations.   Concludes  that ALINE  ET  VALCOUR
lends  itself  to  more than  one  reading:   "lecture
moralisante et pathétique;  lecture libertine; lecture
'éclairée',  attentive aux thèmes caractéristiques  du
mouvement  des  Lumières,  comme le refus  des  tabous
religieux  ou  la légitimation du divorce."   Suggests
also the possibility of a feminist reading.

1359.  Fabre,  Jean.  "Sade et le roman noir."  In IDEES SUR LE
ROMAN:   DE  MADAME DE LAFAYETTE AU MARQUIS  DE  SADE.
Paris:  Klincksieck, 1979, pp. 166-194.

This reprint of a communication presented at the Colloquium on the marquis de Sade, Aix-en-Provence, 19 and 20 February 1966. See item 352.

Reviewed by Roland C. Rosbottom, FRENCH REVIEW 55, 4 (1982): 550-551.

1360. Fabre, Jean. Preface to CRIMES DE L'AMOUR. OEUVRES COMPLETES DU MARQUIS DE SADE. Paris: Cercle du livre précieux, 1964, pp. 195-216.

This first-rate preface analyzes Sade's ideas on the novel, then gives an appraisal of each of the eleven "nouvelles" making up the CRIMES DE L'AMOUR that are not presented in their proper order of importance. States: "Peu importe, au fond, le classement. Il ne s'agit pas de noter des exercices, du très médiocre au très bon, mais d'épier comment le plomb se change en or, de suivre le progrès d'une imagination créatrice qui s'exerce d'abord dans le vide, emprunte ensuite à la vieillerie romanesque ou l'affectation à la mode ses clichés et ses oripeaux, puis, peu à peu, s'émancipe et finit par réaliser cet accord entre l'idée artistique et la forme à quoi l'on reconnaît le chef-d'oeuvre. Pour valoriser ensuite tout le reste, il suffit de constater que le pire garantit le meilleur, et le prépare, et que les prétentions ou les erreurs de l'homme de lettres peuvent s'interpréter, dans le cas de Sade, comme les balbutiements du génie." And concludes that with EUGENIE DE FRANVAL, Sade had at last given a convincing illustration of his IDEE SUR LES ROMANS; he had written a masterpiece.

1361. Finas, Lucette. "Le choc de la baguette sur la peau du tambour." OBLIQUES 12-13 (1977): 65-77.

Gives a detailed analysis of FLORVILLE ET COURVAL. Insists in particular on Sade's expertise in handling misinformations and double meanings. In this type of Oedipus Rex of the feminine gender, Florville kills her mother, sleeps not only with her father but also with her son who is the father of the child she kills, and that is only a part of the events, handed her by fate and that occur while she is totally ignorant of her blood connections. In fact nothing in the novel is what it appears to be. Even names are misleading, for Courval is used for four people.

1362.  Fink, Béatrice.  "The Banquet as Phenomenon or Structure in Selected 18th-Century French Novels."  STUDIES ON VOLTAIRE AND THE EIGHTEENTH CENTURY 152 (1976):   729-740.

Investigates the "Banquet" generally as a "signifier" with multiple "signifieds" in eighteenth century French fiction but states that no repast can stand up to Sade's eating extravaganzas.  "Sadian fiction features megameals which energize its creatures and synergyze its fabric. . . . An important characteristic of Sadian prose is its alimentary parameter.  Nutrients enable the libertine to function like a well-lubricated machine.  Abnormal eating provides the wherewithal for dominance.  Meals serve as behaviour regulators or modifiers.  Food may be a sublimating agent but is primarily a necessary ingredient for sex:  he who does not eat cannot perform."

1363.  Florence, Jean.  "Sade et la littérature."  VIE INTELLECTUELLE, 15 February 1911, p. 11.

Discusses sadism in Sade's works and notes that inconsistencies fill his novels where the main idea is to prove that murder, sodomy, and incest are good and where the marquis only succeeds in boring us.

1364.  Foucault, Michel.  LES MOTS ET LES CHOSES, UNE ARCHEOLOGIE DES SCIENCES HUMAINES.  Paris: Gallimard, 1966.

States that, with Sade, the reign of representative discourse ended and that "possibly JUSTINE and JULIETTE are in the same position on the threshold of modern culture as that occupied by DON QUIXOTE between the Renaissance and Classicism."  English version, THE ORDER OF THINGS, was edited by R. D. Laing, and published by Random House in 1973.

1365.  Giraud, Raymond.  "The First JUSTINE."  YALE FRENCH STUDIES 35 (Winter 1965):  39-48.

Calls the first JUSTINE "an exceedingly distasteful story";  yet contends that "despite its many crudities and considerable intellectual confusion" it is a remarkable work.  By accepting Justine's own evaluations of her suffering, the reader finds

sympathy curtailed. She survives the worst
mishandling relatively unscathed and, always
forgiving, she is ready for conversation with her
tormenters "right after the perpetration of some
particularly ghastly assault on her body." Concludes
that "Sade's principal revelation is not the physical
abuses suffered by Justine, but the embarrassing
spectacle of what the sadist himself undergoes."

1366.  Heine, Maurice. "Le Marquis de Sade et le roman noir."
       NOUVELLE REVUE FRANCAISE 239 (1930): 190-206.

       Discusses the definition of the Gothic novel given by
       Sade in his CATALOGUE RAISONNE published in 1788. The
       marquis was well informed about English letters but
       does not seem to have been influenced by readings of
       English authors, since the plan of his most important
       work was already set in 1785; however, he may have
       been learning from the same models as his British
       contemporaries.

1367.  Heine, Maurice. "Le Plan primitif des INFORTUNES DE LA
       VERTU." OBLIQUES 12-13 (1977): 111-120.

       Gives a step-by-step creative methodology of the
       marquis de Sade's JUSTINE. First, there is a résumé
       of the topic in just four lines. Then there is an
       enumeration of the misfortunes of his character,
       Justine, and a progressive enlargement of each of the
       new headings. Also included are photocopies of Sade's
       manuscript, which is annuled after each expansion.

1368.  Heine, Maurice. "Promenade à travers le roman noir."
       MINOTAURE 5 (1934): 1-4.

       Defines the ROMAN NOIR as a "novel of terror and
       wonder" and, after commenting on the unduly pejorative
       connotation of the word "noir," presents several
       illustrations and a definition of BURLESQUE NOIR,
       REALISME NOIR, GOTHIQUE NOIR, FANTASTIQUE NOIR.

1369.  Heine, Maurice. "Actualités de Sade IV: De JUSTINE à
       LA NOUVELLE JUSTINE à travers les 'Petites feuilles'
       inédites." LE SURREALISME AU SERVICE DE LA REVOLUTION
       5 (May 1933): 4-10.

       Gives many details concerning the composition of the
       JUSTINE of 1791. And furnishes a complete outline,

divided into sixteen notes, found in one hundred
eleven separate sheets sold at auction in Paris on 1
June 1926.

1370. Henniger, Gerd. MARQUIS DE SADE WERKE. Ausgewälht
übersetzt, mit Dokumentation und Nachwort. Augsburg:
Verlag Kurt Desch, 1965. 398 p.

Translation into German of JUSTINE, JULIETTE, LA
PHILOSOPHIE DANS LE BOUDOIR, ALINE ET VALCOUR, and LES
IDEES SUR LE ROMAN.  As an introduction gives a short
biography of Sade:  his youth (1740-1750);  his
schooling and military service (1750-1763);  his
marriage and the Arcueil affair (1763-1768);  the
Marseille affair (1769-1772); his fugitive years at
Lacoste and in Italy (1772-1778); his time as a
prisoner at Vincennes, the Bastille, and Charenton,
with a list of the works written during that period
(1778-1790); his activities during and after the
Revolution (1790-1800); and the last fourteen years
until his death (1801-1814).

1371. Klossowski, Pierre. "Justine et Juliette." Preface to
LA NOUVELLE JUSTINE.   In OEUVRES COMPLETES DU MARQUIS
DE SADE.   Vol. VI.    Paris: Cercle du livre précieux,
1963.

Compares JUSTINE and JULIETTE, two novels "à thèse,"
and suggests that the intent of these works is to
demonstrate that the adhesion to atheism demands an
absolute amorality and, as a positive consequence of
this atheism, Sade develops a metaphysic of universal
prostitution. All of this stems from a contradictory
principle: "La jouissance dans la destruction de
l'objet de la jouissance." Concludes that both
Justine and Juliette are in fact pleading for an
atheistic reason.

1372. Laborde, Alice M. "Sade: La dialectique du regard: La
marquise de Gange." ROMANIC REVIEW 60 (1969): 47-53.

Assigns a special place to LA MARQUISE DE GANGE in the
works of the marquis de Sade. Mentions that author
borrowed from classicism some forms of symbolism
sometimes found in Racine. Stresses the fact that the
world depicted by Sade is a world of abnormals and
lunatics; discusses at length the role played by the
eyes, the look, and, by extension, appearances: "Le

rôle joué par la vue dans ce roman dépasse toutes les
normes habituelles.   Il ne s'agit pas seulement de
décrire pour que le lecteur voie,  imagine d'une façon
frappante les scènes qui lui sont proposées;  il faut
dire  encore qu'une force,  un pouvoir symbolique sont
impartis à l'oeil.   L'oeil est le reflet des pensées,
des désirs et de la personnalité des personnages.  Les
effets  de  la vision sur les héros  et  ses victimes
forment   l'essentiel  du  message  de  Sade  dans  ce
roman. . . .   Le  thème  des  apparences   trompeuses
revient comme un leitmotiv."

1373.  Laborde,  Alice.   "Sade:   LA MARQUISE  DE  GANGE."
       SYMPOSIUM 23 (Spring 1969):   38-45.

       Sees  in that last work of Sade the same philosophical
       preoccupations  as  in  some  of  his  earlier  works:
       recurrent   is  the  theme  of  unhappy  virtue   and
       persecuted  innocence.    States  that LA MARQUISE  DE
       GANGE  was  probably written between 1807 and 1812  at
       Charenton.    Like  other Sadian characters,  the main
       character is blind.  This explains in part the limited
       importance Sade gives to psychological analysis in his
       novels;  however,  Sade excels in tactical  maneuvers:
       "A en juger par la correspondance du marquis, on reste
       convaincu,  en effet,  que les exercices de persuasion
       qui  remplissent  ses lettres furent  l'occasion d'un
       entrainement intensif.   On retrouve, d'autre part, le
       même  souci d'organisation qui caractérise les  autres
       contes  et  romans  de l'auteur.   Le héros  avant  de
       s'engager  dans l'execution de ses  noirceurs  déclare
       explicitement  ses  intentions  et  présente  même  un
       raccourci  de sa technique.   Il y a concordance entre
       la machination du monstre et la machination esthétique
       du créateur."

1374.  Laborde,  Alice M. SADE ROMANCIER.   Boudray:   La
       Baconnière, 1974. 193 p.

       States that,  along with demystification of our  moral
       and social codes,  Sade also questioned systematically
       the  means  of  expression at the  writer's  disposal.
       Concludes that Sade, by not imitating what is commonly
       called  reality  but  by  integrating  his  scientific
       knowledge,  his  philosophical interests and  esthetic
       intentions,  successfully  produced  a  coherent  but
       complex  and  dynamic creation.   Suggests  several
       avenues for further research.   "Cette oeuvre est  une

mine à peine reconnue. Le temps est venu de
l'explorer et de l'exploiter." Includes a fine
bibliography. See annotations of Chapters IV, V, VI,
under titles "Le Rituel sadique," "Le Tempts Sadien,"
and "La Notion d'isolisme in items ." See items 1285,
1782, and 975.

Reviewed by Johannes Thomas, ROMANISCHE FORSCHUNGEN
(1975): 167-169; Béatrice C. Fink, FRENCH REVIEW 49
(1975): 792-793; Anne Lacombe, ESPRIT CREATEUR 16,
no. 1 (Spring 1976): 80-81; J. S. Spink, FRENCH
STUDIES 30 (1976): 475-476; Françoise Laugaa, Traut,
REVUE D'HISTOIRE LITTERAIRE DE LA FRANCE 76 (1975):
484.

1375. Lacombe, Anne. "LES INFORTUNES DE LA VERTU, le conte et
la philosophie." L'ESPRIT CREATEUR 15 (1975): 425-
437.

Begins with an analysis of Sade's approache to the
novel as a new genre revolving around the notion that
virtue should be punished. To avoid repetition Sade
attempts to introduce varieties in the manner that
Justine meets her tormentors (and punishments for her
virtuous attitude). Indicates three elements which
make up the narration: 1) the plot with its enormous
potential as the story of Justine; 2) the remarks made
by Justine; 3) the discourse made by the libertines.
Concludes this outstanding article with an analysis of
the ending: "[Justine] est éliminée de la face du
monde par une phénomène naturel, comme si sa vertu
était vraiment une offence à la nature, et comme si
Sade voulait donner une dimension cosmique à ce
dénouement; car ce châtiment est logique et nécessaire
à l'interieur de la thèse des libertins qu'il vient
confirmer de manière éclatante. . . . Ce premier
dénouement sadien et fulgurant semble malheureusement
gâté et affaibli par un second dénouement présenté
comme la conséquence logique du premier. . . . Contre
toute cohérence psychologique Juliette se laisse
impressionner par l'example de sa soeur et décide de
renoncer au monde. . . . C'est du mauvais
Prévost. . . ."

1376. Lacroix, Paul. "Le marquis de Sade." In CURIOSITES DE
L'HISTOIRE DE FRANCE. Paris: Adolphe Delahaye
libraire, 1858, pp. 225-243.

In the fifth "Dissertation" discusses the publication of JUSTINE and observes that there might be a possibility that several non-fiction characters were used by Sade as models for the heroes of his books. Mentions in particular the Marechal of Retz, strangled during the reign of Louis XI, who had actually done, or so history has it, some of the atrocities depicted in Sade.

1377. Lafarge, Catherine. "Les Délices de l'amour de Restif de la Bretonne: Attaque efficace contre Sade?" In TRANSACTIONS OF THE FOURTH INTERNATIONAL CONGRESS ON THE ENLIGHTENMENT. STUDIES ON VOLTAIRE AND THE EIGHTEENTH CENTURY 153 (1976): 1245-1253.

Contrasts L'ANTI-JUSTINE OU LES DELICES DE L'AMOUR written by Restif de la Bretonne with Sade's JUSTINE. Declares that one of the main differences between the two works is the total absence in L'ANTI-JUSTINE of any philosophical discourse. On the contrary, Restif's aims are clearly stated: "Exciter les sens endormis de ceux qui voudront bien le lire." In other words, the two authors are different in their approach to the novel: "Dans les romans de Sade on s'intéresse aux rapports entre les personnages car ceux-ci ont parfois une vérité psychologique. . . . [Mais] L'ANTI-JUSTINE est un ouvrage salace et parodique, débarrassé de tout discours philosophique, composé d'une suite interminable de scènes orgiaques et écrit dans un style obscène. . . ." Concludes that Restif's attack on Sade qualifies only as a prank.

1378. Lebrun, A. "Sade et le roman noir: les dessous d'une mode." EL TECHO DE LA BALENA, April 1966.

1379. Leduc, Jean. "JUSTINE OU LES MALHEURS DE LA VERTU de Raban." REVUE D'HISTOIRE LITTERAIRE 71 (1971): 683-688.

Reviews a book entitled JUSTINE OU LES MALHEURS DE LA VERTU, written not by Sade but by Raban and probably published in 1836. This work does include a preface by the marquis de Sade and many similarities of plot. However, author concludes that: "L'intérêt du roman Raban ne réside évidemment pas dans sa qualité littéraire. Il est plutôt dans un témoignage quasi inconnu, semble-t-il, de l'influence du marquis de Sade dans la première moitié du dix-neuvième siècle."

1380.  Lee, Vera.  "The Sade Machine."  STUDIES ON VOLTAIRE AND
THE EIGHTEENTH CENTURY 98 (1972):  207-218.

Considers  the  intrinsic merit of Sade's "machine" and
develops criteria for appraisal.  Finds the structure
of his novels "both simple and apparent:  a visual
description  of  vice  alternates  with  the  verbal
justification of vice.  The physical and the abstract
succeed each other with see-saw regularity.  Unity and
continuity  are achieved only through this  mechanical
repetition throughout the works."  But argues that "on
the  philosophical side,  there is little hint of  any
logical development of ideas,  but,  rather,  an
oscillation  between one magnetic pole of a theory and
its  antithesis or counterpole."  Concludes  that  the
Sade  machine  is  "essentially an  onanistic  device,
originally  designed  to deal with  the  author's  own
sexual phantoms and fantasies."

1381.  Lély, Gilbert.  "Histoire secrète d'Isabelle de Bavière,
reine de France."  OBLIQUES 12-13 (1977):  155-161.

Describes  the manuscript of the historical  essay  on
Isabelle de Bavière which is presently in the archives
of  Xavier de Sade.  It contains a preface  in  which
Sade  wrote  that  he wanted to use  the  novel  genre
wisely  in that work:  "un sage et rare emploi de  la
manière du roman."

1382.  Lély, Gilbert.  Preface to LA MARQUISE DE GANGE.  Paris:
Union Générale d'Editions, 1971, pp. 7-12.

In this introduction to LA MARQUISE DE GANGE,  a novel
published anonymously,  states  that there can be  no
doubt about the paternity of the work:  it belongs to
Sade.  Also published in 1961 in the Ed. J. J. Pauvert
and  in  1967 in the OEUVRES COMPLETES DU  MARQUIS  DE
SADE, (Paris:  Cercle du livre précieux).

1383.  Lynch,  Lawrence W.  "Sade:  More Rules for the Novel."
In  EIGHTEENTH CENTURY FRENCH NOVELISTS AND THE NOVEL.
York,  S.C.:  French Literature Publishing, 1979, pp.
155-183.

Investigates  the most prevalent forms of  eighteenth-
century  novels and discusses some of Sade's views  of
his contemporaries.  Quotes well known sources such as

Georges May and Jean Rousset, who have done similar
analyses. Illustrates some of the contradictory
practices current among eighteenth-century authors who
denounced novel writing as a pernicious activity and
then indulged in the writing of novels themselves.

1384. Mauriac, Claude. "Sade déifié." In HOMMES ET IDEES
D'AUJOURD'HUI. Paris: Albin Michel, 1953, pp. 117-
130.

After reading and re-reading LES 120 JOURNEES DE
SODOME, LA PHILOSOPHIE DANS LE BOUDOIR, and JULIETTE,
states:

1) "Il me parut une fois de plus difficilement
compréhensible qu'ait semblé si riche à de bons
esprits l'effarante monotonie de cet érotisme
appliqué, presque toujours, non seulement sans
grandeur, mais encore sans génie, même et surtout dans
le Mal" (p. 119):

2) "Non qu'il faille dénier à Sade une certaine
grandeur et, assurément, du génie" (p. 119).

3) "Mais son génie, pathologique dans ses origines,
poétique dans sa forme et scientifique dans ses
conséquences est incontestable" (p. 128).

4) "Quoi qu'il en soit, nous n'en avons pas fini avec
les dieux de nos athées" (p. 130).

1385. May, Georges. "Novel Reader, Fiction Writer." YALE
FRENCH STUDIES 35 (December 1965) 5-11.

Because Sade was important in the history of moral and
psychological ideas and because he exposed his
theories in the novel, "raises the question of whether
his place in the history of the development of the
novel is not equally eminent." But concludes that
while Sade achieved "distinction as a philosopher, as
a moralist, as a poet, indeed, even as a prophet," and
in spite of the fact that his work was intensely
original, he still cannot claim any fame as a
novelist, even though he was one of the first writers
ever "to chose the novel as a medium through which to
express a startingly original and revolutionary view
of man and the universe."

1386. Mercier, Roger. "Sade et le thème des voyages dans
      ALINE ET VALCOUR." DIX-HUITIEME SIECLE (1969): 337-
      352.

      Discloses the list of travel books transferred, along
      with Sade, to the Bastille (1784) and assumes that the
      marquis was already then reading informative material
      to be incorporated in his novels. Human passions
      reach an unsavory extreme in his works whose structure
      is similar to that of numerous eighteenth-century
      works: "ALINE ET VALCOUR présente donc un caractère
      burlesque et parodique, mais la construction de
      l'intrigue n'est pas marquée par la négligence
      insouciante que l'on trouve habituellement dans les
      romans de ce genre, elle repose au contraire sur des
      correspondances habilement ménagées."

1387. Miller, Nancy K. "JULIETTE and the Posterity of
      Prosperity." L'ESPRIT CREATEUR 15 (1975): 413-424.

      Describes the transformation of Juliette and her
      apprenticeship to learn the type of life she espoused.
      Her self-development is achieved by a reversal of the
      valorization assigned to the cultural and literary
      conventions encoding femaleness, the positively marked
      status of daughter, wife, and mother. Denying all the
      values we hold dearest, her final victory is
      symbolized when she throws her own daughter into the
      fire and amounts to her total emancipation from the
      role structure of the family. However, "Juliette is
      constantly rewarded for her progress in transgression.
      Every crime affords her new respect." Concludes that
      Juliette is not punished for her sins (as Merteuil was
      in LES LIAISONS DANGEREUSES) because she is beyond the
      reach of society; once Juliette "has delivered herself
      of internalized oppression, she is free of
      opposition."

1388. Miller, Nancy K. "Novels of Innocence: Fictions of
      Loss." EIGHTEENTH-CENTURY STUDIES 11 (1978): 325-339.

      States that "the novels of innocence that attach the
      reader require the loss of illusions that comes from
      the sense of a text, of reading." Hence, Justine,
      like Cécile de Volanges in LES LIAISONS DANGEREUSES,
      an easy victim who clings to her ignorance, can be no
      more in the fiction than a thread in the larger
      context of textual strategy.

1389. Monsour, Bernard. "Sade et le roman." ARCHE 22
      (December 1946): 145-147.

      Investigates the stand taken by Sade as a critic,
      especially in connection with his work, IDEES SUR LES
      ROMANS.

1390. Nicoletti, Gianni. "Antropologia aristocratica: tra
      Laclos e Sade." In INTRODUZIONE ALLO STUDIO DLLO
      ROMANZO FRANCESE NEL SETTECENTO. Bari, Italy:
      Adriatica Editrice, 1967, pp. 169-194.

      Studies the French eighteenth-century novels from
      Prévost to Sade. Includes Crébillon fils, Madame de
      Graffigny, Jean-Jacques Rousseau, Laclos, and Sade.

1391. Pasi, Carlo. "Justine e il suo doppio." SAGGI E
      RICERCHE DI LETTERATURA FRANCESE 15 (1976): 183-207.

      Sees in Justine both the center of an insolvable
      conflict and the complementary side of Juliette:
      "L'uno e il riflesso rovesciato dell'altro." In the
      latter an arrogant libidinal attitude is a life force;
      in the former, virtue acts as a vibration of death.
      Sensibility, on the other hand, can be both a
      predisposition to virtue as well as vice. But the
      nucleus of sadistic erotism is narcissism: "Il
      sadismo nasce della negazione dell'altro. E il
      derivato del narcisismo primario. . . . La dualità di
      Justine si rispecchia nella dualità di Juliette. La
      corrente narcisistica circola nei due personaggi in
      maniera alternata." Concludes that Justine is the
      principle of reality through which it is possible to
      recuperate the principle of pleasure (Juliette).
      Through the removal (of Justine) Juliette reconquers
      for her own conscience the liberty of the inconscient.

1392. Paulhan, Jean. "Notes on LES INFORTUNES DE LA VERTU."
      NOUVELLE REVUE FRANCAISE 204 (September 1930): 414-17.

      On the occasion of the publication by Maurice Heine of
      LES INFORTUNES DE LA VERTU (Fourcade) laments that so
      few of Sade's works were in print.

1393. Perkins, M. L. "The Psychoanalytic merveilleux:
      Suspense in Sade's FLORVILLE ET COURVAL." SUB-STANCE
      13 (1976): 107-119.

Summarizes Sade's formula "for creating and maintaining suspense" thus: "while insisting to the utmost on the existential reality of the unusual and mysterious aspects of fated human experience under description, the novelist should at the same time invite the reader to find a parallel explanation for the extraordinary events of the story by the suggestion that the action may be given a symbolic, that is, emotional, psychological meaning." Suggests that the potential for interpretation in Sade is virtually limitless and, in his analysis, shows "the extreme depth and intricacy of Sade's knowledge of human nature and his power to derive from it a new form of suspense or what may be called psychoanalytic merveilleux." First-rate article.

1394. Robbe-Grillet, Alain. "L'ordre et son double." MAGAZINE LITTERAIRE 114 (June 1976): 22-23.

This article was originally a preface to LA NOUVELLE JUSTINE, published by J. J. Pauvert in the complete works of Sade in 1967.

1395. Rosbottom, Ronald C. Review of Jean Fabre, IDEES SUR LE ROMAN: De Madame de Lafayette au Marquis de Sade. (Paris: Klincksieck, 1979. 319 p.). In FRENCH REVIEW 55, no. 4 (1982): 550-551.

Gives a very favorable review of Jean Fabre's IDEES SUR LE ROMAN. Stresses the fact that Sade himself had an essay entitled IDEES SUR LE ROMAN and that Fabre rehabilitates this novelist, arguing that "[Sade] transformed, through parody and innovation, narrative fiction, paving the way for the transition to the romantic, Symbolic, and Surrealist fiction of the nineteenth and twentieth-centuries."

1396. Rustin, Jacques. "Definition et explications du roman libertin des Lumières." TRAVAUX DE LINGUISTIQUE ET DE LITTERATURE PUBLIES PAR LE CENTRE DE PHILOLOGIE ET DE LITTERATURE ROMANES DE L'UNIVERSITE DE STRASBOURG 16, no. 2 (1978): 27-34.

Somewhat misleading title: while in principle this is a study of the libertine novel of the eighteenth-century, it is in fact a restricted study that covers

a period ending with 1761, the year of the publication
of LA NOUVELLE HELOISE.

1397.   Sade, Madame de.   "Suite de réflexions sur le roman
        d'Aline et de Valcour." LETTRES NOUVELLES 1 (1953):
        198-204.

        Publishes the report written in June 1789 by Madame de
        Sade after reading her husband's manuscript, ALINE ET
        VALCOUR.  In this remarkable essay, Madame de Sade,
        the first (partial) reader of the marquis, makes some
        telling remarks:   "De quoi voulez-vous que l'on se
        serve pour juger un ouvrage qui est une production de
        l'esprit?. . . La sodomie est un crime contre la
        nature, puisqu'elle empêche la reproduction. . . . La
        nature n'a qu'une voix, dites-vous, qui parle à tous
        les hommes.  Pourquoi donc que ces hommes pensent
        différemment? . . . J'aime à la folie tout ce qui
        vient de toi."

1398.   Sexton, Joseph M., Jr.   "Sade as an Epistolary
        Novelist." LES BONNES FEUILLES 3, no. 1 (1974): 13-
        26.

        Attempts to assess the merits of Sade as an epistolary
        novelist with an analysis of ALINE ET VALCOUR, a
        "dynamic type of epistolary novel" of the "polylogue"
        variety.   Concludes that "though the novel is
        structurally weak in parts, due to the author's
        inconsistent use of epistolary forms, ALINE ET VALCOUR
        does have a powerful aesthetic unity brought about by
        an ingenious merging of both form and theme. . . .
        Through an inventive diversity of epistolary
        techniques, Sade offers the reader a startlingly
        pessimistic vision of a world whose moral certitudes
        have crumbled and where the only happiness is that
        which is illusory and momentary."

1399.   Stevenson, Lionel.   "Variétés of the Novel." STUDIES IN
        BURKE AND HIS TIME 13 (1972): 2251-2259.

        "A review essay of 12 eighteenth-century novels, 1760-
        1800, that form part of the Oxford English Novels
        series.  The novels reveal the moods, popular tastes,
        attitudes, and themes current during that period of
        turmoil, change, and conflict.   Sentimental
        humanitarianism, emotional excess, sadism, satiric
        rationalism, ironic comedy, Tory dogma, and doctrines

of liberty and equality all can be found somewhere in the 12 novels. The authors represented are William Beckford, Frances Burney, William Godwin, Richard Graves, Thomas Holcroft, Elizabeth Inchbald, Henry Mackenzie, Ann Radcliffe, Clara Reeve, Charlotte Smith, Tobias Smollett and Horace Walpole." Quoted from A. E. Wiederrecht in HISTORICAL ABSTRACTS, item 15.

1400. Thomas, Johannes. Review of SADE ROMANCIER, by Alice Laborde in REVUE FRANCAISE 87 (1975): 167-169.

1401. Uzanne, Octave. Préface sur l'oeuvre de D. A. F. de Sade. IDEE SUR LES ROMANS. Paris: Rouveyre, 1878.

Includes in this annotated edition of IDEE SUR LES ROMANS a short biography of Sade, along with some bibliographical information. Also includes some letters of Sade written between 1790 and 1793 and addressed to the Comédie Française.

1402. Veasey, R. G. "Libertinism and the Novel." In FRENCH LITERATURE AND ITS BACKGROUND--THE EIGHTEENTH CENTURY. Edited by John Cruickshank. London: Oxford University Press, 1968, pp. 148-162.

States that eighteenth-century libertinism developed "from a social game of love into a desperate and cruel battle of the sexes." In the novels of the period, women were in general trapped, prisoners of the male. In a discussion of literary production by Crébillon fils, Duclos, Laclos, and Sade, concludes that the "scenes of torture and extreme sexual perversion in Sade's novels complete the circle which began with the elegant yet patently cruel encounters of Crebillon's characters. From the beginning, libertinism contained the seeds of this total breakdown and negation of positive social values."

1403. Versini, Laurent. "De quelques noms de personnages dans le roman du XVIIIe siècle." REVUE D'HISTOIRE LITTERAIRE DE LA FRANCE 2 (1961): 177-187.

Studied the literary onomatopoesis of names in the eighteenth-century novels. Suggests that the resemblance was intentional. Cites especially syllables like VAL and COUR, i.e. Valcour and Valcourt, Valrose, Valmont, Valville, Clairval,

Fierval, Saint Val; or in the case of some heroines, the syllable "ange" as in Solange, Volange, Marsange, Senange, Volnange, and so on. Notes that the personalities of these characters were interchangeable. Not until the nineteenth century do we encounter in literature heroes of the stature of a Vautrin or a Fabrice with a unique personality and a unique name.

1404. Villers, Charles de. "Lettre sur le roman intitulé JUSTINE OU LES MALHEURS DE LA VERTU." LE SPECTATEUR DU NORD 4 (1977): 407-414.

This essay, in epistolary form, was addressed to an unknown lady. Reviews the novel JUSTINE, which he appraises as both a product and an instigation of the French revolutionary crisis. Also published, with a preface by Augustin Poulet-Malassis, in limited edition of 150 booklets of 27 pages in Paris, by J. Baur, in 1877.

1405. Werner, Stephen. "Diderot, Sade and the Gothic Novel." STUDIES ON VOLTAIRE AND THE EIGHTEENTH-CENTURY 114 (1973): 273-290.

Sees the Gothic novel, defined as a "mood of melancholy gloom, perverse eroticism, and delight in the supernatural," cutting across assorted fiction of the eighteenth-century. States that both Diderot and Sade make different and highly inventive use of the Gothic. Finds the beginnings of French Gothic with Prévost's CLEVELAND and Madame de Tencin's works, whereas Diderot's vision of the Gothic "relates to philosophe convictions about the equilibrium of nature." But the negation in Diderot's works is not similar to that of Sade. Concludes that "the general movement implied in French Gothic is evident. It goes from passive acquiescence to nature to an increasingly more confident way of dealing with it. It develops ideas about freedom which will culminate in Sade's ruthless assertions about how freedom is to be achieved through the negation of consciousness, self, and human life."

# K. POETRY

1406. Anonymous. "Review of Marquis de Sade, La Vérité,"
Paris: J. J. Pauvert. 1961. 30 p. STUDI FRANCESI 7
(1963): 563.

States that only 500 copies of this interesting and
precious work were published. The exact title of the
work is "La Vérité, pièce trouvée dans les papiers de
la Mettrie." Includes a poem of 136 alexandrines with
many corrections and cancellations. Sade is surely
the author of that piece; the use of La Mettrie's name
can be attributed to a safety factor. This poem
condenses Sade's doctrine and contains an
antireligious admission and an apology for integral
explosion. It is probably a work composed in 1788
during a stay at the Bastille. The manuscript was at
one time a part of the collection LA SICOTIERE, but
the review does not mention where it is at present.

1407. Breton, André. CLAIR DE TERRE. Paris: Editions des
cahiers d'art, 1934, p. 165.

Includes a poem about Sade:

Le marquis de Sade a regagné l'intérieur du volcan
en éruption
d'où il était venu.

1408. Brochier, Jean-Jacques. "Le langage et la démesure: le
poète." GAZETTE DE LAUSANNE 30 (February 1965): 18.

Not available.

1409. Cassou, Jean. "Poésie." NOUVELLES LITTERAIRES, 22
August 1930, p. 12.

Deals with the "poetic" aspects of Sade's writings.

1410. Char, René. "Sade." In COMMUNE PRESENCE. Paris:
Gallimard, 1964, p. 111.

Originally published in the collection LE MARTEAU SANS
MAITRE; here under the rubric, "HAINE DU PEU D'AMOUR"
is the poem entitled "Sade":

> Le pur sang ravi à la roseraie,
> Hèle les désirs écartés,
> Empire de la rose deshabillée,

1411. Chaumely, Jean. "Présentation d'un poème inconnu du marquis de Sade suivi d'une lettre de Mme de Sade." LES LETTRES NOUVELLES, April 1953, pp. 193-204.

Presents a poem by the marquis de Sade and remarks written by Madame de Sade on the novel ALINE ET VALCOUR.

1412. Chevé, Emile. VIRILITES. Paris: A. Lemerre, 1882.

Publishes a long poem entitled "Le Fauve," which compares human beings to ferocious animals who enjoy the sight of suffering in others. Alcide Bonneau describes the work as an apology of Sade.

> Oh! qu'il est dans le vrai, ce marquis, ce Satan,
> Qui mariant le sang, la fange et le blasphème,
> D'un Olympe de boue effroyable Titan,
> Dans la férocité mit le plaisir suprême!
> ...
> Marquis, ton livre est fort, et nul dans l'avenir
> Ne plongera jamais aussi bas sous l'infâme:
> Nul ne pourra jamais après toi réunir,
> En un pareil bouquet, tous les poisons de l'âme.

1413. Depaze, Joseph. LES QUATRE SATIRES OU LA FIN DU XVIIIe SIECLE. Paris: Le Moller, an VIII, pp. 20-21.

Outlines in satyrical form Sade's doctrine and concludes:

> Telle est, de point en point, son infâme doctrine.
> L'ami de la morale, en parcourant JUSTINE,
> Noir roman que l'enfer semble avoir inventé,
> Se trouble, et malgré lui demande, épouvanté,
> Comment le monstre affreux qui traça des peintures
> Ne l'a pas expié dans l'horreur des tortures?

1414. Eluard, Paul. Untitled. OBLIQUES 12-13 (1977): 141.

Reprints one page of "L'évidence poétique," published in LA VIE IMMEDIATE by Gallimard in 1968, pp. 9-17.

1415. Fleischmann, Wolfgang B. "The Divine Marquis under the Shadow of Lucretius." ROMANCE NOTES 4 (1963): 121-126.

Compares and contrasts Lucretius's DE RERUM NATURA with Sade's poem "LA VERITE." Both poems, of about equal lengths, "treat of two identical principal themes (condemnation of religion; glorification of physical love)." Sees in Sade's interpretation an important conceptual link between classic and romantic images of DE RERUM NATURA and believes that the Marquis de Sade was a pivotal, prophetic figure in the history of ideas. Reviewed anonymously in STUDI FRANCESI 7 (1963): 562.

1416. Herold, Jacques. Frontispice au poème La Vérité, eau forte, chez J. J. Pauvert, 1961. Listed by F. Rosart (in OBLIQUES 12-13 [1977]).

1417. Lély, Gilbert. "Le Château-Lyre." MA CIVILISATION. Paris: Maeght, 1947, pp. 57-67.

Publishes several poems dedicated to Sade and the castle of La Coste, and an essay in the vocative: "Adieu, Sade, voici l'aurore, Notre Dame de Lumière (sous sa robe de carmélite brûle une entaille impolluée); voici le Lubéron, galbe de vos désirs, le mont des sodomies limpides, l'épouse de l'azur, éprise aussi de vous."

1418. Roudaut, Jean. "Les exercices poétiques au XVIIIe siècle." CRITIQUE, June 1962, pp. 533-547.

Discusses eighteenth-century poetry, which is seen as a spiritual exercise of language and never as an expression of surreality. While this article was written after the publication by the Editions J. J. Pauvert (1961) of Sade's previously unpublished poem, "La vérité," it does not specifically relate to Sade's poetry.

1419. Swinburne, Algernon Charles. APOLOGIE DE SADE (In French). London: n.p., 1916.

In extremely poetic terms, describes Sade, the man-
phallus, at once sinister and incandescent, who,
beyond the pale of the Revolution, stood out amongst a
star-studded list of illustrious writers. "Approchez
et vous entendrez palpiter dans cette charogne boueuse
et sanglante des artères de l'âme universelle, des
veines gonflées de sang divin. Ce cloaque est tout
pétri d'azur; il y a dans ces latrines quelque chose
de Dieu."

1420. Villers, Charles de. "Sur la manière essentiellement
différente dont les poètes français et allemands
traitent l'amour." In Edmond Eggli L'EROTIQUE
COMPAREE. Paris: Librairie universitaire J. Gamber,
1927, pp. 176-198.

Contrasts the literary production of German and French
authors and concludes that licentious mores helped to
degrade both the language and the literature of
eighteenth-century France whereas the idealist
tradition of Kant influenced the German authors.

# L. POLITICS

1421. Agulhon, M. "Le colloque sur le marquis de Sade à la Faculté des Lettres d'Aix-en-Provence, février 1966." PROVENCE HISTORIQUE, January-March 1966, pp. 109-111.

Reports on the Sade Colloquium which took place in February 1966, at the Centre d'études et de Recherches sur le XVIIIème siècle at Aix-en-Provence. Presided over by André Bourde, the meeting lasted two days and was followed by a visit to the castle at Lacoste which belonged to the Sade family. Reports that during the congress the main topics of discussion were 1) the political atmosphere in Provence and 2) the state of prisons and imprisonment under the Old Regime.

1422. Astorg, Bertrand d'. "Sade." In INTRODUCTION AU MONDE DE LA TERREUR. Paris: Editions du seuil, 1945, pp. 1-66.

Compares Sade first to a youthful Saint-Just who at age twenty wrote ORGANT, a poem of 7,000 lines, and states that in both authors is found a concern for the elaboration of a new morality. Then contrasts Sade's political views with those of William Blake and Saint-Just. These three men in their revolutionary works demanded for mankind: "une liberté de chair, d'esprit et de destin qui ne lui a encore jamais été accordée." But points out that Sade was a dissident in his revolt. During the Terror, when killing became a safe and legal act, Sade refused to participate and advocated clemency.

1423. Baccolo, Luigi. "Sade e la Rivoluzione." TEMPO PRESENTE, June 1968, pp. 21-30.

States that Sade's revolutionary activities lend themselves to ambiguity. "Come dice Blamont in ALINE ET VALCOUR, bisogna 'sistematizzori' i propri vizi. E come dice Juliette, in una societa la spada sta meglio nelle mani dei singoli individui, con i loro interessi personali, che nelle mani della giustizia in cui si accumulano gli interessi di tutti i legislatori che dal tempo dei tempi dominano il mondo. E la libertà dell'eros che conta, la sola in definitiva su cui il Sade marchese e il Sade cittadino patevano trovarsi d'accordo."

1424.  Barba, Vincenzo.  SADE:  LA LIBERAZIONE IMPOSSIBLE.
       Florence: Nuova Italia. 1978, 317 p.

       Another top-notch publication from Italy by the author
       of  INTERPRETAZIONI DI SADE,  item 1552.  Includes  a
       biographical essay and appraisal of Sade's works.    16
       page  bibliography.    Reviewed by Emile Namer in REVUE
       PHILOSOPHIQUE, April-June 1979, pp. 226-227.

1425.  Baudot,  Marc-Antoine.    NOTES  HISTORIQUES  SUR  LA
       CONVENTION NATIONALE,   LE  DIRECTOIRE,  L'EMPIRE  ET
       L'EXIL DES VOTANTS.  Geneva:  Slatkine, 1974, p. 74.

       Accuses  Sade  of  being the author  of  books  "d'une
       monstrueuse  obscénité  et d'une  morale  diabolique."
       Also sees Sade as perverted but not crazy, even though
       he  was transferred to Charenton and declared  insane.
       Concludes  that  the story of persons declared  insane
       for political reasons is yet to be written.

1426.  Benedetti,  E.   Review of "Le marquis de  Sade,  auteur
       politique,"  by Gabriel Habert.   STUDI   FRANCESI  4
       (1960):   160.

       Reviews  article  in REVUE  INTERNATIONALE  D'HISTOIRE
       POLITIQUE  ET CONSTITUTIONNELLE 8 (1957):    147-213.
       Gives a list of classic authors whose books were found
       in  Sade's  library and states that the main  idea  of
       Sade's  system  can  ultimately  be  that  of  use  in
       political  science.   Concludes, "Si  il  sistema  di
       Rousseau poteva culminair in un socialismo utopistico,
       quello di Sade sfociava in un vago ordine comunistico,
       in  una  società egualitria.   Nell'ultima  parte  del
       saggio,  l'Autore si occupa delle idee economiche, del
       razzismo  e delle teorie premalthusiane del  Marchese,
       del suo disprezzo aristocratio per i GENS DE  ROBE,  e
       infine  delle  sue  particolari  idee  in  materia  di
       criminologia."

1427.  Blanchot, Maurice.  "L'Inconvenance majeure." Preface
       to FRANCAIS ENCORE UN EFFORT POUR ETRE  REPUBLICAINS.
       Paris: J. J. Pauvert, 1965, pp. 9-51.

       Gives  some  information intended to help  the  reader
       understand  this  text,  which  was  originally
       incorporated  by Sade in LA PHILOSOPHIE DANS  LE
       BOUDOIR.   In this first-rate article,  author states:
       "Avec  Sade--et à un trés  haut  point de  vérité

paradoxale--, nous avons le premier exemple de la manière dont écrire, la liberté d'écrire, peut coincider avec le mouvement de la liberté réelle, quand celle ci entre en crise et provoque une vacance d'histoire. . . . Pour se faire une idée des conceptions politiques de Sade, je crois qu'il suffit de citer peu de textes. Le titre même de l'opuscule, marqué par une invisible ironie, nous parle assez clairement. Il dit qu'il ne suffit pas d'être en république pour être republicain; ni d'avoir une constitution pour être en republique; ni enfin d'avoir des lois pour que l'acte constituant, ce pouvoir créateur persévère et nous maintienne en état de constitution permanente. Il faut faire un effort, et toujours encore un effort--là est l'invisible ironie."

1428. Bonnet, Jean-Claude. "Sade historien." In SADE, ECRIRE LA CRISE: COLLOQUE DE CERISY. Paris: Belfond, 1983, pp. 133-147.

States that, with perverse distortions, Sade reduces history to a cruel system which revolves around and repeats the mechanism of horror. ISABELLE DE BAVIERE illustrated that principle. Concludes: "Sade écrivant l'histoire d'Isabelle, c'est comme si Alfred Hitchcock nous racontait la vie de Staline. Paradoxalement, cette jouissance stérile de l'histoire qui se développe en un plaisir enfantin du massacre a un fort rendement historique et libère une vérité inouie sur le XVe siècle. Inversion criminelle du discours historique finalisé, cette histoire libinale se maintient à la surface logique des évènements. Appliquée à l'histoire, l'écriture sadienne s'allège et approfondit sa souveraine netteté."

1429. Borderie, Roger. "La question de Sade." OBLIQUES 12-13 (1977): 1-3.

Explains why this double issue of OBLIQUES is begun with a text by Pierre Guyotat: "une écriture qui ne soit ni une paraphrase, ni une exegèse du texte sadien mais qui exerce (sur la matière verbale cette fois) la violence créatrice que Sade avait jadis introduite dans le 'récit.'" Comments that in his work at "la section des Piques," Sade saved more heads than he immolates in his fiction.

1430. Bouloiseau, Marc. "Aux origines des légendes contre-révolutionnaires: Robespierre vu par les journaux satiriques (1789-1791)." ANNALES HISTORIQUES DE LA REVOLUTION FRANCAISE 30 (1958): 28-49.

"Satirical journals ran a systematic and unscrupulous campaign of denigration against patriot deputies, 1789-1791. The campaign against Maximilien Robespierre (1758-1794) began in November 1789 and reached its peak in mid- and late-1791. He was portrayed initially as a mediocre charlatan and demagogue, then, as he became more prominent, as an ambitious, corrupt sadist, driven by madness to destroy everything. Based on collections of journals in the Bibliothèque Nationale, the Bibliothèque de l'Arsenal, and the Bibliothèque le Pelletier." (Quoted from HISTORICAL ABSTRACTS [D. J. Nicholls] item 15).

1431. Brahimi, Denise. Review of SADE ET L'ESPRIT REPUBLICAIN, edited by Jacques Viard. In DIX-HUITIEME SIECLE 6 (1974): 350-351.

Proceedings of the Colloquium of Orleans which took place on 4 and 5 September 1970, (Paris: Klincksieck, 1972, 465 pp.) Includes one article about Sade by Jacques Roger and states about that work: "Sade, don't J. Roger étudie quelques récits, a le mérite de mettre en cause l'association trop rituelle entre république et vertu."

1432. Calder-Marshall, Arthur. "The Fate of a Fantasist." TIMES LITERARY SUPPLEMENT 76 (1977): 208.

Presents a mini-biography of Sade and states: "His PHILOSOPHY IN THE BOUDOIR and THE NEW JUSTINE took on a new dimension. Sexually as perverse as ever, they were denunciations of a tyranny of republicanism (and so, for posterity, of all totalitarian tyrannies, communist, fascist or personal)."

1433. Camus, Albert. "Absolute Negation." In THE REBEL. Translated by Anthony Bower. New York: Vintage Books, 1956, pp. 36-47.

Feels that Sade is admired today for reasons that have nothing to do with literature. Sade's inordinate thirst for a life he could not have led him to dream of universal destruction, negating a God which oppresses and denies mankind. Explains Sade's success today by "the dream that he had in common with contemporary thought: the demand for total freedom, and dehumanization coldly planned by the intelligence . . . two centuries ahead of his time and on a reduced scale, Sade extolled totalitarian societies in the name of unbridled freedom--which, in reality, rebellion does not demand."

1434. Dalmasso, Gianfranco. LA POLITICA DELL'IMAGINARIO: ROUSSEAU-SADE. Milan: Jaca Book, 1977. 160 p.

Interesting little book which discusses the place of imagination in politics. Suggests that the transgression of the laws is imaginary and therefore impossible. Also presents essays on enjoyment and language; pleasure and transgression; and the possibility of freedom of enjoyment in a republic. Concludes: "La libertà, e l'uguaglianza, che costituiscono l'atto politico, sono legate strutturalmente al desiderio e alla realtà dell' imaginario."

1435. Darnton, Robert. "Les papiers du marquis de Sade et la prise de la Bastille." ANNALES HISTORIQUES DE LA REVOLUTION FRANCAISE, October-December 1970, p. 666.

Reproduces a letter concerning the events of 14 July 1789 written by "Commissaire Chesnon" to Jean-Charles-Pierre Lenoir, of the Paris Police from 1774-1775 and 1776 to 1785. These papers were among those of J. Ch. Renoir and part of a lot of Manuscripts No. 1423 at the BIBLIOTHEQUE MUNICIPALE of Orléans. Recounts the retrieval of Sade's papers from the Bastille by Madame de Sade.

1436. Delon, Michel. Review of SADE, J'ECRIS TON NOM LIBERTE, by Jean Cherasse et Geneviève Guicheney. DIX-HUITIEME SIECLE 9 (1977): 460.

Briefly reviews the book by Cherasse and Guicheney (published by Pygmalion in 1976) and states: "Le texte vaut comme document sur la survivance aujourd'hui du mythe surréaliste de Sade. On doit également noter quelque fragments épistolaires inédits tirés de la collection X de Sade et quelques belles illustrations."

1437.  Delon, Michel.  Review of SADE ET SES MASQUES, by Roger
       Lacombe.  ANNALES  HISTORIQUES  DE  LA  REVOLUTION
       FRANCAISE, July-September 1977, pp. 482-483.

1438.  Delon, Michel.  "Sade thermidorien."  In SADE, ECRIRE LA
       CRISE:  COLLOQUE DE CERISY.  Paris:  Belfond, 1983,
       pp. 99-115.

       Suggests that Sade's works do not form a homogenous
       whole born of internal, personal needs but rather
       constitute a sort of itinerary, a constant effort to
       adapt to the order of the day:  "Force est de
       constater l'hétérogenéité des discours idéologiques
       brassés par la fiction sadienne qui les réduit tous à
       des stratégies de pouvoir."  Attempts to correlate
       some of Sade's texts to the political climate of the
       time.  But concludes with a warning of the necessity
       to read between the lines:  "Sade tente d'exprimer les
       plus vieux privilèges dans le vocabulaire des droits
       de l'homme, de dire le particularisme en termes
       d'universalité.  Son effort superpose l'élitisme du
       libertin et celui du poète maudit, comme si pouvaient
       coincider la réaction féodale et le sacre de
       l'écrivain."

1439.  Eluard, Paul.  "L'Intelligence révolutionnaire du
       Marquis de Sade."  CLARTE 6 (February 1927):  34.

       Sees Sade as a materialistic thinker, with a
       revolutionary intelligence, and a precursor of
       Proudhon, Fourier, Darwin, Malthus, and modern
       psychiatry, and "l'apôtre de la liberté la plus
       absolue, qui voulut que tous les hommes remontassent
       le cours de leurs instincts et de leur pensée, afin
       d'avoir le courage de se considérer tels qu'ils sont
       et de ne se plier qu'à des nécessités réelles."

1440.  Favre, Pierre.  SADE UTOPISTE: SEXUALITE, POUVOIR ET
       ETAT DANS LE ROMAN "ALINE ET VALCOUR."  Preface by J.
       de Soto.  Paris:  Presses universitaires de France,
       1967.  107 p.

       Examines two utopii, Butua and Tamor, described by
       Sade in detail and affording an overview of Sade's
       political stand:  "Se prêtant singulièrement, du fait
       de leur autonomie, à une étude fouillée des positions
       doctrinales de leur auteur, elles permettent

l'approche apparemment la plus ferme de la pensée
politique de Sade." Concedes that Sade did not
construct a coherent political system but concludes:
"Certaines de ses méditations et protestations,
percutantes sans doute parce que naissant d'une
expérience douloureusement vécue, peuvent fort bien
trouver une place dans une idéologie et dans des
réalisations politiques. Ainsi, ses suggestions quant
aux lois, ses réquisitoires contre les systèmes
pénaux, pour se limiter à deux exemples, n'ont rien
perdu de leur intérêt." In his conclusion, P. Favre
does not make any distinction between Sade, the
writer, and Sade, the man.

1441.  Faye, Jean-Pierre. "Changer la mort et la politique."
       OBLIQUES 12-13 (1977): 47-57.

       Attempts to reassess Sade's political activities and
       to contrast them with those of Robespierre and Saint-
       Just. "[LES ECRITS POLITIQUES] nous sont nécessaires
       pour voir s'aiguiser, par eux, tout à la fois les
       paradoxes du discours sadien et son hors-discours, qui
       le traverse par les contradictions de la Révolution,
       cette Révolution qui pourtant est parvenue à abolir la
       pratique tortionnaire en Europe, jusqu'au moment de
       l'avènement hitlérien et des procès staliniens, des
       guerres impérialistes et des internements
       psychiatriques spéciaux. La topographie entière du
       discours révolutionnaire n'a pas encore été
       rigoureusement explorée dans son mouvement générateur:
       depuis les plaidoyers contre la peine capitale de
       Duport et Robespierre, jusqu'au réquisitoire
       robespierriste prononcé pour imposer la mort de
       Danton."

1442.  Fink, Béatrice C. "The Case for a Political System in
       Sade." STUDIES ON VOLTAIRE AND THE EIGHTEENTH CENTURY
       88 (1972): 493-512.

       Questions the contention that because there are so
       many logical inconsistencies in his works, Sade may
       not be "qualified for membership in the fraternity of
       respectable political philosophers," the criteria for
       serious political philosophy "being a preoccupation
       with the phenomenon of power in society." Sees in his
       writings a strong Hobbesian influence and a
       significance in his denunciation of organized
       religion, and believes that Sade's uniqueness is in

the fact that he attacks lay morality by making
improper behavior commonplace. Hence he reinterprets
eighteenth-century moral relativism by giving a
special meaning to the repetitions found in his works.
While admitting some "shortcomings and ambiguities" in
Sade's political thoughts, nonetheless supports the
proposition that Sade deserves to be taken seriously
as a political thinker. "A political reading of his
works . . . reveals enough substance, originality and
coherence to warrant a reassessment of his meaning and
stature in the continuum of Western political
philosophy."

1443.  Glass, James M. "The Modernity of the Marquis de Sade:
A Question of Action and Life-style." POLITICAL
STUDIES 19 (1971): 303-315.

"Suggests that the study of de Sade may help focus
some meaning on the implications of the current
development of 'counter-cultures.' Much that
resembles de Sade's theory of rejection stands at the
core of the attempt of the 'youth culture' to redefine
and locate satisfying modes of Being. Considers
particularly de Sade's theory of authenticity, his
discussion of the nature of the psyche, his conception
of destruction and cruelty, and his views on the
French Revolution. Unlike the visions of Rousseau and
later of Marx, de Sade saw no possibility of man's
building a moral context for his existence, and thus
effectively challenging its present absurdity. His
radical alienation stood in stark contrast to the
conception of political possibility." (Quoted from M.
Harrison, in HISTORICAL ABSTRACTS item 15).

1444.  Goulemot, Jean-Marie. "Lecture politique d'ALINE ET
VALCOUR: Remarques sur la signification politique des
structures romanesques et des personnages." In LE
MARQUIS DE SADE. Paris: Librairie Armand Colin,
1968, pp. 115-139.

Proceedings of colloquium on the Marquis de Sade, Aix-
en-Provence, 19 and 20 February 1966. Analyzes Sade's
political thoughts in ALINE ET VALCOUR, a novel
written in 1788 which predicted, according to Sade,
the Revolution of 1789. However, the book was
published in 1793. Yet, it is more than a
philosophical work, and, unlike Sade's other novels,
which are monodic, it presents several visions. In

this polyphonic structure, each of the characters represents a different view: juxtaposed are the world of the absolute despot, that of the parasite, and that of the utopic feudal aristocrat. "Un point semble acquis: la dénonciation des Grands, qui apparaissait primordiale dans un premier niveau de lecture, a fait place à une mise en cause de la bourgeoisie. . . . Par une fixation due à son drame personnel, mais aussi par reflexe de classe, Sade rend les bourgeois parlementaires responsables du despotisme. . . . Mais dans le même temps, Sade est obligé de reconnaître à l'idéologie bourgeoise, telle qu'il l'imagine, une vérité. Elle est adaptée au monde réel et à son système économique."

1445. Gripari, Pierre. "Sade et la liberté." In CRITIQUE ET AUTOCRITIQUE. Lausanne: Eds. L'Age de l'Homme, 1981, pp. 135-139.

1446. Habert, Gabriel. "Le marquis de Sade, auteur politique." REVUE INTERNATIONALE D'HISTOIRE POLITIQUE ET CONSTITUTIONNELLE 27-28 (1957): 147-213.

Recapitulates some of the most common themes and ideas in Sade's works and clears the way for some new interpretations. Also discusses Sade's stand against the law and his stand on the judicial code and on a social contract. Compares Sade's ideas with the political thoughts of Rousseau, Montesquieu, Macchiavelli and Swift.

Reviewed by E. Beneditti, STUDI FRANCESI 4 (1960): 160.

1447. Lély, Gilbert. "Sade et la berline de Varennes, 24 juin 1791." MONDE NOUVEAU 104 (October 1956): 137-144.

Discusses the ADRESSE AU ROI DES FRANCAIS written by Sade and later noted in a letter to Gaufridi dated 5 December 1791. Whether or not Sade really threw that pamphlet on 24 June 1791 into the coach of the unfortunate Louis XVI is open to question.

1448. Manuel, Louis-Pierre. In LA BASTILLE DEVOILEE OU RECUEIL DE PIECES AUTHENTIQUES POUR SERVIR A SON HISTOIRE. Paris: Desenne, 1790.

Discussed the role played by Sade during the attack and fall of the Bastille fortress.

1449. Mascolo, Dionys. "Effrayante liberté." LE NOUVEL OBSERVATEUR, 16 March 1966, p. 38.

In answer to criticisms directed against THE NOUVEL OBSERVATEUR, a leftist publication accused of quoting Sade too often, author explains the meaning of "left," a political stand which demands liberty before all else even when that liberty can be--as in the case of Sade--frightening or even dangerous. Sade himself did not invent anything; he simply saw what is--and has always been--in all of us; furthermore, he had the strength to be free to the ultimate degree.

1450. Mead, William. "The marquis de Sade: Politics on a Human Scale." L'ESPRIT CREATEUR 3 (1963): 188-198.

Believes that Sade's political system was neither reasonable nor admissible but still worthy of attention because it is "a permanent gesture of defiance." States that Sade incorporated in his writings concepts of Montesquieu's natural law, Rousseau's social contract, Helvetius' considerations of the relativity of manners: "His thought in its elements may well be that of an entire century, but it comes to us distorted and altered by the very intensity with which he made each separate element his own and somehow unified what everyone could think in terms of what only he could feel." Concludes with the suggestion that the "integral" man will be quite different from us: "The imperious dictates of his nature, the impossibility for him of existing without satisfying his needs, will cause him to look upon a fixed government, with permanent laws and institutions, as an instrument of slavery."

1451. Peise, L. "Rovère et le marquis de Sade." REVUE HISTORIQUE DE LA REVOLUTION FRANCAISE 6 (1914): 70-81.

Discusses the stormy and brief relationship between Sade and Rovère, the Marquis de Fontvieille who acquired a maison-basse at Lacoste. Also publishes several letters revealing the nature of the transaction. Eventually, it seems, the Sade family bought back the property. The arrangement between Rovère and Sade was strenuous, and Rovère claimed that Sade was "l'être le plus vil, le plus abject, le plus infâme qui (il) connaisse."

1452. Pennequin, Jean. "D. A. F. de Sade, Pétition de la Section des Piques aux representants du peuple français." S.L.: Fata Morgana, 1976. (Listed by F. Rosart in OBLIQUES 12-13 [1977].)

1453. Roger, Jacques. "Sade et l'esprit républicain." In L'ESPRIT REPUBLICAIN. Paris: Klincksieck, 1972, pp. 189-199.

Proceedings of the Colloquium of Orléans, which took place on 4-5 September 1970. Investigates the works and stand of the marquis, not as a novelist but as a politician.

Reviewed by Denise Brahimi in DIX-HUITIEME SIECLE 6 (1974): 350-351.

1454. Royer, Jean-Michel and Siméon, Jean-Claude. "Le pamphlet: de Sade à Mitterand." LE CRAPOUILLOT 70 (1983): 4-8.

Special issue devoted to pamphlets published from the eighteenth-century to modern times. Begins with quotations from Sade's ADRESSE D'UN CITOYEN DE PARIS AU ROI DES FRANCAIS, dated 24 June 1791. Also includes an excerpt from a petition for the SECTION DES PIQUES dated 15 November 1793.

1455. Taylor, Robert E. Review of SADE ET SES MASQUES, by Roger Lacombe. In THE EIGHTEENTH CENTURY: A CURRENT BIBLIOGRAPHY (1979): 372.

States that "this study offers some remarkably fresh views on some of Sade's political thinking. Considering all sides of Sade and seeking political overtones throughout his works, Roger G. Lacombe has thrown light on the influence on Sade of certain political upheavals in Sweden, citing precise sources for the first time. Indeed, there is such a wealth of Swedish political history that Sade himself is scarcely mentioned in some chapters. But Lacombe shows how Sade turned the details of one Swedish revolt into a fictional episode in JULIETTE, and in ERNESTINE and OXTIERN. . . . Argues convincingly that

Sade's principal source of information was a booklet by Cadet-Gassicourt, LE TOMBEAU DE JACQUES MOLAY." Concludes with an appraisal of the second part of the book, which he considers disappointing.

1456. Wainhouse, Austryn. Foreword to JULIETTE. New York: Grove Press, 1968, pp. vii-x.

Reviews the publication history of Sade's JULIETTE. Concludes with the statement: "As a thinker, as a pamphleteer, as secretary and then president of his section in Paris, as a magistrate, Sade took an active part in the Revolution, and certainly took his risks: his concern with the Revolution was intense. . . . The Marquis de Sade wanted what no mere formal rearrangement could provide, what no modification of material and relative conditions can alone satisfy; he wanted a permanent insurrection of the spirit, an intimate revolution, a revolution within. He wanted what today revolution no longer holds impossible but holds to be a starting point as well as a final end: TO CHANGE MAN."

## M.   PREFACES AND POSTFACES

1457.  Adam, Antoine.   Préface aux LETTRES DE VINCENNES.   In
OEUVRES COMPLETES.   Vol. XXX.   Paris:   J. J. Pauvert,
1966, pp. i-xxi.

1458.  Aury, Dominique.   Préface au HISTORIETTES, CONTES ET
FABLIAUX.   In OEUVRES COMPLETES.   Ed. Jean-Jacques
Pauvert.  Vol. VII.  Paris:   1967.

1459.  Barret, Gaston.   JUSTINE.   Paris:   Ed. de la vieille
France, 1950.

Listed by F. Rosart in OBLIQUES 12-13 (1977).

1460.  Bataille, Georges.  Preface to JUSTINE, OU LES MALHEURS
DE LA VERTU.   Paris:  Jean-Jacques Pauvert, 1955, pp.
viii-xli.

1461.  Bataille, Georges.   "On Reading Sade."  Preface to ONE
HUNDRED AND TWENTY DAYS OF SODOM, OR THE ROMANCE OF
THE SCHOOL OF LIBERTINAGE.   Paris:  Olympia  Press,
1954.

1462.  Blanchot, Maurice.   "Essai sur Sade."  Postface à CHOIX
D'OEUVRES.   Paris:  Club Français du livre, 1953.

1463.  Blanchot, Maurice.   "L'Inconvenance majeure."  Preface
to FRANCAIS ENCORE UN EFFORT POUR ETRE  REPUBLICAINS.
Paris:  J. J. Pauvert, 1965, pp. 9-51.

1464.  Blanchot, Maurice.   Preface to ECRITS POLITIQUES.   In
OEUVRES COMPLETES DE SADE.   Vol. IX.   Paris:  J. J.
Pauvert, 1967.

1465.  Blanchot, Maurice.   "Sade."  Preface to LA NOUVELLE
JUSTINE.   In OEUVRES COMPLETES DU MARQUIS DE SADE.
Vol. VI.  Paris:  Cercle du livre précieux, 1963.

1466.  Bloch, Iwan (Dr.) (pseudonym for Eugen Dühren).
Foreword to CENT VINGT JOURNEES DE SODOME.   Paris:
Club des Bibliophiles, 1904;  Berlin:  Max Harrwitz,
1904.

1467.  Bonneau, Alcide.  Preface to JUSTINE OU LES MALHEURS DE
LA VERTU.  Paris:  Isidore Liseux, 1884.

1468.  Bonnefoy, Yves.  "La Cent vingt et unième journée."
       Postface to VIE DU MARQUIS DE SADE,  by Gilbert  Lély.
       In  OEUVRES  COMPLETES DU MARQUIS DE  SADE.   Vol. II.
       Paris: Cercle du livre précieux, 1962, pp. 677-685.

1469.  Bourdin, Paul.  Introduction to CORRESPONDANCE  INEDITE
       DU  MARQUIS  DE  SADE,  DE  SES  PROCHES,  ET  DE  SES
       FAMILIERS.  Paris:  Librairie de France, 1929; Geneva:
       Slatkine 1970.  450 p.

1470.  Brochier, Jean-Jacques.  "Sade et le langage."  Preface
       to  OEUVRES COMPLETES DU MARQUIS  DE  SADE.   Vol. XV.
       Paris: Cercle du livre précieux, 1964, pp. 511-519.

1471.  Caradec, François.   Notes for DIALOGUE ENTRE UN PRETRE
       ET UN MORIBOND.   Paris:   Les Presses Littéraires  de
       France, 1949.

1472.  Carteret, J. G.   Introduction  to MONSIEUR NICOLAS  by
       Restif de la Bretonne.  Paris: Michaud, n.d.

1473.  Chaprong, Henri.  HISTORIETTES. . . .  Paris:   1926.
       Listed by F. Rosart in OBLIQUES 12-13 (1977).

1474.  Chauvet.  L'ETOURDI.  Brussels: s.n. Summer 1882.

1475.  Chery.  JUSTINE.  En Hollande: chez  les  libraires
       associés, n.d.  Listed by F. Rosart.

1476.  Crosland, Margaret.   Introduction to SELECTED LETTERS.
       London: Peter Owen, 1965.

1477.  Daumas, Georges.   Preface  to  JOURNAL  INEDIT.   DEUX
       CAHIERS RETROUVES DU JOURNAL INEDIT DU MARQUIS DE SADE
       1807, 1808, 1814.  Paris: Gallimard, 1970.  183 pp.

1478.  Degrave,  Philippe.  LES  INFORTUNES.  Paris: Cercle
       européen du livre, 1970.

1479.  Dühren, Eugen (Dr.).  NEUE FORSCHUNGEN UBER DEN MARQUIS
       DE  SADE  UND  SEINE  ZEIT,   MIT  BESONDERER
       BERUCKSICHTIGUNG  DER SEXUALPHILOSOPHIE DE SADE'S  AUF
       GRUND  DES NEUE ENDECKTEN ORIGINAL-MANUSCRIPTES SEINES
       HAUPTWERKES Berlin:   Druck von Pass und Garleb, 1904,
       p. i-xxxii.

1480.  Esposito, Gianni.   OEUVRES.   Paris:  Club français du
       livre, 1953.

Listed by F. Rosart in OBLIQUES 12-13 (1977).

1481. Fabre, Jean.   Preface to ALINE ET VALCOUR.   OEUVRES
      COMPLETES DU MARQUIS DE SADE.   Vol. IV.   Paris: Cercle
      du livre précieux, 1964, pp. xi-xxiii.

1482. Fabre, Jean.   Preface to CRIMES DE L'AMOUR.   OEUVRES
      COMPLETES DU MARQUIS DE SADE.   Paris: Cercle du livre
      précieux, 1964, pp. 195-216.

1483. Fedida,   Pierre.   "Un érotisme de tête."   OEUVRES
      COMPLETES DU MARQUIS DE SADE.   Vol. XV.   Paris: Cercle
      du Livre précieux, 1967, pp. 613-625.

1484. France, Anatole.   "Notice."   In DORCI OU LA BIZARRERIE
      DU SORT.   Paris:   Charaway, 1881, pp. 7-29.

1485. Galey, Matthieu.   Preface to LA PHILOSOPHIE DANS LE
      BOUDOIR.   OEUVRES COMPLETES DE SADE.   Vol. IV.   Paris:
      Cercle du livre précieux, 1967, pp. i-ix.

1486. Gillibert,   Jean.   "Sade,   sadiste,   sadique-essai
      psychanalytique."   Preface   to   LES 120   JOURNEES   DE
      SODOME.    OEUVRES   COMPLETES   DU   MARQUIS   DE   SADE.
      Vol. XIII.   Paris:   Cercle  du livre précieux,   1967,
      pp. 279-288.

1487. Gourari, Liliane.   LES INFORTUNES. . . .   Paris:  Le
      globe, 1947.   Listed by F. Rosart.

1488. Hamel, Reginald.   Introduction to LA PHILOSOPHIE DANS LE
      BOUDOIR in OEUVRES COMPLETES.   Vol. I.   Montreal:
      Editions du Bélier, n.d.

1489. Heine, Maurice.   "Avant-propos."   In DIALOGUE ENTRE UN
      PRETRE ET UN MORIBOND.   Paris: Stendhal, 1926, pp. 9-
      32.

1490. Heine, Maurice.   Avertissement.   OEUVRES CHOISIES  ET
      PAGES MAGISTRALES DU MARQUIS DE SADE.   Paris: Editions
      du Trianon, 1933, pp. 55-66.

1491. Heine, Maurice.   Foreword to CENT VINGT JOURNEES  DE
      SODOME OU L'ECOLE DU LIBERTINAGE.   Paris:   S.  and C.
      aux dépens des bibliophiles souscripteurs,   1931.

1492.  Heine,    Maurice.    Foreword  to  HISTORIETTES,    CONTES,
       FABLIAUX.  Paris: Simon Kra, 1927.

1493.  Heine,  Maurice.    Preface  to CENT ONZE NOTES  POUR  LA
       NOUVELLE JUSTINE.    Paris:  Le Terrain Vague, 1956, no
       pagination.

1494.  Heine,  Maurice.    Preface  to  CENT VINGT  JOURNEES  DE
       SODOME.    OEUVRES  COMPLETES  DU  MARQUIS  DE  SADE.
       Vol. 13.    Paris:  Cercle du livre précieux,  1964 and
       1967.

1495.  Heine,  Maurice.    Preface to DIALOGUE ENTRE UN PRETRE ET
       UN MORIBOND.    OEUVRES COMPLETES DE  SADE.    Vol. VII.
       Paris: J. J. Pauvert, 1967.

1496.  Heine,  Maurice.    Preface to DIALOGUE ENTRE UN PRETRE ET
       UN  MORIBOND.    OEUVRES COMPLETES DU MARQUIS DE  SADE.
       Vol. XIV.  Paris: Cercle du livre précieux, 1967.

1497.  Heine,  Maurice.    Preface  to  INFORTUNES DE LA  VERTU.
       Paris: Editions Fourcade, 1930, pp. 1-24.

1498.  Heine,  Maurice.    Preface  to  INFORTUNES DE LA  VERTU.
       OEUVRES  COMPLETES  DU  MARQUIS  DE  SADE.    Vol. XIV.
       Paris: Cercle du livre précieux, 1963 and 1967.

1499.  Heine,  Maurice.    La Nouvelle JUSTINE OU LES MALHEURS DE
       LA  VERTU.    OEUVRES  COMPLETES DU  MARQUIS  DE  SADE.
       Vol. III.    Paris:  Cercle du livre précieux, 1963 and
       1966.

1500.  Heine,    Maurice.    Foreword  to  HISTORIETTES,    CONTES,
       FABLIAUX.  Paris: Simon Kra, 1927.

1501.  Herold,  Jacques.    LA  VANILLE ET LA MANTILLE.    Paris:
       Drosera, 1950.

1502.  Hesnard,   André   (Dr.).     "Rechercher  le   semblable
       découvrir  l'homme  dans Sade."  OEUVRES COMPLETES  DU
       MARQUIS DE SADE.    Vol.  III.    Paris: Cercle du livre
       précieux, 1963 and 1966, pp. 13-25.

1503.  Hesnard, André (Dr.).    "Réflexions sexologiques à propos
       des  120 JOURNEES."  OEUVRES COMPLETES DU MARQUIS DE
       SADE.    Vol.  XIII.    Paris: Cercle du livre précieux,
       1964 and 1967, pp. xvii-xxiii.

1504.  Hugo,   Valentine.   EUGENIE  DE  FRANVAL.   Paris:   G.
       Artigues, 1948.

1505.  Hull, Allan.  Introduction to JUSTINE.  London: Spearman
       Holland, 1964.

1506.  Jacob,  Paul  L.   INTRODUCTION A UN CHOIX  D'OEUVRE  DU
       MARQUIS DE SADE.   Brussels:  Chez tous les libraires,
       1870.

1507.  Kerberoux,  Jean.   LES  CRIMES  DE  AMOUR.    Genève:
       Crémille, 1973.  Listed by F. Rosart.

1508.  Klossowski, Pierre.   "Esquisse  du système  de  Sade."
       Preface to CENT VINGT JOURNEES DE SODOME.   In OEUVRES
       COMPLETES  DU MARQUIS  DE  SADE.   Vol. XIII.   Paris:
       Cercle du livre précieux,  1964 and 1967,  pp.  xliii-
       lxxxi.

1509.  Klossowski,  Pierre.   Introduction to ALINE ET VALCOUR.
       In OEUVRES COMPLETES.  Paris: J. J. Pauvert, 1963.

1510.  Klossowski,  Pierre.   "Justine et Juliette."  Preface to
       LA NOUVELLE JUSTINE.   In OEUVRES COMPLETES DU MARQUIS
       DE SADE.   Vol. VI.   Paris: Cercle du livre précieux,
       1963.

1511.  Klossowski,  Pierre.   Preface to ALINE ET VALCOUR.   In
       OEUVRES COMPLETES DE SADE.  Vol. IV.  Paris: Cercle du
       livre précieux, 1967.

1512.  Klossowski,  Pierre.   "Sade et l'homme normal."  Preface
       to  LA  NOUVELLE JUSTINE OU LES MALHEURS DE LA  VERTU.
       In  OEUVRES COMPLETES DU MARQUIS  DE  SADE.   Vol. XI.
       Paris: Cercle du livre précieux, 1967.

1513.  Klossowski,  Pierre.   "Sade et la Révolution."  Preface
       to  LA  PHILOSOPHIE  DANS  LE  BOUDOIR.   In  OEUVRES
       COMPLETES  DU  MARQUIS  DE  SADE.   Vol. III.   Paris:
       Cercle du livre précieux, 1963.

1514.  Klossowski,  Pierre.   "Sous  le masque de  l'athéisme."
       Preface to  LES  CRIMES  DE  L'AMOUR.   In  OEUVRES
       COMPLETES DU MARQUIS DE SADE.   Vol. X.  Paris: Cercle
       du livre précieux, 1967.

1515.  Lannes,  Denis.   EMILIE  DE  TOURVILLE.    Paris:  Le
       François, 1945.

1516. Lély, Gilbert. "A huit rais d'or." Preface to EUGENIE
      DE FRANVAL. Paris: Georges Artigues, 1948, pp.

1517. Lély, Gilbert. Foreword to HISTOIRE SECRETE D'ISABELLE
      DE BAVIERE. Paris: Gallimard, 1953, pp.

1518. Lély, Gilbert. Foreword to LA MARQUISE DE GRANGE.
      Paris: Pierre Amiot, 1957.

1519. Lély, Gilbert. Foreword to MONSIEUR LE 6, LETTRES
      INEDITES (1778-1784). Paris: Julliard Sequana, 1954,
      pp. 9-46.

1520. Lély, Gilbert. "Introduction aux CENT VINGT JOURNEES DE
      SODOME." MERCURE DE FRANCE 331 (1957): 497-504.

1521. Lély, Gilbert. Introduction to NOUVELLES EXEMPLAIRES.
      Paris: Club Français du Livre, 1958, pp.

1522. Lély, Gilbert, ed. LETTRES CHOISIES. Paris: Union des
      Grandes Ecoles, 1969.

1523. Lély, Gilbert. MARQUIS DE SADE, L'AIGLE, MADEMOISELLE
      . . . Paris: Georges Artigues, 1949.

1524. Lély, Gilbert. "Notes for LE CARILLON DE VINCENNES
      LETTRES INEDITES. Paris: Arcanes, 1953.

1525. Lély, Gilbert. Preface and notes to CAHIERS PERSONNELS,
      1803-1804. Paris: Corréa, 1953, pp. i-xviii.

1526. Lély, Gilbert. Preface to LA MARQUISE DE GANGE. Paris:
      Union Générale d'Editions, 1971, pp. 7-12.

1527. Mandiargues, André Pieyre de. Preface to HISTOIRE DE
      JULIETTE. In OEUVRES COMPLETES DE SADE. Vol. XIX.
      Paris: Cercle du livre précieux, 1967.

1528. Maulnier, Thierry. Preface to INFORTUNES DE LA VERTU
      Paris: J. Valmont, 1947.

1529. Nadeau, Maurice. MARQUIS DE SADE, OEUVRES. Paris: La
      jeune Parque, 1947.

1530. Naville, Pierre. "Sade et la philosophie." In OEUVRES
      COMPLETES DU MARQUIS DE SADE. Vol. XI. Paris: Cercle
      du livre précieux, 1964, pp. 11-23.

1531. Pastoureau, Henri. Notes for CENT ONZE NOTES POUR LA NOUVELLE JUSTINE. Paris: Eric Losfeld, 1956, pp. 1-4.

1532. Paulhan, Jean. "Du bonheur dans l'esclavage." Préface à Reage (Pauline): HISTOIRE D'O. Paris: J. J. Pauvert, 1954.

1533. Paulhan, Jean and Heine, Maurice "Introduction and Notice to Sade." In SADE, D. A. F. LES INFORTUNES DE LA VERTU. Paris: Editions du point du jour, 1946, pp. i-xliii, 1-34.

1534. Paulhan, Jean. Preface to ALINE ET VALCOUR OU LE ROMAN PHILOSOPHIQUE. Paris: Pauvert, 1955.

1535. Pauvert, Jean-Jacques. "Introduction." CHOIX D'OEUVRES. Paris: Club du Livre, 1953, pp. 3-63.

1536. Perceau, Louis. "Le marquis de Sade et le sadisme." Preface to LA PHILOSOPHIE DANS LE BOUDOIR. Sadopolis [sic]: aux dépens de la Société des études sadiques, n.d.

1537. Perceau, Louis. "Notice." In LE BORDEL DE VENISE by Alphonse-Donatien de Sade. Venice: Aux dépens des philosophes libertins, s. d., pp. 1-4.

1538. Pia, Pascal. "Le Marquis de Sade." Preface to ERNESTINE. Paris: au Cabinet du Livre, 1926.

1539. Profühl, Gaston. Notes bibliographiques pour les ESCRITS POLITIQUES ET OXTIERN. Paris: J. J. Pauvert, 1957.

1540. Ramon, L. J. (Dr.). "Notes sur M. de Sade." In CAHIERS PERSONNELS (1803-1804). Paris: Corréa, 1953, pp. 41-47.

1541. Robbe-Grillet, Alain. Preface to LA NOUVELLE JUSTINE. In OEUVRES COMPLETES DE SADE. Vol. XV. Paris: Cercle du livre précieux, 1967.

1542. Schuwer, Camille. "Sade et les moralistes." In OEUVRES COMPLETES DU MARQUIS DE SADE. Paris: Cercle du livre précieux, 1964, pp. 25-51.

1543. Thierry-MauPnier. Preface to LES INFORTUNES DE LA VERU. Paris: J. Valmont, 1947.

1544. Tort, Michel. "L'effet Sade." In OEUVRES COMPLETES DU MARQUIS DE SADE. Vol. XVI. Paris: Cercle du Livre précieux, 1967, pp. 583-620.

1545. Uzanne, Octave. Préface sur l'oeuvre de D. A. F. de Sade. IDEE SUR LES ROMANS. Paris: Rouveyre, 1878.

1546. Wainhouse, Austryn. Foreword to JULIETTE. New York: Grove Press, 1968, pp. vii-x.

1547.  Alquié, Ferdinand.  THE PHILOSOPHY OF SURREALISM.  Ann Arbor, Michigan:  University of Michigan Press, 1965, p. 31.

Translated from the French, LA PHILOSOPHIE DU SURREALISME (Paris:  Flammarion, 1955) by Bernard Waldrop.  Mentions that in the MANIFESTO, André Breton finds "some surrealism in Swift, Sade, Chateaubriand, Constant, Hugo, Desbordes-Valmore, Bertrand, Rabbe, Poe, Baudelaire, Rimbaud, Mallarmé, Jarry, Nouveau, Saint-Pol-Roux, Fargue, Vache, Reverdy, Saint-John Perse, and Roussel."

1548.  Baccolo, Luigi.  "Rileggendo Sade."  PONTE 21 (1965):  828-833.

States that 150 years after his death Sade is far from having realized his last wish--namely to erase his memory from the minds of men.  Surprisingly enough, in spite of the fact that his work is in great part pornographic and his philosophy too personal and vindictive, Sade is still read.  Asks if it means, as suggested by the title of Simone de Beauvoir's article, that we should burn Sade?  Answers that, in fact, some works like L'HISTOIRE D'O or Bourget's CRUELLE ENIGME are more dangerous than Sade. Concludes that there are greater dangers than Sade in men's contemporary universe:  "La stupidità del cinematografo americano, la prattezza badiale del divertimento televisio, la publicità offensiva certo cantaurorume aguaiato che tende (o quantomeno arriva) a degradare il concetto stesso e l'immagine dell'uomo--questo oltraggio quotidiano e impunito perpetrato ai danni dell'intelligenza e del pensiero, sara in definitiva meno grave per le sorti dell' umanita che l'erotismo di Juliette."  And author concludes:  Who knows if [all that] is not even worse [than Sade's works]?

1549.  Bagnall, Eric.  Review of THE THOUGHTS AND THEMES OF THE MARQUIS DE SADE, by Lorna Berman.  MODERN LANGUAGE REVIEW, October 1974, pp. 876-877.

Gives a very poor review of Berman's book first published in 1971.  "Dr. Berman's translation tends to

be literal . . . insensitive to say the least . . .
but far more seriously, it is unreliable. . . ."

1550. Baird, Julian. "Swinburne, Sade, and Blake: The
Pleasure-Pain Paradox." VICTORIAN POETRY 9 (1971):
49-75.

"POEMS AND BALLADS may be unified by the exploration
in the separate poems of various aspects of love and
lust, pleasure and pain, God and nature, virtue and
vice. These concerns engaged Swinburne intellectually
in his reading of Sade and Blake. He saw the former
as an unsuccessful rebel against Christian notions of
asceticism. The latter is presented in Swinburne's
study of him (which he was working on concurrently
with the composition of POEMS AND BALLADS) as
rejecting the notions of a transcendent deity and of
the dichotomy between body and soul in human nature,
together with the traditional moral implications
derived from these notions. 'A Ballad of Life' and 'A
Ballad of Death,' the opening poems, are thematically
prefatory to the volume and correspond to Blake's
SONGS OF INNOCENCE and SONGS OF EXPERIENCE. They also
reveal Swinburne's concurrent interest in Lucretia
Borgia and his admiration for her--in Blakean terms--
as emancipated from the tyranny of asceticism. In
'Laus Veneris,' the third poem in the volume,
Swinburne uses Tannhauser as a persona to explore
subtly the relationships between eroticism,
asceticism, guilt, and emancipation in a Blakean-
inspired inversion of good and evil, heaven and hell."
(Quoted from MLA abstracts, 1971, Vol. II, pp. 15-16).

1551. Bakari, Salih al. "Fi-al-Dhikra al-Sadisah Liwafal Taha
Hussayn." AL-FIKR 25, no. 1 (1979): 30-40.

On the sixth anniversary of Taha Hussayin's death,
writes an evaluation of the work of this author who
was greatly influenced by European culture and
especially by Baudelaire and the esthetic of evil.
Relates only tenuously to Sade but listed in MLA 1979,
No. 11722. (Comment by Mohammed Haddar.)

1552. Barba, Vincenzo. INTERPRETAZIONI DE SADE. Rome:
Savelli, 1979. 224 p.

In this erudite and very readable anthology of
criticism on Sade, Barba presents synopses and

passages in Italian translation (from the French by Elsa D'Ambrosio and by Ciro Perrotta from the English) of some of the best articles published on Sade. While relatively few prominent eighteenth- and nineteenth-century authors are included, the list of twentieth-century scholars is studded with big names; surprisingly few Italian authors/critics are included even though the book itself is a commentary on the interest Sade has generated in Italy. A first-rate reference book for any serious study of Sade.

1553. Barthel, Georges. Review of JOURNAL INEDIT. DEUX CAHIERS RETROUVES DU JOURNAL INEDIT DU MARQUIS DE SADE. In DIX-HUITIEME SIECLE 4 (1972): 444-445.

Gives a poor review of this publication by Gallimard with a preface by Georges Daumas: "l'appareil critique est quasi inexistant, et, de ce fait, le JOURNAL est bien souvent totalement incompréhensible."

1554. Basil, Guy. "Sur les traces du 'Divin Marquis'?" STUDI FRANCESI 14 (1970): 63-71.

Recounts a story presented by Fleury in his MEMOIRES in which the main character would have been the marquis de Sade. While some facts seem to fit well with what is known of the life of Sade, other details do not belong in the same frame. The complete text of Fleury's story is included.

1555. Bataille, Georges. LA LITTERATURE ET LE MAL. St. Amand: Gallimard, 1957, pp. 119-148.

Gives credit to Jean Paulhan, Pierre Klossowski, and Maurice Blanchot for having recognized the genius, the significant value, and the literary beauty of Sade's works. Pictures Sade as an atheist who had the lifelong occupation of enumerating the possible ways of destroying human beings while enjoying the thought and sight of their sufferings and deaths. Yet stresses the fact that Sade himself, in spite of several entanglements with the police, was never charged with any real crime. "Il eut souvent maille à partir avec la police, qui se méfia de lui, mais ne put le charger d'aucun crime véritable."

1556.  Batlay, Jenny H. and Fellows, Otis E. "Diderot et Sade:
       Affinités et divergences." L'ESPRIT CREATEUR 15
       (1975): 449-459.

       Gives several examples suggesting that Sade owes
       Diderot a large debt and that the marquis may not have
       broken as much ground as is usually believed: "Le
       marquis se croyait nouveau, dans l'expression de
       tendances qui remontent au deluge! Ce n'était que le
       sombre cri d'une sexualité brutale poussée jusqu'à ces
       extremes conséquences. L'éclectisme de Diderot
       comprenait Sade ainsi que bien d'autres
       contemporains."

1557.  Belaval, Yvon. "Sade le tragique." CAHIERS DU SUD 285
       (1947): 721-724.

       Entire issue devoted to Sade with subtitle "Approches
       de Sade." Claims that only tragedy could define Sade.
       His works were rigorously scientific, as was noted by
       Dühren, Apollinaire, Heine; yet he was taken to be
       insane. Sade's so-called "inventions" have been
       realized, if anything, too well. Sade's personal
       engagement was a contradiction between necessity and
       freedom and his entire production is only a passionate
       interrogation by a man about his own destiny. In the
       case of Sade, it was a tragic one.

1558.  Bellmer, Hans. JUSTINE. Paris: Presse du livre
       français, 1950.

       With drawings in the erotic mode typical of the
       artist.

1559.  Berman, Lorna. "The Marquis de Sade and His Critics."
       MOSAIC I, no. 2 (1968): 57-73.

       Analyzes the reactions and attitudes of readers/
       critics toward the marquis's writings. Considering
       that pornography is produced by the "fragmentation of
       sex" and that Sade's depictions are not fragmentary--
       "Sade tells all and is completely open and frank"--
       Sade's prose is simply "clinical." Therefore, "it
       would seem that those who have banned Sade's works
       have done so precisely out of fear of just such a
       latent destructive impulse in human nature." Believes
       that several factors have impaired the objectivity of
       a number of Sade's critics, not the least of which is

the "fear of being identified in the public mind with
the propensities, acts and concepts which have become
associated with his name." Severely criticizes Simone
de Beauvoir, who misquoted Sade by omission, and
concludes: "Of course, all attitudes and reactions to
the works of Sade, however prejudiced, are of
interest."

1560. Biou, Jean. "Le Saint-Roi et le Divin Marquis."
RAISON PRESENTE 22 (April-June 1972): 57-72.

Contrasts the Marquis de Sade's views with those of
King Louis IX of France--Saint-Louis--who was harshly
condemned by Sade in ALINE ET VALCOUR: "C'est une
chose vraiment singulière que l'extravagante manie qui
a fait louer par plusieurs écrivains, depuis quelque
temps, ce roi cruel et imbécile, dont toutes les
démarches sont fausses, ridicules ou barbares; qu'on
lise avec attention l'histoire de son règne et l'on
verra si ce n'est pas avec justice que l'on peut
affirmer que la France eut peu de souverains plus
faits pour le mépris et l'indignation. . . ." Takes
this comment by Sade seriously and shows how inane is
the stand taken by historians when judging Saint-
Louis--one of the most cruel kings France ever had--
and relates this entire debate to Sade's political
thoughts: "Pour Sade l'antilégiste et son maître, la
société générale du genre humain est une pure chimère
et l'utilitarisme social une escroquerie puisque les
intérêts particuliers sont toujours contraires à
l'intérêt général, que les riches exploitent les
pauvres et que les gouverants oppriment les
gouvernés."

1561. Biou, Jean. "Deux oeuvres complémentaires: LES
LIAISONS DANGEREUSES ET JULIETTE." In LE MARQUIS DE
SADE. Paris: Armand Colin, 1968, pp. 103-114.

Proceedings of Colloquium on the Marquis de Sade, Aix-
en-Provence, 19 and 20 February 1966. Compares and
contrasts LES LIAISONS DANGEREUSES of Laclos and
JULIETTE of Sade. Uses Hegelian vocabulary and
analysis to consider Valmont and Merteuil as masters
of a consciousness that exists for itself, but which
is mediated with itself through other consciousness,
and demands, therefore, a social and human world. In
opposition, the world of JULIETTE is a universe where
the Other--l'Autre--no longer exists, where there is

no humanity. Furthermore, while Laclos's novel
progresses according to projected and/or hampered
plans, these novels of Sade are made up of a
succession of episodes which can be added or
subtracted without changing the meaning of the work.
This type of structure is perfectly suitable for the
expression of a libertine's conception of happiness,
that is, multiplication of similar events.

1562.  Blanchot, Maurice. SADE ET LAUTREAMONT. Paris: Edition
       de Minuit, 1949, pp. 219-265.

       This article was originally published in TEMPS MODERNE
       under the title "A la rencontre de Sade." See
       annotation to item 1225.

       Reviewed by Franco Fé in IL PONTE 31 (1975) 296-297.

1563.  Blin, Georges. LE SADISME DE BAUDELAIRE. Paris: José
       Corti, 1948.

       Compares and contrasts the "sadisme" of Sade with that
       of Baudelaire. Asserts that main difference is in
       their approach to nature. Sade tends to serve and
       magnify nature; in Baudelaire the intention is to
       correct nature. For Sade: "Le meurtre rend
       disponible de l'énergie bloquée ou séquestrée; c'est
       donc bien toujours la négation qui fournit à la
       dialectique son ressort et son dynamisme, et si, pour
       Sade, la destruction n'est pas un crime, c'est parce
       que, à ses yeux, le crime n'est pas un acte de
       destruction." For Baudelaire: "S'il a raffiné sur
       l'art de se donner le mauvais rôle, s'il s'est offert
       aux coups et voué à l'échec, c'est au fond dans un
       esprit de sacrifice orgueilleux sans doute, et de
       tragique conscient. S'il a accepté de faire souffir,
       c'est dans la mesure où il tenait que tout homme est
       en faute, et par nature débiteur, que faire le malheur
       de son prochain, c'est une façon de pouvoir à son
       salut."

1564.  Bourde, M. A. "Allocution." In LE MARQUIS DE SADE.
       Paris: Librairie Armand Colin, 1968, pp. 7-8.

       Proceedings of the Colloquium on the Marquis de Sade,
       Aix-en-Provence, 19 and 20 February 1966. Brief words
       of welcome from the President of the Centre Aixois
       d'Etudes et de Recherches sur le XVIII$^e$ Siècle.

1565.   Brandt, Per Aage. "Don Juan ou la force de la parole. Essai sur le contrat." POETIQUE 12 (1972): 584-585.

Mentions that Sade has greatly influenced interpretation of classical texts and gives a new reading of Molière's DON JUAN: "Depuis Sade, le texte classique devient autrement lisible: on dirait que son humanité éclate et que la voix de ses lettres sonne à partir d'un concavité impossible à prendre pour le coeur de l'univocité."

1566.   Breton, André. ENTRETIENS 1913-1952. Paris: Gallimard, 1952, pp. 41, 66, 92, 141, 209, 249, 261, 264, 194.

Numerous references to Sade throughout these interviews. Tends to promote a morality based on desire and sees in Freud, Fourier, and Sade three great emancipators of desire.

1567.   Breton, André. MANIFESTE DU SURREALISME. Paris: J. J. Pauvert, 1962, p. 41.

In the first MANIFESTE DU SURREALISME (published 1924) Breton stated: "Sade est surréaliste dans la sadisme."

1568.   Breton, André. LES PAS PERDUS. Paris: Gallimard, 1964, pp. 10, 42, 199.

Indicates the debt Apollinaire owed Sade.

States: "Les moralistes, je les aime tous, particulièrement. Vauvenargues et Sade. La morale est la grande conciliatrice. L'attaquer, c'est encore lui rendre hommage."

1569.   Brochier, Jean-Jacques. "Un grand rhétoricien des figures érotiques. Entretien avec Roland Barthes." MAGAZINE LITTERAIRE 114 (June 1976): 24-25.

Interviews Roland Barthes who describes Sade as "un homme qui par l'écriture construit des structures romanesques extrêmement bien faites qui sont aussi des structures érotiques . . . [et qui] produit quelque chose de très rare dans la littérature, dans la rhétorique: une écriture parfaitement dénotée. Quand il décrit, dans une phrase, un acte érotique, il n'y a

absolument   aucune  connotation.   La   phrase   est
tellement    mate   qu'aucun   symbolisme   ne   peut
intervenir."   Yet,  in  spite of the  obvious  riches
contained  in the marquis's writings,   states that  it
takes courage and a sense of the urgency to  intervene
in the field of Sadian literature.

1570.  Brousson,  Jean-Jacques.   "La Nuit du marquis de Sade,"
       In LES NUITS SANS CULOTTE.   Paris:  Flammarion, 1930,
       pp. 139-199.

       Begins  with an excerpt from DIALOGUE ENTRE UN  PRETRE
       ET UN MORIDOND.   Recounts an apocryphal  conversation
       between  Sade and Abbé de Fénelon which is supposed to
       have  taken place while they were on their way to  the
       guillotine.   Also describes a meeting with "filles de
       joie."  Pornography in the worst possible taste.

1571.  Brumfield,  William  C.   "Thérèse  Philosophe  and
       Dostoevski's Great Sinner."  COMPARATIVE LITERATURE 32
       (1980):  238-252.

       Investigates  an  enigmatic mention of the marquis  de
       Sade  in  a  notebook  entry  dated  1864  written  by
       Dostoevsky and declares that "while it seems  unlikely
       that  we  shall ever have definitive  knowledge  about
       Dostoevsky's  acquaintance with the writings of  Sade,
       it can be assumed beyond reasonable doubt that he read
       the trashy little books. . . ."  One of these, THERESE
       PHILOSOPHE,  whose  authorship  is attributed  to  the
       marquis d'Argens,  seems  to have greatly  influenced
       Dostoevsky,  but the relationship with or influence of
       Sade appears tenuous at best.

1572.  Bryan,  C.  D.  B.   THE MARQUIS DE SADE.  Fort Collins,
       Colo.:  Colorado State University Press, 1967, p. 27.

       This is the fourth annual writer-in-residence lecture,
       sponsored by the university's Fine Arts Series.   Says
       simply that Sade was "insane,  filthy-minded,  vicious
       and fascinating."  Passes in review the most important
       recent publications on and by Sade, who is compared to
       D.  H.  Lawrence and Henry Miller.   Concludes:  "Why
       read JUSTINE?   The  reader  who  completes  it  has
       achieved  a  herculean accomplishment.   The  plot  is
       hopeless. . . .   The tortures are repetitive.  Sade's
       anality  and  coprophilia  are  revolting.   His
       viciousness,  cruelty  and negative vision of man  are

disturbing. But Sade, nevertheless, provides a fascinating insight into a criminal's mind."

1573. Buisson, Françoise. "Les bougres, ou les derniers archanthropes." OBLIQUES 12-13 (1977): 19-22.

Believes that Sade's work has gained a new status, giving it the worth attached to what is supposed to represent reality and lending strength to the figure of Sade himself as a symbol, begun on paper, of a social revolutionary. Sade dehumanized man, took away his thoughts and emotion. He was master of form and substance. But his art was in the manner in which he went about this dehumanization. In contemporary mores, men are dehumanized with the efficiency of the factory, no longer cutting off a person's head but simply destroying his mind. Sade would dissect a body on an anatomy table; now it is done on an autopsy table.

1574. Camus, Michel. "La question de Sade." OBLIQUES 12-13 (1977): 1-3.

Introduces this double issue of the journal devoted to Sade. Stresses the contradictory aspect of Sade's legation. "Son oeuvre et sa correspondance ne sont au fond que du langage, corps de langage appartenant au corps du monde et, comme lui, infiniment muet, infiniment parlant . . . qu'une oeuvre aussi contestataire, la plus contestataire qui fut jamais, ait attendu près d'un siècle et demi pour sortir de l'Enfer de quelques bibliothèques privées et devenir publique, cela ne saurait être le résultat du hasard mais bien l'action d'une lente et redoutée prise de conscience dont le sens, sauf à en soupçonner la nécessité absolue, reste toujours en question."

1575. Camus, Michel. "Sade au chateau de Cerisy." In SADE, ECRIRE IA CRISE: COLLOQUE DE CERISY. Paris: Belfond, 1983, pp. 11-12.

Introduction to the proceedings of the colloquium entitled SADE, ECRIRE LA CRISE, which took place from 19 June 1981 to 29 June 1981 at the International Cultural Center of Cerisy-la-Salle. This colloquium was organized by Michel Camus and Philippe Roger. Explains the metaphysical title of the colloquium by the fact that the "living pictures" of Sade's books do not belong to any kind of stageable reality except that of his books.

1576. Carter, Alfred Edouard. THE IDEA OF DECADENCE IN FRENCH LITERATURE, 1830-1900. Toronto: University of Toronto Press, 1958, pp. 31-37.

Traces the influence of the Latin historians Sade, who had read them, and in turn, the influence of Sade on some writers of the Romantic school: "The syndrome of decadence may be said to come into existence when the marquis de Sade's influence [played] on the exhausted sensibility of Romanticism."

1577. Cerruti, Giorgio. "LE PARADOXE SUR LE COMEDIEN et LE PARADOXE SUR LE LIBERTIN de Diderot et de Sade." REVUE DES SCIENCES HUMAINES 146 (1972): 235-251.

Compares the paradoxical literary universe of Diderot with that of Sade. There exist many similarities in their materialist approach to life, but one can only talk of coincidences rather than influences because, while Sade may have been acquainted with the ENCYCLOPEDIE, it is virtually certain that he never read Diderot's PARADOX SUR LE COMEDIEN: "Tout au plus peut-on parler pour Sade et Diderot de coincidences entre le développement de leur pensée, coincidences d'autant plus intéressantes qu'elles sont involontaires; souvent les audaces de la pensée de Diderot s'apparentent à certains developpements sadiens ultérieurs." Yet both writers seem to have been concerned with a problem of equilibrium between passion and reason: "le dilemme et le dialogue entre le coeur, la sensibilité et la raison a été exploité et résolu de façon différente, mais également paradoxale par Diderot et Sade; on pourrait ajouter, en guise de conclusion, que ce dilemme est propre à tout artiste confronté au problème de la création et à tout homme qui veut donner à sa vie une valeur esthétique."

1578. Cerruti, G. Review of SADE ET SES MASQUES, by Roger Lacombe. STUDI FRANCESI 19 (1975): 363.

Brief review in Italian of Lacombe's book on Sade. States nothing new except announcement of another publication on Sade.

1579.  Cha, Michel.   LEGENDE DE SADE.   HISTOIRE D'UN MYTHE DE
       L'EROTISME.   (Thèse de 3ème cycle, Université de Paris
       VII, 1976, 162 p.)

       Unpublished dissertation from the University of Paris.

1580.  Champagne, Roland A.   "The Metamorphoses of  Proteus:
       Roland  Barthes' SADE,  FOURIER,  LOYOLA."  HELICON  1
       (1975): 21-33.

       This review of Barthes's article appeared in a journal
       published in Calcutta, India, and was not available at
       this time.

1581.  Champarnaud, François.   "La JUSTINE de Sade vue par la
       bande dessinée."   CRITIQUE 38 (1982): 871-875.

       Discusses  the  adaptations of JUSTINE into two  comic
       strips  and states about the first by Gilbert  Garnon:
       "Le  sang,  le sperme et la merde paraissent  être  au
       centre  de son ouvrage. . . .  L'humour de Garpon  est
       court,  faute  d'avoir  choisi un point de vue sur  LA
       NOUVELLE JUSTINE de Sade.  C'est un échec."  About the
       second,  by Guido Crépax:  "Il n'est pas la peine  de
       rappeler la finesse du dessin de Crépax, son goût pour
       le détail juste,  la notation historique et exacte, la
       mise en page variée et astucieuse.   Mais le talent de
       Crépax se révèle ici à plusieurs niveaux.  D'abord, il
       a  su  construire  son récit en  reprenant  le  double
       encadrement qu'avait donné Sade à son conte.  Un cadre
       philosophique. . . .  Un cadre dramatique. . . .  La
       bande  dessinée  de  Crépax  est  rigoureusement
       construite.  Comparée à celle de Garnon, à chaque page
       sa supériorité éclate."

1582.  Char, René.  "Hommage à D.A.F. de Sade."  RECHERCHE DE LA
       BASE ET DU SOMMET.   Paris: Gallimard, 1965, pp. 105-
       106.

       Begins this homage to Sade with a quote:   "A signaler
       à Paris vers la fin du XVIIIe siécle (Sade) et vers la
       fin du XIXe siècle (Lautréamont) une courte apparition
       de  la  pierre philosophale."  Continues:   "Quelle
       existence  particulièrement  bien comprise arrivera  à
       percevoir  à  l'heure d'un couchant exceptionnel  les
       vibrations de l'insolite monument dressé sur une grève
       de pierres hantées à la limite des eux mortes,  entre
       deux  rivages  à  jamais arides? . . .  Le  temps  m'a

prouvé par la suite que mon existence à ce moment-la
pouvait tout au plus déserter deux nuages et une épave
encore à découvrir. Une obscurité croissante
semblable à celle qui règne sur les visions, tombe
dans les yeux de Pilar. A l'horizon, des mains
téméraires ont soulevépour le plaisir les lourdes
pierres horizontales.

"Sade, l'amour enfin sauvé de la boue du ciel,
l'hypocrisie passée par les armes et par les yeux, cet
héritage suffira aux hommes contre la famine, leurs
belles mains d'étrangleurs sorties des poches."

1583. Collier, Peter. Review of INTERSECTIONS: A READING OF
SADE WITH BATAILLE, BLANCHOT, AND KLOSSOWSKI. MODERN
LANGUAGE REVIEW 77 (1982): 967.

Review of Jane Gallop's INTERSECTIONS: A READING OF
SADE WITH BATAILLE, BLANCHOT, AND KLOSSOWSKI,
University of Nebraska Press, 1981.

1584. Coulet, Henri. LE ROMAN JUSQU'A LA REVOLUTION. Paris:
Armand Colin, 1967, pp. 482-496.

Contrasts and compares Sade and Restif de la Bretonne.
There is non-negligible common ground between them:
both lived during a period of excessive sensibility,
moral confusion, unleashed violence, and both were
egocentric; their works had an unrestrained quality.
Gives a good bird's eye view of Sade's production and
states: "Sade est un philosophe qui connait
parfaitement la pensée de son siècle et apporte aux
questions qu'elle se posait sur la nature, sur le mal,
sur la société, sur Dieu, des réponses radicales;
c'est aussi un psychologue, le premier qui ait osé
appliquer à un domaine interdit les procédés d'analyse
et de classement du rationalisme expérimental;
enfin,c'est un créateur dont l'imagination a inventé
quelques-unes des scènes les plus stupéfiantes qu'on
puisse rencontre dans le roman français du XVIIIe
siècle."

1585. Crickillon, Ferry. "Actualité de Sade." MARGINALES 137
(March 1971): 22-24.

In this short article, notes that Sade's works have
somehow managed to obtain a popularity which is hardly
deserved: "La légende escamote le témoignage;

l'oeuvre, pas ses outrances, engendre un mythe qui de loin la dépasse."

1586. Crocker, Lester G. AN AGE OF CRISIS, MAN AND WORLD IN EIGHTEENTH-CENTURY FRENCH THOUGHT. Baltimore: Johns Hopkins University Press, 1959, pp. 212-213.

Many references to the marquis de Sade but states in particular: "Once more we find in the marquis de Sade the ruthless logical exploitation of radical views which had given their very proponents pause. A man of widest philosophical culture, Sade was thoroughly familiar with the writings of his century and of earlier times. He seems to unite the statements of Deslandes, La Mettrie and Helvetius: men will always oppress and exploit others; pleasure is most exquisite when it derives from cruelty; murder (preferably by torture) is the greatest source of pleasurable excitement. This is a law of nature, and man is incapable of extirpating it."

1587. Dabadié, Maité. "Le Colloque à la Faculté d'Aix-en-Provence sur le Marquis de Sade." LE CERF VOLANT 54 (1966): 58-60.

Reviews the assorted presentations made at the colloquium of February 1966 on Sade, his work, and his influence. Presided over by Jean Fabre, the conference welcomed philosophers and litterateurs to discuss works which were then still censored. "Etonnante époque que la nôtre où les hommes de science et de la technique veulent pour connaître, déchirer les enveloppes du cosmos et poussent les autres à s'enfoncer dans le labyrinthe de la pensée pour une plus grande quête de la vérité."

1588. Debout, S. "Légitime défense--légitime entente: Sade et Fourier." LIBRE 1 (1977): 202-246.

States that history is not made by sleeping men but by men with dreams who have the power to create new realities. Both Sade and Fourier were those kinds of men but Sade went further than Fourier in his investigation of spiritual, natural and social evil. He also questioned the relationship between power and rational order, and complicity between domination and servitude. Concludes that Sade wanted to give back to men the power of primitive instincts and that he saw in his dreams more than regressive thoughts.

"Sade rapporte son discours, et tout ce qui est, à des émotions ou à des passions dévorantes, sans partage, et qui resteraient impuissantes s'il ne mettait à leur service les institutions et les régles, la fonctionalité rationnelle dont il inverse par la même le sens exhibé. Fourier, tout à l'inversion, voit dans le moindre élan passionnel un pouvoir de lien."

1589.   Delon, Michel. "Candide et Justine dans les tranchées." STUDIES ON VOLTAIRE AND THE EIGHTEENTH CENTURY 190 (1980): 241-243.

Attempts to delineate national values such as they are pictured in 18th-century French literature. Voltaire is seen as representative of a positive trend of nationalism while Sade would be situated at an opposite pole. Concludes with a question on the different forms nationalism has taken in the literary heritage.

1590.   Delon, Michel. "Les historiennes de Silling." In L'HISTOIRE AU XVIII$^e$ SIECLE. Aix-en-Provence: Edisud, 1980, pp. 101-113.

Proceedings of the Colloquium of Aix-en-Provence, 1, 2, and 3 May 1975.

1591.   Delon, Michel. "Sade face à Rousseau." EUROPE 522 (1972): 42-48.

Makes a comparison between Rousseau and Sade at the professional and personal levels and contrasts some aspects of LA NOUVELLE HELOISE with those of ALINE ET VALCOUR. Concludes that it could almost be said that Rousseau and Sade were, like Diderot and Rousseau, two brother enemies.

1592.   Delon, Michel. Review of LECTURES DE SADE, by Françoise Laugaa-Traut. In DIX-HUITIEME SIECLE 8 (1976): 504.

States: "Le grand mérite de F. Laugaa-Traut est de porter une attention scrupuleuse à la textualité de tous les énoncés ainsi qu'à leur insertion dans tel ou tel type de discourse (journalistique, juridique, médical, universitaire, psychanalytique)."

1593.   Deprun, Jean. "Sade et l'abbé Bergier." RAISON
        PRESENTE 67 (1983):5-11.

        Investigates the relationship and influence of the
        Abbé Bergier on Sade's materialist philosophy. States
        that Sade bought in 1769 LE DEISME REFUTE PAR LUI-MEME
        and L'APOLOGIE DE LA RELIGION CHRETIENNE CONTRE
        L'AUTEUR DU CHRISTIANISME DEVOILE, ET CONTRE QUELQUES
        AUTRES CRITIQUES, and also probably acquired the
        REFUTATION DU SYSTEME DE LA NATURE which contains much
        of the philosophy advocated by the marquis.
        Concludes: "Il nous semble pourtant significatif que
        le mouvement de sa réflexion--et de ses phantasmes--
        antihumanistes ait coincidé, au moins partiellement,
        avec la démarche purement tactique de Bergier."

1594.   Didier, Béatrice. "MADAME PUTIPHAR, roman sadien?"
        Preface of MADAME PUTIPHAR by Petrus Borel. N.p.:
        Regine Deforges, 1972, pp. vii-xx.

        This essay was later reprinted in part III, chapter 4
        of SADE: UNE ECRITURE DU DESIR (see item 1596).
        Stresses the importance of Sade as an influence on
        romantic writers, especially Lamartine and
        Chateaubriand and discusses the parallels that can be
        made between Sade's biography and the plot of MADAME
        PUTIPHAR. States: "Petrus Borel ne s'est pas
        contenté de faire apparaître l'image de Sade, il a
        prêté à son personnage principal une partie de la
        biographie du marquis, en particulier, ce qui fut la
        vie même de l'auteur de JUSTINE, l'incarcération
        continuelle et injustifiée; mais l'analogie va plus
        loin: tout le dénouement si pathétique semble avoir
        été inspire par la fin de la vie de Sade à l'hôpital
        des fous à Charenton."

1595.   Didier, Béatrice. "Sade et Don Juan." OBLIQUES 5,
        (1974): 67-71.

        Contrasts the attitude of a libertine with that of a
        Don Juan and suggests that they are quite different;
        the former is intent on pleasure, no matter how
        acquired, while the latter prefers a pursuit, a hunt.
        The women in Sade's novels are either libertines
        themselves or victims; Don Juan only seduces women in
        order to abandon them. Though noting that the
        behavior of the Sadian hero is not at all that of a

seducer, suggests that both are essentially mythical representations of the revolutionary characterization of desire.

1596. Didier, Béatrice. SADE. UNE ECRITURE DU DESIR. Paris: Denoël-Gonthier, 1976. 208 p.

"Constantes," Part I of this book contains several articles published in assorted journals: "Sade dramaturge de ses 'Carceri'" in NOUVELLE REVUE FRANCAISE; "Le château intérieur de Sade" in EUROPE; and "Inceste et écriture chez Sade" in LES LETTRES NOUVELLES. See annotations to items 943, 1247, and 1760. Part II, "Variations," discusses some of the main works of Sade; Part III, "Prolongements" discusses several authors who owe much to Sade but failed to acknowledge their debt: Chateaubriand in MARTYRS: Benjamin Constant in ADOLPHE; George Sand in INDIANA; Petrus Borel in MADAME PUTIPHAR, and Jules Valles in l'ENFANT. Concludes with a 20-page overview of Sade's popularity today, examining the paradox which is his history: "Il a passé quarante ans de sa vie en prison, occulte, bailloné par son siècle. . . . Pourtant il semble qu'il ait été le phare le plus brûlant, le plus éclairant de ce siècle des Lumières. Cette dialectique de l'obscurité et de la clarté se retrouve dans la destinée de sa gloire après sa mort."

Reviewed by Jean-Marc Gebaude in REVUE PHILOSOPHIQUE DE LOUVAIN 75 (1977): 529-530; Jean Delon, DIX-HUITIEME SIECLE 9 (1977): 459-460; and Claude Mauriac, LE FIGARO LITTERAIRE 1559 (3 April 1976): 14.

1597. Doyon, René-Louis. DU MARQUIS DE SADE A BARBEY D'AUREVILLY. Paris: La Connaissance, 1921.

Another publication which stresses Sade as a precursor of specific writers, especially those who wrote about "evil" and diabolical influence.

1598. Duchet, Claude. "Flaubert, premier lecteur de Sade." LA QUINZAINE LITTERAIRE 324 (1980): 13-15.

Conjectures that in the nineteenth century, Flaubert may have been Sade's first and perhaps only true reader: "un intelligence hantée par M. de Sade. . . . Sade, auquel revient toujours, comme fasciné, l'esprit de Flaubert. . . . Sade qu'on trouve à tous les bouts de Flaubert comme un horizon. . . . Il y a vraiment chez Flaubert une obsession de Sade. . . ." Concludes that there is in the works of Flaubert something "invisible" which is due to Sade's presence in the works of the nineteenth-century author.

1599. Duchet, Claude. "L'image de Sade à l'époque romantique." LE MARQUIS DE SADE. Paris: Colin, 1968, pp. 219-240.

Proceedings of the colloquium on the marquis de Sade which took place in Aix-en-Provence on 19 and 20 February 1966. Appraises Sade's influence during the Romantic period and states three conclusions: 1) Sade's literature was known especially during the period after 1834 and the publication of Janin's essay. 2) Sade, the man, belongs to the realm of myth, a monster or a madman. 3) The most important and most interesting conclusions are indications suggesting a period of total refusal of sadism: "on pourrait parler d'une influence négative."

1600. Dulaure, Jacques A. HISTOIRE PHYSIQUE, CIVILE, ET MORAL DE PARIS. Vol. VI. Paris: Guillaume, 1821, p. 224.

Gives a very brief judgment of Sade.

1601. Dupré, Gilbert. "Le marquis de Sade." OEUVRES LIBRES 136 (1957): 27-76.

Assesses the works of the marquis de Sade and evaluates some of his critics as well: P. Klossowski, Maurice Heine in particular. Interesting but out-of-date.

1602. Durozoi, Gérard. "Note sur Sade et Bataille." OBLIQUES 12-13 (1977): 79-81.

Compares and contrasts the writings of Bataille and Sade and finds that they have much in common: "de part et d'autre, il y a une inhabituelle monotonie, une ressassement inlassable. . . . chez Sade comme chez Bataille, non-respect de la traditionnelle séparation entre théorie et fiction: les deux textes sont également anomiques par rapport à la dichotomie qui exige (depuis Platon) l'absence de communication entre 'pensée' et 'littérature.'" Concludes with a

quote from Bataille, L'EROTISME: "c'est devant nous-
mêmes que nous tremblons."

1603.  Durrell, Lawrence. THE ALEXANDRIA QUARTET. London:
       Faber, 1962.

       See commentaries by J. McMahon for comparison with the
       works of Sade, item 1673.

1604.  Ellrich, Robert J.  Review  of  LE MARQUIS  DE  SADE,
       COLLOQUE D'AIX-EN-PROVENCE.   FRENCH REVIEW 44 (1970):
       618-620.

       Gives  a review of LE MARQUIS DE SADE,  edited by Jean
       Bio et al., (Paris:  Armand Colin, 1968).   Regrets
       that "certain 'non-academic' Sadians were unwilling to
       associate themselves with an 'academic' study of their
       author," and  were  therefore  absent  at  the  Sade
       Colloquium which  took  place  at  Aix-en-Provence  in
       February 1966.   Believes that "what to do with  Sade"
       was  clearly  on the minds of the group  assembled  at
       that meeting.   Concludes:   "For many reasons we need
       more  work  on Sade.   The  papers  and  discussions
       contained  in  this colloquium provide an  encouraging
       example  of  the ways in which historians of  culture,
       students  of literature,  and psychologists  can  work
       together  to advance our understanding of a figure who
       cannot be understood by any one of those groups. . . .
       Perhaps  the most valuable residuum of the reading  of
       these  acta  is  the heightened  awareness  of  Sade's
       relationship  to his own time on the one hand,  and of
       his 'relevance' to our own time on the other."

1605.  Ersch, J. S.   "Sur Sade."   LA  FRANCE  LITTERAIRE  3
       (1798):  221-222.

1606.  Fabre, Jean.  "Sade et le roman noir."  In LE MARQUIS DE
       SADE.  Paris:  Armand Colin, 1968, pp. 253-278.

       Traces  and recounts the history and tradition of  the
       "roman noir" but states that, while there are elements
       of  roman noir in Sade's work,  the author goes beyond
       that genre.  Sade incorporated some elements of it but
       he  also created a literary universe which  bears  his
       poetic stamp.   EUGENIE DE FRANVAL,  ALINE ET VALCOUR,
       the second JUSTINE are poems.   However, concedes that
       in  works like HISTOIRE DE JULIETTE,  LES  CENT  VINGT
       JOURNEES,  or in LA PHILOSOPHIE DANS LE BOUDOIR,  Sade

"s'emmure en lui-même, prisonnier, bien plus férocement que de n'importe laquelle de ses geôles, de son hyperbole onirique et de sa vaticination forcenée. Nous sommes alors non seulement au-delà du roman noir, mais au-delà de toute littérature, dans un univers dont l'inventeur se condamne à la solitude, où tout étant dépassé, l'idée, le verbe, la colère, le désir, le rêve, tout risque de s'abolir dans le néant." Concludes that the works of Sade are not reducible to a type of roman noir.

1607.   Faye, Jean-Pierre. "Au secours de Sade." ESPRIT 29 (1961): 623-626.

Quotes alternately from the works of Louis-Ferdinand Céline and from those of Sade and invites us to ponder on a "parallèle plein de sens." Concludes that between Céline and Sade there is at least "une curieuse rencontre" (from a political point of view).

1608.   Fayolle, Roger. "Etre professeur de lettres, hier et aujourd'hui." LITTERATURE 19 (October 1975): 8-15.

Cites Pierre Clarac and Pierre Brunel, who recommend that, when choosing authors to be taught in schoolrooms, one pick "representants de l'humanité éternelle" (including Sade): "Ce qui donne au divin marquis sa valeur irremplacable, c'est l'audace de son entreprise."

1609.   Fé, Franco. Review of LAUTREAMONT E SADE, by Maurice Blanchot. IL PONTE 31 (1975): 296-297.

Reviews briefly the book LAUTREMONT E SADE, by Maurice Blanchot, originally published in 1948 but translated into Italian only in 1974. Observes: "Diciamo solo che di Sade è qui messo in risalto l'ostinato sforzo di supreare i limiti terreni, di di sperimentare tutto per mettersi al sicuro da tutto, per negare gli uomini, la natura e Dio e arrivare a quel punto supremo che è 'l'uomo unico nel suo genere.'"

1610.   Fiedler, Leslie. "Prototypes and Early Adaptations." In LOVE AND DEATH IN THE AMERICAN NOVEL. New York: Criterion, 1960, pp. 101, 114, 117.

States that "the primary meaning of the gothic romance, then, lies in its substitution of terror for love as a central theme of fiction. The titillation of sex denied, it offers its readers a vicarious participation in a flirtation with death--approach and retreat, the fatal orgasm eternally mounting and eternally checked. More than that, however, the gothic is the product of an implicit aesthetic that replaces the classic concept of nothing-in-excess with the revolutionary doctrine that nothing succeeds like excess. . . . the supremely disgusting art of JULIETTE or THE ONE HUNDRED AND TWENTY DAYS OF SODOM . . . represents the final abomination for which the gothic yearns. . . ."

1611. Fink, Béatrice. "Utopian Nurtures." STUDIES ON VOLTAIRE AND THE EIGHTEENTH-CENTURY 19 (1980): 664-671.

States that "food and its concomitants are components of French Enlightenment utopias on the level of construct as well as on that of myth." Investigates Morelly's BASILIADE (1735), Mercier's L'AN 2440 (1770), Fénelon's TELEMAQUE (1669), Sade's ALINE ET VALCOUR (1795). The latter is characterized by "rampant cannibalism" and underlines Butua's "antithetical character with respect to the other texts." But concludes that a common denominator is to be found in all the texts studied: The consumer of all these utopias "react against culture by their resort to 'natural' foods."

1612. Fowler, Albert. "The Marquis de Sade in America." BOOKS ABROAD 31 (1957): 353-356.

See also article by Ryland, item 621.

Comments on Sade's popularity following the 1952 publication of Edmund Wilson's "The Vogue of the Marquis de Sade," but this article is less a study of Sade in America than a comparison of Rousseau's and Sade's political attitudes and conceptions of natural man. Concludes that "neither Sade nor Rousseau was mad, but they were not entirely sane, and the modern age which is so concerned with their ideas of freedom shares in large degree their devotion to the natural man, benign as Rousseau saw him, malign as Sade saw him."

1613.  Fowler, Albert. "Rousseau and Sade: Freedom Unlimited." SOUTHWEST REVIEW 43 (1958): 205-211.

Contrasts Sade with Rousseau in order to investigate "the tradition of naturalism, a lingua franca extending across frontiers of nation, class, and generation." Emphasizes the fact that its adepts are men with strange and eccentric desires: "So numerous and evident are these instances of instability, physical as well as mental, among the naturalists that genius throughout this period has overtones of disaster."

1614.  Fowlie, Wallace. AGE OF SURREALISM. Bloomington, Ind.: Indiana University Press, 1950, pp. 78-82.

Gives much credit to Sade as an influence on some of the surrealist/symbolist writers and poets: "No such figure as Herodiade can exist alone. She must have ancestors and descendants." Names the marquis de Sade's stories, such as JULIETTE and JUSTINE, where "voluptuousness is achieved in scenes of crime and destruction."

1615.  France, Anatole. "Notice." In SADE, D.A.F. DORCI OU LA BIZARRERIE DU SORT. Paris: Charaway, 1881, pp. 7-29.

"Rather general, with many of the inaccuracies of the period. Yet A. France, speaking as critic, is fair to Sade, recognizes his intelligence, critical judgment, and defends him against those who were comparing him to Gilles de Retz." (Quoted from Cabeen, item 8).

1616.  Galey, Matthieu. "Le mythe Sadien." LA REVUE DE PARIS, 75 (1968): 112-121.

Also published as a preface to LA PHILOSOPHIE DANS LE BOUDOIR (ed. J.J. Pauvert). Gives a history of the interest suggested among writers by the work of Sade. Names in particular, Lamartine, Lautréamont, Baudelaire, Barbey d'Aurevilly (who was not too flattering) Sainte-Beuve (who granted Sade one of his Lundis), Gustave Flaubert (one of the most enthusiastic), Edmond de Goncourt (who advised reading Sade), Apollinaire ("une mine à exploiter"), and Maurice Heine (who dedicated his life to research on Sade), P. Klossowski, M. Blanchot, and G. Bataille among the moderns, to name but a few mentioned.

1617.   Gallop, Jane.   INTERSECTIONS:   A READING OF SADE WITH
        BATAILLE, BLANCHOT, AND KLOSSOWKI.   Lincoln, Neb.:
        University of Nebraska Press, 1981.   135 p.

        This is a doctoral dissertation.   See annotation to
        item 880.   Reviewed by Peter Collier, MODERN LANGUAGES
        REVIEW 77 (1982):   967; Ann Smock, SUB-STANCE   35
        (1982):   72-73; M. B. Holland, FRENCH STUDIES 36
        (1982):   360;  and Jefferson Humphries, L'ESPRIT
        CREATURE 4 (Winter 1963):   84-85.

1618.   Garai, J.   "L'Invasion du sadisme."   LE NOUVEAU CANDIDE,
        9 October 1966, pp. 4-8.

        Stresses Sade's influence in the history of ideas
        because he catalogued perversions at a time when most
        writers were still collecting herbarium:   "(Sade) se
        dresse au carrefour de deux siècles comme un énorme
        défi aux moeurs et au bon sens."   Deplores the fact

        that sadophilia and sadology occupy such a large place
        in our lives.

1619.   Garçon, Maurice (Maître).   "Sade, Paulhan, et le
        Président." L'EXPRESS, 4 January 1957, p. 25.

        Speech delivered to the courts by the counsel for the
        defense, attorney Maurice Garçon, on the occasion of
        the publication of twenty-eight books written by Sade.
        One of the witnesses for the defense was Jean Paulhan,
        who had written a short dissertation on Sade.   He
        disputed the ambiguity of the notion of morality:
        "L'importance de Sade, à la fois comme écrivain--c'est
        un trés grand écrivain--et comme philosophe, me paraît
        si considérable qu'interdire les livres de Sade
        reviendrait à peu près, étant donné que nous lisons
        tous les jours des oeuvres de ses disciples, à
        interdire le livre et à permettre la même chose dans
        des journaux quotidiens.   Il y aurait là quelque chose
        d'extrèmement choquant."

1620.   Gassin, Jean.   "Le sadisme dans l'oeuvre de Camus."   LE
        REVUE DES LETTRES MODERNES 360-365 (1973):   121-144.

        Believes that inclination to sadism--not defined--is
        found in the male heroes in Albert Camus's works.
        That tendency would be most prevalent in their sexual

lives:    "Frustrés et doutant d'eux-mêmes,  ces hommes
sont  alors  la  proie  de  leurs  pulsions  sadiques.
Celles-ci,   pour  s'actualiser,   trouvent  dans   la
sexualité des héros le terrain de choix. . . ."

1621.  Gaudon,  Jean.  "Lamartine lecteur de Sade."  MERCURE DE
       FRANCE 343 (1961): 420-438.

       Examines Alphonse de Lamartine's poem,  LA CHUTE  D'UN
       ANGE, and compares it with Sade's JUSTINE, citing some
       direct  "borrowings."   Stresses  the fact  that  many
       traits of LA CHUTE D'UN ANGE can be interpreted from a
       Sadian  perspective.   Affirms  in  conclusion   that
       Lamartine's  poem could well be subtitled LES MALHEURS
       DE LA VERTU.

1622.  Glaser, Horst A.  "Literarischer Anarchismus bei de Sade
       und Burroughs:   Zur methodologie seiner  Erkenntnis."
       In  LITERATURWISSENSCHAFT  UND  SOZIALWISSENSCHAFTEN:
       GRUNDLAGEN  UND MODELLANALYSER.   Edited by Thomas  W.
       Metscher et al. Stuttgart: Metzler, 1971, pp. 341-356.

       This  bold  essay  by  a  young  scholar  in   German
       literature consists of two parts:   1) a  programmatic
       statement  on the need for a new radical sociology  of
       art   which  combines  close  textual  and  structural
       analysis  with  broad  dialectical  categories,  2)  a
       tentative   application   of   these   priniciples   in
       comparative  remarks on the work of Sade  and  William
       Burroughs.   "With  their utopian ideal of  anarchism,
       both S. and B. are bent on the destruction of anything
       that  can be called a barrier,  i.e.,  social, moral or
       even   psychological  laws.   They  want  to   destroy
       everything that  obstructs  their  wild  and  extreme
       individualism,  i.e.,  the  world of facts  and  their
       rationality" (pp. 348-49).  From a neomarxist point of
       view,   S.'s   novels   are   seen   as   philosophical
       anticipations  of the French Revolution,  because they
       draw  the most radical conclusions from  18th  century
       rationalism.   Specifically,  they  are to be read  as
       sarcastic  parodies of Rousseau's moral and  political
       philosophy  (pp.   349-50).   By  contrast,   B.'s
       experimental  novel NAKED LUNCH (1959) is  interpreted
       as  the self-destructive rebellion of  an  avant-garde
       writer   against   the  conformist  and   destructive
       tendencies  of late capitalist society (pp.  351-56).
       However,  while  S.'s thought is basically progressive
       and   potentially  liberating,   B.'s  tends   to   be

regressive in its complete irrationality and is to be considered symptomatic of capitalist decadence.

1623. Goldschlager, Alain. "L'image sadienne dans l'oeuvre de Stendhal." REVUE BELGE DE PHILOLOGIE ET D'HISTOIRE 57 (1979): 612-627.

Attempts to delineate the ties that bound Stendhal to Sade. Discusses in particular their common pessimism toward love, the attraction they both had for beings marginal to society. But mainly stresses "l'engagement politique de Stendhal et de Sade [qui] se fonde sur une conception commune de la société et de l'impossiblité pour l'homme de se réaliser dans les normes étroites et insensées qu'elle impose. . . . Ce que nos deux auteurs ne peuvent accepter dans la société de leur temps, c'est l'orientation religieuse de la morale et des lois. Athées tous les deux, ils luttent contre le pouvoir et l'oppression de l'Eglise. Cette lutte se mène sur tous les fronts--politique, morale, éthique, théosophique--et par tous les moyens--la polémique, l'ironie, le sarcasme. Athées, ils le sont sans concessions mais luttent dans des contextes différents. . . ."

1624. Goldschlager, Alain. "Sade et Chateaubriand." NINETEENTH-CENTURY FRENCH STUDIES 2 (1974): 1-12.

Attempts to change the myths connected with Chateaubriand, who presents a much more complex image than that of a man imbued with Christian faith, poetical delirium, and lyrical metaphors. Rather many comparisons between him and Sade can be made. Both were aristocrats with good educations. But both "furent marqués par des tabous, des préjugés sociaux, religieux et sexuels identiques." Concludes that as surprising as it might be, this tie between the two writers reveals much to be learned: "Elle change et enrichit l'image de Chateaubriand, image sclérosées par trop d'analyses orientées. Elle humanise Sade et le réintègre à sa place méritée d'écrivain--au sens le plus élevé du mot--et de miroir d'une époque."

1625. Hayman, Ronald. "Holes and Corners: Sade and the Structuralists." ENCOUNTER, July 1976, pp. 71-76.

A misleading title unless John Fraser, Balzac, Apollinaire, and Swinburne have of late made it to the rank of the structuralists. Author does mention Sade, Barthes, and "jouissance." Concludes: "Though Dr. Martin writes very well about Mallarmé and Ponge, he might have done more to fortify his main argument if he had ventured far enough into the no man's land to risk a comparative piece of practical criticism on texts by Wittgenstein and Chomsky."

1626.   Heine, Maurice. "Actualités de Sade." LE SURREALISME AU SERVICE DE LA REVOLUTION 2 (October 1930): 3-5.

Almost two hundred years after the birth of the marquis de Sade, proposes to bring to light on a regular basis some hitherto unknown facts and texts relating to the marquis. Presents a letter dated 4 October 1779 written by Sade to Martin Quiros. Includes a text of René Char, a letter (written by Maurice Heine) to M. Abel Hermant of the French Academy, and a review of LES INFORTUNES DE LA VERTU, published by Fourcade. The "Actualités de Sade," numbered I, III, and IV, were also published by Gallimard in 1950 in Heine's THE MARQUIS DE SADE, ed. by Gilbert Lély, pp. 75-104.

1627.   Heine, Maurice. "Sade." In TABLEAU DE LA LITTERATURE FRANCAISE, XVIIe ET XVIIIe SIECLES." Paris: Editions de la Nouvelle Revue Française, 1939, Paris: Gallimard, 1962, pp. 369-372.

1628.   Hénaff, Marcel. "Les âges de la lecture sadienne." ROMANSK INSTITUT KOBENHAVNS UNIVERSITET 68 (November 1979): 1-51.

1629.   Hénaff, Marcel. "Réponses à Yvon Belaval et Ebbe Spang-Hanssen." ROMANIC REVIEW 16 (1981): 190-192, 195-196.

1630.   Henric, Jacques. "L'Intolérable et l'Infâme." OBLIQUES 12-13 (1977): 39-45.

Contrasts Sade, "L'Intolérable pour toute communcauté," to Robespierre, "L'Infâme parce qu'il reste le modèle du héros révolutionnaire." Sade was behind bars under every regime in France and firmly believed that this demonstrated the danger of the abuse of power personified by Robespierre who is sometimes remembered as a Christ-like figure even though he was a guilty power. Sade is often blamed

for the faults of the society he wrote about but his
literature reflects to some extent the craziness of
the time.

1631. Henry, Charles. LA VERITE SUR LE MARQUIS DE SADE.
Paris: E. Dentu, 1887.

Proposes to tell the truth and publishes anonymously
the first, if weak, defense of Sade. The identity of
the writer of this essay was revealed by Lucien
Descaves in an article published in JOURNAL, 24 April
1930.

1632. Holland, M. B. Review of INTERSECTIONS by Jane Gallop.
FRENCH STUDIES 36 (1982): 360.

Review of INTERSECTIONS: A READING OF SADE WITH
BATAILLE, BLANCHOT, AND KLOSSOWSKI by Jane Gallop,
published by the University of Nebraska Press, 1981.
Observes that "Gallop's work will satisfy no
one. . . . Nevertheless, in her lively exploration of
the ins and outs of whoring and sodomy, she intimates
a fundamental pattern of textual behavior which no
theory of fiction has yet defined or even truly
recognized. Gallop has written a daringly original
book, and one which, having blazed its trail, may well
remain as a landmark."

1633. Hoog, Armand. "Sade et Laclos." LA NEF 14 (1946): 113-
116.

Compares Laclos's philosophy with that of Sade and
contrasts some of the most obvious differences between
the two authors, with Laclos coming out second best.

1634. Humphries, Jefferson. Review of INTERSECTIONS, A
READING OF SADE WITH BATAILLE, BLANCHOT AND
KLOSSOWSKI. L'ESPRIT CREATEUR 22, 4 (Winter 1983):
84-85.

Reviews very briefly this "courageous and important
little" book by Jane Gallop published by University of
Nebraska Press in 1981. States: "To engage in
literary activity is, whether one likes it or not, to
enter into the most perversely unpragmatic, purely
pleasure-oriented domain there is, aside from raw sex.

And yet, as such, literature, like sexual libertinage, is a hyperbolic exemplar of all human endeavor and human life."

1635. Hurtret, M.  "Le marquis de Sade."  MEMOIRES DE LA FEDERATION DES SOCIETES D'HISTOIRE ET D'ARCHEOLOGIE DE L'AISNE 1 (1966): 26-27.

1636. Illuminati, Augusto.  SOCIETA E PROGRESSO NELL'ILLUMINISMO FRANCESE.  Urbino:  Argalia, 1972, pp. 249-255.

Makes some interesting comparisons among De Maistre, Sade and Kant.

1637. Jackson, Robert Louis.  "Dostoevski and the Marquis de Sade."  RUSSIAN LITERATURE N.S. 4 (1976): 27-45.

Refuses the concept of Dostoevski as a Russian Sade, as advocated by Ivan Turgenev, but mentions several references made to Sade by some of the heroes in Dostoevski's novels. However, believes that the total nihilism of Sade is only occasional in Dostoevski. Concludes:  "In the final analysis, the challenge of Sadean man and philosophy could only be met by one who recognized man's earthly truth as well as his passion for transcendence, one who has explored the Sadean abyss, yet, like Dante, had reached the 'other shore.' Such a genius was Dostoevski, one who wove the diverse threads of an entire epoch--beginning with the Enlightenment and ending with the age of nihilism--into an unforgettable epic design."

1638. Jacob, A.  "SADE, FOURIER, LOYOLA."  HOMME ET LA SOCIETE 26 (1972): 253-256.

Reviews of essays by Roland Barthes written in 1971.

1639. Janin, Jules.  "LE MARQUIS DE SADE SUIVI DE LA VERITE SUR LES DEUX PROCES CRIMINELS DU MARQUIS DE SADE, PAR LE BIBLIOPHILE JACOB.  Paris:  Chez les marchands de nouveauté, 1834.

Gives an apocryphal biography of Sade.  Also some bibliographical details.  Reviewed by J. Piazzoli in CATALOGUE DE LIVRES ANCIENS. . . .  Milan:  Librairie Dumolard Frères, 1878, p. 396.

1640. Jannoud, Claude. "Roland Barthes réunit dans une même lecture Sade le maudit, Fourier l'utopiste et Loyola le jésuite." FIGARO LITTERAIRE, 3 December 1971, p. 24.

Review of SADE, FOURIER, LOYOLA by Roland Barthes who, he says, has collected in the same essay, Sade: the damned, Fourier: the utopist, and Loyola: the Jesuit.

1641. Jean, Marcel and A. Mazei. "Sade, l'homme and Sade, le poète et le savant." In GENESE DE LA PENSEE MODERNE. Paris: Correa, 1950, pp. 29-42.

Sees in Sade a precursor of the romantic movement which he greatly influenced. Also treats of Lautréamont, Rimbaud, Mallarmé, Jarry, Apollinaire, and Roussel, seven "essential writers."

Reviewed by P. Lebesque in OISE LIBEREE, 22 July 1950, pp. 59-60; by C. Mauriac in TABLE RONDE, July 1950, pp. 109-118; A. P. in PARU, June 1950 pp. 59-60.

1642. Jean, Raymond. "L'Imitation de Sade." EUROPE 522 (1972): 88-105.

Reappraises the surrealist revolt as an imitation and emulation of Sade. In turn, because of the surrealists' influence, several readings of Sade's writings are now possible: at the historical, political, philosophical, clinical, or even flatly pornographic level. Takes as a specific example of influence the work of André Breton and 1) cites several surrealist authors; 2) investigates the literary relationship between Apollinaire and Sade after the publication of the LETTRES A LOU (from Apollinaire to Louise de Coligny-Châtillon). Considers these letters as a precise example "particulièrement significatif, de la façon dont Sade, par des voies obliques, a pu agir sur la conscience érotique de certains écrivains."

1643. Jean, Raymond. "Sade et le surréalisme." LE MARQUIS DE SADE. Paris: Colin, 1968, pp. 241-251.

Proceedings of the colloquium of Aix-en-Provence of 19 and 20 February 1968. States that Sade's books can be approached through many angles--historical,

political, philosophical, clinical, pornographic--but
feels that the most rewarding interpretation, because
it is so rich in possibilities, is a "surrealistic"
reading. Quotes several successors of Sade who were
influenced by his writings.

1644. Jelenski, Constantin.   Introduction to HANS BELLMER.
Edited by Alex Grall.   New York:   Macmillan Company,
1973, pp. 1-23.

Sees a rapprochement between the artistic and
philosophical values depicted in Sade's writings and
Bellmer's drawings.   States that "art which sets free
is rarely the work of a free man, but rather of a man
obsessed by the confining walls that curb his desire,
frustrate or waylay him. It is the work of a prisoner
digging an imaginary road to freedom . . . the Doll
which Bellmer began to construct at thirty-one was an
attempt to create in his imagination what only murder
could have achieved in real life:   the illusion of
grasping the essential being in the throes of
death. . . . Can the imagination not find in her
existence the joy, the exaltation and the fear for
which it was searching?   For Bellmer, this impulsion
is no ordinary 'compensation'. . . . He is a
materialist, like Sade, and believes that all forms of
expression (posing, sound, words, graphics, the
creation of objects) are the workings of the same
group of mechanisms. . . . Bellmer belongs to that
proud race, now rare, who refuse to consider the
forbidden as a necessary adjunct of exaltation. He is
of the same race as Sade. . . ."

1645. Klossowski, Pierre. "L'androgyne dans la représentation
sadienne." OBLIQUES 12-13 (1977): 245-247.

This was excerpted from "Sade ou le philosophe
scélérat" published in TEL QUEL 28 (Winter 1967):   3-
22, item 973.

1646. Klossowski, Pierre.   "Sade et Fourier." TOPIQUE 4-5
(October 1970):   79-98.

Investigates the attitudes of both Sade and Fourier as
related to the sexual drive in specific economic
contexts.   Although he finds Fourier and Sade at
opposition to one another, characterized by what he
calls "céladonisme," feels that both writers, in fact,

tend to put value on price--Fourier on virtue, Sade on the currency spent: "Supprimez le numéraire et vous aurez la communication universelle entre les êtres. Par cette sorte de défi, Sade prouve justement que la notion de valeur et de prix est inscrite dans le fond même de l'émotion voluptueuse, et que rien n'est plus contraire à la jouissance que la gratuité."

Also stresses the mediating role of money between the closed world of abnormalities and the normative world.

1647. Klossowski, Pierre. "Sade y Fourier." PLURAL: CRITICA, ARTE, LITERATURA 11 (1972): 29-34.

Excerpt from the essay "Sade et Fourier" published by Fata Morgana, item 1646.

1648. Klossowski, Pierre. LES DERNIERS TRAVAUX DE GULLIVER suivi de SADE ET FOURIER. Montpellier: Imprimerie de la Charité, 1974, pp. 33-77.

Begins with the question: "How is economy, independently of the law of supply and demand, an expression, representation, and interpretation of the affective life of the individual and of society?" Takes as a testimony of social upheavals the events that occurred during Sade's and Fourier's lifetimes. Asserts that, in order to understand how sensuous emotion can only be an object of mercantilism and become an economic factor in our industrialized epoch, one must consider what is meant by sexuality and eroticism. Concludes: "Sade veut démontrer que de part et d'autre il ne s'agit que du même maître qui se cache sous le couvert des institutions et qui, dans la SOCIETE DES AMIS DU CRIME, se manifeste sous son vrai visage. Ce maître, c'est encore une fois la monstruosité intégrale: et le numéraire, le signe honteux de sa propre richesse, devient signe de sa gloire. C'est par le numéraire dépensé pour le phantasme que la société clandestine imaginées par Sade tient en otage le monde des sublimation institutionnelles."

1649. Klossowski, Pierre. SADE, MON PROCHAIN. Paris: Editions du Seuil, 1947.

"Worth of essay is in its provocativeness; winner of PRIX SAINTE-BEUVE in 1947." (Quoted from Cabeen, item 8.)

Reviewed by G. Bataille in CRITIQUE 15-16 (1947): 147-160; and in CRITIQUE 17 (1947): 304-312; by M. Blanchot in TEMPS MODERNES 25, October 1947, pp. 597-598; by Gaeton Picon in FONTAINE 62 (1947): 646-654.

1650. Konczacki, Janina M. Review of WIEK MARKIZA DE SADE by Jerzy Lojek. In THE EIGHTEENTH CENTURY, A CURRENT BIBLIOGRAPHY. New York: AMS Press, 1978, pp. 440-441.

See item 1668 for annotation.

1651. Lacan, Jacques. "Kant avec Sade." CRITIQUE 19 (April 1963): 291-313.

Also included as an afterword to LA PHILOSOPHIE DANS LE BOUDOIR. In OEUVRES COMPLETES DU MARQUIS DE SADE. Vol. III. Paris: Cercle du livre précieux, 1966, pp. 553-576.

1652. Lacan, Jacques. "Kant avec Sade." In ECRITS II. Paris: Seuil, 1971.

This masterly--and difficult--essay attempts to show that LA PHILOSOPHIE DANS LE BOUDOIR, coming eight years after THE CRITIC OF PRACTICAL REASON, not only is in complete agreement with it but further more completes it. Investigates the relationship of happiness/pleasure to the law. States: "Si le bonheur est agrément sans rupture du sujet à sa vie, comme le définit très clairement la CRITIQUE, il est clair qu'il se refuse à qui ne renonce pas à la voie du désir" [sic]. Concludes "que le fantasme sadien trouve mieux à se situer dans les portants de l'éthique chrétienne qu'ailleurs, c'est ce que nos repères de structure rendent facile à saisit. . . . L'apologie du crime ne le pousse qu'a l'aveu detourne de la loi."

See also article "Paraphrase de Kant avec Sade," item 1653.

1653. Lacan, Jacques. "Paraphrase de Kant avec Sade." SCILICET, 2-3 (1970): 283-324.

This long, difficult essay was published annonymously though it has been assigned to Lacan. The reader is advised to have Lacan's essay "Kant avec Sade" to which references are made in front of him for comparison purposes. Forty-seven paragraphs are discussed and commented on i.e. Paragraph £5: "Kant avec Sade": "LA PHILOSOPHIE DANS LE BOUDOIR vient huit ans après LA CRITIQUE DE RAISON PRATIQUE. Si après avoir vu qu'elle s'y accorde, nous démontrons qu'elle la complète, nous dirons qu'elle donne la vérité de la CRITIQUE." Paragraph £5 in "Paraphrase": "LA PHILOSOPHIE DANS LE BOUDOIR vient huit ans après la CRITIQUE DE LA RAISON PRATIQUE (celle-ci est de 1788, l'autre de 1796, quand Sade, sauvé de justesse après Thermidor, use de la liberté de publier). Si nous voyons qu'elle s'y accorde, que c'est du même sujet que toutes deux traitent, et que la PHILOSOPHIE complète, sur ce sujet, la CRITIQUE, au sens où elle lui apporte quelque chose qui lui manque, nous dirons qu'elle en donne 'la vérité',--la clef susceptible d'ouvrir ce sur quoi la CRITIQUE se ferme."

1654.  Lacombe, Roger G. SADE ET SES MASQUES. Paris: Payot, 1974. 271 p.

Sees Sade as a writer interested mainly in diversity in time and space and, therefore, one of the intiators of the comparative method. Discusses the possible sources of Sade, in particular LE TOMBEAU DE MOLAY for L'HISTOIRE DE JULIETTE, but concedes that the characters and details of the story are the marquis's own invention. Analyzes in depth Sade's concept of utopia, his concern for criminal justice, his stand against capital punishment, his theories on libertinage. Concludes with an important statement on Sade as a precursor: he was a pioneer in a sexual revolution with all its political, religious, and moral implications. In the realm of physiology, credits Sade for having prepared the way for the Kinsey reports; in abnormal psychology, claims that Sade accurately appraised, well ahead of his time, the importance of genetic background in the study of sexual deviations. On many issues, sees Sade as extremely modern, especially as an advocate of organized peace. In this way, he can be viewed as anticipating such organizations as the United Nations.

Reviewed by G. Cerruti, STUDI FRANCESI 19 (1975): 363; M. Delon, ANNALES HISTORIQUES DE LA REVOLUTION FRANCAISE, July-September 1977, pp. 482-483; M. Delon, DIX-HUITIEME SIECLE 8 (1976): 504-505; and Robert E. Taylor, EIGHTEENTH-CENTURY CURRENT BIBLIOGRAPHY, (1974), p. 372.

1655. Lafourcade, Georges. "Sade et Swinburne." In JEUNESSE DE SWINBURNE, 1837-1867. Paris and Strasbourg: Les belles lettres, 1928, pp. 264-267, 354-358.

Refers briefly to Sade, who apparently influenced Swinburne. The latter was acquainted with the marquis's works and is quoted as saying: "I think your remarks on JUSTINE the most sensible I ever heard. They quite give my own feeling, with which I never found any one to agree before; usually that work is either a stimulant for an old beast or an emetic for a young man, instead of a valuable study to rational curiosity."

1656. Lafourcade, Georges. "William Blake et le marquis de Sade." CONFLUENCES 1 (1943): 156-162.

Discusses the influence Sade had on one of his contemporaries: William Blake. This is also mentioned by Vincenzo Barba in INTEPRETAZIONI DI SADE item 1152.

1657. Laugaa-Traut, Françoise. LECTURES DE SADE. Paris: Colin, 1973. 370 p.

Presents excerpts, preceded by commentaries, from most important secondary sources published on Sade. Difficult reading, because none of the essays are in complete form, but valuable, especially since, to date, this is the only one of its kind. Well researched.

Reviewed by Daniel R. Dupêcher, OEUVRES ET CRITIQUEES. Vol. III, no. 7 (Summer 1978): 141-144.

1658. Lehmann, A. G. "Surrealism, Love, and the Marquis de Sade." LISTENER, 4 February 1960, pp. 212-214.

Reports on a BBC radio broadcast transmitted on 18 January 1960 which once more relates the Surrealists to Sade. See item 1671.

1659. Lély, Gilbert. "Le marquis de Sade et Rétif de la
       Bretonne." MERCURE DE FRANCE 331 (1957): 364-366.

       Discusses the antagonism between Sade and Rétif de la
       Bretonne, which even shows up in their respective
       writings.

1660. Lély, Gilbert. Preface and notes to CAHIERS PERSONNELS,
       1803-1804. Paris: Corréa, 1953, pp. i-xviii.

       Describes in detail the papers collected by Sade as
       NOTES LITTERAIRES and partially published as CAHIERS
       PERSONNELS. Among the manuscripts were included
       forty-two excerpts from the novel DELPHINE, written by
       Madame de Staël, which illustrate two main themes:
       1) adversity and 2) debilitating old age. Asserts,
       however, that these assorted notes, as important and
       significant as they are, do not totally complete the
       picture of Sade's literary preoccupations around 1804.

1661. Lély, Gilbert. "Sade a-t-il été jaloux de Laclos?"
       NOUVELLE REVUE FRANÇAISE 1 (1953): 1124-1129.

       A short article which suggests that Sade might have
       been jealous of Laclos because the former failed in
       his IDEE SUR LES ROMANS to mention the latter and then
       proceeded to outline plans for a new novel which
       closely resembled LES LIAISONS. Considers this to be
       especially curious since the two men had spent seven
       months imprisoned together and must have discussed
       their literary plans.

1662. Lély, Gilbert. "Panorama de Sade." GAZETTE DE LAUSANNE
       30 (6 February 1965): 19.

1663. Lemaître, Maurice. LE BOUDOIR DE LA PHILOSOPHIE
       LETTRISTE, D'APRES SADE. Paris: Centre de Créativité-
       Eds. Lettristes, 1978.

1664. Lepage, Jacques. "Notes pour un dossier d'érotologie:
       Çiva, Sade et Novalis." MARGINALES 137 (1971): 52-54.

       Sets down a few precepts concerning erotica and
       contrasts the views of Novalis who, he says, defined
       evil as free will, with that of Sade who embraced a
       view closer to the Hindu triad personified as Civa.

1665. Levimakarius, L. "Sade et Pasolini dans le cercle de la transgression." HOMME ET SOCIETE 41-4 (1976): 273-275.

Discusses the film SALO directed by Pasolini and compares its mode of transgression with that of Sade.

1666. L'hoir, Maurice. PAGES CURIEUSES. Paris: La Grille, 1926.

1667. Lobet, Marcel. "Du mal de Sade à l'ennui de Benjamin Constant." REVUE GENERALE BELGE 100 (September 1964): 21-33.

Compares today's mal du siècle with that of the eighteenth century, especially as it takes shape in Sade. States that the aim of Sade, a man controlled by boredom, is to do evil for the sake of evil in a sort of intellectual absolute which Lobet connects with romantic types like Chateaubriand, Sénancour, and Benjamin Constant. Concludes with an overview of two centuries of literature consecrated to personal emancipation and sees in Benjamin Constant the literary transition between the psychological frivolity of the 18th century and the more incisive tragedies of this century's children.

1668. Lojek, Jerzy. WIEK MARKIZA DE SADE; SZICE Z HISTORII OBYCZAJOS I LITERATURY WE FRANCJI XVIII WIEDU. Lublin: Wydawnictwo Lubelskie, 1972, pp. 227-430.

Includes four sections entitled The Century of the Marquis de Sade: Studies on Mores and Civilization during the Eighteenth-Century; Crébillon fils and His Contemporaries or Smiling Libertinage; Restif de la Bretonne or Condemned Libertinage; The Marquis de Sade or Human Nature Unveiled.

1669. Mardore, M. LA PREMIERE COMMUNION. Paris: Gallimard, 1962.

This work, which utilizes the plot of EUGENIE DE FRANVAL, was, according to Giorgio Cerruti, inspired by Sade.

1670. Martin, René. "Le Marquis de Sade: Disciple de
      Lucrèce?" In INFLUENCE DE LA GRECE ET DE ROME SUR
      L'OCCIDENT MODERNE. Edited by Raymond Chevalier.
      Paris: Belles Lettres, 1977, pp. 227-39.

      Points out several similarities in outlook between
      Sade and his epicurean ancestor, Lucretius. The main
      themes mentioned as common to both writers are:  1) a
      sensualist epistemology;  2) a viewing of death as  a
      source for life;  3) a consistent denial of religious
      beliefs;  4) and  the necessity to substitute laws  of
      nature    for    religious    rulings.    Concludes:
      "l'important, c'est de constater qu'entre 1780 et 1790
      les thèmes épicuriens les plus orthodoxes tiennent une
      place  non négligeable dans la pensée du marquis,  qui
      est  le  premier  à s'en rendre  compte puisque  nous
      l'avons vu se glorifier de son 'épicurisme.'"

1671. Matthews, J. H.  "The Right Person for Surrealism."  YALE
      FRENCH STUDIES 35 (December 1965):  89-95.

      Reviews a talk by a BBC broadcaster, A. G. Lehmann,
      published  in  the LISTENER on 18  January  1960,  who
      related Sade to the surrealists on the occasion of the
      "Exposition internationale du Surréalisme,  1959-1960"
      (with emphasis on eros).  Feels that Sade  indeed
      enjoyed  "an incontestable reputation among surrealist
      writers and painters" and, as suggested by Lehmann, he
      "set little store by conventional norms of sanity,  or
      conventional   artistic   and   moral   ideas,   or,
      significantly,  by  the  approval of his  fellow-men."
      States also that two of the most fervent defenders  of
      Sade--Maurice  Heine and Gilbert Lély--were members of
      the surrealist circle.  Concludes that it is perfectly
      logical that the surrealists should have admired  Sade
      and  followed  in  his footsteps for they  "have  long
      since  given ample proof of their  complete  disregard
      for   criticism  directed  against  their  unshakable
      confidence  in  the validity of desire  as  motivating
      force of all human activity.   For them the world Sade
      depicts  is one in which desire is placed before moral
      and social constraint.  It is, therefore, an exemplary
      fictional   universe   in   which   violently   anti-
      conventional  attitudes confront  all that  tends  to
      combat  the  free expression of desire,  and  does  so
      triumphantly."

1672.  Matthieu, Galey.  "Le Mythe sadien."  REVUE DE PARIS 75,
       no. 2 (1968):  112-121.

       "An assessment of the reputation of the Marquis de
       Sade from his contemporaries to present day figures,
       with conflicting opinions quoted from Baudelaire,
       Larousse, Sainte-Beuve, Flaubert, Sartre, and Barthes.
       Concludes that Sade has become a modern myth, a
       repository for all the meanings his writings have
       acquired."  Drawing, nine notes.  (Quoted from L. R.
       Atkins, HISTORICAL ABSTRACTS, item 15.)

1673.  McMahon, Joseph.  "Where Does Life Begin?"  YALE FRENCH
       STUDIES 35 (December 1965):  96-113.

       Compares the work of Sade to that of Lawrence Durrell
       in the ALEXANDRIA QUARTET.  Believes that the common
       thread between Sade and Durrell is the effort made by
       both to use the imagination as the mediator between
       individual consciousness and reality.  Sees Sade as an
       example of an imagination obsessively applied to
       reality because reality is there in its singular
       unpleasantness.  Unlike Sade, Durrell wants more
       tenderness in a disorderly world.  Sees Sade as
       rejecting tenderness as an emotion to be sought in
       sexual relations or anywhere else.  Believes that
       Sade's characters hate women and prefer to use them.
       Says that for Sade, need is very important.  Need must
       be satisfied and when it is not, we are frustrated by
       a reality that is false.  Concludes that for Sade
       there is no other reality than that offered by
       imagination.  However, ALEXANDRIA QUARTET seems to
       justify believing that real life begins on the other
       side of the imagination where we see life as an
       unending attempt to produce an impossible balance
       between what the world offers and what we would like
       to contribute.

1674.  Mercken-Spaas, Godelieve.  "Some Aspects of the Self and
       the Other in Rousseau and Sade."  SUB-STANCE 20
       (1978):  71-77.

       Compares two seminal texts of Rousseau and Sade in
       order to investigate how these authors demarcate
       possible elaborations of the self/other relationship.
       First states that both authors pay tribute to the
       republican form of government, but here ends their
       common grounds.  For Rousseau, "once society is

formed, laws become unavoidable [but] . . . Sade
rejects the universality of a legal system."
Furthermore, "Self and Other are within the same
category for Rousseau and in opposing categories for
Sade." Concludes: "The coincidence of creation and
destruction which characterized the Sadian writing,
opposes it strongly to the Rousseauvian text. Sade
produces numerous characters in order to allow
continual destruction, whereas Rousseau creates few
characters but does not subject them to destruction.
The economy of characters, overabundant in Sade,
limited in Rousseau, is in inverse proportion to the
importance of the other."

1675.  Miller, Nancy K. "JUSTINE, or, The Vicious Circle."
       STUDIES IN EIGHTEENTH CENTURY CULTURE. Edited by
       Ronald C. Rosbottom. Vol. 5. Madison: University of
       Wisconsin Press, 1976, pp. 215-228.

       Attempts a simutaneous confrontation of sexuality and
       textuality in Sade's works. To prove her point,
       chooses the second edition of JUSTINE, the most
       controversial of all the editions. Believes that the
       key to this version of the work is that the structure
       is designed in a circular way, to support opposing
       values of the time. Truth suffers in the process of
       illumination. Justine does not grow as a character
       because her suffering was designed to support the
       system in which she exists. In the book, action is
       privileged at the expense of the character. Justine
       is victimized because in conformity with the role of
       the victim, Justine submits, hence the circularity.
       Her life is the story. When there is no more story to
       tell, Justine dies. Believes that there is disparity
       at the end of the novel between the code and its
       message. Lists several circular themes: 1) the
       automatic opposition that takes place continuously in
       Justine's life, i.e., her good deeds are always
       punished; 2) the chain reaction set in motion by her
       first sexual encounter. "And the end of the novel is
       a model of literary construction: just as the
       beginning of Justine's suffering is marked by the
       separation of two sisters, an end to suffering is
       brought about by their reunion."

1676.  Mitchell, Jeremy. "Swinburne, the Disappointed
       Protagonist." YALE FRENCH STUDIES 35 (December 1965):
       81-88.

Reviews the attitude of Swinburne toward Sade. Swinburne considered JUSTINE a literary failure because crime repeated extensively is not necessarily great crime. Also criticized Sade's philosophy, which is no more, as Swinburne sees it, than phallic worship. Yet praises Sade as a poet especially in the eighth part of ALINE ET VALCOUR. Swinburne was greatly absorbed with the sea and complained that it was regrettable that Sade had not imagined any torture done at sea. However, Swinburne succeeded in doing just that: "Sometimes sea, love, ecstasy, and masochism become entwined" in Swinburne's writing.

1677. Montel, Jean-Claude. "Sade, encore un effort." EUROPE 522 (1972): 15-23.

Contrasts the motivation of French eighteenth-century libertines with that of Chinese libertines in books like KING PING MEI and JEOU P'OU T'OUAN. Discusses Sade's pamphlet entitled "Français encore un effort si vous voulez être républicain," which contains an idée-force: the nonprescriptive right to pleasure for all individuals. Concludes that there is something phony about libertines who only rejoice in the death of others.

1678. Namer, Emile. Review of SADE, by Vincenzo Barba. REVUE PHILOSOPHIQUE, April-June 1979, pp. 226-227.

Review of SADE: LA LIBERAZIONE IMPOSSIBILE, item 1424, published in 1978 by Nuova Italia. States that author attempts to delineate Sade's thoughts and interprets his works in terms of the totality of his production.

1679. Nodier, Charles. In SOUVENIRS, EPISODES, ET PORTRAITS DE LA REVOLUTION ET DE L'EMPIRE. Vol. II. Paris: Levasseur, 1831, pp. 52 and 60.

Gives a description of Sade which might be imaginary.

1680. OBLIQUES 12-13 (1977). Numéro Spécial SADE.

This voluminous issue of OBLIQUES was entirely devoted to Sade. Includes many superb articles too numerous to list and a lengthy bibliography by F. Rosart. In his review M. Delon states: "Le volume apparaît finalement comme un cénotaphe: beau monument en marbre rouge pour un corps perdu et une oeuvre insaisissable, toujours deplacée, ailleurs. Sade OBLIQUE, en ligne de fuite."

Reviewed by M. Delon in DIX-HUITIEME SIECLE 10 (1978): 507.

1681.  Oliver, A. Richard. "Charles Nodier and the Marquis de Sade." MODERN LANGUAGE NOTES 75 (1960): 497-502.

Sets the record straight on the meeting of Sade with Charles Nodier. Claims that this meeting could not have taken place because the two men were never in the same prison at the same time. Backs up his contention with written proof and concludes that Nodier himself, who "attempted to whitewash to a degree de Sade's notorious reputation as a pervert and amoralist" probably started the myth in order to minimize his own irregularities in the Palais Royal gardens.

1682.  Ormesson, Jean d'. "Logothètes et littéraires." NOUVELLES LITTERAIRES 2309 (December 1971): 8.

Reviews SADE, FOURIER, LOYOLA, by Roland Barthes, originally published by the Editions du Seuil in 1971.

1683.  Palmer, Jerry and Fletcher, Ian. FIERCE MIDNIGHTS: ALGOLAGNIAC FANTASY AND THE LITERATURE OF DECADENCE. New York: Holmes & Meyer, 1980. 216 p.

1684.  Pasi, Carlo. "Sotto il segno della crudeltà: Sade e Artaud." MICROMEGAS 1 (September-December 1947): 23-40.

Discusses silence as a measure of cruelty in both Sade and Artaud. For Sade silence is a form of suffocation, an oppression imposed by the walls of a cell. It is an imposition from the "outside" and the need to find an exit is repeated--in writing--like a mania. For Artaud, on the other hand, the threat of silence is an internal asphyxia which blocks the functions of thought. Since writing is born out of suffering, both Sade and Artaud know the urgency of communication. The cruelty stems then the need to impair the integrity of "the Others." Concludes that, if Sade can have influenced Artaud, it is only through

Artaud that we can talk of a theatrical dimension in Sade: "E in tal senso, oggi, Sade, potrebbe apparire l'anticipatore del teatro di Sade." Another first-rate article from Italy.

1685. Pasi, Carlo. SADE E ARTAUD. Roma: Bulzoni, 1979. 192 pp.

Reviewed by Enrico Guaraldo in RIVISTA DI LETTERATURE MODERNE E COMPARATE 33 (1980): 157-179.

1686. Pastoureau, Henri. "Sade, précurseur d'une Weltanschauung de l'ambivalence." NEF 7 63-64 (1950): 39-46.

"Well documented article on the balanced passive and active algolagnic character of Sade's writing." (Quoted from Cabeen, item 8).

1687. Pastoureau, Henri. Notes for CENT ONZE NOTES POUR LA NOUVELLE JUSTINE. Paris: Eric Losfeld, 1956, pp. 1-4.

In the "Avertissement de l'Editeur" discusses several of the "Notes" published under the title "Actualité de Sade" in LE SURREALISME AU SERVICE DE LA REVOLUTION, by Maurice Heine.

1688. Pastoureau, Henri. "Lexigraphe préalable." In CEREMONIAL SADE. Edited by Alain-Valéry Alberts and Jean-Jacques Auquier. Brussels: Aelberts & Auquier, 1970, pp. 13-17.

Includes a lexicon which contains only four letters: S, A, D, E, used to define sadism in line with the ceremonial published by Aelberts and Auquier.

1689. Pastoureau, Henri. "Entretien sur Sade avec Gilbert Lély." PARU, No. 56, 15 December 1949.

1690. Patri, Aimé. "Notre frère damné." L'ARCHE 26 (1947): 152-157.

Presents some interesting commentaries on Klossowski's SADE MON PROCHAIN and relates it to the stand taken by Georges Bataille on Sade. Rather tenuous argumentation.

1691.   Patri, Aimé.   "Critique et histoire littéraire."   PARU
        61 (June 1950):   59-60.

        Reviews the book GENESE DE LA PENSEE MODERNE by Marcel
        Jean and Arpad Mazei (Correa, 229 p.) which is a study
        devoted to seven wise men "sept sages":    Sade,
        Lautréamont, Rimbaud, Mallarmé, Jarry, Apollinaire,
        Roussel.    States:    "il serait à souhaiter que les
        essais critiques aient toujours cette richesse de vues
        et cette hardiesse de pensée."

1692.   Paulhan, Jean.   "Il marchese di Sade e la sua complice
        ovvero la rivincita del pudore." VERRI 32 (1971): 20-
        46.

        See item 995 for annotation of French version.

1693.   Pauvert,   Jean-Jacques.    L'AFFAIRE   SADE.    Paris:
        Pauvert, 1957.   187 p.

        This is a complete report of the legal action against
        the  publishing firm Pauvert after the publication  of
        Sade's works.  Defense attorney was Maurice Garçon.

1694.   Pauvert, Jean-Jacques.   "Une interview exclusive  avec
        G. Pompidou." LE FIGARO LITTERAIRE, 1 September 1966,
        p. 9.

        See item 1700.

1695.   Perceau, Louis.   "Notice."   In LE BORDEL DE VENISE by
        Alphonse-Donatien de Sade.   Venice:   Aux dépens des
        philosophes libertins, s. d., pp. 1-4.

        This  edition  of THE BORDEL DE VENISE was  ornamented
        with   watercolors   "aquarelles   scandaleuses,"   by
        Couperin  and  included  a  notice by Louis  Perceau
        reproduced  here  in  its  entirety:    "LE BORDEL DE
        VENISE,   ouvrage  fort  recherché aujourd'hui,   fut
        publié, pour la première fois, en 1921, 'pour quelques
        amateurs'  en un volume in-8 carré de 4 +  64  pages,
        plus   une   page   blanche  et  une  page  pour   la
        justification avec une couverture illustrée et tiré  à
        200 exemplaires numerotés.  Les magnifiques aquarelles
        qui  ornaient cette édition et qui en font un des plus
        beaux  illustrés  de  luxe publiés  sous  le  manteau,
        étaient dues à un artiste de grand talent,  qui mourut
        malheureusement  à l'heure où s'achevait le tirage  du

volume. C'est sur ces mêmes clichés qu'ont été tirées
les gravures de cette seconde édition. Le texte est
extrait de L'HISTOIRE DE JULIETTE, qui est l'un des
principaux romans du marquis de Sade. Ajoutons, pour
terminer, que l'histoire du BORDEL DE VENISE se
déroule régulièrement, débbarassée des digressions et
des enchevêtrements qui sont de règle dans les romans
du divin marquis."

1696. Petriconi, Hellmuth. "Laclos und Sade." DIE VERFUHRTE
UNSCHULD. Hamburg: n.p., 1953, pp. 72-98.

Compares and contrasts the theme of seduced innocence
in Laclos and Sade.

1697. Pia, Pascal. "Lire Sade au XIXe." MAGAZINE LITTERATURE
114 (June 1976): 19-21.

Considers Sade's ill fame in the nineteenth century
and mentions a judgment brought against his works in
1815 by the Cour Royale of Paris and again ten years
later, when all of Sade's books were condemned.

1698. Pia, Pascal. "Sade au XXe siècle." CARREFOUR, 24 July
1963, p. 20.

Reviews two publications, HISTOIRE DE SAINVILLE ET DE
LEONORE (collection 10/18) and LETTRES CHOISIES (J. J.
Pauvert). Also gives an appraisal of the reception of
Sade's works eighty years after Apollinaire's
prediction that our century would take notice of the
marquis's production. Concludes from the reading of
these letters that Sade showed some impertinence:
"Son ton de hauteur et d'insolente ironie, Sade l'a
conservé toute sa vie. Il est probable que cela n'a
pas arrangé ses affaires, mais rien ne permet de
croire qu'il ne l'ait pas prévu. Passé trente-cinq
ans, il semble ne s'être jamais amadoué que lorsque
aucun intérêt personnel ne l'y incitait. En 1792, par
exemple, loin de chercher à se venger de sa belle-
famille, il s'interdit tout ce qui aurait pu nuire à
ces Montreuils qu'il déteste. Dans son bourbier,
comme il dit, il avait ses élégances."

1699. Piovene. "Hitler et Sade." LA STAMPA, 24 September
1965.

Believes that Sade foresaw the possibility of a
holocost because he understood the inhumane nature of
man.

1700.  Pompidou, Georges. "Interview." LE FIGARO LITTERAIRE,
1<sup>er</sup> septembre 1966, p. 9.

Brief allusion to Sade in an interview conducted by
J. J. Pauvert. Question: "Que pensez-vous du sort
fait aujourd'hui à l'érotisme après tant de savants
commentaires sur la littérature et le mal, Sade ou
Gilles de Rais?" Answer: "L'érotisme m'ennuie. Il a
sa signification, bien sûr, et des sectateurs de grand
talent. Il est peu d'artistes qui ne lui aient fait
sa part. Mais, à dose répétée, ou élevé à la hauteur
d'une philosophie de l'art ou de la vie, il a bien du
mal à se frayer une voie entre la pornographie et la
démence. Et la littérature érotique est d'une
intolérable monotonie. Voyez Sade, précisement,
malgré son indiscutable génie. J'ajoute que la place
prise par l'érotisme dans l'art, la pensée et la
littérature aujourd'hui, comme dans la vie d'ailleurs
ne présage rien de bon, pour parler comme le docteur
Knock. Les sociétés où l'érotisme s'étalait ont
toutes mal fini."

1701.  Pomeau, René. "Sade (1740-1814)." In LITTERATURE
FRANCAISE. Edited by Antoine Adam. Paris: Larousse,
1967.

See item 775.

1702.  Porter, C. A. RESTIF'S NOVELS, OR AN AUTOBIOGRAPHY IN
SEARCH OF AN AUTHOR. New Haven: Yale University Press,
1967, pp. 384-390.

Examines the reasons why Restif de la Bretonne wrote
L'ANTI-JUSTINE. The first might be as an antidote to
the work of Sade and the second an "erotikon épicé"
for a tired husband. States that the basic trouble
with L'ANTI-JUSTINE "is the piling up of obscenity and
irreverence with absolutely no intent other than
delight in being bad."

1703.  Pouillart, Raymond. "Maurice Maeterlinck: Subconscient
et 'sadisme.'" LES LETTRES ROMANES 27 (1973): 37-61.

Attempts to analyze sources and influences on the author Maeterlinck. "Sadism" in this context is not limited to sexual life. Its meaning is much more general and relates to Sade only tenuously. Rather, sadism is traced back to the Germanic influence of Ruysbroeck.

1704. Praz, Mario. "All'insegna del divin marchese." In LA CARNE, LA MORTE E IL DIAVOLO NELLA LETTERATURA ROMANTICA. Milan: Società editrice la cultura, 1930, pp. 91-184.

See item 1705.

Reviewed by L. A. MacKay in CANADA-FRANCAIS 14 (October 1933): 32; NEW REPUBLIC 76 (27 September 1933): 193; NEW STATESMENT AND NATION 6 (29 July 1933): 137; SATURDAY REVIEW OF LITERATURE 10 (12 August 1933): 47; H. Tronchon in REVUE DE LITTERATURE COMPAREE 13 (1933): 214-215; W. Troy in NATION (New York) 137 (11 October 1933): 417-418; TIMES LITERARY SUPPLEMENT, 20 July 1933, p. 492.

1705. Praz, Mario. "The Shadow of the Divine Marquis." In THE ROMANTIC AGONY. New York: Meridian Books, 1950, pp. 95-186.

Describes authors who, in their writings, implied that virtue leads to misery and ruin, vice to prosperity and, therefore, found it necessary "to practice vice because it conforms to the laws of nature, evil being the axis of the universe," in the tradition begun by Sade.

1706. Rabkin, Leslie Y. and Brown, Jeffrey. "Some Monster in His Thought: Sadism and Tragedy in OTHELLO." LITERATURE AND PSYCHOLOGY 23 (1973): 59-67.

Proposes to illuminate in new ways the atmosphere of OTHELLO by using sadism as a key variable. Relates sadism to feelings of helplessness and "futility as regards [one's] own life." In a tenuous conclusion affirms: "This is why 'jealousy is the most important affective manifestation of sadism': jealousy allows one to blame the exploiter and the self . . . and lets him adopt a cynical view of a hopeless existence which is highly consonant with his own projected feelings of worthlessness."

1707.  Rachildre.  LA MARQUISE DE SADE.  Paris:  Ed. Monnier &
       Cie, 1887.  379 p.

       Novel  which begins with the quotation  "Aimer,  c'est
       souffrir"  [sic].    However,  it  has  very  little
       relationship  with  the true life of the  marquise  de
       Sade, wife of Donatien Alphonse de Sade.

1708.  Regard, Michel.  "Balzac et Sade."  L'ANNEE BALZACIENNE
       2 (1971):  3-10.

       Demonstrates  that there are many similarities in  the
       materialism  of  Sade  and  Balzac  and  states:   "La
       ressemblance  des deux écrivains est si prononcée  que
       parfois  on croirait que Balzac a trempé sa plume dans
       l'écritoire du Marquis. . . . L'érotisme, qui est pour
       Sade la forme sous laquelle l'instinct s'exprime  avec
       le  plus  d'aisance,  occupe une large place  dans  LA
       COMEDIE HUMAINE. . . ."  Also attempts to show that in
       the  nineteenth century, gold replaced libertinage as a
       corrupting  agent  and  that  since  the  "letters  de
       cachet"  were replaced by a civic code,  secret crimes
       became  even  more  necessary  in  order  to  build  a
       foundation for the dialectic between vice and virtue.

1709.  Restif de la Bretonne, Nicolas-Edme.  L'ANTI-JUSTINE OU
       LES  DELICES DE L'AMOUR PAR M.  LINGUET.   Paris:  La
       Bibliothèque privée, 1969.

       Written in reaction to Sade's JUSTINE,  L'ANTI-JUSTINE
       is a pornographic work which totally misses the point.

1710.  Revol,  Enrique-Luis.  CAMINOS DEL EXCESO:  WILLIAM BLAKE
       Y EL MARQUIS DE SADE.   Córdoba:  República Argentina,
       1964.

       Begins  this  comparative study on William  Blake  and
       Donatien  de Sade with a quote from Blake:   "The road
       to  excess leads to the palace of knowledge."   Entire
       second  section of work devoted to  Sade's  modernity.
       Concludes:   "Se entiende, por lo tanto, a qué se debe
       que  el  materialista frances sean,  sobre todo  desde
       principio de este siglo,  objeto de verdaderos  cultos
       en  ciertos  grupos intelectuales asi como  objeto  de
       constante  estudio por parte de la critico más atenta.
       Ambas  figuras tienen vigencia plena en la medida  que
       Occidente   no   llega  todavia  a  una   conciliación

dialectica de razon e imaginación, de materia y energía, es decir, en la medida que Occidente se niega a reconocer un camino seguro entre estos dos 'caminos del exceso' que abrieron Blake y Sade."

1711.  Richard,  Oliver A.   "Charles Nodier and the Marquis de Sade."   MODERN LANGUAGE NOTES 75 (June 1960):   497-502.

Discusses once more the supposed meeting of Charles Nodier and Sade and questions the origin of the myth. Suggests that perhaps "to minimize his own irregularities in the Palais Royal gardens, Nodier felt it necessary to whitewash to a degree de Sade's notorious reputation as a pervert and amoralist.   The plea for more tolerant and understanding legislation with regard to cases of this nature,  however, we must take more seriously:   Nodier was one of the first to oppose capital punishment,  he was one of the earliest articulate feminists,  and in general he begged for a more humane legal system to be administered by understanding and sympathetic judges."

1712.  Roger,  Philippe.   "La trace de Fénelon."  SADE, ECRIRE LA CRISE:  COLLOQUE DE CERISY.  Paris:  Belford, 1983, pp. 149-173.

States that Sade had such strong dislikes for some writers that he sometimes tore up their books. However, he was also deeply influenced by authors not usually associated with him.   Such is the case of Fénelon whose traces appear in ALINE ET VALCOUR,  LA PHILOSOPHIE DANS LE BOUDOIR, HISTORIE DE JULIETTE, IDEE SUR LES ROMANS and in the  CORRESPONDANCE. Projected by Sade was a "REFUTATION DE FENELON." Concludes:   "En Fénelon,  et plus encore dans le fénelonisme des Lumières,  c'est le XVIIIe siècle 'superficiel, mou, humain' qu'il traque, avec ce reste d'impatience aristocratique qui le sauve de l'air du temps."

Also includes introduction,  stressing the fact that the main theme of the Cerisy colloquium, which took place from 19 June 1981 to 29 June 1981, was not focused on one special topic but rather "l'atmosphère du colloque a été, sinon idyllique,  du moins irénique--rerum concordia discors."

1713.  Rumazo, Lupe.  "La presencia del sadismo en Sabato."
       CUADERNOS HISPANOAMERICANOS:    REVISTA MENSUAL  DE
       CULTURA HISPANICA 270 (1972): 551-558.

       Discusses sadism in the works of Ernesto Sábato,
       especially in EL TUNEL, and compares his brand with
       that of other writers, such as Salvado Elizondo in
       FARABEUF.  Recognizes that the sadism of Sabato takes
       on a somewhat different form:  "El sadismo de Sabato
       no se plasma asi fundamentalmente en la pareja; es un
       trasfondo de la humanidad y una posibilidad verídica
       de actuación."

1714.  Runte, Roseanne.  "La Fontaine:  Precursor of the
       Eighteenth-Century Libertine."  EIGHTEENTH-CENTURY
       LIFE 3 (1976):  47-51.

       "Analyzes the types of libertines depicted in the
       stories of Jean de la Fontaine.  His discreet
       insinuation of eroticism clearly influenced the
       licentious tales of Duclos, Voisenon, Crebillon fils,
       and even the Marquis de Sade.  La Fontaine is linked
       to the libertine tradition by his own legendary
       exploits, his philosophy, and his choice of
       situations, characters, vocabulary, and style.

       Appendix on the use of the device of the veil."
       (Quoted from J. D. Falk, in HISTORICAL ABSTRACTS, item
       15.)

1715.  Ryland, Hobart.  "Anatole France, Le Marquis de Sade et
       Courtilz de Sandras."  KENTUCKY FOREIGN LANGUAGE
       QUARTERLY 4 (1957): 200-204.

       Mentions that around 1880, Anatole France discovered a
       collection of twenty-six unpublished tales by Sade and
       that he chose to publish one of them, DORCI OU LA
       BIZARRERIE DU SORT, with a preface containing
       information on its author.  Anatole France, the
       marquis de Sade, and Courtilz de Sandras all wrote
       stories featuring a bed with pulleys.

1716.  Sainte-Beuve.  "Jugement sur Sade."  LA REVUE DES DEUX
       MONDES 3 (1843):  5-20.

       Sees a little of Sade in several well-known authors
       and states ·that Byron and Sade were perhaps the
       greatest inspirations of our times, even though one

wrote in an open and the other in a clandestine fashion.

1717. Sartre, Jean-Paul. "Sartre répond." LA QUINZAINE LITTERAIRE, 15 October 1966; also in L'ARC 30 (1966).

1718. Saulnier, V.I. LA LITTERATURE DU SIECLE PHILOSOPHIQUE. Paris: n.p., 1948, pp. 91-93.

Expostulates on Choderlos de Laclos, Restif de la Bretonne, and the Marquis de Sade:  a shameful trio.

1719. Schlesinger, P. "Proudhon et Sade." MERCURE DE FRANCE 312 (1951): 373-374.

Notices that Proudhon had some ideas found in Sade. First, both felt that the right to propriety is the right to steal.  Second, both reported that Egyptian women prostituted themselves publicly to crocodiles. Comments: "Heureux crocodiles."

1720. Schmidt, Albert-Marie. "Duclos, Sade et la littérature féroce." REVUE DES SCIENCES HUMAINES 62-63 (1951): 146-155.

Attempts to establish a precise comparison between Duclos's HISTOIRE DE MME DE LUZ and Sade's JUSTINE. Both are examples of virtuous women pursued by misfortune.  Claims that the work of Sade is a parody of that of Duclos:  "Mais à quoi bon multiplier les exemples d'une rhétorique perverse qui dérive sans conteste de celle qu'inventa Duclos?"

1721. Schmidt, Albert-Marie. "Pierre Cuisin petit sadiste malgré lui." LES LETTRES NOUVELLES, June 1960, pp. 157-161.

Discusses the works of one of Sade's emulators, Pierre Cuisin (1777-1845), and suggests that scholars should investigate the style--"pre-romantisme narquois, cruel et galant"--of this ignored admirer of Sade.

1722. Scully-Hudon, E. "Love and Myth in the LIAISONS DANGEREUSES." YALE FRENCH STUDIES 11 (1953): 25-58.

Starts with a comparison of Laclos's LES LIAISONS DANGEREUSES and the Marquis de Sade's JUSTINE. Goes on to mention Goethe's ELECTIVE AFFINITITES, Henry

James's THE AMBASSADORS, Samuel Richardson's CLARISSA,
André Gide's LES FAUX-MONNAYEURS, Ovid's THE ART OF
LOVE, C. S. Lewis's THE ALLEGORY OF LOVE, and ends
quite unexpectedly with two lines from Mallarmé.

1723.  Steinhagen, Harald.   "Der junge Schiller swischen
       Marquis de Sade und Kant. Aufklärung und idealismus."
       DEUTSCHE VIERTELJAHRSSCHRIFT 56 (1982): 135-157.

       Gives    a    summary   in   English:    "The    essay    is
       thematically    centered    around    the    'dialectics    of
       enlightenment.'    It   demonstrates   that   the   young
       Schiller  makes  poetic  use  of  the  same  pure  formal
       reason  the  practical  use  of  which  he  criticizes  in  the
       enlightened  materialist,  Franz  Moor  (and  Sade).  Thus,
       Schiller's  idealistic  attempt  to  refute  radically
       enlightened thoughts does not succeed."

1724.  Stringer, Patricia.   "Restif  de  la Bretonne and  the
       Subject of Evil."  ROMANCE NOTES 16 (1975): 592-598.

       Suggests that what is "striking about Restif is not so
       much the novelty of what he produced,  but rather  the
       similarities  between  his  works  and  those  of  his
       contemporaries,  Rousseau  and  Sade."  Also  mentions
       Restif's obsession with evil and concludes that he was
       "much  more  interested  in  tendencies  explored  and
       described by Sade than he ever dared to reveal."

1725.  Switzer, Richard.  "Racine, Sade, and the Daisy Chain."
       In STUDI  OFFERTI A ROBERTO RIDOLFI DIRETTORE DE  "LA
       BIBLIOFILIA."   Edited by Berta Maracchi  Biagiarelli
       and Dennis E.  Rhodes.  Florence:  Olschki, 1973,
       pp. 2063-2069.

1726.  Thévenot  de Morande,  Charles.  "Sur Sade."  In LA
       GAZETTE  NOIRE  PAR UN HOMME QUI N'EST  PAS  BLANC  OU
       OEUVRES  POSTHUMES  DU  GAZETIER  CUIRASSE.  London:
       Printed a hundred leagues from the Bastille, 1784.

1727.  Thody, Philip.  "Problems and Themes:  Evil."  JEAN
       GENET:  A  STUDY OF HIS NOVELS AND PLAYS.  New York:
       Stein and Day, 1969, pp. 25-26.

       Contrasts  Genet to Sade,  who in his way was striving
       after a version of the good:  "the freeing of  Nature
       from artificial trammels. . . .  Genet,  by contrast,
       has  no  concept of goodness and no desire to  achieve

it.   He is aiming at absolute evil, and the inclusion
of any rational argument,  of any search for pleasure,
would   introduce   positive qualities   into   what   must
remain an entirely negative world."

1728.  Tondeur,    Claire-Lise.     "Flaubert  et  Sade,    ou  la
        fascination  de l'excès."   NINETEENTH-CENTURY  FRENCH
        STUDIES 10 (1981-1982):  75-84.

        Discusses  common themes  found  in Sade  and  Flaubert.
        Both     authors    seem   to   have   had   an    encyclopedic
        obsession, a fascination with excess.  Also present in
        their works are numerous descriptions of violent acts;
        SALAMMBO, for instance, can be read as an anthology of
        atrocities.     Finally,   Sade  and  Flaubert  have  a
        predilection for the enclosed space.

        Concludes   that,   while   Flaubert  may  have   been
        fascinated  by Sade,  he was also repulsed  by  his
        obsession with evil,  the manifestation of an inverted
        moralism,  which  the author calls a reincarnation  of
        Catholicism.

1729.  Valsenestre,    Jeanne de.     "Maistre François Rabelais et
        M.  le  comte  de  Sade,  amplification  en  forme  de
        parallèle."  CAHIERS  DU  COLLEGE DE  PATAPHYSIQUE  15
        (1954): 61, 67.

        Draws parallels between Rabelais and Sade.   Both  are
        adept  technicians of imaginary solutions,   and  both
        ignore nature as it is normally understood.   But Sade
        constructs prodigious castles,  closed,  isolated, out
        of reach of the common man and far from the control of
        the police, while Rabelais dreams of breaking the ties
        which  bind him to Theleme--with its  open  doors--and
        longs  for  journeys to foreign lands where nature  is
        not itself.

1730.  Vercruysse,   J.    "Fragments inédits d'un roman perdu de
        Sade:   LE PORTEFEUILLE D'UN HOMME DE LETTRES."  REVUE
        D'HISTOIRE  LITTERAIRE DE LA FRANCE 68  (1968):   633-
        637.

        Mentions   a   lost   epistolary   novel   of  Sade:    LE
        PORTEFEUILLE  D'UN  HOMME DE LETTRES and  includes  an
        unpublished  fragment,  the thirtieth  letter,  titled
        "Pholoé  à  Zénocrate."

Briefly reviewed by F. B. Crucitti Ullrich, STUDI
FRANCESI 38 (1969): 357.

1731. Viel-Castel, Comte Horace de. "Souvenirs sur Sade." In
MEMOIRES. Edited by L. Leouzon Le Duc. Vol. 1.
Paris: Chez tous les libraires, 1883, p. 93.

Contends that Sade's works did untold harm not only
because reading them is pernicious but also because so
many writers were influenced by them. Among others,
cites Victor Hugo in NOTRE DAME DE PARIS, Jules Janin
in L'ANE MORT, Theophile Gauthier in MADEMOISELLE DE
MAUPIN, Georges Sand, Eugene Sue, Alfred de Musset and
Alexandre Dumas: "Tous jettent un morceau de sa
débauche dans leurs productions."

1732. Vier, Jacques. "Le marquis de Sade." In LITTERATURE A
L'EMPORTE PIECE. Paris: Editions de Cèdre, 1969,
pp. 69-84.

Reprinted in HISTOIRE DE LA LITTERATURE FRANCAISE:
DIX-HUITIEME SIECLE, vol. 2, 1970, pp. 476-491. Even
though author does not profess high regard for Sade,
includes him in his history of French literature,
perhaps an indication that Sade has come a long way
from his season "en enfer."

Reviewed by A. Egret, LA PENSEE CATHOLIQUE 124 (1970):
100-104; and B. A. Pocquet de Haut Jusse, ANNALES DE
BRETAGNE 76 (1969): 605.

1733. Villers, Charles de. "Lettre sur le roman intitulé
JUSTINE OU LES MALHEURS DE LA VERTU." LE SPECTATEUR DU
NORD 4 (1977): 407-414.

This essay, in epistolary form, was addressed to an
unknown lady. Reviews the novel JUSTINE, which he
appraises as both a product and an instigation of the
French revolutionary crisis. Also published, with a
preface by Augustin Poulet-Malassis, in limited
edition of 150 booklets of 27 pages in Paris, by J.
Baur, in 1877.

1734. Weinhold, Ulrike. "Das Universum in Kopf: De Sade und
der junge Hofmannsthal." NEOPHILOGUS 63 (1979): 108-
119.

Compares Sade's work with that of Hugo von
Hofmannsthal, even though at first glance this
comparison might be hard to understand. Both are
"decadent" writers, but there is a difference: Sade's
libertines need and do evil willingly as a means of
representation of free spirit whereas Hofmannsthal's
decadent heroes must first fight and overcome the
knowledge that what they are doing is evil. States:
"De Sade Perverse können in ihrem Bewusstein das
Mittel nicht tilgen, im Bewusstsein der
Hofmannsthalschen Feingeister ist es zunachst
verschwunden oder nur latent vorhanden." Concludes
that indeed in Sade and the young Hofmannsthal we do
find two levels of modern attitudes "in denen sich die
Tendenz, einer entfremdeten und damit zum Mittel
degradierten Aussenwelt mit der Erschaffung eines
inneren Universums zu antworten, nachdrücklich
abzeichnet."

1735.  Wilson, Edmund. "D. A. F. Sade, The Vogue of the
       Marquis de Sade." NEW YORKER, 18 October 1952, pp.
       163-176.

       See item 1737.

1736.  Wilson, Edmund. "On de Sade's Letters." NEW YORKER, 10
       January 1953, pp. 76-79.

       Review of Geoffrey Gorer's article published in the
       NEW YORKER, 18 October 1952, pp. 163-176.

1737.  Wilson, Edmund. "The Vogue of the Marquis de Sade." In
       EIGHT ESSAYS. New York: Doubleday, Anchor, 1954,
       pp. 167-180.

       Originally published in the NEW YORKER, 18 October
       1952, pp. 163-176. Reviews the recent fortune of
       Sade's works. States that Guillaume Apollinaire, by
       publishing a selection of the marquis's works, brought
       Sade "into general currency." Gives a history of
       criticism beginning with the most important authority
       on Sade, "a writer named Maurice Heine, a former
       communist of a very ancient vintage, since he was
       eliminated, in 1923, from the staff of the communist
       HUMANITE when he opposed the suppression of free
       discussion in the councils of the party. Heine's
       interest in the queer marquis was evidently partly
       inspired by his passionate libertarianism, for the

marquis, in his dubious way, was a fierce libertarian
too. Heine virtually devoted his life to running down
and publishing Sade's work and vindicating his
reputation." Continues by giving a very biased view
of Sade and his critics' lives and works. Along the
way, comments on three recent publications on Sade,
especially those of Gorer and Praz.

1738. Young, George J. "Sade, los decadentistas y Bradomin."
CUADERNOS HISPANOAMERICANOS 298 (1975): 112-131.

Presents a thorough study of Sade's influence on a
Spanish writer, Ramón Maria del Valle-Inclan, and
compares the life of the hero of the series CORTE DE
AMOR, the marquis of Bradomin, with that of Sade.
Discusses "decadence writers" who, with Sade as a
model, "rivalizaban por el honor de haber escrito
escenas de la más insólita perversión." Lists among
them, Barbey d'Aurevilly, Maurice Barres,
Chateaubriad, Percy Shelley.

1739. Zimmerman, Marc. "Sade et Lautréamont (sans Blanchot):
Starting Points for Surrealist Practice and Praxis in
the Dialectics of Cruelty and Humour Noir." BOUNDARY
5 (1977): 507-528.

Begins with the conjecture that, in Sade, cruelty is a
praxism Then proceeds to ask questions: "What does
this praxis mean? How does it work and to what does
it lead? And what relation does it have to the
surrealism that will later emerge? Is the relation to
be found in terms of another relations? The relation
between cruelty and Humour Noir?" Attempts in article
to give answers and concludes: "The effort to reduce
Sade (and Lautréamont) to humour noir or cruelty would
deprive their work of all seriousness and possibility,
free them from reprimand and value. . . . We know the
therapeutic value of writing and how Sade may have
saved himself by words--but: when and how do we make
our tie to life? . . . The ambivalence expressed here
should provide a close that leaves all doors open."

1074. Omitted.

## O. TECHNIQUE AND STYLE

1741. Amette, Jacques-Pierre. "Apprendre à lire." QUINZAINE LITTERAIRE 132 (1 January 1972): 15-16.

Reviews Roland Barthes' book, SADE, FOURIER, LOYOLA, stressing Barthes' talent as a critic. About the essay on Sade, states: "En courts paragraphes, par une sorte de combinaison d'insistances, Roland Barthes poursuit les écarts qui demarquent l'oeuvre de Sade de celle produites par ses contemporains. Les transgressions sadiennes sont mises à jour, articulées, et ordonnées dans leurs niveaux. . . . A cette exploration des transgressions, s'ajoute une recherche de définition d'une écriture véritablement terroriste, révolutionnaire: irrécupérable par la petite bourgeoisie."

1742. Aron, Jean-Paul. "Le fou rire du marquis de Sade." LE NOUVEL OBSERVATEUR 603 (31 May 1976): 74-75.

Reviews LA PHILOSOPHIE DANS LE PRESSOIR (Grasset, 1976) by Philippe Roger and discusses the paradox of Sade's humour so ably discussed by Roger: "Merci à Philippe Roger d'avoir mis en évidence l'humour de Sade: d'emblée c'est l'intrinsèque du libertinage qu'il appréhende . . . vous, curieux ou vicieux qui sado-masochisez à l'occasion, je conseille de lire, et vite, le livre de Philippe Roger."

1743. Bataille, Georges. "Le secret de Sade." CRITIQUE 15 (1947): 147-160.

Recognizes that in 1947 the worth of the marquis de Sade's literary skills and his genius were only beginning to emerge. Wonders about the possible ties between Sade's ideas and the meaning of the French Revolution: "On voit qu'un auteur et un livre ne sont pas immanquablement les heureux résultats d'un temps calme. Tout se lie dans le cas présent à la violence d'une révolution . . . ce que Sade eut le rage ou l'obligation de ressasser était la destruction dans la créature humaine d'un élément humain, de cette dignité operatoire dont nous privent au dernier degré des hurlements de douleur et d'effroi. . . ." Concludes that Sade's discovery, his secret, is the possibility,

the affirmation, that there exist in all of us some
definite masochistic tendencies.

1744.  Beausobre de, Julia.  "Creative Suffering."  THEOR THEOR
       12 (1978): 111-121.

1745.  Berman, Lorna.  THE THOUGHT AND THEMES OF THE MARQUIS DE
       SADE.  Kitchener, Ontario: Ainsworth, 1972.  725 p.

       Attempts in this long labor of love (begun in 1954,
       published in 1971) to classify the thoughts and themes
       found in Sade's works according to 235 topics.  But
       first gives summary of his main publications,
       including circumstances of writing and publishing.
       Also recounts important events in Sade's life and
       includes an index of characters and a listing of
       writers mentioned in Sade's works.  Sade was obviously
       well read.  This concordance is incomplete but could
       be a useful reference tool.  Among conclusions drawn
       from this study, the following: "One can take very
       little of Sade's work literally or at face value, as I
       have shown in the previous section.  There is scarcely
       an argument for which one could not find a refutation
       elsewhere in his work . . . [which] illustrates . . .
       the meaninglessness of all words and acts in
       themselves alone and the ease with which anything can
       be proved or justified simply by bandying words
       about. . . ."

1746.  Biou, Jean.  "Review of THE THOUGHTS AND THEMES OF THE
       MARQUIS DE SADE by Lorna Berman."  REVUE D'HISTOIRE
       LITTERAIRE DE LA FRANCE, January-February 1974, pp.
       113-114.

       Proposes to answer his own question:  "D'où vient que
       ce séduisant ouvrage laisse insastisfait?" Proceeds to
       explain with proofs of lacunae and inaccuracies.

1747.  Blanc, Henri.  "Sur le statut du dialogue dans l'oeuvre
       de Sade."  DIX-HUITIEME SIECLE 4 (1972): 301-314.

       Discusses the status of "dialogue," defined as oral
       and verbal REPRESENTED communication, in two works of
       Sade, LES INFORTUNES DE LA VERTU and LA PHILOSOPHIE
       DANS LE BOUDOIR.  Believes that "derrière l'apparente
       platitude d'un pastiche du discours vertueux, le récit
       (de Justine) tente en fait d'équilibrer trois sens
       labiles:  un monologue de la femme vertueuse revêtue

des armes dangereuses de la première personne, qui
surmonte les 'sophismes' tentateurs du crime,
disséminés dans une troisième personne
multiple. . . ." Concludes that as early as 1787
there existed two facets in Sade's production, the
utopic and didactic monologue and a "bakhtinien" type
dialogue, more preverse and subtle.

1748.   Blanchot, Maurice. "L'Expérience-limite. L'insurrection
de la folie d'écrire." L'ENTRETIEN INFINI. Paris:
Gallimard, 1969, pp. 323-342.

In order to simplify matters, gives three ways in
which Sade's work explores the excesses of reason.
1) Sade makes a census of human deviant behavior.
2) The second notion is of a dialectical nature: "Je
ne vois nul anachronisme à appeler dialectique au sens
moderne la prétention essentiellement sadique de
fonder la souveraineté raisonnable de l'homme sur un
pouvoir transcendant de négation, pouvoir qu'il ne
manque de reconnaître au principe de la plus claire et
de la plus simple raison positive." 3) Writing is
Sade's madness. "Quelque chose de plus violent se
fait jour dans cette fureur d'écrire: une violence
que ne réussissent pas à épuiser ni à apaiser tous les
excès d'une imagination superbe ou féroce, mais
toujours inférieure à l'emportement d'un langage qui
ne supporte pas d'arrêt, pas plus qu'il ne conçoit de
terme." Very readable essay.

1749.   Blanchot, Maurice. "Français, encore un effort."
NOUVELLE NOUVELLE REVUE FRANCAISE 26 (1965): 600-618.

Suggests that the work of Sade must be read in its
entirety rather than a fragment at a time. Adds that
reading Sade is difficult. Explains how in his work,
the author has explored the excesses promulgated in
the name of reason. To simplify, he names only three
of them. The first has an encyclopedic overtone. It
is a census of human possibilities, especially those
that could be labeled aberrations. The second has a
dialectical emphasis: "Je ne vois nul anachronisme á
appeler dialectique au sens moderne la prétention
essentiellement sadique de fonder la souveraineté
raisonnable de l'homme sur un pouvoir transcendant de
négation, pouvoir qu'il ne manque pas de reconnaitre
au principe de la plus claire et de la plus simple
raison positive . . . pouvoir infini de negation (qui)

exprime et tour à tour annule, par une experience
circulaire, les notions d'homme, de Dieu, de Nature,
pour finalement affirmer l'homme intégral. . . ."
Finally, Blanchot says that reason in Sade also
examined itself in the writing effort, and writing is
Sade's madness. Concludes that one need not read a
lot of Sade's political works in order to have an idea
of his political stand. There does not exist a single
free government, because everywhere man is and will be
victim of the laws, which are even more dangerous than
any and all individual impulses. States that for Sade
a truly revolutionary regime is one that exhibits a
total absence of laws. In such a context men could
tell all--true liberty is that possibility, to be able
to tell all.

1750.  Blanchot, Maurice. "The Main Impropriety." YALE FRENCH
       STUDIES 39 (1967): 50-63.

       This is an excerpt, translated by June Guicharnaud,
       from "L'inconvenance majeure," first published as a
       preface to Sade's FRANCAIS, ENCORE UN EFFORT POUR ETRE
       REPUBLICAIN (J. J. Pauvert, 1965).

1751.  Bonnet, Jean-Claude. "La harangue sadienne." POETIQUE
       XII, no. 49 (February 1982): 31-50.

       In the 18th century, when historical methods were
       loosely defined, Sade developed his own original style
       of history, a kind of conciliation between erudition
       and philosophy: "Sade imite le savoir historique dans
       sa recherche patiente de la verité, tout en
       pervertissant les procedures par la gaieté d'un texte
       souverain, dont la meilleure trouvaille consiste en
       l'utilisation systématique des 'embrayeurs' habituels
       du discours historique, et particulièrement la
       critique et la correction des historiens
       précédents. . . . Prenant au mot ceux qui dénoncent
       l'apathie des historiens, Sade réveille le discours
       historique par le coup de fouet d'une éloquence
       forcenée. . . . La harangue généralise le
       fonctionnement machinique du discours libertin."

       This article is the expanded version of the last half
       of a paper presented at the Cerisy Colloquium. See
       also "Sade historien," item 1428.

1752.  Brochier, Jean-Jacques. "La circularité de l'espace."
       LE MARQUIS DE SADE. Paris: Colin, 1968, pp. 171-188.

       Proceedings of colloquium on the marquis de Sade, Aix-
       en-Provence, 19 and 20 February 1966.  States that
       while there appear to be many similarities between the
       "roman noir" and Sade's works, elements in both do not
       fill the same function.  Sade's novels are not
       intended to terrify but are rather intended as novels
       of concentrated evil.  The importance of location is
       emphasized.  Numerous descriptions are given of
       enclosed spaces from which escapes are impossible.
       Filling a double purpose, these out-of-the-way
       places--concentric circles or high-perched castles--
       are both a refuge from pursuers and a prison for those
       inside.  "Cet espace clos instaure un nouvel
       ordre . . . le règne de l'ordre des mots . . . [avec]
       la possibilité d'une transgression infinie. . . .
       D'autre part, comme le mot, pour Sade, est la chose,
       d'une certaine manière, et même plus que la chose,
       toute la construction de son univers romanesque tient
       dans la dialectique entre les orgies et les
       raisonnements, dont les rapports seuls traduisent et
       créent l'univers du libertinage, de l'Unique et de la
       totalité.  L'orgie se fait raisonnante, et le
       raisonnement orgiaque.  Enfin, troisième
       caractéristique de cet ordre, c'est ce frémissement du
       langage. . . . Ce monde des mots est enfin un monde
       parfaitement clos, un système achevé, l'espace du
       ressassement. . . ." And this enclosed space is both
       the death of the world and the birth of the book.

1753.  Brochier, Jean-Jacques. "Sade et le langage." Preface
       to OEUVRES COMPLETES DU MARQUIS DE SADE. Vol. XV.
       Paris: Cercle du livre précieux, 1964, pp. 511-519.

       Sees in Sade's thoughts the essence of Hegelian
       philosophy.  States that all the oppositions between
       individual and society, good and evil, determinism and
       freedom are outlined by the marquis.  Language is the
       sole mediator that Sade has at his disposal to create
       a reality which is not destroyed by simply negating
       it.  Also states that through language, which is more
       destructive than the action itself, Sade reaches an
       almost perfect negation.  Concludes that "La
       contradiction à laquelle se heurtait Sade entre la
       realité exitentielle qu'il avait à communiquer (et le
       système qui en découlait) et l'insuffisance

fondamentale du langage, qui de surcroit impose un nouveau déterminisme à une pensée qui les refuse tous à priori, cette contradiction ne peut être résolue que par le consomption de l'oeuvre, le jeu de mots et la contradiction ouverte entre les termes, l'humour noir. Le language ne permet une communication qu'à partir du moment ou il s'anéantit: Sade est un poète."

1754. Cerruti, G.    Review of SADE ET SES MASQUES,  by Roger Lacombe.  STUDI FRANCESI 19 (1975):  363.

Brief  review  in Italian of Lacombe's book  on  Sade. States  nothing  new except  announcement  of  another publication on Sade.

1755. Daix, Pierre.  "De Sade à Guyotat ou les conditions de l'intelligibilité."    LES  LETTRES    FRANCAISES,    28 October 1970, pp. 3-4.

Reviews  Sade's JOURNAL  INEDIT  edited  by  Georges Daumas.  Objects to the presentation which is somewhat falsified.    Says  that Sade's text cannot be read  as one  reads  Hugo's CARNETS INTIMES--the  former  was imprisoned,  the  latter  was free--and conditions  of production  enter  into the  interpretation.    Similar network  of thoughts can be applied to Guyotat's  EDEN EDEN EDEN.    Concludes  that  logically  one  should examine  the  text  in  terms  of writing  compulsion generated in the author.

1756. Damisch, Hubert.    "L'écriture sans mesures."  TEL QUEL 28 (Winter 1967): 51-65.

Concedes that what Sade wrote about constitutes a sort of  crime that perpetuates itself.   Compares the form of Sade's work to its content:  "N'admirons-nous donc, dans son oeuvre,  que le crime qui en fait  proprement la matière, et la beauté froide, presque classique, eu égard à la forme qui est sienne,  qui vient à ce texte de  la  passion qui tient son auteur?"  Believes  that the disgressions and regressions are part of a  bigger scheme,  a  properly ordered disorder which intends to be  "natural," typical of what is in nature as opposed to culture.    States:    "le précepte de l'IDEE SUR LES ROMANS qui veut que 'les épisodes naissent toujours du fond du sujet et q'ils y rentrent' nous donne,  si  on le  prend  à la  lettre,  la  clé  de  la  structure spécifiquement  TRAGIQUE  de  l'ériture  de  Sade."

Concludes that order has no place in Sade's style of enjoyment: "C'est que l'ordre n'a point de part dans des jouissances à tel point déréglées et compliquées qu'elles ne trouvent plus à se fixer et qu'il faut attendre de les voir se consumer d'elles-mêmes pour que puisse rétablir, après coup, une autre façon d'ordre qui n'emprunte ni ne prête rien au desir. Parvenue à ce point, l'écriture de Sade ne retentit plus seulement de la fureur des passions: elle s'emplit du BRUIT qui se fait dans le langage quand se dénoncent les appartenances secrètes du désir, et peut-être ses alliances naturelles." First-rate article.

1757. Delon, Michel. Review of SADE: UNE ECRITURE DU DESIR by Béatrice Didier. DIX-HUITIEME SIECLE 9 (1977): 459-440.

Briefly reviews the book by Beatrice Didier (published by Denoel-Gonthier in 1976): "L' information est sérieuse et discrète, la rédaction aisé."

1758. Delon, Michel. Review of SADE, L'OEL DE LA LETTRE by Chantal Thomas. DIX-HUITIEME SIECLE 11(1979): 514-515.

States: "Refusant de soutenir une thèse, de se livrer à une lecture unifiante ou rédutrice, C.T. entend 'se glisser sans effort sur le texte.'"

1759. Deprun, Jean. "Quand Sade récrit Fréret, Voltaire, et d'Holbach." OBLIQUES 12-13 (1977): 263-266.

Tries to show that Sade borrowed more than he admitted and, by modern standards, more than he should have. From the point of view of quantity, Sade tended to shorten the text he borrowed; but since he excised what was most potent, his text improved in terms of quality. Furthermore, Sade gave to the reworked material an additional degree of harshness. Gives some telling examples of borrowing from Fréret, Voltaire, and D'Holbach.

1760. Didier, Béatrice. "Inceste et écriture chez Sade." LETTRES NOUVELLES, May-June 1972, pp. 150-158.

Appraises Sade's writing as a means to go beyond a taboo, and as with incest, to do something which

should not be done.   Incest (and writing) permits him
to   negate both a social order and a religious order:
"L'écrivain s'affronte à un interdit,   en sachant très
bien que là (comme son personnage par   l'inceste),   il
remet en question tout le systéme social, tout le code
des signes."

1761.  Duvernois,   Pierre.     "L'emportement   de   l'écriture:
Roland Barthes et SADE,   FOURIER,   LOYOLA."   CRITIQUE:
REVUE     GENERALE     DES     PUBLICATIONS     FRANCAISES     ET
ETRANGERES   28 (1972):   595-609.

In this first-rate essay,   comments on Barthes's SADE,
FOURIER,   LOYOLA   and   states that Barthes adopts   the
Sadian dialectic of the body,   pleasure/desire in   his
language:     "L'articulation   de   la pensée   de   Roland
Barthes   se   fait   autour   du   désir   exprimé,   voulu,
réclamé pour l'écriture.   Le rapport désir/besoin est
dialectisé, il y a un glissement de l'un à l'autre."

1762.  Eaubonne,   Françoise d' (pseudonym for Martine   Okapi).
"Sade   ou l'horrible travailleur."   In   LES   ECRIVAINS
EN CAGE.   Paris: André Balland, 1970, pp. 67-89.

Discusses several writers who have spent much of their
time   in jail:     "Genet ou le voleur inclément,   Oscar
Wilde   ou l'enchanteur pourrissant,   Dostoevski ou   le
salaud malgré lui,   Silvio Pellico ou Fedor le   Petit,
Sade   ou l'horrible travailleur,   Fray Juan ou la nuit
obscure,   Verlaine   ou l'ébauche du crime."   A   fairly
long chapter on Sade compares the marquis's   solipsism
to that of Berkeley,   which, she feels, is grounded on
the most irrefutable experience, each person's own.

1763.  Finas,   Lucette.   "Sade, théoricien du roman."   L'ACTION
LITTERAIRE 15 (1965):   11-12.

Three   main questions occupied Sade:   word etymology,
sources of romanesque genre,   and the art of   writing.
Suggests   that Sade,   by his own admission,   is moral
because   he   described   crime   in a   way   intended to
terrify his readers:     "Jamais je ne peindrai le crime
que sous les couleurs de l'enfer."

1764.  Fink,   Béatrice.   "La Langue de Sade."   In EROTICISM IN
FRENCH LITERATURE.   FRENCH LITERATURE   SERIES,   1983,
pp. 103-112.

Sees in the sadian word a weapon which participates in eroticism just as appropriate organs do. The combination of three registers, authorized language, forbidden language, and scientific language, makes up the Sadian text. Concludes that "le lexique érotique de Sade constitue donc un langage qui est en fait un métalangage. L'érotigramme qu'il agence défigure l'idéogramme de la classe dominante et déforme la courbe selon laquelle se dessine le progrès linguistique."

1765. Fink, Béatrice C. "Food as Object, Activity and Symbol in Sade." ROMANIC REVIEW 65 (1974): 96-102.

Investigates the use of a structural component of Sade's writings—food—as mimesis, praxis, and semiosis. Eating for the Sadian libertine is more than a nutritional activity; first it is socially significant; it also provides a means to establish a hierarchy of an acceptable code of ethics. Special effects are provided by excesses, not by hallucinogenics and narcotics. Even blasphemy can be committed by putting the Eucharistic host to unmentionable uses. Concludes by mentioning also that "the over-abundant consumption of human flesh is an obvious derivative—and sublimation—of the destructive urge" (which represents for sadian libertines) "a ritualistic absorption of others. . . . Sacrilegious as an activity, eating takes on the significance of a religious rite when, like the mandrake root, it becomes the magic key for passage to the world of omnipotence."

1766. Fink, Béatrice C. "Narrative Techniques and Utopian Structures in Sade's ALINE ET VALCOUR." SCIENCE-FICTION STUDIES VII (1980): 73-79.

States that ALINE ET VALCOUR, the only novel declared philosophical by its author, "may be read as a pronouncement on the interplay of forces that are released in group dynamics." The insertion of Tamoé's utopian structure has a narrative function, that of a yardstick measuring the imperfections of the established order. Concludes: "One of utopia's less explored functions may thus be that of structural signifier in the dialectical movement of the text. In the case of ALINE ET VALCOUR, this particular function reaches a peak. Within its category of inserted structures, Tamoé alone is fully developed along utopian lines, and the text it relates to is more diversified in its narrative techniques. Sade may be diabolical but he is also devilishly adroit."

1767. Foucault, Michel. "La pensée du dehors." CRITIQUE, 229 (June 1966): 523-546.

Attempts to give a definition of "thought from the outside"--a kind of language where the subject doing the uttering is excluded--and finds paradoxically a possible example in Sade's repetitive monologues. Expands on the difficulty of giving this type of thought a language not lapsing into interiorization when it becomes reflexive. States: "le langage n'est ni la vérité ni le temps, ni l'éternité, ni l'homme, mais la forme toujours défaite du dehors; il fait communiquer, ou plutôt laisse voir dans l'éclair de leur oscillation indéfinie, l'origine et la mort." Hence if language can thus be reduced each beings who, when saying "I talk," is by the very uttering affirming his own vanishing and his future "apparation" (undefined).

1768. Gallop, Jane. "Impertinent Questions: Irigaray, Sade, Lacan." SUB-STANCE 26 (1980): 57-67.

Reviews Luce Irigaray's book, SPECULUM (Editions de Minuit, 1974), which begins with detailed reflections on Freud but turns out to be a reflection on Lacan and Sade. States: "Irigaray can see Sade but not Lacan as an ally, although she classes Sade and Lacan as phallocratic colleagues. Lacan finally breaks his alliance with Sade, nearly dumping Freud in the frantic attempt to assert difference." The impertinent questions revolve around the need of Sade's text "to await Irigaray's embarrassing questions, impertinently exposing the phallic religion masked as libertinism."

1769. Gallop, Jane. "'BS.'" VISIBLE LANGUAGE: THE RESEARCH JOURNAL CONCERNED WITH ALL THAT IS INVOLVED IN OUR BEING LITERATE 11 (1977): 364-387.

Proposes to read Sade, as suggested by Roland Barthes, according to the principle of the delicate S (DELICAT-ESSE). Proceeds to interpret the text SADE, FOURIER, LOYOLA and states that Barthes chooses not to read

Sade according to a project of violence.  Furthermore,
Barthes sees in Sade "only the violence encompassed by
the system—ordered,    arranged violent acts.    He
ignores the violations to the system,   thus dismissing
Sadian  violence as co-opted and  uninteresting. . . .
Fourierist  pleasure  is camped under  the  banner  of
delicatesse  rather  than that of violence.    So  when
Barthes  chooses to read Sade according to a  principe
de  delicasse rather than a project  of  violence,  he
gives Sade a Fourierist reading."

1770.  Guicharnaud, Jacques.   "The  Wreathed  Columns  of  St.
       Peter's."    YALE  FRENCH STUDIES 35  (December  1965):
       29-38.

Montesquieu visited the Uffizi Museum in Florence  for
several weeks in 1728 and recounted his experiences in
his work, VOYAGES.  Guicharnaud contrasts this highly
detailed and  aesthetic description  of  the  Uffizi
collection    against    the    sensual,   superficial
interpretation offered by Sade's characters.    As they
stroll through the gallery, only the sexual or violent
aspects  of the pieces catch Juliette's eye,  and  she
responds to them on a purely sensual level.  The works
chosen symbolize  the  main  themes  of  the   novel,
"sacrilege,    the    spectacle   of   death,    sexual
perversions,  the  glorification of feminine  volupté,
murder,  incest,  slavery,"  which construct the  main
idea of the book as a whole,  "the natural alliance of
sex and  destruction."   Sees Sade's description  as
purposefully selective.   Each object introduced  into
the  reader's  imagination is an implement  of  Sade's
conception of the world and of human nature,  in which
erotic  and destructive forces are  paramount.   Feels
that   Sade's   literary  style  is   graceless   and
repetitive,   insistently symbolizing his conception of
human nature as lustful and aggressive.

1771.  Guyotat, Pierre.   "Tombeau  pour cinq  mille  soldats."
       OBLIQUES 12-13 (1977):  4-5.

Gives  an  embryonic  example  of a text  which  will
eventually be published as LE TOMBEAU.  The editors of
OBLIQUES  explain  that  this text was  chosen  to  be
included  in  an issue on Sade because Guyotat  is  as
violently  creative with verbal matter as Sade was  in
time  past with recitative.  "Tot ça d'jeansharrassés
qu'enjamb't les parapets d'la Femm' Sauvaj', d'un'

dobl' chorba te y raman'au vié a d'un blanc qu'te leur
fas tranchier te l'man' en vent' o vont, fessaill'
dentur' écartés mâm' pogn' sos mazda, vié coïllassat
palpétris pogn' conchiassée d'ex-gindr'viendu sondeur,
passer sos maîtr', comptant, a, tracé lastex
s'éffaçant à l'aîn', enjamber du pet jusqu', par
terrass'o décop't'ac leur pied dallaj'd'or songé mac
en cosy, chaq' en odeur d'spécialité, précipit' au
pavé son nu-cerveau, rat' entraill' por chacals,
buccoïllassat por macs, oreill', mans por rimas,
genoux, front por mufti, anus hyènnargué d'un étron
qu'en sort trop fras, rast'ombilic tétons talons
piétiné émeutiers, oeil treturé en man
d'aveugl' . . ., a t', v'lue qu't'sonj' ton anus en
boch'd'ç' Djillali d'sonj', r'mords m'l'vié . . .,
mords . . ., r'mords . . ., a, d'mon déqueu mac, j't'
cop' langu' qu'veut putan parler maît' . . ., me mort,
ç'au blond d'm'codr' tes parties vevant' en
boch' . . ., mords'm' jusqu' mon coeur . . ., manj'm'
jusqu'ton gosier l'avant-chié qu'm'fat bander mes
boyaux. . . ."

1772.  Hackel, Roberta J. DE SADE'S QUANTITATIVE MORAL
       UNIVERSE: OF IRONY, RHETORIC, AND BOREDOM. The
       Hague: Mouton, 1976. 101 p.

       Sees in many of Sade's stylistic patterns an
       illustration of a contrapuntal exposition of vice and
       virtue. Melodramatic cliches are repeated so often
       that they prevent the reader from identifying with
       virtue and at times even allow him to identify with
       vice, so that we witness a reversal of values. Just
       as the vicious characters reason away their criminal
       acts, so the virtuous learn to defend their passions.
       "Sade thus gives an ironic twist to popular ideas of
       his age. . . . Sade's irony is brought to bear on
       several levels. He begins his work by categorically
       attributing specific moral roles to the virtuous and
       vicious protagonists. He then proceeds to switch the
       moral vocabulary and have the characters take on the
       attributes of their opposites. . . . In the end,
       Sade's work becomes a purely creative act in which
       verbal dexterity is as much a means of sustaining a
       moral universe as any didactic intent."

1773.  Harari, Josué V. "Exogamy and Incest: De Sade's
       Structures of Kinship." MODERN LANGUAGE NOTES 88
       (1974): 1212-1237.

Begins with the premise, rejected by Sade, that in Occidental culture "desire and knowledge are incompatible." Also opposed by Sade were an arbitrary concept of norm and a notion of truth which he held to be meaningless. States that it is in order to demystify and demythicize our cultural foundations that Sade dwelt at such lengths in transgressions of all types, especially incest. Investigates all the many taboos connected with incest, which is also seen as a problem connected with language: "The register of Sadian incestuous perversions can never take on its full meaning because our system of language does not possess constitutive elements which can express the category of the monstrous. What incest does introduce into everyday language is the 'non-language' of monstrosity which can result only in expulsion and death. Thus de Sade's task is as violent as it is impossible. . . . Sadian writing actualizes, and perpetuates violence . . . engendered through the mediation of writing."

1774.  Harari, Josué V.  "Reply to Ms. Jane Gallop."  MODERN LANGUAGES NOTES 89 (1974):  1046-1048.

Answers Jane Gallop's reviews published in MODERN LANGUAGE NOTES, of Mr. Harari's article, "Exogamy and Incest." States: "Ms. Gallop's blindness to the text of the article is gravest when she accuses me of 'repeated substitutions . . . between Sade and Sade's fictional libertines,' I say gravest, since it betrays first, unfamiliarity with a terminology that Ms. Gallop should well know as a specialist of modern French criticism."

1775.  Hassan, Ihab.  "Sade: Prisoner of Consciousness."  TRI-QUARTERLY 15 (1969):  23-41.

Begins with a bird's-eye view of Sade's life and states that Sade started "his true life of crime behind prison bars, through fantasy, through a new kind of literature" which reveals the darkness in our dreams and thus makes history prophecy.  "Paradox and duplicity riddle Sade's ideas as well as his life. His ideas are not seminal, but they have the partial truth of excess, the power of release. They constitute a dubious paradigm of consciousness. We perceive the outlines of that consciousness as we move

from his exoteric to his esoteric works, from his
avowed to his underground publications. The movement,
regardless of chronology, is toward total
terror. . . . But Sade's contribution to literary
history does not exhaust itself in romantic decadence.
It depends, rather, on his effort to supplant the
sentimental novel, and to give Gothic fiction new
authority. During his own lifetime the morality of
the bourgeois novel spent itself; revolutionary
thought demanded new values. Sade calls hell to the
rescue, thinking thus to redeem the reality of
fiction. He even assumes a larger task which he never
quite realizes: the creations of the modern
novel. . . . In the end, however, Sade limits his
relevance to us because he demands to be taken only on
his own terms. The Sadian Self permits no encounter,
no negotiation. It solves the problem of evil by
converting all pain, whether inflicted or received,
into a source of personal pleasure." But concludes
that Sade concocted the perfect crime: the one which
"perpetuates itself even when the agent has ceased to
act: the crime of the imagination."

1776. Hénaff, Marcel. "Sade: L'Espace du tableau et
l'imaginable." REVUE ROMANE 11 (1976): 267-285.

This article was reprinted as chap. 4 of the book,
SADE: L'INVENTION DU CORPS LIBERTIN (item 1212).
Attempts to define the mechanism of a sadian text
which is intended by Sade to affect/injure the
reader's body. Whereas numerous authors of the
Enlightenment (Crébillon, Duclos, d'Argens, La
Morlière, et al.) made ample use of the
marvelous/legendary, Sade refused to dwell in the
fantastic—for him all that could be imaginary was in
fact imaginable: "Tout est dit, même l'interdit; il
n'y a pas d'au-delà du tableau; le désirable coincide
avec le pensable. . . . Ce qui importe à Sade c'est
que l'inconditionnel du désir devienne une structure
possible du 'monde réel', c'est-à-dire s'inscrive dans
les formes de la société telles qu'elles sont
historiquement reçues. Aussi même dans les programmes
les plus déments, on reste dans les frontières de la
Raison, c'est-à-dire du Référent; on n'esquive pas
l'Institution: on l'utilise, on la détourne. . . .
Mais ce monde objectif n'en reste pas moins celui que
le texte délimite et produit comme la pellicule
référentielle indispensable au cadrage du récit."

1777. Hénaff, Marcel. "Tout dire ou l'encyclopédie de
      l'excès." OBLIQUES 12-12 (1977): 29-38.

      A longer version of this essay was reprinted as  chap.
      II of SADE: L'INVENTION DU CORPS LIBERTIN (item 1212).
      Differentiates  between saying it all--describing  the
      totality  of  what has to be englobed--and  saying  it
      all--not  hiding anything to the point of  excess,  of
      uncovering everything.  The first translates for Sade
      into "encyclopedia," the  second  as  perversion  or
      writing a complete repertory of perversions.  The work
      that  best fits this definition is LES 120 JOURNEES DE
      SODOME,  which combines the features of a  dictionary
      and  some  elements  of  the  recitative,  and  thus
      particularizes  each passion.   "Dans LES 120 JOURNEES
      comme  dans  JULIETTE tout se passe sur  le  scène  du
      RECIT;  tout  ce  qui est visible doit  être  dicible.
      Cette  mise  à nu sans réserve,  cette exposition  sans
      mesure,  c'est  ce qui définit l'espace de  l'obscène.
      La  tentative est tellement radicale qu'elle ne  cesse
      de  s'opérer sur ses propres limites. . . .   Trahison
      de  classe et trahison de culture dans une  corruption
      généralisée  de  la  language,  le  TOUT  DIRE  est
      formellement  le  crime qui engendre tous  ceux  qu'il
      énonce.  C'est le crime sadien pas excellence.  Il n'y
      en a du reste point d'autre."  First-rate article.

1778.  Henric, Jacques.  "Sade, Lély, language, désir."  ART
       PRESS INTERNATIONAL 12 (November 1977):  16-17.

       Gilbert  Lély  answers questions asked  by  J.  Henric
       concerning language and desire in Sade.

1779.  Ivker, Barry.  "On the Darker Side of the Enlightenment:
       A  Comparison of the Literary Techniques of  Sade  and
       Restif."  STUDIES  ON  VOLTAIRE  AND  THE  EIGHTEENTH
       CENTURY 79 (1971):  199-218.

       Stresses the difference in literary technique found in
       Sade  and Restif de la Bretonne.   Feels that  "Sade's
       works  show little inventiveness with regard to  form"
       and  sees  in  him  no more than  the  "spiritual  and
       intellectual  heir  of  the  literary and  philosophic
       tradition  of  libertinism."   On  the  other  hand,
       Restif's  attention to "the details of the demi-monde,
       of  his COEUR-MIS-A-NU,  will involve a dissection  of
       the  real  world  in  a  form beyond  the  confines  of

fiction, at least of fiction as it had been written up to that time." Concludes that "there is thus no comparison possible between the outrages perpetrated by Sade's libertines, even in LES 120 JOURNEES DE SODOME, and the endless humiliations exacted upon Ingenue, the insane jealousy and sense of inadequacy of Moresquin, his hatred for Ingenue's rich, successful father, his total incapacity for accepting or understanding signs of tenderness. . . . Restif's use of both physical and psychological detail places him outside the tradition of the conte philosophique . . . and thus with Restif we see the possibilities of future development in stylistic technique."

1780. Juin, Hubert. "Sade entier." EUROPE 522 (1972): 10-15.

Regrets that Sade is so misunderstood and so badly misread. States that Sade's philosophy cannot be resumed because it is always in a forth and back motion, conquering a few inches of ground on the way forward to its aim: freedom only to go back. "Pour cela, (Sade) est écrivain prodigieux: il a porté le langage qui était le sien et celui de son siècle, cet instrument dont il a hérité, à un singulier point d'incandescence." Concludes that Sade has become one of the most important writers to come out of the eighteenth-century.

1781. Kristeva, Julia. DESIRE IN LANGUAGE: A SEMIOTIC APPROACH TO LITERATURE AND ART. New York: Columbia University Press, 1980. 305 p.

Sprinkles her text with references to Sade: "a naturalist discourse appears as joy ripped with pain. . . . Sade was the stage director for pain as the scene of unconsciousness and jouissance" (p. 184). "Poetic language includes the language of . . . Sade" (p. 5). "All of the most important polyphonic novels are inheritors of Menipeau, carnivalesque structure: . . . .those of Sade." (p. 79). "Barthes' studies of Fourier and Sade suggest the possibilities open to this biological-corporeal, transsymbolic, and transhistorical cathexis" (p. 112). Lists Sade, along with Rabelais, Swift, and Kafka, among major writers.

1782.  Laborde, Alice M.  "Le Temps sadien."  FAR-WESTERN FORUM
       1 (1974): 89-94.

       Believes that Sade rejected not only all the moral
       conventions that weave man's mentalities but also the
       customary reactions to the notions of time.  States
       that each of the described activities would imply some
       physical and psychological reactions which exclude,
       even annihilate, each other and would render
       impossible the contiguity of the acts in the reported
       time lag.  Interprets some of the tentatives of the
       libertine as a mode of capturing time and rendering
       the moment eternal.  Concludes that "l'acte érotique,
       tout en condamnant celui qui s'y soumet à une forme de
       mort, à une annihilation de son temps intime, lui
       offre aussi la possibilité de se dépasser et, ce
       faisant de se projeter dans un au-delà de temps quasi
       infini."

1783.  Laufer, Roger.  "Le vertige du libertin: Sade."  MANUEL
       D'HISTOIRE DE LA FRANCE.  Edited by Pierre Abraham and
       Ronald Desné.  Vol. III.  Paris: Editions Sociales,
       1969, pp. 409-419.

       Gives biographical data on Sade followed by succinct
       appraisal of author's works.  Explains that many of
       Sade's paragraphs cannot be quoted because of the
       taboo tied to the vocabulary--which Sade uses
       gratuitously--of the sexual act.  Hence Sade offends:
       "La violence que Sade fait au langage est celle même
       qu'il fait aux sentiments.  L'étrange puissance
       poétique de sa pornographie vient de ce que les fêtes
       de l'amour physique avec ses mots se déroulent chez
       lui à la lumière de la raison dans un décor souvent
       néo-classique et artificiel."

1784.  Lély, Gilbert.  D. A. F. DE SADE.  Paris: Pierre
       Seghers, 1948.

       Presents excerpts from Sade's writings; gives a brief
       biography and a bibliography of works on Sade.

1785.  Lély, Gilbert.  "Une supercherie littéraire de Sade:
       Isabelle de Bavière."  MERCURE DE FRANCE 340 (1960):
       476-488.

Because of some new evidence, announces that this publication replaces the chapter on pp. 644-649 in VIE DU MARQUIS DE SADE (1952, Vol. II). The manuscript of ISABELLE DE BAVIERE was mentioned in 1825 in Michaud's BIOGRAPHIE UNIVERSELLE. The work was finished on 24 September 1813. In order to render authenticity to this work, Sade falsified history and gave non-existent proofs to lend veracity to the facts submitted. "Mais pour avoir, en maints endroits, sous couvert d'archives sans existence, exposé comme véritables des mobiles et des causes tirés de son imagination algolagnique, Sade ne nous en offre pas moins, grâce à des matériaux positifs utilisés de main de maître, un ample et saisissant tableau du règne de Charles VI." During the fifty years between her marriage and her death, Isabelle, according to Sade, prostituted herself with Craon, so that he would kill "le connétable de Clisson." She had Louis d'Orléans assassinated, along with his wife. She then had intimate relations with her sons. She poisoned three of her own children. She also disguised herself as a professional whore in order to copulate with thieves, robbers, and the like.

1786.  Lobet, Marcel. "De la Bastille de Sade à la chambre insonore de Proust." CLASSIQUE DE L'AN 2000. Paris: Editions de la Francité, 1970, pp. 125-128.

Discusses briefly the road to productivity in some writers.

Reviewed by A. de Kerchove, REVUE GENERAL BELGE 107, no. 4 (1971): 101-104; Raymond Deschamps, REVUE NATIONALE 43 (1971): 186-187; and A. Soreil, LA VIE VALONNE 45 (1971): 198-200.

1787.  Lund, Mary Graham. "The 'Confession' as a Novel: The Century of de Sade." MODERN AGE 8 (1963): 38-44.

Divulges that "the vocabulary of Sade is that of guilt. But the unique passion of the novels is INDIFFERENCE. Nothing proves his failure so completely as the tragic monotone in the repetition of the luxuries and the vices of Sodom . . . the results of his search still lie, in part unread, in the archives of the British Museum" [sic].

1788.  Margolin, Jean-Claude.  "Lectures de Sade."  ETUDES
       FRANCAISES 3 (1967):  410-413.

       Reviews briefly the five articles on Sade's thoughts
       published in TEL QUEL (1967): Klossowski, "Sade ou le
       philosophe scélérat"; R. Barthes, "L'arbre du crime";
       P. Sollers, "Sade dans le texte"; H. Damish,
       "L'écriture sans mesures"; and M. Tort, "L'effet
       Sade." Objects to the inclination these critics have
       to see in Sade a writer worth writing about. States
       that there is a danger of not comprehending the true
       meaning of Sade if one does not analyze properly or if
       one tries to read his work simply as romantic myth--
       traps that none of the five authors reviewed has
       fallen into.

1789.  Martinon, Jean-Pierre.  "La Représentation de interdits
       et la poétique du malsaint."  DIX-HUITIEME SIECLE  9
       (1977):  81-89.

       Describes the Sadian spaces as the frame and staging
       of the ethical and erotic evocation of desire.
       Opposes the open space of Julie's "Elysée" in LA
       NOUVELLE HELOISE to the labyrinthian architecture of
       Sadian enclosed space. The geometry of Sade's
       constructed enclosure is a reflection and a necessity
       for optimal conditions of pleasurable enterprises.

1790.  Miller, Nancy K.  "JUSTINE, or, The Vicious Circle."
       STUDIES IN EIGHTEENTH CENTURY CULTURE.  Edited by
       Ronald C. Rosbottom. Vol. 5. Madison: University of
       Wisconsin Press, 1976, pp. 215-228.

       Attempts a simultaneous confrontation of sexuality and
       textuality in Sade's works. To prove her point,
       chooses the second edition of JUSTINE, the most
       controversial of all the editions. Believes that the
       key to this version of the work is that the structure
       is designed in a circular way, to support opposing
       values of the time. Truth suffers in the process of
       illumination. Justine does not grow as a character
       because her suffering was designed to support the
       system in which she exists. In the book, action is
       privileged at the expense of the character. Justine
       is victimized because in conformity with the role of
       the victim, Justine submits, hence the circularity.
       Her life is the story. When there is no more story to
       tell, Justine dies. Believes that there is disparity

at the end of the novel between the code and its
message. Lists several circular themes: 1) the
automatic opposition that takes place continuously in
Justine's life i.e., her good deeds are always
punished; 2) the chain reaction set in motion by her
first sexual encounter. "And the end of the novel is
a model of literary construction: just as the
beginning of Justine's suffering is marked by the
separation of two sisters, an end to suffering is
brought about by their reunion."

1791.  Parant, Jean-Luc. "Enfin pouvoir nous échapper avec
       eux." OBLIQUES 12-13 (1977): 340-341.

       This is excerpted from JOIE DES YEUX, published by
       Editions Christian Bourgois, 1977. Was included in
       the special issue of OBLIQUES dedicated to Sade. Here
       are a few lines taken from that text:

       "colorés comme la lumière et que le sexe était terne
       comme la terre dans l'obscurité et que nous ne
       pouvions engendrer que la nuit et que si nous pouvions
       nous accoupler avec les yeux nous deviendrions
       subitement enceints de la tête et nous ferions naître
       en un instant un être ailé qui s'échapperait dans
       l'espace et qui ne pourrait plus quiter le ciel car la
       tête est un ventre et ses yeux un sexe pour le feu et
       nous sommes pris ici au globe dans sa surface même
       recouverts de la nuit pouvant tout juste écarter deux
       fentes pour découvrir le jour deux fentes trop petites
       pour y passer entier se jeter dans la lumière et
       sortir complètement dehors et il fait jour mais c'est
       seulement de très loin que nous en prenons conscience
       et il ne fait pas jour nous sommes toujours dans la
       nuit il n'y a que nos yeux qui sont dans le jour nous
       baignons entièrement dans l'obscurité en pleine
       lumière et seulement la vue s'y trouve y est et nous
       ne pouvons pas y aller les fentes sont trop petites
       pour y passer nous resterons toujours dans la nuit
       tant que les paupières ne se seront pas."

1792.  Paz, Octavio. "L'au-delà érotique," ARGUMENTS 21
       (1861): 2-4.

       Shows the continuous process of invention which is
       found in Sade. "Il imite et il s'invente; il invente
       et il s'imite. Expérience totale et qui jamais ne
       s'achève en son entier, car son essence consiste à

être toujours au-delà. Le corps d'autrui est un
obstacle ou un pont; dans l'un comme dans l'autre cas
il faut le franchir. Le désir, l'imagination
érotique, la voyance érotique traversent les corps,
les rendent transparents ou les anéantissent. Au-delà
de toi, au-delà de moi, par le corps, dans le corps,
au-delà du corps, nous voulons voir quelque chose. Ce
quelque chose est la fascination érotique."

Also published in OBLIQUES 11-12 (1977): 233-35.

1793. Pfersman, Andreas. "L'ironie romantique chez Sade." In
SADE: ECRIRE LA CRISE. Paris: Belfond, 1983,
pp. 85-98.

Attempts to trace the development of Sadian irony in
the successive publications of the three versions of
JUSTINE. Sees a relatively conventional irony in LES
INFORTUNES with "potentialisation" of the work in LES
MALHEURS DE LA VERTU. Concludes: "La
'potentialisation' de l'oeuvre naît donc dans LA
NOUVELLE JUSTINE au moment historique précis où une
société déchue se voit évincée par un nouvel ordre
civil, ce qui donne une nouvelle fois à penser que la
transformation du corps social affecte aussi le corps
du roman sadien, par la médiation de son organisation
esthétique."

1794. Pleynet, Marcelin. "Sade: Des Chiffres, des lettres, du
refermement." TEL QUEL 86 (1980): 26-37.

Investigates the charges that Sade is illegible and
countercharges that it is because Sade is legible that
his works have been banned. Asks again the question
of Sade's standing in literature, a standing which has
been distorted by the connotation of the adjective
"sadistic." States that when imprisoned, and only
then, Sade did begin his romanesque writings. He
first wrote DIALOGUE ENTRE UN PRETRE ET UN MORIBOND,
but his first novel was LES 120 JOURNEES DE SODOME
which introduces a real criminal society. Concludes
that "Le premier roman que Sade écrit alors qu'il est
enfermé à Vincennes puis à la Bastille, n'est autre
que l'ensemble des histoire monstrueuses d'un
refermement, n'est autre que l'ordre comptable de la
société et de sa loi. . . . Du compte des victimes
obligées des 120 JOURNEES, au compte soigneusement
établi des pratiques sexuelles du prisonnier de

Vincennes  et de la Bastille,  nous voyons bien que le
rapport  dépasse  la simple anecdote  biographique  et
qu'il y a quelque part identité entre le  renfermement
de  l'écrivain  dans  les  prisons  monarchiques  et
réplublicaines,  et les mises en scéne du renfermement
romanesque,  comme si pour Sade une même loi régissait
le réel et le fictif."

1795.   Proust, Jacques.   "La diction sadienne, à propos de la
marquise de Gange."  In SADE, ECRIRE LA CRISE.  Paris:
Ed. Belfond, 1983, pp. 31-46.

Questions the authenticity of the story in LA MARQUISE
DE GANGE.   Was it written by Sade?  Was it based on a
real  event,  a  "cause célèbre"  of  the  times
incorporated  by other authors in some of their works,
i.e.  LES CAUSES CELEBRES,  by Gayot de Pitaval (1734-
1743),  HISTOIRE  DE LA MARQUISE DE GANGE,  by Fortia
d'Urbain (1810)?   Also questions the role of the main
character in Sade's interpretation, which is different
from that of the others.   "Le premier texte [D'Urban]
met l'accent sur l'horreur du spectacle, et le courage
physique de la femme martyrisée.   Le second [Sade] au
contraire  en atténue les effets,  au détriment d'une
créature  assez  sotte  ou  assez  aveuglée  par  la
superstition  pour songer encore à épargner celui  qui
la tue."  Concludes that Sade wrote tongue-in-cheek in
order to satirize rather ferociously public opinion.

1796.   Queneau, Raymond.  "Sur Sade."   BATONS,  CHIFFRES ET
LETTRES.   Paris:  Editions Gallimard,  1950, pp. 214-
216.

This  essay  was  also  reproduced  in  the  NOUVEL
OBSERVATEUR 68 (March 1966).

Believes  that there is much in Sade that  anticipated
the Nazi horrors that it is now no longer known as the
wild  imagination  of  a hallucinating writer  but  as
realities practiced by thousands of fanatics.

1797.   Riffaterre,  Michel.   "Sade, or Text as Fantasy."
DIACRITICS 2,  no.  3 (1972): 2-9.  (Revised review of
Barthes's SADE, FOURIER, LOYOLA, 1971).

Reviews Barthes's book,  SADE, FOURIER, LOYOLA (Ed. du
Seuil,  1971).   States  that the sadian text presents
enormous  difficulties  of  interpretation but  that

Barthes's application to Sade's works of the interpretative method he developed in S/Z is a "rare opportunity to explore literary and critical discourse together since Barthes's reading and Sade's writing betray elective affinities." Points to several misinterpretations that "[results] from superimposing the wrong code into the text" and to "fragmentary and random reading." Objects to Barthes's violation of his own principles, namely, that "everything, to be pertinent, must remain within the limits of the text." Believes Barthes erred because he mixed reading with empirical psychology: "This holds Barthes's analysis at the level of fantasies, although his metalanguage is aimed at the text."

First-rate essay.

1798. Robbe-Grillet, Alain. "Sade et le joli." OBLIQUES 12-13 (1977): 59.

Presents a study of Sade's attitude toward prettiness or "le joli." Sade described with fine clarity the traits of his characters but not, as might be expected, to emphasize the violence of his statements. On the contrary, the violence is there only to emphasize the "joli." "Il est si manifeste que Sade est ému, charnellement, par la joliesse que l'on est tenté de dire tout le contraire: le ruisselet de sang n'est là que pour mettre en valeur la perfection des courbes les plus délicates, la souffrance ne sert qu'à faire trembler d'émotion le tendre ourlet des lèvres, briller davantage la profondeur des yeux, bouger plus exquisement les reins; la torture n'est en somme qu'une amoureuse exarcerbation des caresses qui leur rendent un juste hommage. . . ."

1799. Rode, Henri. "Chroniques." CAHIERS DU SUD 301 (1950): 530-531.

Reviews LES CRIMES DE L'AMOUR, published by Sagittaire. Discusses the impossibility of fitting the works of the marquis de Sade in the usual literary molds. Everywhere Sade belongs to the exception. "Sade n'est en fin de compte que lui-même, inassimilable à tout, sauf à notre curiosité saisie. . . . Son message, qu'il souhaite lui-même voir oublié nous parvient à travers le jour de la chambre des tortures et sa valeur humaine n'est autre

que poétique à l'excès. . . . On admire d'abord le
conteur dont la saveur n'est plus à dire. Et que tant
de licence, de rondeur, d'intelligence sensuelle aient
été aussi salutaires, comment en douter? Sade
décomprime la morale et défait les bandelettes
d'Adolphe, il pressent l'éclosion d'Emma Bovary. Il
tranche le déversement de la marmelade romantique.
Dans ces historiettes rapides, magistralement
distriates, et bien menées, il fait déjà office de
dompteur et d'éclaireur, et qu'un Apollinaire, un
Breton, un Eluard et quelques autres saluent en lui un
libérateur n'est pas, dans l'ordre des valeurs
spirituelles, son moindre titre de gloire."

1800.  Roger, Philippe. "D. A. F., le corps et le texte." LA
        QUINZAINE LITTERAIRE 282 (1 July 1978): 18.

        Reviews two recent publications, SADE: L'INVENTION DU
        CORPS LIBERTIN, by Marcel Hénaff; and SADE, L'OEIL DE
        LA LETTRE, by Chantal Thomas. Asserts that these two
        books have little in common except that in both, in
        spite of divergent points of view, Sade is
        recognizable. "Le texte sadien, Marcel Hénaff le
        note, est une monnaie qui a beaucoup circulé . . . il
        fait surgir la figure de Sade telle que l'a dessinée
        la modernité. . . . Tout autre est l'OEIL DE LA
        LETTRE de Chantal Thomas: bel emblème d'une critique
        qui, sans perdre de vue la lettre, ne serait pas
        seulement poéticienne. . . . Marcel Henaff éclaire un
        Sade qui nous guérit de cette ancestrale peur et du
        plaisir: son dernier mot, au bas de la dernière
        page--'m'affole.'"

1801.  Rosset, Clement. "L'Ecriture violente." NOUVELLE REVUE
        FRANCAISE 328 (1980): 60-65.

        Believes that the literary genius of Sade consists in
        the presentation of an always laughable reality in
        comparison with the all-powerful strength of the
        written word. Rather than attempting to transcribe
        empirical data, the only reality accepted is whatever
        is written, so that the literary object is not only
        present but the only one having existence. For Sade,
        then, the literary object has, in platonic terms, not
        only the "being" of "not being" but also the "being"
        of "Being." Concludes "pur effet littéraire en quoi
        se résume, au moment où on l'écrit, l'effet de vérité,
        comme s'y résume l'effet de réel."

1802. Smock, Ann.   "Review."  SUB-STANCE 11,  no. 35 (1982):
      72-73.

      Review  of  INTERSECTIONS:   A READING  OF  SADE  WITH
      BATAILLE,  BLANCHOT,  AND  KLOSSOWSKI,  by Jane Gallop
      (University of Nebraska Press,  1981).   Declares that
      "INTERSECTIONS,   as  its  title  indicates,   is   an
      intertextual  undertaking which pays  no  particular
      respect to the integrity of given authors nor observes
      the boundaries framing one work and separating it from
      another.    Instead,   it  considers texts and the names
      attached to them to be effects of a lively network  of
      multiple   relationships. . . .   INTERSECTIONS   is
      characterized  by  the indeterminate relation  between
      'major'  and  'minor'  engagements  of  the  issues  it
      engages.   Once  again,  the book is  itself . . . an
      enjoyable   joke   about   the   minorness   of   its
      majorness. . . ."

1803. Solier,  René de.   "Sade ou l'avocat des formes."   LES
      CAHIERS DU SUD 285 (1947):  725-728.

      Also  published  in OBLIQUES 12-13  (1977):   227-228.
      States  that  Sade has  assembled  with extraordinary
      success,  a composite of the bizarre:   "le roman noir
      athée,"  where  the  supernatural is replaced  by  the
      concentrationary  absolutism of human gesture.   "Sous
      ce  puzzle,  à  travers  le  carroyage  des  éléments
      prisonniers,  Sade persuade que l'événement historique
      a,  pour corollaire,  un événement mental et charnel qui
      résulte d'une rupture.   Nous sommes en présence d'une
      rhétorique  de  l'excès."   Concludes  that  Sade's
      achievement is in the obsession he creates with forms:
      his  repetitions become a movement,  a driven force in
      spite of the boredom and tiredness they provoke in the
      reader.

1804. Sollers,  Philippe. "Sade dans le texte."  L'ECRITURE ET
      L'EXPERIENCES DES LIMITES.   Paris: Editions du Seuil,
      1971, pp. 48-66.

      See item 1805.

1805. Sollers,  Philippe.   "Sade dans le texte."  TEL QUEL 28
      (Winter 1967): 38-50.

Also published in LOGIQUES (1968): 78-96, and in
L'ECRITURE ET L'EXPERIENCE DES LIMITES (Paris: Seuil,
1971), pp. 48-66.

States that at the junction of desire and logos, the
writings of Sade as an act of transgression, is the
negation of language within language. What is
asserted is the language of desire, which reaches a
cosmogonic level forgotten or abolished in our
culture. In other words, order comes out of chaos,
just as anarchy precedes all laws. Concludes:
"Ecrire dans le seul but de détruire incessamment les
règles, les croyances qui cachent l'écriture du désir,
écrire non pour exprimer ou représenter . . . mais
pour détruire à la fois la vertu et le vice, leur
complicité, par un crime à tel point cause et effet de
lui-même qu'il ne puisse plus être caractérisé; écrire
est alors un crime pour la vertu comme pour le crime."

Reviewed by J. Fremon in ETUDES 335 (1971): 308-309.

1806. Somville, Pierre. Review of SADE, FOURIER, LOYOLA, by
Roland Barthes. REVUE INTERNATIONALE DE PHILOSOPHIE
27 (1973): 542-543.

Contends that Roland Barthes affirms quite clearly his
literary epicurism in this work which forms "une
concaténation de jouissances." Deciphers the three
separate texts and discloses that "La congruence est
effectivement remarquable: nous voyons peu à peu se
dessiner, puis s'imposer irrésistiblement, des
parallèlismes de syntaxe logique très révévelateurs
dans la taxonomie de ces trois langages, caractérisés
chacun, précisément, par une sorte de rage
classificatrice."

1807. Swabey, Marie C. "The Comic as Nonsense, Sadism, or
Incongruity." JOURNAL OF PHILOSOPHY 55 (1958): 819-
833.

Investigates the nature of the comic which "besides
involving emotional and physiological responses,
requires logical and metaphysical comprehension, a
normative intellectual insight which grasps what is
worthy of laughter, what state of affairs is laughable
and not merely what makes us as organic creatures
laugh." A philosophical essay relating only tenuously
to Sade and sadism.

1808.  Temmer, Mark J.  "Style et rhétoric."   YALE  FRENCH
       STUDIES 35 (December 1965):   20-28.

       Feels that Sade is paradoxical and  exasperating.   In
       order  to  read  him,  one  must  calmly  analyze  his
       passions,  which  are  distorted  views  of  universal
       passions.   One  must  also  consider  his  form  and
       diction, his poor style.  Sade's nihilistic views lead
       him to see God and Nature as evil.  His philosophy was
       the dehumanization of man,  which he expressed by  the
       destruction  of nature through man.   Wonders  whether
       the  flaw in Sade's style is due to the subject matter
       or  to Sade himself.   Death and destruction can  be
       represented  in  a  poetic,   symbolic  form  (as  in
       Shakespeare)  or  can  be represented by  speaking  as
       energetically  as  possible and making  language  come
       alive (as in Sade).   And as long as he is  energetic,
       Sade  is a good stylist.   Author believes that Sade's
       works  are the most ill-composed in French  literature.
       They  lack unity and they do not appeal to the senses.
       His  works lack conciseness and  are  boring.   States
       that  "his  bodily  imprisonment was paralleled  by  a
       spiritual  neurosis which impeded the fashioning of  a
       personal  style."   In  other  words,  when  Sade  had
       contact with the outside world, his work improved.

1809.  Thomas,  Chantal.  SADE,  L'OEIL DE LA LETTRE.   Paris:
       Payot, 1978.  180 p.

       Proposes a reading apprenticeship of Sade's text:   "A
       travers  leurs multiples variantes,  nos  lectures  de
       Sade trahissent toutes pour cette force de destruction
       le  même  désir angoissé.   Au point où il n'y a  plus
       qu'à se perdre et disparaître, nous continuons de nous
       servir  du  langage  comme d'un  instrument  qui  nous
       permettrait  à la fois de dire cette perte et de  nous
       en préserver."  Does not attempt to elucidate a Sadian
       philosophy  nor  to  present  structural  analysis  of
       Sade's works but,  in this palimpsest,  peels off  for
       Sade's  heliotropic  system  a  suitable  and  equally
       heliotropic  critical  analysis:   "La  liberté  d'un
       immaitrisable     mouvement     de     glissements,     de
       déplacements,  de métamorphoses hante toute l'écriture
       de  Sade  et  sa vie."  States that  the  practice  of
       rhetorical  art  constitutes  in  Sade  the  dominant
       passion and one onto which all the other passions  are
       grafted.   First-rate  analysis of Sade's  "écriture."

Reviewed by Philippe Roger in LA QUINZAINE LITTERAIRE 282 (1 July 1978): 8; and Michel Delon in DIX-HUITIEME SIECLE 11 (1979): 515-516.

1810. Thomas, Chantal. "Isabelle de Bavière: dernière héroine de Sade." SADE, ECRIRE LA CRISE. Paris: Ed. Belfond, 1983, pp. 47-66.

Appraises Sade's techniques as an historian. Not content to simply report the facts, Sade brought proofs to back his statements; however, the proofs are the products of his own fertile imagination, though they give an evaluation of what history should be, according to Sade. It appears again that "les femmes sont plus cruelles que les hommes." Sade puts much of the responsibility for Charles VI's madness on mistreatment and persecutions at the hands of his wife, Isabelle de Bavière. By extension, Sade would be saying that all the troubles of France are caused by its malevolent queen. However, author concludes that "Les démonstrations qu'il établit, et dont l'évidence lui semble relever d'une 'vérité géometrique', évoquent au lecteur familier de ses calculs signalistes la déraison de leur évidence mathématique."

1811. Torchia, Francesco. "Per una lettura testuale della PHILOSOPHIE DANS LE BOUDOIR di D. A. F. de Sade." NUOVA CORRENTE: RIVISTA DI LETTERATURA 75 (1978): 42-68.

Attempts a textual reading of LA PHILOSOPHIE DANS LE BOUDOIR. Makes some interesting observations concerning the monotonous repetitions in Sade's text: "La funzione della ripetizione speculare: un sistema di specchi quale quello approntato da Sade annulla ogni cristallizzazione dell'immagine, cioè ogni funzione semplicemente omologica rinviando l'imago di specchio in specchio moltiplica la differenza assoluta di ogni movimento." In a rather surprising conclusion states that sadian monstrosity is not in Sade but in the representation of the times: "Ma più profondamente quel testo monstruoso, per l'appunto, coglie lo sfaldamento del metafisica della rappresentazione classica, e scrive tra le sue pagine la verità dell'unica legge possibile: quella del desiderio."

1812. Tort, Michel. "L'effet Sade." TEL QUEL 28 (1967): 66-83.

> Attempts to isolate within the logic of Sade's text the formal structures which distinguish it. Believes that the organization principle of that logic is to be found in Sade's imagination. Defines "l'effet Sade" as the decisive function given to the imaginary representation incorporated in the structural format of the sadian production. Concludes that though the sadian discourse revolves on the intention of telling it all--whatever comes to the imagination--this extreme freedom is still subjugated to the insistence of desire. First-rate article.

> Also published in OEUVRES COMPLETES DU MARQUIS DE SADE. Vol. XVI. (Cercle du livre précieux, 1967, pp. 583-620.)

1813. Vercruysse, J. Review of SADE, by Jean-Jacques Brochier. In DIX-HUITIEME SIECLE 2 (1970): 360.

> Answers the question "Is Sade a classic writer?" in the affirmative. States: "Une initiation claire et agréable à un auteur difficile. . . . En quelques pages, M. Brochier a rendu l'essentiel de la pensée sadienne."

1814. Wolf, H. J. "Pour un examen du vocabulaire sadien." LE FRANCAIS MODERNE: REVUE DE LINGUISTIQUE FRANCAISE 45 (1977): 48-51.

> Examines the sadian vocabulary but to illustrate his point mentions three examples drawn from Sade's poem "La Verité." These examples are 1) enculer; 2) se masturber; 3) masturbateur. Concludes that lexical researches should be done on the works of Sade.

## P.  THEATER

1815.  Adrien, Philippe.  L'OEIL DE LA TETE:  EFFET SADE.  Play
produced in Paris and in Brussels, 1975.

Mentioned by Michel Delon, item 1815.

1816.  Adrien, Philippe.  SADE DANS LE XVIII SIECLE, REPRESENTE
DU  7 NOVEMBRE AU 8 DECEMBRE A LA  SALPETRIERE.
Critique et propos recueillis par Nathalie Godard.
ART PRESSE, No. 20, September–October 1975.

1817.  Aelberts,  Alain-Valery,  and Auquier, Jean-Jacques.
CEREMONIAL POUR SALUER D'ERUPTION EN ERUPTION  JUSQU'A
L'INFRACASSABLE  NUIT  LA  BRECHE  ABSOLUE  ET  LA
TRAJECTOIRE DU MARQUIS DE SADE.  Brussels:  Aelberts
and Auquier, 1970.  67 p.

Includes  an  unpublished poem by Gilbert Lély  and  a
preface  by  Henri Pastoureau.  Illustrated by  Jorge
Camacho  and  Jacques Herold.  Surrealist  scenario
honoring Sade.  Each scene is subtitled--for instance,
Tableau 13:  "L'oiseau-feuille traverse  la  pluie."
Tableau 14:  "Les chiens ont dévoré le crépuscule."

Reviewed  by  Michel Delon in DIX-HUITIEME  SIECLE  11
(1979):  422.

1818.  Almeras,  Henri D.,  and d'Estrée,  Paul.  LES THEATRES
LIBERTINS AU XVIII SIECLE.  Paris:  Daragon,  1905,
p. 13.

Lists  nothing  specific  on Sade  but  discusses  the
specialists  of  "pièces  grivoises,"  "scènes
croustilleuses," "la magnière [sic] dont elles étaient
rendues,  la  franche gaîté qu'ils y mettaient,  les
ordures  gaillardes dont ils  savaient  l'assaisonner,
enfin jusqu'à leur prononciation vicieuse et pleine de
cuirs,  faisaient  rire à crever tous les seigneurs de
la Cour qui n'étaient pas tout à fait dans  l'habitude
d'être  grossier,  z'et [sic] de voir chez le Roi  des
joyeusetés aussi libres."  In other words, the Marquis
de  Sade was  not alone in his times with  a  special
liking for saucy stories.

1819.  Anonymous.  "Sur Marat-Sade."  LE NOUVEL-OBSERVATEUR, 28
September 1966, LE MONDE, 16 September 1966.

1820. Artaud, Antonin. "Le Théâtre de la cruauté." NOUVELLE
REVUE FRANCAISE, 229 (October 1932): 603-614.

This first manifesto of the theater of cruelty lists
in its nine works, including a tale written by the
Marquis de Sade: "un conte du marquis de Sade, où
l'érotisme sera transposé, figuré allégoriquement et
habillé, dans le sens d'une extériorisation violente
de la cruauté du côté sang, et d'une dissimulation du
reste."

1821. Beaujour, Michel. "Peter Weiss and the Futility of
Sadism." YALE FRENCH STUDIES 35 (December 1965):
114-119.

Reviews the play MARAT/SADE by Peter Weiss. States
that while some critics have "pigeonholed" MARAT/SADE
as "theatre of cruelty," it lacks too much to be a
"happening." Without suspense, and with too much
unrestricted folly, the play cannot even boast of a
little sadism. Concludes that the "unbounded freedom
of Sade's imagination, and the assumed freedom of
Marat, the revolutionary, have no great weight when
confronted with necessity. They are the phony
freedoms of intellectuals." Hence the play is for
this critic a paradox in its theme and a failure in
its performance.

1822. Bouër, André. "Le marquis de Sade et le théâtre."
REFLETS MEDITERRANEENS, April-May 1958, pp. 24-26.

States that consultation of the catalog of Sade's
library holdings shows that Sade admired the theater
of his time. If Sade did not bring any novelty to the
theater, as he did to the novel, he contributed nevertheless to some originality in stage setting (i.e., in
the preface of MISANTHROPE PAR AMOUR he suggested, in
order to tie the two acts together, having mimes
perform in front of the curtain at intermission).
Gives a succinct history of Sade's successes and
failures in the theater and concludes with an overview
of the theater at Charenton where Sade did direct his
own theater group and had some of his own plays
performed.

1823. Brega, Gian Pietro. "L'anticipazione del teatro di
Sade." SIPARIO, June 1965, pp. 2-4.

States that the violence found in much of Sade's novels is not present in his theater. In OXTIERN, the most "dignitosa" of his plays, only one of the nine characters can be seen as a typically Sadian hero. Only once did Sade affront his theater with as much courage as he shows in his novels; that play is "Josephine, ou l'Espouse malheureuse," where one can see the influence of LES JOURNEES DE FLORIBELLE. Concludes that "la qualità spectacolare di vali azioni sceniche, non deve però farcene dementicare le premesse filosofiche, quel perserguire la regione fino alle sue colonne d'Ercole, oltre le quali si promette apunto la visione dramatica; una meta raggiungibile solo dopo che sia stato percorso l'intero periplo della queste premesse che liberano la scena or giastiche di JUSTINE e delle 120 JOURNEES da ogni scoria sadica, e ne fanno si primi esempi di quel teatro sadiono al quale si sono avvicinati teorici e scrittori moderni, da Buchner a Artaud, dai surrealisti a Genet, da Beckette a Gelber." Follows a translation of the Roland Episode from the 1791 version of LA NOUVELLE JUSTINE.

1824.   Brochier, Jean-Jacques. "Charenton et le théâtre." OBLIQUES 12-13 (1977): 174-176.

Cites some of the plays produced by Sade at Charenton. Most of them were written by contemporaries of Sade, e.g., L'ESPRIT DE CONTRADICTION, MARTON ET FRONTIN, LES DEUX SAVOYARDS. Sade himself wrote only a few: LA FETE DE L'AMITIE, L'HOMMAGE DE LA RECONNAISSANCE. This text was also published as a preface to Sade's THEATER, Edition Jean-Jacques Pauvert, 1970.

1825.   Brookes, J. "Producing MARAT/SADE." HOSPITAL AND COMMUNITY PSYCHIATRY 26, no. 7 (1975): 429-435.

Reenacts the play MARAT/SADE in contemporary setting—another theater produced in a psychiatric hospital.

1826.   Bussotti, Sylvano. "Notes pour la mise en scène de 'La Passion selon Sade,' mystère de chambre." LE THEATRE 1 (1968): 89-99.

Writes a series of notes and commentaries for staging a "mystère de chambre," LA PASSION SELON SADE, and defines his work as a "Concerto Figure." Concludes "en choisissant d'interpréter le premier role masculin de ce mystère, en choisissant d'assumer par son corps même le poids de toute la représentation, l'auteur pense démythifier l'acte intellectuel qu'il veut réduire à la dimension d'un geste éphémère."

1827. Dupré, Gilbert. "Le théâtre malade de la culture. Censure, information et conjoncture." PARTISANS 36 (March 1967): 18-19.

Complains that while officially theater censorship no longer exists, there are in fact many impediments to theater production, not the least of which is funding. In the case of the play by Peter Weiss, MARAT/SADE, gives an interesting sypnosis of a correspondence between Bertrand Flornoy (who wanted to ban the staging of the play) and M. A. M. Julien, the director of the Sarah-Bernhardt theater (who had included that production in the program for that season).

1828. Esquirol, Jean-Etienne. DES MALADIES MENTALES CONSIDERES SOUS LES RAPPORTS MEDICAUX, HYGIENIQUE ET MEDICO-LEGAL. Vol. II. Paris: J. B. Baillères, 1838, p. 561.

Mentions Sade's theater at Charenton, the mental hospital.

1829. Frantz, Pierre. "Sade: texte, théâtralité." In SADE, ECRIRE LA CRISE: COLLOQUE DE CERISY. Paris: Belfond, 1983, pp. 193-218.

Examines two divergent attitudes toward Sade's theater, that of Gilbert Lély who thought Sade had no talent at all as a playwright and that of Jean-Jacques Brochier, who saw in Sade's dramaturgy the necessary complement to his other productions. Attempts to demonstrate that "l'écriture du marquis joue AVEC et CONTRE le théâtre." States that Sade as a playwright is a heretic refusing the inheritance of theatrical types defined in the classical comedy by a hypertrophia of passion in a character. Concludes: "Dans ces agencements machiniques, la théâtralité est donnée comme achèvement impossible. Au fil du texte, le lecteur lui aussi est entrainé à défaire et à déborder ses représentations."

1830. Freed, Donald. "Peter Weiss and the Theatre of the Future." DRAMA SURVEY 6 (Fall 1967): 119-173.

Gives much credit to Peter Weiss for the new trend in contemporary experimental theater which combines paradoxical mixture such as Artaud's theater of cruelty and involvement with Brechtian estrangement or alienation. This applies especially to MARAT/SADE.

1831. Goulemot, Jean-Marie. "Le marquis de Sade, ses pompes et ses oeuvres, selon PETER WEISS." LA PENSEE 134 (August 1967): 104-114.

Attempts to study the impact made by Peter Weiss's play on the popularity of the Marquis de Sade. Notes that the confrontation with Marat which is depicted in the play is totally imaginary and stems only from the fact that Sade was the one who spoke at Marat's funeral. Concludes that MARAT/SADE "reste la mise à jour des mécanismes de confiscation d'une révolution faite par et pour le peuple, la dénonciation de l'oppression bourgeoise, et de ses alibis les plus grossiers. . . . La fatalité historique, qui, selon Sade, voue toute révolution à l'échec, fait de sa dénonciation un jeu gratuit, propre à séduire les mieux intentionnés comme les plus cyniques."

1832. Guaraldo, Enrico. Review of SADE/ARTAUD, by Carlo Pasi. RIVISTA DI LETTERATURE MODERNE E COMPARATE 33 (1980): 157-159.

1833. Guyaux, André. "Théâtre de Sade." REVUE D'HISTOIRE DU THEATRE 31 (1979): 46-51.

Believes that for Sade the theater was a literary fantasm and that he never reached the glory of the dramatic author, to which he aspired: "Le théâtre de Sade plutôt que celui qu'il écrivit, est une oeuvre virtuelle, irréalisable à son époque et peut-être aujourd'hui encore. Cette virtualité apparaît à la fois dans le caractère théâtral (de scènes et de mises en scènes) de l'oeuvre romanesque de Sade et dans le caractère décevant de son oeuvre et de sa carrière théâtrales." Among his papers were found outlines of projected plays. Published here is the plan for a verse comedy in one act entitled MELINDE OU L'HEUREUSE INFIDELITE.

1834. Hampshire, Stuart. "The Theatre of Sade." In MODERN WRITERS AND OTHER ESSAYS. London: Chatto and Windus, 1969, pp. 63-70.

Comments on the play MARAT/SADE, by Peter Weiss, an original idea of "extraordinary brilliance: to make Sade the centre, and the commentator, of a play within a play, which would illustrate the full range of theatrical effects which the modern stage, after Buchner, Pirandello, Brecht, and Genet, can now provide."

1835. Heckroth, Hein. THEATRUM SADICUM DER MARQUIS DE SADE UND DAS THEATER. Emsdetten: Lecte, 1963. 341 p.

Contributes the illustrations of this oversize book on Sade's theater. Rather puzzling is the fact that while many of Sade's plays are so run-of-the mill, without even a "sadistic" tinge, some of the drawings included in this beautiful book are of the obscene variety.

1836. Heine, Maurice. "Dramaturgie de Sade." LE MINOTAURE 1 (February 1933): 12-19.

Discusses Sade's interest of long standing in the theater. Believes that the performances conducted by Sade at Charenton had a therapeutic effect on inmates willing to attend or perform in the plays. Also gives an abstract of a comedy entitled ZELONIDE with a footnote from the author giving the proposed title of that play as SOPHIE ET DESFRANS.

1837. James, Norman. "The Fusion of Pirandello and Brecht in MARAT/SADE and THE PLEBEIANS REHEARSE THE UPRISING." EDUCATIONAL THEATRE JOURNAL 21 (1969): 426-438.

Compares Peter Weiss's play MARAT/SADE, with one written by Gunter Grass, THE PLEBEIANS REHEARSE THE UPRISING. As Pirandello had done in SIX CHARACTERS IN SEARCH OF AN AUTHOR, both Weiss and Grass are able "to convey a world in which there are no fixed points in space and time, but in which various points in space and time illuminate each other, any given point, including the present, achieving whatever reality it has in terms of its relations to other points." Also states that one can recognizes the influence of Brecht on Weiss's play, which could not have been written on

so many alienating levels without this able precursor.
Concludes: "Weiss transcends, in ways foreshadowed by
Pirandello as well as Brecht, the limitations of a
stage illusion. . . . Not only is Weiss's technique
more complex than that of Grass. It should already be
apparent that he uses it to give us a more complex
view than that of Grass of the historical events he
depicts."

1838.  Keller-Schumacher, Brigitte.  DIALOG UND MORD: EINE
       INTERPRETATION DES MARAT/SADE VON PETER WEISS.
       Frankfurt: Athenum. 1973, 434 p.

1839.  Lacombe, Anne.  "Du théâtre au roman: Sade."  STUDIES
       ON VOLTAIRE AND THE EIGHTEENTH CENTURY 129 (1975):
       115-143.

       Studies the influence the theater may have had on the
       novel in the eighteenth century.  Investigates more
       specifically the relationships between the plays
       written by Sade during the period he devoted to LES
       120 JOURNEES DE SODOME and LES INFORTUNES DE LA VERTU.
       While Sade may have been reluctant to express in the
       theater some of his deepest obsessions, perhaps for
       reasons of propriety, it seems, that Sade learned from
       Racine, Prévost, and Richardson that dramatic interest
       is only to be found in the misfortunes of virtue, a
       contention which he would use as a moral justification
       for some of his productions.

1840.  Macchia, Giovanni.  "Il diavolo in biblioteca."  IL MITO
       DI PARIGI: SAGGI ET MOTIVI FRANCESI.  Turin: Giulio
       Einaudi Editore, 1965, pp. 257-262.

       Discusses for the most part three "devils in the
       library"--Baudelaire, Apollinaire, and Sade--and the
       interest, emphasized by Apollinaire, that Sade had in
       the theater.  Sade's motivation to become not only a
       playwright but an actor was suppressed when he was
       free; but it became a reality, an obsession, when he
       was at Charenton.  His aptitudes were encouraged by
       the director of the institution, M. Royer-Collard.

1841.  Manz'ie.  "Le théâtre de Sade."  LA QUINZAINE
       LITTERAIRE 113 (1 March 1971): 10.

       To the question "What is the mystery of Sade's
       theatre?" answers: "C'est le nécessaire négatif, le

repoussoir de l'oeuvre romanesque; c'est Sade blanc, Sade noir. L'un complète l'autre, le permet et le justifie. . . . Tandis qu'il [Sade] refuse toute contrainte de sa force vitale, de 'l'énergie qu'il a reçu de la nature', il a besoin d'une place dans la société. Tout se passe alors comme s'il offrait un 'paraître' public . . . comme s'il offrait à ses semblables un personnage qui ne les dépareille pas." This article was written shortly after the publication by J. J. Pauvert of four volumes of Sade's THEATRE.

1842. Mays, James. "Pons Asinorum: Form and Value in Beckett's Writing, with some Comments on Kafka and De Sade." IRISH UNIVERSITY REVIEW 4 (1974): 268-282.

Investigates the different meanings given to the word "form." It can be interpreted as structure, organic form, pure form, symbolic form, proportional form, significant form. Sade's 120 DAYS OF SODOM, "a demonstration of writing which is not literature," is a book doomed to failure; in spite of its encyclopedic format it can only be incomplete. Concludes: "The 120 DAYS OF SODOM is the only piece of writing outside Beckett's own in which an ever-restless, totally irreconcilable content is set against such an arbitrarily but beautifully exact and incongruous form, in a way that encompasses such anger and such anguish."

1843. Mère, Charles. LE MARQUIS DE SADE. Paris: Librairie Théâtrale, 1921.

This was a dramatic production, in two acts, presented in Paris on 5 February 1921 at the Grand Guignol theater.

1844. Miller, Leslie L. "Peter Weiss, Marat, and Sade: Comments on an Author's Commentary." SYMPOSIUM 25 (1971): 39-58.

Discusses two contemporary theatrical productions, Hochhuth's DER STELLVERTRETER (1963) and Peter Weiss's DIE VERFOLGUNG UND ERMORDUNG JEAN PAUL MARATS DARGESTELLT DURCH DIE SCHAUSPIELGRUPPE DES HOSPIZES ZU CHARENTON UNTER ANLEITUNG DES HERRN DE SADE, and states that "thematically these two plays have little in common; both, however, depict historical events and figures and both raise controversial moral and political issues upon which their respective authors have commented at length in a number of essays and interviews." Furthermore, believes that Weiss's choice of Sade "as a counter-figure to Marat in the drama seems to invite confusion and ambiguity." Though author affirms that the deep perception reflected in Weiss's drama is likely to generate interest, also suggests that Weiss "seemed unable to interpret his own plays other than in the somewhat unconvincing terms of the commentaries discussed (in the article)."

1845.  Mishima, Yukio, pseud. MADAME DE SADE. Tokyo: C. E. Tuttle Co., 1971.

A play translated from the Japanese by Donald Krene.

1846.  Montagna, Bonatti G.   Review of L'ANTICIPAZIONE DEL TEATRO DI SADE by G. P. Brega.   STUDI FRANCESI 11 (1967): 559.

This is a review of an article "L'Anticipazione del teatro di Sade" published in SIPARIO, June 1965, pp. 2-4.   Quotes the author as saying that Sade's theater is neither aristocratic nor revolutionary, neither republican nor monarchial.

1847.  Parham, Sidney F.  "Marat/Sade: The Politics of Experience, or the Experience of Politics?"   MODERN DRAMA 20 (1977): 235-250.

Praises Peter Weiss's play, MARAT/SADE, because it is a "fashionable mixture of all the best theatrical ingredients around--Brechtian, didactic, absurdist, theatre of cruelty." It is also a very successful experiment in stereometric time which allows us to see both sides of several double binds. The central one is an oppressive situation: "The current oppressive regime must be replaced. It can be replaced only through violent revolution, but violent revolution breeds oppressive regimes. . . . The situation of the patients is an exact parallel to this political situation. They are in an oppressive situation; their attempts to escape that oppression confirm Coulmier in the diagnosis of madness and justify further repression."

1848. Roubine, Jean-Jacques. "Oxtiern, melodrame et palimpseste." REVUE D'HISTOIRE DU THEATRE 22 (1970): 266-283.

After numerous failures in the theater, LE PREVARICATEUR, JEANNE LAISNE OU LE SIEGE DE BEAUVAIS, LE BOUDOIR OU LE MARI CREDULE, AZELIS OU LA COQUETTE PUNIE, LE SUBORNEUR--Sade obtained a relative success in OXTIERN, an adaptation of his novel ERNESTINE. OXTIERN was first played 22 October 1791 at the Théâtre Molière; but in order to accommodate the demands of the theater-going public, Sade amputated most of his play's dramatic elements, which were unacceptable on the stage because spectators could not have accepted the horrors of wronged innocence. In so doing, Sade removed the "sadistic" elements of his play which, therefore, became commonplace.

1849. Seelman-Eggebert, Ulrich. "Das Theater des marquis de Sade." NEUE ZURCHER ZEITSCHRIFT, n° 53, 1 October 1972.

1850. Sichère, Bernard. "Le théâtre Sadien." OBLIQUES 12-13 (1977): 187-188.

Discusses the theatrical presentations directed by Sade at Charenton, a kind of learned delirium directed at an insane audience by insane performers in an alienated world. To the question "Who is crazy?" answers: "La réponse est claire: ni le fou, ni le libertin qui en jouit, ni le spectateur qui jouit en secret de cette jouissance, mais la machine sociale qui produit le fou et le pervers et qui fonde l'anomalie à côté de la norme."

This article is reprinted from L'AUTRE SCENE 7 (1973): 28-39.

1851. Sontag, Susan. "Marat/Sade/Artaud." PARTISAN REVIEW 32 (1965): 11-22.

Reprinted in AGAINST INTERPRETATION (New York: Dell Publishing, 1961), pp. 163-174. Author states that "theatricality and insanity--the two most potent subjects of the contemporary theater--are brilliantly fused in Peter Weiss' play, THE PERSECUTION AND ASSASSINATION OF JEAN-PAUL MARAT AS PERFORMED BY THE INMATES OF THE ASYLUM AT CHARENTON UNDER THE DIRECTION

OF THE MARQUIS DE SADE." Disagrees with the statement read all too frequently that "while MARAT/SADE is, theatrically, one of the most stunning things anyone has seen on the stage, it's a 'director's play,' meaning a first-rate production of a second-rate play." Investigates also the influence of Artaud and Brecht on the Weiss-Brook production. Concludes that "certain features of MARAT/SADE are reminiscent of Brecht's theater--constructing the action around a debate on principles and reasons; the songs; the appeals to the audience through an M.C. And these blend well with the Artaudian texture of the situation and the staging."

1852. Taberner-Prat, Josemaria. UBER DEN MARAT/SADE VON PETER WEISS: ARTISTISCHE KREATION UND REZEPTIVE MISSVERSTANDNIS. Stuttgard: Heinz, 1976. 419 p.

1853. Tonelli, Franco. "From Cruelty to Theatre. Antonin Artaud and the Marquis de Sade." COMPARATIVE DRAMA 3 (1969): 79-86.

Links the plays of Artaud's theater of cruelty to the novels of Sade. Feels that the "dramatic energy" in Sade's writings is dissipated in his plays, which were adapted to the needs of the stage. Gives as an example OXTIERN, which loses some of its impact because some of the monologues reveal pity and love-- two feelings "alien to sadism," whereas Artaud, in his plays, wanted to show "a brutal stylization of the very essence of eroticism . . . in its original state without any moral, psychological, or sociological contingency dissipating its primal originality." Concludes that "for Sade, as for Artaud, art has as its aim the violent revelation of the ultimate reality of existence. This is probably the context in which Artaud saw Sade's work and the reason he included it in its proposal."

1854. Vinot-Préfontaine. "Le marquis de Sade et Jeanne Hachette." BULLETIN DE LA SOCIETE ACADEMIQUE ARCHEOLOGIQUE D'OISE 87 (20 October 1864): 2.

Brief note reproduced here in its entirety: "Il s'agit d'une pièce en cinq actes, JEANNE HACHETTE OU LE SIEGE DE BEAUVAIS, que son auteur, le fameux marquis de Sade, célèbre par ses excentricités lubriques, présenta en 1791 à la Comédie Française qui la refusa et rendit le manuscript à son auteur.

Pour quelles raisons, le divin marquis--dont les occupations étaient d'un autre genre--s'intéressa-t-il à Jeanne Hachette et à Beauvais? Tout simplement parce que sa femme, fille du seigneur de Marseille-en-Beauvais, descendait, d'ancienne et trés honorable famille de la bourgeoisie beauvaisine. Dans une lettre, Sade relate la visite qu'il fit à Beauvais pour sa documentation aux archives de la ville.

"Qu'est devenu le texte de sa pièce? M. Vinot Préfontaine qui a déjà obtenu d'intéressants renseignements de l'archiviste de la Comédie Française, va poser la question à L'INTERMEDIAIRE DES CHERCHEURS ET CURIEUX et ne désespère pas de la retrouver."

1855. Waldrop, Rosemarie. "Marat/Sade: A Ritual of the Intellect." BUCKNELL REVIEW 18, no. 2 (1970): 52-68.

Questions the polarity of the two main characters in Peter Weiss's play MARAT/SADE and wonders whether we as spectators can "be at the same time detached and critical (as Brecht would have us) and totally involved (as Artaud would try to make us)." Believes that the key to the play rests on the relationship between Marat and Sade, representing a series of antitheses, i.e., "confrontations of the individualist with the socialist, the pessimist with the optimist, the sensualist with the man of principle, the contemplative man with the man of action." In the end concedes that these opposites (including death, which is not an end) are irreconcilable. "Weiss does not try to round things off. The questions remain open and the stage goes into chaos. Sade is laughing triumphantly as life and impulse defeat the attempts at establishing order."

1856. Weiss, Peter. LA PERSECUTION ET L'ASSASSINAT DE JEAN-PAUL MARAT RESENTES PAR LE GROUPE THEATRAL DE CHARENTON SOUS LA DIRECTION DE M. DE SADE. Paris: Editions du Seuil, 1965.

See item 1857.

1857.  Weiss, Peter. THE PERSECUTION AND ASSASSINATION OF
       JEAN-PAUL MARAT AS PERFORMED BY THE INMATES OF THE
       ASYLUM OF CHARENTON UNDER THE DIRECTION OF THE MARQUIS
       DE SADE.  English version by Geoffrey Skelton.  Verse
       adaptation by Adrian Mitchell.   Introduction by Peter
       Brooks.  New York:  Atheneum, 1966.

       The  play  recounts the staging in an  insane  asylum,
       Charenton,   of  an  assortment  of  plays  under  the
       direction of the Marquis de Sade.   This play within a
       play  was  brilliantly directed by  Peter  Brook,  who
       first  presented  it  in  London  in  August   1964.
       According  to  Susan  Sontag,  "what  Brook  has  put
       together  is particularly brilliant and inventive--the
       rhythm of the staging, the costumes, the ensemble mime
       scenes.  In every detail of the production--one of the
       most  remarkable elements of which is  the  clangorous
       tuneful  music  (by Richard Peaslee) featuring  bells,
       cymbals,  and  the  organ--there is  an  inexhaustible
       material  inventiveness,  a relentless address to  the
       senses."

       Reviewed  by Susan Sontag in  AGAINST  INTERPRETATION,
       pp. 163-174.

Réseau de bibliothèques
Université d'Ottawa
Échéance

Library Network
University of Ottawa
Date Due